Operation Carder Kaos

He didn't just chase cybercriminals—he became one of them.

In this electrifying blend of true crime, cyber espionage, and undercover spycraft, former U.S. Secret Service Agent Richard LaTulip recounts his covert mission to infiltrate one of the world's most dangerous online criminal networks.

Assuming a false identity, LaTulip embedded himself deep inside the digital underground, building trust with elite carders, traffickers, and hackers, while secretly gathering the intelligence that would bring them down.

Operation Carder Kaos offers a rare inside look at the murky world of cybercrime, where deception is currency and exposure can be deadly. It's a high-stakes, real-world thriller about betrayal, digital warfare, and the price of living two lives.

For readers of spy thrillers, cybercrime exposés, and intelligence memoirs, this is the true story they've never heard—told by the agent who lived it.

Security, Audit and Leadership Series

Series Editor: Dan Swanson, Dan Swanson and Associates, Ltd., Winnipeg, Manitoba, Canada.

The scope and mandate for internal audit continues to evolve each year, as does the complexity of the business environment and speed of the changing risk landscape in which it must operate. The fundamental goal of this exciting series is to produce leading-edge books on critical subjects facing security and audit executives and practitioners. Key topics addressed include Leadership, Cybersecurity, Security Leadership, Privacy, Strategic Risk Management, Auditing IT, Audit Management and Leadership, and Operational Auditing.

Digitalization and Women's Rights: Volume 1
By Muharrem Kılıç and Sezer Bozkus Kahyaoglu

Analysis of Threat Perceptions: NATO and Türkiye's Cyber Terrorism Policies
By Mehmet Emin Erendor

Members, Methods, and Measures: Unlocking the Secrets of IT Leadership
By Thomas E. Armstrong

Philosophy.exe: The Techno-Philosophical Toolkit for Modern Minds
By Matthias Muhlert

Guardians of the Digital Age: Securing the Future
By Elçin Biren

Ironwill 360° Leadership: A Blueprint for Level 5 Unicorn Leadership
By Douglas P. Pflug

Behavioral Insights in Cybersecurity: A Guide to Digital Human Factors
By Dustin S. Sachs

Integrated Assurance: Unified Risk Strategy
By Patrick Hayes

Preparing for Sustainability Audits: A Practical Guide for IT Sector
By Mahsa Fidanboy

Scaling Pyramids: Leadership Lessons from a Mid-Level Bureaucrat
By Christopher Stitt

Program Architecture: Fight the Good Fight
By Gideon T. Rasmussen

Operation Carder Kaos: How One Agent Penetrated the Underground Economy
By Richard K. LaTulip

For more information about this series, please visit: https://www.routledge.com/Security-Auditand-Leadership-Series/book-series/CRCINTAUDITA?

Operation Carder Kaos
How One Agent Penetrated the Underground Economy

Richard K. LaTulip

CRC Press
Taylor & Francis Group
Boca Raton London New York

CRC Press is an imprint of the
Taylor & Francis Group, an **informa** business

Designed cover image: Mauricio Dreher

First edition published 2026
by CRC Press
2385 NW Executive Center Drive, Suite 320, Boca Raton FL 33431

and by CRC Press
4 Park Square, Milton Park, Abingdon, Oxon, OX14 4RN

CRC Press is an imprint of Taylor & Francis Group, LLC

ISBN: 978-1-041-07749-7 (hbk)
ISBN: 978-1-041-08206-4 (pbk)
ISBN: 978-1-003-68039-0 (ebk)

DOI: 10.1201/9781003680390

Typeset in Sabon
by codeMantra

To the agents who walk the line between order and chaos —

This story is for those who serve in silence, sacrifice in
shadows, and never stop chasing the truth.

And to Eliis, Michael, Samantha, and my family—thank you for your unwavering support during the long hours it took to bring this story to life.

Contents

Foreword

In the mid-2000s, Rich, serving as a Special Agent with the U.S. Secret Service, embarked on a covert mission to infiltrate international credit card fraud networks thriving on the dark web. However, that's not when I first met Rich. Rather, it was in 2023 when Rich was a student, and I was his professor, in the Master of Science in Cybersecurity Policy and Governance program at Boston College. Having known Rich as a student and then reading this book, I still find it difficult to reconcile the professional, courteous, and insightful student with the undercover Special Agent described in these pages. This stark contrast is a testament to his remarkable ability to adapt and seamlessly blend into any environment, much like a chameleon.

While working undercover, Rich's journey took him from encrypted online forums to face-to-face encounters with cybercriminals across the globe. Along the way, he collaborated with foreign law enforcement agencies, navigated cultural and legal complexities, and built trust with individuals whose livelihoods were rooted in crime and deception.

With all its twists and turns, this book reads like a gripping crime novel, with one key exception—it's all true! From the outset, readers are drawn into the high-stakes realm of undercover cyber investigations, where the boundaries between law enforcement and criminality blur. The cost of doing the job is measured not only in risk but also in the relentless challenge of maintaining and managing an undercover persona.

The story is fast-paced and full of tension: covert meetings, sudden betrayals, internal pressures within the Secret Service, and the pressure of sustaining a false identity while managing personal relationships back home. What truly makes this narrative compelling is its emotional depth. Rich's undercover life demanded immersion in morally ambiguous environments. Drinking, gambling, and transactional relationships were not optional—they were operational necessities. Unlike the imagined world of spies and secret agents, the adrenaline here was genuine, as were the regrets, the isolation, and the strain placed on personal relationships and within the Secret Service.

Equally revealing is the portrait of the institution behind the mission, the U.S. Secret Service. The story highlights how government bureaucrats, focused on their own career ambitions and standing, often fail to provide genuine and moral support to those conducting operations. As a Special Agent, Rich faced ongoing bureaucratic obstacles, including limited funding, internal politics, isolation, and leadership that often prioritized appearances over real outcomes. These challenges not only slowed progress and impeded the case but also put Rich at risk while working undercover, making each step toward success an uphill battle.

This highly personal account by Rich is not sanitized. It is raw, reflective, and uncomfortable, and that authenticity makes it essential reading not only for those interested in cyber criminals living on the dark web but also for anyone interested in learning about criminal investigations, undercover work, and the human cost of justice from the perspective of someone who has lived it. Rich's story is one of persistence, compromise, and victories earned through sacrifice, while marked by scars.

If you are searching for a gripping "true" crime story that reads like fiction yet resonates with the weight of lived experience, you will find it here!

Forward by: Kevin R. Powers

Kevin is the Founder, Faculty Director & Lecturer-in-Law for the Master of Legal Studies in Cybersecurity, Risk & Governance at Boston College Law School. He also serves as a Cybersecurity Research Affiliate at the MIT Sloan School of Management and a Lecturer for MIT Sloan's Executive Education Cybersecurity Programs.

Book teaser—at the very end

Yet, while I waited for the new crop of leaders to emerge, my journey was far from over. Before they are put in place, I will be pulled into darker days and across a treacherous new landscape. It begins in Estonia, where talented hackers set their sights on the heart of global markets. I'll be forced to face threats unlike any I've seen before. But as I hunted the hackers, lurking behind me and hiding in the shadows, they were not adversaries, but allies, or so I thought.

The lines began to shift, and the world I thought I knew slowly turned against me. These chapters are yet to be written... but when they are, it's going to be one hell of a ride.

Preface

This book reflects a personal journey and an undercover operation that occurred over two decades ago. It is a recounting of my memories, not an official record, and as such, it is based on my perspective of events as I experienced them. No non-public case materials, files, or documents from any government agency were used in the creation of this book. What follows is not a verbatim account but a reflection on those moments, filtered through the lens of time and memory. All conversations, descriptions, and interpretations are based solely on my memory and perspective; they should not be read as exact transcripts or official accounts.

The details shared in this book, while based on real experiences, do not delve into the full scope of procedures typically followed in government operations. Much like in films or books, routine actions such as report writing or reviewing mountains of legal documents have been omitted to maintain the flow of the narrative. Standard procedures, although followed during the operation, are not elaborated upon unless they directly impact the storyline or provide deeper insight. These omissions are made for the sake of storytelling, much like how mundane actions are left out in art unless they serve a specific purpose.

It is essential to note that the U.S. Secret Service (USSS) did not offer, suggest, or send me to a formal specialized undercover training course designed to teach survival skills, share lessons learned, or provide practical experience for long-term assignments before or during this case. As a result, the survival skills I applied were based on instincts and adaptability. While I consulted with supervisors to ensure my work aligned with mission objectives, the strategies, decisions, and survival techniques I relied upon were my own—developed in real time out of necessity, not drawn from any formal program. Even when the Service later formalized its undercover training, my experiences and ideas remained separate from those efforts, underscoring how independent my actions were from any structured doctrine.

The decisions I made in the field were shaped by supervisory guidance, operational realities, and necessary compromises. While I was instrumental in shaping the day-to-day operations, my decisions were always made with consideration for what was acceptable within the mission's context, even when taken in the heat of the moment. Every action I took was grounded in the training I had received and the guidance communicated to me at the time, following policies and practices to the best of my abilities.

As for the USSS's involvement with this book, I submitted the manuscript for review as required by pre-publication guidelines. However, the USSS neither endorsed nor participated in its production, nor did they approve or support its content. To aid my recollection, I filed multiple FOIA requests for case materials and photographs, but all were denied. Therefore, I reiterate that no official case materials or classified information, beyond what exists in the public domain, were used in writing this book. The views and experiences presented are mine alone and do not represent the official position of the USSS or any other agency.

Some characters in this book are based on online monikers used in the public domain during the operation. Characters such as Maksik are publicly known due to media coverage and press releases issued by organizations such as the U.S. Department of Justice. Other characters are based on real individuals, but their names, attributes, and actions have been fictionalized for narrative purposes. Any resemblance to real people, living or dead, is coincidental. For clarity and narrative flow, some characters have been combined or adjusted. With regard to foreign operations, I have taken every precaution to protect identities and safety by changing names and descriptions.

Throughout the operation, all actions were coordinated locally and approved at multiple levels. No unilateral operations were carried out, and no laws or regulations were knowingly violated. The dangerous nature of undercover work sometimes required unconventional actions to maintain my cover and ensure my safety. These were taken with careful consideration of mission goals and circumstances. At times, instructions I received from supervisors conflicted with operational realities. When I believed directives jeopardized my safety or the mission, I resisted or adapted them while remaining true to the spirit of their intent.

This book is, above all, a personal account of one agent's experience in a high-stakes undercover operation. It is not an official history or a detailed record. I have made every effort to ensure no sensitive information is disclosed and that the safety and privacy of all involved are protected. While some details have been simplified or adjusted for narrative clarity or privacy, I have aimed to provide an accurate and factual account to the best of my recollection.

Finally, I emphasize that this book is a work of non-fiction. It is not intended to serve as an official account of any government agency's actions or policies. Any views or opinions expressed here are my own, and I take full responsibility for its content. My hope is that readers will gain a unique perspective on the complexities of undercover work and the challenges faced by those who take on such dangerous roles in service of the public.

To those who read this book, I hope it offers a rare glimpse into operations seldom shared or reflected upon. My wish is that readers not only gain an appreciation for the intricate nature of such missions but also walk away with lessons that may help them navigate their own journeys, whether in law enforcement, security, or life itself.

Acknowledgments

This book is the result of not only years of undercover work but also the encouragement and support I received long after the mission ended.

To my wife Eliis—thank you for your patience, insight, and quiet strength during the writing of this book. You stood by me as I revisited difficult chapters of my life, and your support helped bring this story to the page.

To the U.S. Secret Service, thank you for the privilege of serving and for entrusting me with a mission as complex and consequential as Operation Carder Kaos. While many of the people I worked with cannot be named, you know who you are and I carry deep respect for your professionalism and commitment.

To Sone, thank you for standing by me during the operation itself. Your presence and support in those critical moments helped sustain both the mission and me personally at a time when trust was rare and pressure was constant.

To Dan Swanson at Taylor & Francis—your belief in this project and your editorial guidance made all the difference. Thank you for giving this story a platform and helping shape it into a meaningful narrative.

To Kevin Powers and the faculty at Boston College Law School, thank you for leading the Cybersecurity Policy and Governance program with purpose and vision. Your instruction and insight broadened my understanding of the policy landscape and reinforced the power of personal narrative in driving national and global security conversations.

To my colleagues at Recorded Future, thank you for continuing to value intelligence, integrity, and mission-focused work. Your support has been instrumental in helping me bridge the lessons of the past with the realities of today's cyber threat landscape.

And finally, to the readers—especially those in law enforcement, national security, or cybersecurity—thank you for joining me on this journey. I hope this book serves as both a cautionary tale and a tribute to those who carry out their work with purpose, sacrifice, and honor.

Author Biography

Richard K. LaTulip is a retired U.S. Secret Service Agent with over two decades of experience investigating cybercrime, conducting international undercover operations, and leading digital forensics teams. He served as a cybercrime liaison and diplomat in Estonia and was the lead undercover agent in the groundbreaking mission known as Operation Carder Kaos—a story he reveals for the first time in this book.

LaTulip holds a Master's degree in Cybersecurity Policy and Governance from Boston College and serves as Field Chief Information Security Officer at Recorded Future, a global leader in threat intelligence. He is a frequent public speaker and expert witness on issues ranging from insider threats to intelligence-driven risk management.

Operation Carder Kaos is his debut book—an unflinching, real-world account of double lives, digital deception, and what it takes to bring the world's most elusive cybercriminals to justice.

Abbreviations

Abbreviation	Meaning
ASAIC	Assistant Special Agent in Charge
AML	Anti-money laundering
APT	Advanced Persistent Threat
ATM	Automated Teller Machine
ATSAIC	Assistant to the Special Agent in Charge
AUSA	Assistant United States Attorney
BAC	Blood Alcohol Concentration
CI	Confidential Informant
CISO	Chief Information Security Officer
CNP	Card Not Present (transactions)
CVV	Card Verification Value
D+P	Dumps and PINs (magnetic stripe data+PIN codes used in card fraud)
DCM	Deputy Chief of Mission
DD	Deputy Director
DDoS	Distributed Denial of Service
DEA	Drug Enforcement Administration
DHS	Department of Homeland Security
DNA	Deoxyribonucleic Acid
DOJ	Department of Justice
DUI	Driving Under the Influence
ECSAP	Electronic Crimes Special Agent Program
EU	European Union
Europol	European Union Agency for Law Enforcement Cooperation
FBI	Federal Bureau of Investigation
FINCEN	Financial Crimes Enforcement Network
FSNI	Foreign Service National Investigator
GOV	Government-Owned Vehicle
ICQ	I Seek You (messaging platform)
Interpol	International Criminal Police Organization
IP	Internet Protocol
ISO	International Organization for Standardization
JTTF	Joint Terrorism Task Force
KGB	Komitet Gosudarstvennoy Bezpasnosti
KYC	Know Your Customer
MFA	Multi-Factor Authentication
MLAT	Mutual Legal Assistance Treaty

MSR Magnetic Stripe Reader
MSSP Managed Security Services Provider
NIC Nickname
OFAC Office of Foreign Asset Control
OIA Office of International Affairs
OPSEC Operational Security
OSINT Open-Source Intelligence
PCH Pacific Coast Highway
PII Personally Identifiable Information
PIN Personal Identification Number
RSO Regional Security Officer
SA Special Agent
SAIC Special Agent in Charge
SOC Security Operations Centre
SSN Social Security Number
SUV Sport Utility Vehicle
TTPs Tactics, Techniques, and Procedures
UC Undercover
UK United Kingdom
URL Uniform Resource Locator
USB Universal Serial Bus
USSS United States Secret Service
VPN Virtual Private Network
Wi-Fi Wireless Fidelity

Glossary

9/11 Refers to the September 11, 2001, terrorist attacks on the United States, including the destruction of the World Trade Center in New York City.

9/11 terrorists The individuals affiliated with al-Qaeda responsible for orchestrating and carrying out the September 11 attacks.

Academy A formal training facility for law enforcement personnel, such as the U.S. Secret Service or FBI Academy.

Agent 99 A character from the television series Get Smart, known for her intelligence and poise. Referenced in contrast with operational roles in the book.

Alias A false name used by undercover agents or criminals to conceal identity.

Baccarat A popular card game often played in casinos, referenced in the context of gambling culture.

Backstopping The process of supporting a false identity with documents, activity, and digital artifacts to legitimize an undercover agent's alias.

Bangla Road A prominent nightlife street in Patong Beach, Phuket, known for bars and entertainment venues.

BIN List A list of Bank Identification Numbers used to identify the issuing bank and type of card. Essential for pricing and targeting in carding schemes.

Boondoggle A trip or project that appears to be work-related but is seen as a waste of time or money, often for personal enjoyment.

Boris and Natasha Villains from The Rocky and Bullwinkle Show; used as nicknames for foreign investigators resembling the characters.

Botnet A network of compromised computers controlled remotely, often used to launch cyberattacks or send spam.

Brat Russian slang for "brother" or close associate, often used to imply criminal affiliation or trust.

Bribe An illicit payment offered to influence a person in a position of authority.

Building Seven A World Trade Center building that collapsed on 9/11, formerly housing the New York USSS field office.

Carder A criminal who traffics in stolen credit card data for fraudulent use.

Carderplanet A now-defunct underground carding forum where stolen data and tools were traded.

Carding forum Online communities where cybercriminals buy, sell, and trade stolen financial information.

CardSystems Solutions A U.S.-based payment processing company that suffered a major data breach in 2005.

Cash cow A lucrative criminal operation that consistently generates revenue, such as a high-performing scam or vendor.

Cashing out Converting stolen card data into physical goods or money, often via ATMs or reshipping schemes.

Chargeback fraud When a legitimate transaction is falsely reported as unauthorized to reverse charges, often used to launder money or test stolen cards.

Classic (Credit Card) A low-tier card with minimal benefits, usually the cheapest in carding markets.

Clone A counterfeit card made using stolen magnetic stripe data ("dumps").

Confidential funds Government funds used to support covert operations, often for informants or undercover expenses.

Cooked Slang for tampering with or destroying evidence to avoid detection by law enforcement.

Cotai Strip A luxury gambling and entertainment district in Macau, often referred to as Asia's Las Vegas.

Counterfeit Fake goods or documents, such as cloned credit cards or forged currency.

Countersurveillance Measures taken to avoid being followed, observed, or recorded during an operation.

Credential stuffing An automated attack where stolen usernames and passwords are used to gain access to accounts on different websites.

Credit card data Information encoded in the magnetic stripe or chip of a card, often targeted in cybercrime.

Da Russian word for "yes."

Dark web A portion of the Internet not indexed by standard search engines, where anonymous transactions often occur.

DarkMarket/DumpsMarket Notorious underground forums where carders gathered to buy and sell stolen financial data.

Database A structured set of data; in this context, a stolen database of credit card information.

Deep and dark web The deep web includes non-indexed content; the dark web refers to intentionally hidden online markets used by criminals.

Drop A person or address used to receive illicit goods or funds on behalf of a Carder.

Drop address/Drop A physical mailing address—often fake or used with a fake ID—where fraudulently obtained goods or information is delivered.

Dropbox A cloud-based storage service sometimes used to transfer illicit data.

Dump Stolen credit card magnetic stripe data used to make counterfeit cards.

D+P Dumps and PINs; stolen track data paired with PINs, used for ATM withdrawals.

eBay An online auction and shopping site referenced in context with laundering or reshipping.

E.F. Hutton A financial services brand used metaphorically ("When E.F. Hutton talks, people listen").

Embosser A machine used to raise characters on plastic cards, such as fake credit cards.

Extradition Legal process of transferring a suspect from one country to another for prosecution.

Forensics The application of scientific methods, particularly digital forensics, in criminal investigations.

Fullz A complete data set for identity theft: name, SSN, address, DOB, and financial data.

Garden of Eden A Bangkok entertainment venue referenced in relation to Thailand's adult industry.

Get Smart A 1960s spy comedy referenced throughout the book; source of terms like "Kaos" and "Agent 99."

Getting burned Slang for having one's undercover identity exposed.

Gmail Google's email platform, sometimes used in cybercrime communication.
Google The dominant Internet search engine, also referenced in relation to data gathering.
Ground Zero The site in New York City where the World Trade Center stood before its destruction on 9/11.
Hard disk drive A physical storage device for computer data, often collected during forensic investigations.
Hard disk imaging The process of creating a forensic copy of a suspect's hard drive.
Hmong An ethnic group from Southeast Asia; many were resettled in the United States after the Vietnam War.
ICQ A legacy chat platform popular among cybercriminals for its anonymity.
Informant manager Law enforcement personnel assigned to supervise and manage confidential informants.
Intelligence Information gathered through surveillance, informants, or digital means to support investigations.
James Bond A fictional British spy, referenced as a cultural touchstone for espionage and undercover operations.
Kak Dela Russian phrase meaning "How are you?"
Kaos A fictional evil organization from Get Smart, referenced metaphorically in the book.
Karon Beach A quieter beach near Patong Beach in Phuket, Thailand.
Kills dumps Slang for invalidating stolen credit card data, making it unusable.
Kuku An ICQ notification sound, referenced in the manuscript to signal a message arrival.
LA Los Angeles, California.
Lai Kwai Fong District A nightlife district in Hong Kong.
Magnetometers Security devices used to detect metal, common at government buildings and airports.
Mercado Spanish for "market," often used to describe central gathering areas.
Moderator A person with elevated privileges on a carding forum responsible for access control or trust scores.
MoneyGram A money transfer service often exploited in cyber-enabled fraud.
MTCN Money Transfer Control Number, used to track Western Union and MoneyGram transfers.
Mule A person who moves money or goods in service of fraud or laundering schemes, often knowingly but sometimes unwittingly.
Official U.S. passport A diplomatic or government-issued passport used for official travel.
Old school Slang for traditional or experienced approaches, often referencing legacy techniques in law enforcement.
Operation Firewall A major cybercrime operation led by the U.S. Secret Service, involving Segvec and early carding takedowns.
OPSEC Practices to secure operations and avoid compromise.
Pai Gow Poker A casino card game combining poker and Chinese dominoes, popular in Asian gambling culture.
Patong Beach A major party and nightlife area in Phuket, Thailand.
Phishing A technique used to trick individuals into revealing sensitive information through deceptive emails, messages, or websites.
Phuket An island in Thailand that serves as a key backdrop in the book's events.
Plastic Slang for counterfeit or cloned credit cards made from stolen data.
Policy Could refer to internal law enforcement procedures or broader governmental cybersecurity policy.
Privet Russian for "Hello."

Professional visitor's area A secure, monitored room for official meetings inside a correctional or embassy facility.
Pseudonym A false name used to conceal an identity; commonly used in undercover or cybercriminal contexts.
Red Notice An Interpol request to provisionally arrest an individual pending extradition.
Reseller A person who buys stolen goods or data in bulk and resells them for profit in underground markets.
Ripper A scammer in criminal forums who takes money but doesn't deliver the promised goods or services.
Rocky and Bullwinkle Show An animated series used metaphorically; Boris and Natasha characters reappear in nicknames.
Safe-mail A privacy-focused email service, popular among cybercriminals for anonymous communication.
Script A Carder mentioned as organizing real-world gatherings.
Singha A popular Thai beer.
Skimmer A physical device used to steal card data from ATMs or point-of-sale machines.
Skimming The process of capturing card data using a hidden device.
Skimming device A small, often disguised device used to collect data from card swipes.
Spoofing Faking the identity of a device, caller, or website to mislead victims or systems.
Surfrider The author's undercover alias while infiltrating carding networks.
Swag Promotional merchandise or stolen goods, depending on context.
Task force A coordinated group of personnel from different agencies brought together for a specific mission.
Thailand Country in Southeast Asia, central to the setting of the operation.
Tipping machine A device used to imprint raised characters on credit cards or identification.
Track One Magnetic stripe data on a credit card that includes the cardholder's name and account info.
Track record Reference to a person's history, often criminal, relevant to background checks or investigations.
Track Two Magnetic stripe data that includes card number and expiration, but not the cardholder's name.
Triads Chinese-organized crime syndicates involved in cybercrime, trafficking, and financial fraud.
Try2Check An underground website used to verify the validity of stolen credit card data.
Tsunami Refers to the 2004 Indian Ocean tsunami that severely impacted Phuket and the surrounding region.
Tuk-Tuk A small, three-wheeled motorized taxi popular in Thailand and other parts of Southeast Asia.
Tums Antacid tablets referenced humorously or during stressful scenes.
TurboJet A fast ferry service between Hong Kong and Macau.
Type A personality A behavior type associated with urgency, competitiveness, and stress—common in law enforcement.
Type B personality A behavior type characterized by relaxation, flexibility, and lower stress response.
uBuyWeRush A known vendor or marketplace referenced in the carding and fraud ecosystem.
Undercover The act of operating under a false identity to infiltrate criminal organizations.
Undercover identity A manufactured persona used by law enforcement agents during covert operations.

Underground community Refers to the hidden online world where cybercriminals communicate and transact.

Underground economy A hidden, illicit digital marketplace where stolen data, malware, services, and illegal goods are traded.

Underground forum Online platforms where criminals trade stolen data, tools, or services—typically hosted on the dark web or protected by encryption.

U.S. passport An official identity document used for international travel by U.S. citizens.

Vendor A seller of stolen card data, PINs, or counterfeit cards on underground forums.

Wan Chai District A nightlife area in Hong Kong referenced for context and travel.

Western Union A financial service company used for global money transfers, often exploited in fraud.

Wire A covert audio device used to record conversations or broadcast them to law enforcement teams.

Wire room An intelligence coordination hub within a federal agency, often used for real-time communication during operations.

Yahoo email A widely used email service, sometimes referenced as a medium for illicit communications.

Disclaimer

This book is a personal account based solely on my memories and experiences during an undercover operation that occurred more than two decades ago. It is not an official record, transcript, or history. All conversations, descriptions, and interpretations are based on my recollection and perspective, and should not be read as exact reproductions of events or communications.

No non-public case materials, files, or documents from any government agency were used in the writing of this book. To aid my memory, I filed Freedom of Information Act requests for materials, but all relevant requests were denied. As a result, this work contains no classified information, and nothing beyond what is publicly available. The views and opinions expressed are mine alone and do not reflect the official position of the United States Secret Service (USSS) or any other government agency.

Certain names, attributes, and identifying details have been altered, fictionalized, or combined for privacy, security, or narrative purposes. Any resemblance to real individuals, living or dead, is coincidental. While I have made every effort to provide an accurate reflection of my experience, this book is intended only as a personal narrative, not as an authoritative account of government policies or operations.

TESTAMENT

For years, I lived a double life. By day, I was a U.S. Secret Service Agent. By night, I was someone else entirely—a criminal persona built to earn the trust of carders, hackers, and digital opportunists operating in the shadows of the Internet. What started as an operation soon became something deeper, more personal, and far more dangerous than I ever anticipated.

Operation Carder Kaos was more than a mission. It was a test of endurance, trust, and identity. To survive undercover, I had to speak their language, understand their motivations, and immerse myself in a world where deceit was currency—not just in the shadows of the online cyber underworld, but in face-to-face encounters where digital threats became real-world danger. The boundary between who I was and who I pretended to be blurred, sometimes in ways that took years to reconcile.

I wrote this book not to glorify the operation, but to tell the truth behind it. The late nights, the betrayals, the close calls, and the moments where I questioned whether the mission—and the toll it was taking—was worth it.

This is not just a story about cybercrime. It's a story about adaptation, sacrifice, and navigating a system where right and wrong often aren't as clear as we wish they were.

My hope is that this book sheds light on what it takes to fight crime in the digital age—and the price paid by those who do.

Chapter 1

It was always about the mission

I sat in my hotel bed, gazing into the distance at the Mediterranean Sea. The sun was descending rapidly toward the horizon, eager to reach the water. My thoughts wandered, as this was the first time since arriving in Dubai that I had a moment to think about nothing.

Just as I drifted off to sleep, a knock at the door jolted me awake. My eyes flew open, pulling my mind back from dreams, and I shook off the haze. That knock indicated it was time to get to work. I steadied my nerves as I rose. Reaching the hotel door, I took a deep breath before opening it.

I knew who was on the other side, and as I opened the door, I exclaimed, "Maksik."

Smiling, arms wide open with a bottle of vodka, Maksik replied, "Rich, it's so great to see you again. I brought you a gift. It's a special bottle of vodka from a distillery near my home village."

Maksik passed me the bottle, which I eagerly accepted. I turned to Svetlana, who was smiling and delighted to see me. We leaned in and embraced as I said, "Welcome to Dubai."

Svetlana replied in her best English, "Happy to be here, welcome."

Turning to Maksik, I said, "We should have a shot to celebrate your arrival."

Maksik refused, stating, "No, that bottle is yours. Plus, I'm hungry." He gestured for everyone to join him at the restaurant downstairs.

Who was I to oppose? I put the bottle away and let them lead the way to the elevator. While we walked, I quickly sent a simple message to ATSAIC Carrington: "Target arrived, headed to lobby to eat."

When the elevator doors opened, it signaled our arrival in the lobby. Maksik, Svetlana, and I stepped out and faced two options: a restaurant with white tablecloths or a diner. Maksik turned to me and said, "I'm not a fan of fancy restaurants. Let's head to the diner."

Upon hearing his response, I felt somewhat disappointed. I would have preferred the more upscale restaurant, but I was here for him. If Maksik preferred something ordinary, then ordinary it would be for me. Looking at him, I said, "Lead the way."

As we sat in the restaurant, we discussed the last several months, mostly small talk. The typical "How are you?" "How's Ukraine?" Most importantly, I understood that Maksik learned his lesson from Thailand. Don't pack three thousand dollars in your suitcase because someone will steal it.

The conversation was more interesting when we talked about Maksik's business over several beers. Gaining more trust, Maksik dove deeper into his hacking network, still careful not to divulge any secrets. The names of hackers must be closely guarded. They are the keys to status and wealth.

I initially thought that Maksik and Svetlana, feeling tired after dinner, would head to bed. Based on our experiences in Thailand, this seemed typical for them. However, I was completely mistaken this time.

"Do you want to visit my room? We can take from minibar," Maksik cheerfully suggested.

DOI: 10.1201/9781003680390-1

"You're not tired?" I asked inquisitively.

"No," Maksik explained, "Actually, I'm in mood for more drinks. You'll come, right?"

I was always game for drinks and wouldn't let anyone down now. "Absolutely!"

After finishing our dinner, we all made our way to his room. I mentally cataloged every detail, knowing how crucial they were for Ahmed and the search warrant. I recognized Maksik's tower and confirmed we were in Tower Two. As we neared his room, I took note of the number, "2–2223." The first digit represented the tower, the next two indicated the floor, and the last two were his room number, "23."

When Maksik opened the door to his suite, he said, "Come on in."

Maksik held the door, and as I passed, I kindly said, "Thank you, Sir."

Upon entering, I swiftly scanned the room. I continued to mentally note details, like the position of Maksik's computer, which was artfully positioned at the center of the desk. Although the lid was shut, it remained visible for all to see.

Looking through the patio door at the distant view, I remarked, "Nice room. It even has a view," while noting the Burj Al-Arab in the background.

I was distracting myself rather than truly admiring the view. My police training was taking over. Maksik's laptop was close at hand, yet I fought the temptation to grab it. I understood the operation's objective; it was only a matter of time before the team secured that computer.

"I'll grab you a beer," Maksik said, pulling me away from my thoughts.

Upon accepting the beer, I said, "Thank you." I opened it, raised it high, and added, "для вашего здоровья!"

That was the extent of my Russian, apart from "Привет" and "До свидания." The Secret Service was budget-conscious and didn't allocate funds for Russian language training despite the potential operational personal risks.

However, Maksik tilted his head back with a half-smile and remarked, "I'm impressed. Good job. Cheers." Pointing to the room's safe, Maksik said, "Let me show you something."

Maksik's proposal caught my interest, so I replied, "Certainly! What do you have?"

Maksik opened the room's safe, pulled out what appeared to be official law enforcement credentials, and handed them to me.

Seeing these credentials and knowing they were in Maksik's hands caught me off guard, prompting my curious question, "Are you affiliated with law enforcement?"

Maksik shook his head and replied, "No, but Ukrainian cops can't tell the difference. If they stop me, I show them these; usually, they let me off. Worse case, I give them a hundred euros. What else can they do but take it?"

Fascinated by his insight, I handed him back his phony "credentials" and said, "That's awesome. It's a kind of get-out-of-jail-free card."

Chuckling, Maksik replied, "You're absolutely correct. It's like a get-out-of-jail card."

Maksik invited me to his balcony, and we continued our conversation there. As we gazed into the dark, starry night and admired the glow of the Burj Al-Arab, he brought up Mona.

"You know Mona?" Maksik inquired.

In that instant, I realized that he and Mona had been talking about me. I confidently replied, "Yes, I know her." Playing the uninformed person's role, "You know her as well, correct?"

Maksik replied, "Yes. But I'm curious: what makes you buy her dumps?" He added, "You have me; you can obtain whatever you need from me."

"Are you familiar with Vincent?" I inquired. Noticing Maksik shaking his head in response, I added, "He wanted my opinion. The norm is, Does she sell fresh dumps? Are the prices reasonable? And can she be trusted?"

I internalized the wheel's turning in Maksik's mind. From Maksik's vantage point, he was my supplier of stolen credit card data, not Mona. Before Maksik could speak, I elaborated, "Listen, I could have easily dismissed my friend and said they're great, but that's not who I am. So, I set up another ICQ account and messaged Mona."

As I responded, Maksik nodded in agreement, appreciating my straightforward and honest answer. Such transparency is a rare quality in this business. He then stated, "Mona is my reseller. But I'm curious, how did you know she was my reseller?"

I shrugged my shoulders and replied, "That part was simple; once she presented her BIN list, I realized it wasn't 'her' BIN list. I've seen too many of your BIN lists. I had no doubt—she was a reseller, and you were her supplier."

Maksik's next words really boosted my ego: "I must tell you, Rich, initially, I was perplexed. I wondered how you had discovered it. But after reflecting on it, I was truly impressed that you figured it out. No one else did, yet you managed to do it in record time. Very impressive."

We slowly emptied the mini bar of beer and spirits. We ordered more drinks and began working our way through a fresh bottle of Absolut Vodka. Our discussions varied greatly, covering everything from life's big questions to topics about the online world.

We discussed the ever-present online drama, which included the rippers who worked so easily online. They were always a point of contention. Perhaps it was due to the vodka, but as the evening marched toward the early morning hours, Maksik seemed more serious. He scratched his head and inquired, "Why are you rarely online? Everyone else is online all the time?"

I wasn't mentally prepared for that question. Naturally, I couldn't just say, "Well, Maksik, I have to call Headquarters every day and argue about this case. They don't share my perspective, which makes it a continuous challenge. On top of that, there's local management, report writing, paperwork, post standing, and balancing friends and family. It's a lot to manage. Ultimately, though, it means I'm not online all the time." This wasn't the response, even if it was the truth.

I focused my response on the drama we recently spoke about, saying, "I dislike being online. The drama, the complaints, and the endless 'he said, she said' nonsense—no thank you. I log on, get what I need, and go to work."

Maksik quickly grasped my point about drama: the endless complaints, particularly concerning the dumps. There were always grievances about the quality, with everyone eager to get their money's worth from the vendor. If a single card failed, there was an instant uproar.

Looking down, Maksik said, "Yeah, it's like every card must be valid. I think half my day is swapping bad for new cards. Mostly, I think everyone is a liar. No one wants to pay. They want everything for free." Maksik then turned, recalling something. "How's the database?"—referring to our recent deal for a significant database of stolen credit cards.

I looked at Maksik and said, "It was enough. About forty to forty-five percent of the work; some I get a tank of gas, and others, I hit the jackpot."

Maksik, eager to assist, inquired, "Do you need me to swap out any cards?"

I shook my head and replied, "I'm fine. I nearly got my money back, and I have plenty left. No need to replace anything."

It wasn't that I couldn't have asked Maksik for more dumps, but it was a hassle for me. Also, based on my experience I knew, 10,000 more credit cards would not move the needle regarding his being sentenced to more time in prison. In terms of sentencing, Maksik was nearing the maximum.

Maksik poured another round of vodka. My thoughts raced, reflected, and contemplated the next steps. I was seated across from the most notorious vendor of stolen credits. Online, everyone was eager to befriend him and anxiously awaited his replies. I recognized that progressing to the next level would be a remarkable achievement. I was starstruck and knew I was where I wanted to be.

I took a sip of my vodka, feeling proud of myself, unaware that I was about to face my greatest challenge. It all began with a story.

Wanting to strengthen our bond, I shared, "Maksik, something awful occurred last week. My brother was riding his motorcycle on a crowded road when suddenly, a random car pulled out in front of him. He hit the brakes but couldn't stop in time. He ended up flipping over the car, breaking both his hands and legs. To make matters worse, the motorcycle was wrecked."

I believed this story would strengthen our connection, yet I was taken aback when Maksik recalled a critical detail. He immediately confronted me, saying, "You told me you had no brothers or sisters."

Frozen, I thought, "How the fuck did that happen?"

Chapter 2

How did I get there?

Before that evening, I never imagined I'd find myself on a balcony with one of the most notorious vendors of stolen intellectual property. It felt like a dream come true. Some may blindly call it luck, but I've learned that you create luck by being focused, organized, and dedicated. It's this effort that positions you for success.

However, let's rewind a bit. Let's go back to a time before I became a Secret Service Agent or an undercover operative. Back then, I was just a regular, everyday, normal guy living in suburban America. My hometown was Dyer, situated in the northwestern part of Indiana. I was the youngest, and my brother was older by two years.

My childhood was filled with family vacations focused on discovering America. I clearly remember our road trips across this vast nation; when my brother and I weren't sleeping, we would argue, no fight, in the back seat of our family car. My father did his best to steer with one hand while using the other to keep us separated, all without veering off the road.

We often drove early in the morning and late into the evening. In between, we stopped to see historic locations, national parks, amusement parks, big cities, and small towns. We stayed at motels or hotels along the highway.

My mother used to say, "Boys, look for the sign with the big cloud." It referenced Motel 6, a preferred overnight destination for our family while traveling the highways of America.

It was an opportunity for us to focus on something other than fighting. But let's be honest, my father was tired from driving, big cloud or not; if the sign were lit up in red with the word "Vacancy," we would stop. The issue was that my mother was a clean freak. As nostalgic as it may seem, the roadside hotels weren't always properly maintained. Occasionally, we would walk in and find cockroaches scurrying about.

However, when she lifted the sheets and discovered one in the bed, it was simply a bridge too far. Fatigue or no fatigue, we loaded back into the car and drove to the next "Vacancy" sign. Who can blame her? I wouldn't want to sleep with cockroaches, but I probably would have just grinned and endured it as a child.

With all that travel, even without air-conditioning while driving through the desert, I saw, experienced, lived, and learned about American culture. I was fortunate to enjoy international trips, as my parents occasionally took me to Mexico and Canada. When we weren't exploring the United States, we would visit a nearby lake in Indiana to water ski.

Apart from family trips, my life centered on school, which I found unenjoyable, a sentiment shown in my minimal effort. I generally kept a C average, but now and then, I slipped to a D or F, resulting in one or two weeks of grounding. In the 1980s, being cooped up at home was far from perfect. Everyone else was outdoors, and that's where I wanted to be.

To prevent issues, I figured out how to "alter" my grades from D's or F's to C's or B's. I would erase the actual scores, write in a "new grade," fold the paper just right to conceal the noticeable changes, and hope my parents wouldn't catch on. Even if they did, it didn't affect me; I was

DOI: 10.1201/9781003680390-2

facing grounding regardless, and if it succeeded, I got away without consequences. Surprisingly, whether they were aware, they accepted the altered grades.

The shift from middle school to high school felt monotonous for me. Much like my previous experience, this time was equally uneventful, as I didn't do anything remarkable. I didn't engage in sports, join clubs, or gain popularity, limiting myself to just a few friends. I stayed away from drinking and drugs, yet many assumed I was using. My high school style only fueled this misconception; I sported a mullet, wore hard rock T-shirts, ripped jeans, and high-top sneakers.

Overall, my high school experience felt more like being a guest than a genuine student. I rarely studied, and I often only remembered we had homework when a classmate asked if I had completed it, or worse yet, when the teacher asked for it. This frequently led to a frantic scramble to finish as much as I could in less than two minutes.

I often told my parents I had finished my homework in class or had no assignments. They believed me, at least they wanted to, because, like most parents, they hoped their child was being honest. These days, I see the same excuses coming from my son. The difference is that now parents can check grades online anytime they want. If they're curious enough, they can track everything day by day, something I'm delighted wasn't possible when I was growing up.

High school ended, but my performance was underwhelming. I wanted to attend college, though Ivy League schools were never in the picture. With a 2.0 GPA and average SAT scores, my options were limited. Still, I had a plan.

While Indiana University's main campus was out of reach, its satellite campus in Gary pretty much welcomed all applicants. Furthermore, I learned that if I maintained a 2.0 GPA, I could eventually transfer to Bloomington.

Given my lack of effort in high school, a one-year penalty wasn't bad. Furthermore, how hard could college be, after all, I had scraped by in high school. Once classes started, I decided it was time for a makeover: I ditched the ripped jeans, scaled back the concert T-shirts, and finally cut off the mullet.

Sadly, other than appearance, socially, not much changed. In high school, I rarely attended parties or drank alcohol, which continued at the satellite campus. So far, my college experience has felt like a continuation of high school, and I long for a change.

By the end of the first year, to everyone's surprise, I maintained a 2.0 GPA, applied to the main campus, and got accepted. To discourage me, my parents told me, "I was on my own and would have to pay the bills."

I stayed calm and firm. "I was going to Bloomington, like it or not." But before I left, my parents took me to dinner. Instead of trying to talk me out of it, they said, "We didn't want to go because you thought we'd pay for it. Seeing your commitment, we decided we'll help you out."

I recall my brother exclaimed, "Had I known, I would've gone to West Lafayette!"

College served as a valuable training ground. The experience transformed an awkward, socially inept kid, setting off a journey of maturation and connection with others. During these years, I moved frequently, lived with diverse people, made new friends, experienced heartbreak, began new relationships, and, most importantly, partied. My youth and energy fueled countless nights of partying; however, it quickly became clear that this newfound party lifestyle needed adjustment.

After my second year, I received a letter from the University notifying me that I was being placed on probation due to my low GPA and was at risk of expulsion. I only had one semester to elevate my GPA above 2.0. While I didn't want to sacrifice enjoyment, I recognized the importance of finding equilibrium.

To achieve balance, I stepped away from the Sunday-to-Saturday party scene and focused on studying Monday through Thursday. I only allowed myself to party after my Thursday studies ended unless it was a special occasion, like when a friend visited from back home.

After finding balance, my GPA improved, and I enjoyed my college life until my senior year, when I met Sandy Evans at a fraternity party. We clicked instantly and developed a strong connection. Before I knew it, I graduated in August 1995 with a 2.3 GPA. However, knowing I wanted to work in federal law enforcement, my mother contacted me. "Rich, did you know the Border Patrol carried guns?"

Armed with my degree from Indiana University, I applied, was accepted, and began my first law enforcement position on December 10, 1995, in San Diego, CA. While attending the Border Patrol Academy, Sandy and I were married on February 17, 1996, before a justice of the peace. While many couples celebrate this day, I felt more somber. I wasn't particularly happy or sad.

Reflecting on the past, I'm unsure what led me to marry her; it was probably a mix of influences. The pressure of being away at the academy and the upcoming relocation from Indiana to California might have swayed my decision, especially since she accompanied me, and I felt I "owed it to her." While it appeared to be the correct choice initially, I soon realized it wasn't the best.

Arriving in San Diego, it became evident that Sandy and I were growing apart. While there were enjoyable moments, those were mainly in the past. Instead, we spent hours arguing. I sought refuge in working the midnight shifts to sidestep issues during my tenure with the Border Patrol.

Nevertheless, I remained dedicated to doing my part, hoping to salvage our marriage. Work was unexpected; the primary mission was prevention rather than enforcement. Our instructions were "to park our vehicles near the border and be visible." Leadership believed this would deter migrants from entering the United States illegally.

This initiative, called "Operation Gatekeeper," felt political to me. From where I stood, the official counts seemed to be selective, only those who were "turned back south" were documented. while the fate of those who made it north was largely unrecorded. Watching this unfold left me uneasy, wondering what criteria guided the operation and who, if anyone, was truly being counted.

Over the next two and a half years, I gained valuable experiences, but it quickly became clear that the Border Patrol wasn't the right fit for me. I yearned for a more meaningful and fulfilling role, so I applied to the Secret Service, FBI, and Drug Enforcement Administration.

I waited patiently throughout the lengthy hiring process, which took around sixteen months from application to hire. With each milestone I achieved, I felt increasingly encouraged and excited. Yet, every success brought its own set of challenges.

When I was offered a position, the San Diego Field Office welcomed a new Special Agent in Charge (SAIC), John O'Reilly. He hailed from the New York Field Office and wasn't only tall, muscular, and astute. I met SAIC O'Reilly when he visited my home to discuss the harsh realities of life as a Special Agent.

The interview aimed to inform me about the most grueling aspects of the role and to fulfill the requirement of warning me. Aside from telling me the worst of the worst, SAIC O'Reilly also asked, "Are you interested in working for me in San Diego?"

I replied, "I thought it wasn't an option."

He responded, "Things have changed."

Stumbling over my words, I quickly replied, "Yes, I'd like to stay here and would be happy to work for you."

SAIC O'Reilly said, "Good."

On August 2, 1998, I was sent to Washington, DC, and began training as a Secret Service Special Agent.

Chapter 3

Feeling special, at least for the time

During my interview process, I recall being told by the then ASAIC, "You are continuing with the interviewing process because of your high score on the exam. Typically, this isn't something I witness often when hiring an agent." Hearing this made me feel special.

This ego boost allowed me to imagine how classmates may be mentally and physically. I believed everyone would be "high caliber," "strong," and "run like gazelles." This idea was quickly dashed upon arriving in Washington, DC. Upon arrival, I took the stance of not being too outgoing or talkative. Instead, I observed and welcomed the conversations when they presented themselves.

Most of the conversations were general in context, the type to get to know or feel each other out. The class seating was prearranged, so the people I sat around were with whom I became most acquainted. The first speeches from the instructors were meant to inspire the class. To push us to improve, strive for more, achieve the world, and be the best. They talked about what it meant to be a Special Agent. Listening to the speeches, I felt inspired, but when I looked around, it seemed to me physical fitness wasn't at the forefront of all hiring officials' minds.

During one of the breaks, a recruit approached me and asked "What did you this about his motivational speech?".

"What do you mean," I replied. "I think it was fine."

"Ah," the recruit replied. "It's all bullshit. You don't need to "run," "do pull-ups," or "push-ups."

Hearing this, I was put off, to say the least. Not being one to start a controversy on day one, I replied, "I work out for me, and if needed, to respond when called to help a partner. I would feel awful if I refused some discomfort in my life, meaning working out, and that led to my colleague losing their life." I felt this because I couldn't live with that burden, so I made sure, within reason, I could perform adequately.

Special? From that conversation, it was evident that special wasn't necessarily applicable to everyone. Over the following days, it became clear to me that the hiring standards varied from office to office. While scoring high on the exam might have been expected, in my experience it was not always emphasized. I noticed that some classmates scored lower, occasionally just at or above the minimum threshold, which left me questioning how standards were applied.

Understanding the root cause was critical and probably caused unflattering news media attention. I surmised that when an organization ramps up hiring, standards can naturally shift. This does not imply that the Secret Service recruited candidates who failed to meet the criteria. Instead, it highlights the stark contrast between hiring fifty-two agents and six hundred agents annually.

Another challenge that can affect quality is a shortage of applicants who could successfully navigate all stages of the application process. The most significant hurdles were passing the polygraph and being truthful about drug use, which were frequently interconnected;

 DOI: 10.1201/9781003680390-3

applicants often omitted their drug usage and was sometimes only revealed during the polygraph examination.

Regardless, I was hired at the beginning of a hiring surge and, therefore, a beneficiary. My class was filled with outstanding candidates, and then there were the rest. I was somewhere in the middle. I wasn't going to swim or run the fastest, nor was I going to shoot the eye of a bird at 1,000 feet, or achieve the highest academic grades. I gave one hundred and ten percent and was destined to be upper-middle ranking in the class.

Diving deep into my Academy days and government career, I sought to understand "why" I was the type of person I was and "why" I wasn't the same as the rest. I was looking for a purpose. The Secret Service typically sought out candidates of a specific type, often from the military or former law enforcement backgrounds. I fit into the law enforcement category; however, the most critical category in which most were hired, I knew that I wasn't. I didn't have a Type A personality.

I wasn't high-strung or impatient and didn't easily become stressed, suggesting I was likely more of a Type B personality. I tended to be relaxed, low-stress, even-tempered, adaptable, emotionless, and patient. Initially, I struggled with disorganization, which I only recognized as my caseload increased.

More and more documents got randomly arranged on my desk. When I was tasked with finding anything, it took me time, leading to frustration. Much like college, I needed to find a balance to succeed. Once balance was achieved, I became organized, and with this, I was ready for more sophisticated casework.

One of my Academy instructors, Charlie Stonehouse, was your quintessential Type A personality and what I characterized as your typical New Yorker, driven, outspoken, and intensely focused. SA Stonehouse was from the local field office, and his time there overlapped with John O'Reilly. I wouldn't say they were friends, but it seemed to me that they knew each other. SA Stonehouse, like O'Reilly, was dedicated to fitness and happened to be our health and fitness instructor.

Unlike O'Reilly, SA Stonehouse was a bully and not as sharp; because of this, he used fear tactics to garner respect. It wasn't a quality I admired and avoided repeating during my career. Adding to his lesser qualities, he reminded us daily that he was an agent formerly assigned to the President's Detail.

Charlie Stonehouse was the type of instructor keen on lecturing the class about fitness. He enjoyed lashing out at those he deemed unfit. It was his method to "weed out" the unqualified. It was as if he took joy in berating those for not performing to his expectations. SA Stonehouse even had his catch phrase: "You know there is a special assignment awaiting you; it's called the 'Lady Bird' detail. If you aren't fit, that's precisely where you'll find yourself."

I didn't catch SA Stonehouse's ire for fitness; no, it was another reason. It was trivial, and it was that Type B versus Type A personality came into play. You see, he directed the class to get flat-soled shoes, all black, and "supported" your ankles.

Well, I had black Converse All-Star shoes, except I bought a black permanent marker and colored in the white parts. They became more purple than black but were flat-soled and had "some" ankle support.

These shoes made a good impression on many instructors; however, it was clear, SA Stonehouse didn't appreciate my creativity and originality. In his view, I wasn't "fitting in" or "conforming" with the rest of the group. I almost heard him questioning SAIC O'Reilly: "Does he want to reconsider this particular agent?"

Despite the issue, I graduated from the Academy in February 1999. Before I departed, they gave me my credentials, a laptop, and a Sig Sauer P229. I then boarded a flight and flew to San Diego. I was ready to report for duty.

Chapter 4

When one door closes another opens

Trust is the essential foundation of every relationship. Without it, there is nothing. By December 2000, I realized this critical element was missing from my relationship. This absence led to my wife and me separating and beginning our lives separately. However, our divorce didn't become official until after our daughter was born in October 2001.

Feeling liberated and unburdened, I eagerly returned to the "party" lifestyle I had left behind in Indiana. At the same time, I was dedicated to investigating financial crimes and had built a strong reputation within the banking sector. My contacts consistently referred cases to me, so I rarely needed to answer duty calls.

Living deep in Escondido, far from the freeway, made my daily commute particularly challenging, especially during rush hour. I considered moving closer to San Diego, but lacked the funds due to my divorce. Luckily, I was still young and energetic, and my limited tolerance for traffic prompted me to rethink my habits.

My solution was to change my workout schedule. Instead of working out during the day, I decided to wake up early, around five thirty, to drive to San Diego and hit the gym. If everything went as planned, I would arrive at the office by eight thirty.

During one of these early morning drives, I overheard some disturbing news. Like most days, I listened to music and lost myself in thought. But today, the music abruptly stopped; the DJ calmly announced, "A plane crashed into the World Trade Center, and now back to the music."

The moment the DJ interrupted the music, I felt annoyed—not by what was said, but by the interruption itself. I thought nothing of it with no sense of urgency in their voice. Probably a daredevil pilot flying a Cessna miscalculated a turn and hit the building. But when the music came back on, my mind quickly wandered.

What did the DJ mean by "A plane hit the World Trade Center?" If it was a Cessna, why not say it? Could it be something bigger? What was the damage? Was anyone hurt? Curiosity overwhelmed me. I immediately turned the dial seeking a morning talk show.

I pressed the button, and the next station sprang to life with a DJ explaining the seriousness of the situation in New York. It was a real-time update; the narrative developed as I listened, clarifying exactly what type of plane it was. It wasn't a Cessna; instead, it was a commercial airliner packed with passengers. The damage was significant and, for now, localized to only one of the two towers.

That day's drive quickly became less agonizing as everything faded into the background. Upon arriving at the office, I hurried to our fifth-floor office and turned on the news. Not knowing if anyone was in the office, I yelled, "Anyone here? You need to see this NOW!"

One agent, unaware of the events, stumbled in and asked, "What's going on?"

"Look," I said, pointing to the TV.

As events unfolded, I could only think about helping. I called the one person I knew who had the juice and said, "Send me to New York. I want to help."

DOI: 10.1201/9781003680390-4

SAIC O'Reilly served once at the New York Field Office and had many friends in the Service. He replied, "Let me make some calls."

The FBI wasted no time and immediately issued a nationwide alert. It was all hands on deck; personnel were to report to their local Joint Terrorism Task Forces (JTTF). And San Diego was top of the list since it was a recruitment center and home for four of the 9/11 terrorists.

Soon, SAIC O'Reilly assigned me and several other agents to assist in any way possible. I was eager to help, as this could represent the pinnacle of my career. I made myself available for any assignment, ranging from interviews and surveillance to executing search warrants and subpoenas.

When I got bored, I approached the FBI supervisor and said, "Whenever you need me, I'm here."

After about two weeks of working locally, SAIC O'Reilly called me and said, "You're being reassigned. You leave for New York tomorrow to help at Ground Zero."

To celebrate, a group of us decided to watch the first Monday Night football game post-9/11. Amazingly, the bar was packed. People were ready to turn away from the twenty-four-hour news cycle. When I arrived, the game was mid-first quarter, and our group was near the bar.

After greeting everyone, I turned my attention to getting a beer. But as I stood waiting, I spotted two women sitting nearby. The good news was that I didn't need to move, as the one who caught my eye was almost sitting next to me.

I observed her most appealing attributes as I attempted to make eye contact. Her olive-toned skin shimmered while her dark brown hair cascaded gracefully to her shoulders. Her curves appeared natural and proportionate; her mesmerizing eyes sparkled, and her luscious lips perfectly complemented her. She wore a fitted shirt that slightly rose above her waist, revealing a tattoo.

I turned back toward one of the guys and asked, "Has anyone tried speaking to the two to my right?"

One person replied, "Yeah, but they weren't interested."

Undeterred, I knew an opportunity may present itself, and I wanted to be ready when it materialized. So, I always kept one eye on them. After a few drinks. I pointedly asked, "Are you sure? Did they outright shut you down? Or was it more of a come back later statement?"

Tired of hearing "the guys talk about talking," one female FBI Agent took the lead and said, "Hi, how are you ladies this evening?" Instantly, she sparked the conversation I only dreamed about.

Feeling shy knowing I missed the opportunity, I made a loud, offhand comment, "I feel like I'm on the outside looking in on a good conversation."

Upon hearing me, Rachel laughed and remarked, "Exactly! You're on the outside looking in."

Instantly, I knew I didn't want to waste another second. I stepped in and said, "Hi, my name is Richard LaTulip."

Rachel replied, "My name is Rachel Peters. Nice to meet you finally."

With introductions out of the way, we began a more meaningful one-on-one conversation. Our conversation lasted until the bar closed, but I had one issue. "Tomorrow" was the morning I would be in New York for at least two weeks. This wasn't the perfect scenario, as I preferred an in-person meeting.

Regardless, since Rachel knew I was with a bunch of FBI Agents, who all happened to be working on a vast terrorist investigation, I said, "Rachel, I want to see you again. However, I leave for New York tomorrow. Can I call you while I'm away?"

Rachel said, "Yeah, you can call me," and gave me her telephone number.

Hearing this good news, I decided to make one last attempt to impress her. I handed Rachel my Secret Service business card and said, "Talk to you soon." The next day I left for New York.

Once I returned from New York City, I wanted to pick up where I left off. Rachel and I were to meet in downtown San Diego at the famous party location. The area was referred to as the historic Gaslamp section. Many eclectic bars, restaurants, and shops were located on this street, attracting residents and tourists. The bar was filled with people, and we planned to meet during "happy hour" before the bar became a disco.

As I arrived, while walking past the bar's picture window, I noticed Rachel sitting near it. I waved and motioned that I would be inside shortly. Getting close to the table, Rachel stood up, greeted me, and hugged me, briefly embracing each other. The smell of her perfume was intoxicating, and her beauty was equally still. Rachel wore a sparkling shirt, black skirt, and knee-high boots. Everything complemented Rachel's personality and elegantly brought life to her body.

Rachel inquired, "How have you been? Oh, hold on, how was your trip to New York?"

"New York," I remarked, "was quite an experience. Upon my arrival, they transported us to a merchant ship moored on the east side."

Confused, Rachel asked, "A merchant ship? What were you doing there?"

"That was my hotel," I explained. "It was a far departure from the norm, but hey, at least it wasn't a tent in the middle of Africa where I heard the team had to fend off monkeys eager to take their snacks."

"That's funny," Rachel chuckled, then turned serious. "Tell me, how was Ground Zero? It must have been overwhelming."

"It was," I started. "I was assigned midnights. My partner and I were stationed near Building Seven, where the Secret Service was located. Just before we arrived, the mission transitioned from rescue to salvage. On the pile of rubble, it was surreal. It was one crane stationed above another. The claw dug in and passed the debris from one to the next. All the while, the NY fire department was putting water on it. They explained that, at the core, the fire was still burning. The smell of the burning fire permeated throughout the city. It was a constant reminder of the tragedy. My partner and I were on standby, ready to assist. If the workers found anything, we were the ones they needed to contact."

"Wow, that must have been amazing and sad simultaneously," Rachel lamented.

"It was," I said. "When I wasn't close to Building Seven, I walked about. I stood by the square, where the globe was, and the music played. It continued for the first two days before it suddenly stopped. I stood near that spot one month before, listening to the same music. I took some photos. When I get them developed, I will show you."

"Please do," Rachel replied. "Oh, and do you know the business card you gave me?"

"Yes," I replied.

Rachel replied, "I ripped it up that night you gave it to me."

Astounded, I remarked, "You ripped it up?"

"Don't worry," Rachel replied, "a day later, I kept thinking about you, so I got it out of the trash and taped it back together."

Time passed quickly, and our chemistry was only interrupted when a barback gently asked for the chairs. Fate interjected, and with our chairs taken away, feeling the music, we moved to the dance floor. Once on the floor, we embraced, our bodies moved as one. As we danced, I attempted my best moves, wanting to impress and, simultaneously, knowing I wasn't the best dancer, to make her laugh.

An occasional spin, followed by a twirl, and then a dip, followed by pulling Rachel closer to me. Our hips moved together, peering deep into each other's eyes. Feeling confident, I moved in; Rachel offered no resistance as our lips touched.

Passionately, we kissed; my hand moved down her back, tracing her spine to her hips, moving slightly past to explore her buttocks. After a very short stay, my hands moved back up Rachel's back, ever so slightly touching her with my fingertips, and then I stopped to hold the back of her neck gently. The excitement was palpable, and we both enjoyed the time.

I felt happy hour began moments ago, and the disco raged, but the lights turned on, and the bouncers announced, "Last call!" Hours felt like minutes, our conversation was a flash, and the dancing a distant memory. I would have sworn I had just walked through the front door. But after all of this, the night was far from over. We looked at each other; no words needed to be said; our desire burned deep from inside.

Rachel inquired, "If you're interested, I know a place we can go? It has a wonderful view of the city lights and the bay."

I said, "Absolutely I'm interested!"

With that, we walked to her friend's apartment. Rachel was watching her friend's cat and knew she had the apartment all to herself. Rachel and I could have the privacy not offered in any club, but we desperately sought.

Decency prevented us from getting too personal. Now, no other people were around, lights were turned down, and large picture windows were all around us, a perfect view of the city. It was a clear night, so the city sparkled; the stars and moon were exceptionally bright on this night. The apartment was modestly furnished. It was modern and open the couch and desk naturally surrounded us. To me, boring and plain but about to serve as a stoic witness to love's embrace.

A few minutes were spent looking at the cityscape, quickly shifting our focus back to the moment at hand. We hadn't come here to lose ourselves in the view. Turning toward each other, our eyes met, and I pulled her close in rhythm with the music.

We embraced, letting the energy of the night carry us. The connection between us deepened with every heartbeat, drawing us closer as time seemed to dissolve. Whatever surrounded us faded into the background until nothing remained but the pull we felt toward each other.

When the intensity finally gave way to stillness, we lay side by side, catching our breath. Staring up at the ceiling, the ache in our bodies was little more than a reminder of the moments just passed—already receding into memory. After a quiet pause, our thoughts began to return, and the world slowly crept back in.

Tomorrow would be an early day, maybe now seemed like the right time to move on. With the night already slipping away, we dressed and departed. Once street side, we shared a final kiss, a passionate goodbye, before heading in opposite directions, each carrying the promise to meet again soon.

Chapter 5

Life always has a curve ball to throw

It was Friday night, and I planned to attend a colleague's retirement party. Knowing I was the only Secret Service representative attending, SAIC O'Reilly asked me to present him with a plaque of appreciation. I happily accepted and headed to the party.

These events aren't supercharged, like hanging out with Rachel and her crew. No, they mainly served beer, perhaps a shot of vodka, but overall, it was tame by comparison, lasting only three to four hours. Once the party ended, I decided to visit Rachel.

When I arrived, I sat and conversed with some of the regulars. Over time, we had gotten to know each other, but more importantly, I enjoyed the conversations. When the bar closed, we stayed behind to have one more drink.

After that one drink, Rachel looked at me and asked, "Interested in going to our spot?"

I knew what that meant and replied enthusiastically, "Yes!"

We piled into Rachel's SUV, and she drove us to her friend's apartment. Here, there was no one to bother us—a lesson we learned from our past experiences. On that evening, a neighbor's dog barked uncontrollably as one of San Diego's Finest was patrolling the area. The barking caught their attention. They turned on the patrol car's external lamp, looking for any potential problems.

I knew being parked in the garage was enough to conceal us. However, with the lights shining, we were still startled. Instinct took over as I did my best to cover our naked bodies.

Rachel froze and asked, "Did he see us?"

I peered over her bare shoulder and said, asked, "He is definitely looking for something or someone."

Rachel crouched down as replied, "At least the dog stopped barking."

I laughed, "No shit." Then the light turned off, the engine revved, and the Officer drove off.

Panic subsided as I looked into Rachel's eyes and said, "He's gone.

Rachel turned her head sideways, and before passionately kissing me, replied, "Yes!"

Since we learned from our experience and didn't want to have a repeat issue, we found a "new spot." Like many other special nights, tonight we had our fill of lust-filled backseat SUV sex. As the hours passed and it grew later, we decided it was time to return.

I needed to be dropped off to get my car and return home. At the time, I felt fine, but since it was late on a Friday night, I was undoubtedly tired. Once on the road, I envisioned my bed and the comfort of getting home to some much-needed sleep.

It was a thirty-five-minute drive home from the bar, partly on a highway and the last ten miles on poorly lit, winding backcountry roads. Streetlamps come by infrequently, which meant I had to rely on my headlamps to light the way.

Ten minutes off the highway, my eyelids felt heavy, my energy dissipated, and sleep consumed me. A head nod would jolt me awake, forcing me to shake my head. It was a brief refresh, but it was also temporary. I told myself, "Only five more minutes."

DOI: 10.1201/9781003680390-5

Unfortunately, my "refresh" only lasted one minute. I'd lost my fight, and sleep washed over me. My arms fell from the steering wheel, and the road gently curved to the left. There was no guardrail; however, there was a small, raised curb, and once the car hit the curb, it rocked me from my slumber.

I attempted to understand what was happening, but I had no opportunity to process anything other than trying to grab the steering wheel and slam on the brakes. Nothing I did mattered; driving at fifty-five miles per hour, the car hopped the curb, aligned perfectly, and collided with a telephone pole.

The crash was loud and violent, and it was over as quickly as it began. Immediately, I stepped outside to assess the damage. The car's front end was wrapped around the telephone pole, with the headlights hanging by their electrical wires. Then, panic set in, and I thought, "Oh shit, when I got out of the car, I never put the car in park."

Given the circumstances, it was a ridiculous thought; however, I wasn't processing the situation correctly. This brought me to my next dilemma: Should I run or stay? No one was around; I was alone, and it was early morning. Fleeing the scene was a legitimate option.

As I paced back and forth, considering my options, I wondered, "Where's my backpack?" It contained my gun, radio, badge, and baton; I needed to find it. I checked the car but found nothing. While searching, I thought, "Wow, the sunroof is gone." That's when it struck me: "It must have flown out through it."

I continued my frantic search in the field until finally, there it was, lying about forty feet in front of the car. Relief set in, my shock was wearing off, and I called Rachel. Answering, she said, "What's up?"

I replied, "You won't believe this, but I ran into a telephone."

"On my God!" She exclaimed. "Are you okay?"

"Yes," I responded. "You think you can pick me up?"

"Where are you?" Rachel inquired.

"Main road," I said. "About four minutes from my house."

"I'm on the way," Rachel replied.

Twenty minutes later, I spotted headlamps piercing the darkness. I hoped it was Rachel coming to my rescue following the crash. However, my expectations were shattered when the overhead lights illuminated the area. An officer emerged and inquired, "Have you been drinking?"

Sheepishly, I replied, "I only had three beers tonight."

Given the accident's severity, I should have declined to answer questions. Once the officer finished the field sobriety test, he stated, "You failed and I'm arresting you for suspicion of driving under the influence of alcohol." Later, I would find out my blood alcohol content (BAC) was right at the legal limit, which, at the time, was point zero eight percent.

After the accident, I was ordered to stay home until SAIC O'Reilly called me into the office. There was some concern about whether I was "all right" and if I had sustained any severe injuries. According to the police report, I hit the telephone pole at approximately fifty-eight miles per hour. I never even touched the brakes. The vehicle's airbag deployed, saving me from significant injuries.

I was fortunate that my only injuries were a small cut above my eye, a slightly bruised chest, and a jammed middle finger. Hindsight being twenty-twenty, being asleep, and in a very relaxed state saved me from tensing up, resisting, or straining myself, which, by themselves, could have resulted in more severe injuries.

Nonetheless, I realized some personal items that needed to be recovered were left in the car. When I arrived, I asked to be escorted to the vehicle. While walking, the attendant said, "Man, have you seen the car? It was one of the worst wrecks I've seen in a while. I bet the driver is dead. Do you know if the driver survived the accident?"

I looked at him and said, "I was the driver."

The attendant, his eyes wide with astonishment, exclaimed, "You were the driver? You walked away? Not a scratch on you?"

I acknowledged, "Yes, I had a scratch." I then showed him a cut on my hand and the one above my right eye.

The attendant assessed the damage, glanced at the car, and remarked, "You're one lucky son of a bitch."

I continued, "Yes, I was fortunate to have walked away alive."

With that, I retrieved the items from the vehicle and left.

Several days later, I received that long-awaited call. I was informed that SAIC O'Reilly would see me, so I headed to the office to meet him. Upon my arrival, I felt like an outsider. I knew I had disappointed him. Coworkers cautiously greeted me or outright avoided me.

I walked down the passageway toward SAIC O'Reilly's office. Once inside, SAIC O'Reilly said, "Take a seat."

There was a long pause. Internally, I thought, shall I start? But just like that, SAIC O'Reilly said, "How are you? Are you ok?"

"I'm fine. A small cut on my finger and above my eye. That's it," I replied.

This moment of endearment lasted only as long as my answer. Once I finished, SAIC O'Reilly demanded, "Tell me what the hell happened?"

I explained myself and admitted everything was my fault and my fault alone. I blamed no one for my actions, apologized for a colossal misstep, and accepted whatever punishment SAIC O'Reilly deemed fit. Appropriate or not, I promised I would not fight it.

SAIC O'Reilly looked at me and said, "Give me your gun, credentials, and badge. And go home."

Some weeks passed, and eventually, I was told to return to the office for administrative work. During this time, the Secret Service's investigation of any policy violations, specifically misuse of a government vehicle, paralleled the State's case. This case was managed from Headquarters; however, Amanda Cross was the representative. Her job was to obtain police reports and work with victims, such as the energy company.

Since the Secret Service is self-insured, they are responsible for damages caused by an agent while on duty. However, the bill for damages was significant, and they weren't interested in paying. Now came the conundrum: Could they get me to pay for the telephone pole?

SA Cross's responsibility was simply to inform the victims of their rights and provide them with the proper forms. These forms should have been provided to them. However, as I learned later, she never offered them any forms. The reason: the play to "get my insurance to pay."

As a result, everything was put on hold pending the resolution of the conflict with the insurance company, the energy company, and my lawyer. They also learned that my lawyer was urging me to have the Service acknowledge its responsibilities and pay for the damages. This led ASAIC George Thomas to ask, "What will you do?"

I said, "It was my mistake, and if necessary, I'll cover the cost of the pole."

Once all my local legal issues were resolved in San Diego, I was ordered to return to Headquarters. Here, I would have to explain myself again to two internal affairs agents, Jack Hightower and Cindy Flowers.

They sought answers. I was reminded I was under oath and to start explaining that night. I explained how I represented the Office at a San Diego Police Detective's retirement party and how, after the party, I drove to the bar where Rachel worked. I explained what I drank and where Rachel and I "parked." I told them we returned to the bar afterward, and that is when I departed for my residence.

"Wait," Agent Hightower stated, "Tell this to me again after the bar closed; what did you do?"

I explained, "Rachel and I got into her vehicle and drove to a private street in a local neighborhood."

Agent Flowers, taken aback, snarled, "Of course, no one was in your assigned government vehicle; how convenient."

I replied, "I didn't take the assigned government vehicle because it was too small and not as comfortable; Rachel had an SUV."

Agent Flowers, in disbelief, continued to press, "Ok, let's assume you both didn't get into the assigned vehicle; then what?"

I restated, "We drove together to a side street that was secluded and private."

Agent Flowers was puzzled but had an idea, "Then you continued to drink alcohol?"

This was a simple answer from me, "Nope."

Agent Flowers, now ready to pounce, stated, "Drugs, you both did drugs! Correct?"

"Again," I explained, "We spent about two hours together, no alcohol, no drugs. Then we returned to the bar so I could pick up my government vehicle."

Not ready to believe these statements, Agent Flowers insisted, "You are to expect me to believe, for two hours, you and this Rachel just sat in a car on a dark street, just the two of you, and you didn't drink, didn't do drugs, nothing. I'm expected to believe this."

I thought it was apparent what a man and a woman might do for two hours in an SUV in the middle of the night, on a dark street, in a secluded neighborhood, but Agent Flowers was seeking the "gotcha moment."

I looked at Agent Hightower, puzzled, and said, "Okay, do I need to say this out loud? You actually want me to describe to you what we did for two hours?"

Finally, the light bulb clicked. Agent Hightower understood everything clearly and said, "No, there's no need; we can move on."

Agent Flowers, obviously upset and feeling that "the suspect" was about to break, felt betrayed by her partner. Agent Hightower messed it all up right when the admission of guilt was about to be said out loud. Agent Flowers, countering Agent Hightower's statement, now insisted, "No, you can tell me what the two of you were doing."

It was evident that Agent Flowers, not the sharpest investigator, still needed to be made aware of what was happening. I blurted out, "Do you really want me to say it out loud?"

Agent Hightower interrupted and, at the same time, assured Agent Flowers, "I will tell you later." Then he turned toward me, stating, "No, not required; please continue."

Once the "critical" piece of the investigation was explained to a clueless investigator, I wondered how she would react. Nonetheless, weeks passed, and finally, the verdict arrived: several weeks suspended, to be administered every other pay period.

My past sins were quickly put behind me, but not forgotten. Occasionally, I needed to defend myself. ASAIC Thomas had moved on, and our new ASAIC was Zorn DuBois. ASAIC DuBois was the son of a former pilot, and he consistently tried to live up to his father's standards.

I was relieved that ASAIC DuBois had been assigned to San Diego. Before he stepped into the role, he was just an agent; we worked together on a presidential visit in California. Together, we worked hard but also played hard.

Opportunistic agents shared my "past" with ASAIC DuBois. Others tried to knock me down to position themselves ahead of me. This prompted ASAIC DuBois to come to my office and question me. He asked me, "Rich, are you still drinking and driving a GOV?"

I sadly replied, "Sir, it has been four years since that day. I did my time. I worked my cases, all without a single alcohol-related incident. If I had a problem, don't you think it would have happened by now?"

Chapter 6

A brief history lesson

In my best estimation, crime on the Internet exploded between 1998 and 1999. While it's true that crime via the Internet wasn't new, it needed globalization to truly take hold. As the Internet advanced, so did opportunities for criminal activity. Borders and proximity suddenly mattered little.

The advantage for individuals engaging in online crimes was the absence of law enforcement presence. Law enforcement was not actively monitoring forums or chat rooms because they remained unaware of them. Additionally, they were overwhelmed with traditional access device fraud cases.

As a result, criminal activity had ample opportunity to grow. The Secret Service only became involved in the early 2000s and immediately faced numerous challenges. The first significant arrest was Segvec, who single-handedly peeled back the layers of the onion.

Segvec, desperate to save himself, explained the "what," the "who," and the "how" of the dark web. He described dark web slang and talked about what a "dump," "plastic," or "BIN list" meant to people online. Segvec spoke about what it meant to be a "Vendor," "Carder," or "Ripper."

He spoke about the beginning, noting that not many would-be criminals initially believed the data was real. Consequently, no one would spend a dime. However, that wasn't the only reason.

Can you imagine? "Hi, my name is Dimitry. I live in Vladivostok, Russia. I have dumps. Send me money. Use Western Union. Once I have money, you get dumps in email."

Unfortunately, it didn't work, and hackers were forced to "hand out" dumps for free. Compensation was in line with free, with one hacker telling me, "I got paid in cartons of cigarettes, bottles of vodka, or relatively small amounts of money. The money was little, but the data was significant. It was all I could get in the early."

In the early days, hackers compromised millions of victims' credit cards, and the profits should have equaled the amount. They had a marketing problem. However, the marketing challenge would soon be solved, thus flipping everything on its head.

Motivational videos were created, photos of luxury items shared, and bags of cash advertised. All these were meant to attract new members, and the data was plentiful. Slowly, the question of whether people would take the "leap of faith" and go all in was answered in a resounding "YES!"

Dark web forums were the place to be, and they were springing up everywhere. In these forums, cybercriminals could discuss their tradecraft and tactics. They could freely speak and share their successes and losses. Lessons are learned and shared on these forums so the next person can avoid such problems.

Once all the information was provided, Operation Firewall was launched from the Newark Field Office. Segvec was placed in the starring role; he performed well, albeit

DOI: 10.1201/9781003680390-6

opportunistically, and took advantage of the agents when feasible, as they were primarily young, raw recruits, and still learning the investigative ropes.

At the start of this case, it was pretty complex. There had been no prior investigations of this scale, and the Secret Service offered minimal guidance or training on handling informants. There was guidance on running "informants;" however, in the early 2000s, it was brief and hardly covered any proper "dos" or "don'ts." agents were forced to learn "on the fly," so to speak, and our bench of knowledgeable agents, who could share experience, was sparse.

The Secret Service's frugality compounded the agent frustrations. Hearing about their issues brought back memories. I recall one protection assignment when I was instructed to secure a room for the agent briefing. ASAIC DuBois called me into his office and said, "We'll only be in the room for no more than one hour. We don't need any services, maybe only a few chairs. So, if you can get it on the cuff."

The notion, or at least my interpretation, was that, given it was merely an hour, the hotel ought to sacrifice profits for the prestige of accommodating the Secret Service. It was absurd. This economic stinginess was not limited to protection; it also applied to undercover purchases, which were frequently initiated with the question, "Can't we get it for free?"

When Operation Firewall began developing, I joined our forensics program. I attended a training session in Washington, DC, where I participated in the office "cooler talk" about Operation Firewall. I listened and made a few remarks, but I minded my own business since it wasn't on my doorstep. Besides, I had enough work waiting for me upon my return.

When I did return to San Diego, a new ATSAIC, Dirk Essel, had reported for duty. ATSAIC Essel was slightly overweight and not someone you would place at the top of fitness charts. Lucky for him that SAIC O'Reilly had already retired; otherwise, I wondered if he would have been selected for this assignment.

Outside of physical optics, ATSAIC Essel was a seasoned agent starting his second and likely last management tour. This primarily stemmed from his frustration with a deeply biased promotion process. Regardless, he knew where the bodies were buried due to his tenure.

About my ongoing negotiations with my insurance company, my lawyer had advised, "The Secret Service is responsible. They are the ones you should be suing." But I wouldn't accept that; instead, I sought alternatives. This led him to request the Secret Service's policy on vehicle usage. I barely knew ATSAIC Essel when I walked into his office, interrupting his nap, and asked, "I have a question. Do you know where I can get the Secret Service's policy on GOVs? Oh and our corresponding self-insurance declaration?"

Rubbing the sleep from his eyes, ATSAIC Essel said, "Why do you need them?"

I responded, "My lawyer needs them. I'm not sure, but do you know that several years ago, I was driving my GOV, had a few drinks, fell asleep, and slammed it into a telephone pole. I'm paying for it now, but my lawyer is fighting with my insurance company."

ATSAIC Essel, now fully awake, replied, "What? NO! I'm aware. Why are you paying for the telephone pole?"

Surprised, I responded, "Well, from what I know, SAIC O'Reilly never checked the 'was' or 'wasn't covered' box on the form. It's just open and unresolved. And the energy company wants their money, so I'm paying."

ATSAIC Essel, now upset, said, "Bullshit, the box needs to be checked 'covered'."

Confused, I asked, "Why?"

"Well," ATSAIC Essel replied, "On my last assignment, an agent, driving his GOV, visited his girlfriend. The next morning, he T-bones another car on his way into the office. They checked that box for him and must do the same thing here."

I was astonished that someone was willing to share this information with me. ASAIC Thomas wasn't interested in helping; instead, he frequently asked, "Are you planning to sue the Service?" Now I understand why: "Headquarters was doing all it could to avoid responsibility."

After my conversation with ATSAIC Essel, I walked into the new SAIC's office. His name was José Montaña, and during his last assignment rumor on the street was that the office was a dumpster fire. To avoid getting burned, Montaña left town quickly. When it came to investigations, well, SAIC Montaña was lost, and now it was my time to explain how my past situation had changed thanks to information from ATSAIC Essel. SAIC Montaña listened and then asked for some time to speak with Headquarters.

A few days later, SAIC Montaña brought me into his office and said, "I spoke with Headquarters. You have two choices. The first is to leave everything as is: pay for the telephone pole, and all will be well. The second is to check the box, and the Service pays for the pole. While you think about it, a word of caution. Headquarters said your incident was 'water under the bridge'—nobody recalls it. Opting for the second choice will reopen old wounds, potentially triggering a new investigation. It's your decision; what's your choice?"

Immediately, I felt the bullying from SAIC Montaña. I was faced with two choices: one was to "just take it and be quiet." Thoughts swirled in my mind; feelings of fairness, fair treatment, and anger rushed over me. Fair treatment is necessary for all, regardless of who you are in the Secret Service. However, I soon realized that the world isn't fair, and this incident served as my reminder.

I glared back and declared, "Option two. The Service established a pattern, and why would I be treated differently?"

Soon after my meeting, Headquarters instructed SAIC Montaña to mark the box as "covered." SA Cross was tasked with supplying the appropriate government claim forms to the energy company, as they are entitled to file a claim for reimbursement of damages. After receiving the paperwork, they filed their claims.

Two weeks later, the Secret Service responded in writing. They acknowledged that Special Agent LaTulip was working under the policy. Because I was working according to policy, the Secret Service accepted responsibility for all damages. However, because the energy company failed to file its claim within one year of the accident, it was denied.

In one letter, the Secret Service avoided all responsibility. Despite all the goodwill shown by the energy company, that letter was their final way of saying "fuck you!" The energy company responded by sending me a letter releasing me from all financial responsibility. The telephone pole was now a relic of the past.

With that chapter closed, I focused on cybercriminal investigations. Operation Firewall was in full swing, and offices were taking notice. Over the next several months, I honed my forensic skills. When Operation Firewall ended, it made headlines. National media picked it up, igniting a footrace among government agencies.

Chapter 7

It all started in San Diego

At the office, agents gathered around the water cooler to discuss Operation Firewall. Conversations ranged from the agents challenges to Segvec's remarkable performance. Headquarters was so impressed that it offered Segvec a role as a consultant. They recognized that with the rise of online operations, the Secret Service needed a trusted resource to advise and guide its agents. From then on, Segvec was that resource.

Meanwhile, a Drug Enforcement Administration (DEA) Agent tipped off the San Diego Task Force. An Asian criminal group, using stolen credit cards, was wiping out high-end electronics stores. This was the second tip in as many days.

A few weeks earlier, a banking contact had shared information about a common point of purchase. Since I had received some slack for "taking all the cases," I wanted to share this one. So, I briefed SA Cross on this and let her run with it.

SA Cross and her partner visited the manager of the seafood restaurant, a popular place among the Asian community in San Diego. SA Cross intended to present the compromised credit card information to the manager, requesting a cross-reference with the restaurant's records to identify which server processed the transactions. Whoever that was would be the primary suspect. Unfortunately, they never reached that stage.

I was assigned as the Duty Agent when SA Cross and her partner visited the restaurant. Coincidentally, while SA Cross was on site about to interview the restaurant manager, a concerned citizen entered the lobby and asked, "May I speak with an agent?"

I replied, "How can I help you?"

The citizen explained, "One of your female agents left an item in the women's restroom." She continued, "It's sitting on a toilet."

Understanding the seriousness of the situation, I asked, "Can you show me?"

Relieved, she responded, "Of course, follow me."

I followed her into the hallway and approached the women's restroom door. I then asked, "Could you please check if anyone's inside? I'd prefer not to interrupt anyone."

"Yes, you're right," she replied, stepping inside the restroom. After a glance around, she confirmed, "All clear, you can come in."

As I entered the women's restroom, the concerned citizen pointed and said, "That's it. It's in there."

Upon opening the door, I instantly spotted the item on the back of the toilet. I quickly retrieved it and said, "Thank you for bringing this to my attention."

Looking distressed, the woman responded, "Do you realize how dangerous this is? Someone could have been killed. You people need to do a better job."

I nodded in agreement and replied, "I understand and will speak with the agent immediately. Thank you again."

Returning to the office, I logged into our internal systems and checked our databases. To my surprise, the item was assigned to SA Cross. Suddenly, it hit me, "She's in the field interviewing

DOI: 10.1201/9781003680390-7

suspects." I needed to reach her quickly, so I sent a brief message: "Please call the office now; I need to update you on a situation."

A minute later, my phone rang. I answered and said, "Did you leave something at the office?"

SA Cross replied, "No, I don't think so. Why do you ask?"

"Check your belt," I said. "I think you'll find something missing."

"FUCK, PLEASE TELL ME YOU HAVE IT," SA Cross exclaimed.

Before she could say another word, I replied, "Don't worry. I have it. When you get back, come see me."

SA Cross immediately left the restaurant and returned to the office, leaving the manager's information behind.

By now, ATSAIC Essel had retired, frustrated by the Secret Service's good old boy back-of-the-house policies. His replacement was Rashed Carrington, a former tactical team member. He was gruff, dedicated, hard-working, a non-drinker, and committed to the family life. He was a rare breed in the Secret Service. Initially, ATSAIC Carrington and I were like oil and water; we didn't mix, but as we got to know each other, we became good friends.

As ATSAIC Carrington settled into his new role, I took a closer look at the information provided by the DEA. After cross-checking the data, I confirmed that the group originated from Southeast Asia and preferred purchasing high-end electronics. They mostly targeted "hot" items from Apple, HP, and Samsung. While contemplating how to break into this group, I received another skimming case from my banking contacts.

This one involved a popular bar in Mission Valley, and I started by speaking with the manager. He was eager to help, remarking, "I'm glad you're here. I've had many calls from angry customers. They say that they were used fraudulently after using their credit cards here. Please tell me you can help."

I responded, "That's why I'm here."

I shared with him the data regarding all credit cards used at the restaurant that were later fraudulently abused. The manager reviewed the information and said, "Please give me ten minutes. I'll be right back."

As expected, the manager returned with paperwork, declaring, "I have it! Sofia Rodriguez. She handled nearly all the transactions. She's on shift now. Can you talk to her before she leaves?"

"Yes, bring her to me," I responded.

"Immediately," the manager answered.

Sofia was visibly nervous, likely already aware of why I was sitting at the most remote table. The question-and-answer period was swift, and Sofia explained everything. Miguel Perez was the person she worked for. She knew all his details: where he lived, his car, and how the operation worked. Best of all, she handed over the skimming device and agreed to cooperate.

An old-school San Diego Police Department Detective named David Summers was assigned to assist me. The case evolved quickly and often changed. I focused on adapting to it, moving at the pace of the criminals. However, Detective Summers pushed back, claiming, "We're moving too fast." I countered, "Crime waits for no one," and pushed it forward despite his pleas.

Sofia spoke with Miguel, who agreed to meet that day at 5:00 p.m., just after Sofia's shift. I briefed SAIC Montaña and ATSAIC Carrington on the operational plan. During the meeting, I explained where each agent would be assigned and where our surveillance van would be parked.

While pointing at the map, I said, "The surveillance van will stop here. Agents will spread out across the parking lot and be ready. Sofia will park close to the van. When Miguel calls, she will guide him to her location. However, keep in mind that Miguel is unpredictable and might suggest a different plan. Therefore, we may need to adapt."

SAIC Montaña tilted his head and stuck his tongue in and out, saying, "Why would we move? The van is perfectly positioned. Miguel needs to come to her."

Considering what SAIC Montaña said, I responded, "We must remain flexible. This setup is ideal for a clear shot, but..."

SAIC Montaña interrupted, saying, "No, we don't move. He comes to us, or we leave."

Thoughts raced through my mind. I thought, "This isn't a TV show. Suspects don't follow a script, and cases never conclude in 30 minutes." The political answer was for me to nod and say, "Yes, Sir."

However, I blurted out, "That's not how it works. This isn't television. We can't force him to stand here or go there just for a photo. We need him to accept the skimmer from Sofia; otherwise, we have nothing. If he tells her to move, we move."

Embarrassed, SAIC Montaña replied, "Okay. I just thought it was better not to move."

"Moving on," I said, "Let's go. We have two hours before the meeting."

The call came on cue as the team was positioned in the parking lot near the restaurant.

"Hey, Rich," Sofia said. "Miguel called. He wants to meet at In-N-Out. I guess he's hungry."

"Okay," I replied, frustrated. "Tell him you'll meet him. What time? Is it still the same time?"

Sofia hesitantly responded, "Now."

"Got it," I acknowledged.

I got on the radio and said, "New location: In-N-Out Burger."

A barrage of replies crackled through the radio. ATSAIC Carrington immediately questioned Miguel's intentions, asking, "What's going on? Why does he want to change the meeting place?"

"I don't know," I replied. "He's hungry or something. We need to move; I don't have time for a debate. He's already here."

This small change will present challenges, such as taking a photo or two, but everything will be fine. The In-N-Out wasn't far off—maybe one to two hundred yards from us. Nonetheless, this sent everyone into action, orchestrating and restaging vehicles to get "eyes on" the target. Unfortunately, we didn't know what vehicle Miguel was driving. Luckily, we did know what car Sofia drove, so this was the focal point.

Like clockwork, Sofia pulled into In-N-Out, saw Miguel, and parked beside him. The meeting lasted two minutes: a quick hello, a wave of the hand, and everyone went their separate ways. That was it for me, as I needed to collect the wire we had placed on Sofia.

Everyone else focused on "putting" the target to bed. Before the night turned into day, the target did just that: he drove, the device in hand, to his residence in Vista, California. Now that Miguel brought the skimming device filled with stolen credit card data to his home, I had all the probable cause I needed to obtain a search warrant.

Two days later, the team met near Miguel's home. After the briefing, we took our positions. Ensuring everyone was prepared, the green light was given. In a booming voice, I pounded on the door and said, "Police with a search warrant, demanding entry!" Upon hearing us at the door, Miguel ran to the kitchen. He was too busy to be burdened with other worries.

With no one answering the door, I called for the battering ram. With a few swift thrusts, the door gave way and flew open. Behind the door, frozen, crying, and unable to move was Miguel's son. The door flew open in his face. I could see his look, eyes wide open, scared as hell.

Fortunately, the heavy door narrowly missed him. Quickly, we moved him to safety and rushed into the house. As we proceeded deeper, we evaluated the situation, checking each room. We discovered Miguel in the kitchen. He was preoccupied, intently watching his jump drive melt in the microwave. I lurched forward and moved Miguel away from the microwave.

Once he was cleared out, I turned and glimpsed through the microwave's door window the remnants of a jump drive tangled in its plastic casing. Recognizing its significance, I initially felt disheartened by my loss. Fortunately, the jump drive wasn't the only evidence at his residence.

Miguel was escorted to our office for processing. I read him his Miranda Warning. Miguel knew he was in trouble. This made him willing to talk and cooperate fully.

Miguel shared, "Phitanousone Sayasenh, or Sone for short, is the mastermind behind the largest credit card cashing operation in San Diego."

"I won't even attempt his full name," I replied. "So, Sone, where is he from?"

Miguel explained, "Sone is originally from Southeast Asia but is now a U.S. citizen residing in South San Diego. He has a large crew. I used to work for him but decided to go independent for my profit. Sone previously skimmed cards, but now he purchases "dumps" to buy high-end electronics, like laptops, iPads, and iPhones."

I raised my hand and asked, "Wait a minute. What do you mean by dumps?"

Miguel replied, "Oh, right, you don't know. A dump refers to one stolen credit card. A guy named YouBuyWeRush introduced Sone to someone named Slim or Slimbady. He sells them to Sone. I can buy them from Sone."

Giving it no thought, I asked, "Can you call him now? Say you want to buy fifty dumps?"

"Sure, I have his number," Miguel replied.

Before he made the call, I set up our recording device, had Miguel sign a consent form, and watched as he dialed Sone's number. The phone rang twice before he picked up.

"What's up?" Sone answered.

"Hey man, do you still have that hook?" Miguel inquired.

"Absolutely," Sone responded confidently.

Miguel then asked, "I need to buy fifty from you; is that cool?"

Without any hesitation, Sone replied, "Yeah, man, one hundred each."

"Deal. I'll pick them up in two days," Miguel said before hanging up.

"Wow, that was easy," I remarked.

"I know him. He sells me what I need," Miguel asserted.

"Regarding that," I remarked. "I understand this is moving fast, but we should discuss the money before reaching an agreement. My bosses aren't going to like me spending $5k."

Once our meeting concluded, I focused on handling the paperwork and briefing ATSAIC Carrington, which I knew would be challenging since we had only five hundred dollars in cash. Spending five thousand dollars and letting it "walk" was foreign to most supervisors. They were accustomed to buying busts and recovering the money. Then there was the puzzle of how to increase the confidential funds.

The learning curve was steep but not insurmountable. Once the cash was in our account, I was ready to move forward. Miguel easily adapted to his new role as a confidential informant. His next mission was to meet with Sone and purchase fifty dumps. Once the team was ready, I called Miguel, saying, "Make the deal."

Miguel parked his car on the street in front of Sone's residence. He exited and walked toward the front door. I watched as he approached the door. From afar, I could tell he was nervous, but, understanding his predicament, he knocked on the door. The door opened, and Miguel disappeared into the residence. Now, I had to rely on the wire Miguel was wearing.

The wire transmitted sound over the radio. However, as is often the case with such devices, the quality was hit or miss. Testing is easy in an open area. However, inside a residence, it's a different story. I listened carefully, but the transmission was weak. I picked up a word here and there, and at times, I heard nothing at all.

For the moment, time stood still. I was interested in what was being said inside and concerned that everything was proceeding as planned. I didn't want anything to deteriorate rapidly or for Miguel to be hurt. Working in this capacity is a risk, and it has occurred in the past to informants. No one wants to be found out midstream that they are an informant. The situation can go from ordinary to absolute violence out of anger.

Listening intently, there was a crackle and a bit of conversation, and then Miguel walked out the front door directly to his car. The radio traffic that had been nonexistent one minute ago was now alive with chatter. Our vehicles' engines all came to life. Detective Summers and I followed Miguel to our meeting location.

Once we arrived, I asked, "How did it go?"

Miguel said, "No problems," handing me a five-and-one-quarter-inch computer disk.

"Anything strange?" I asked. "Did he suspect anything?"

"Nope," Miguel replied. "He was chill."

"Okay," I said. "I'll be in touch. Don't go too far."

I looked at the disk, then at Detective Summers, and said, "Now, I have a lot of work to do."

Something television shows fail to highlight. Forty-five minutes of excitement translated into several days of reports, briefings, and more paperwork.

Special Agent Doug Bander was new to the forensics program and known for his passion for working overtime. While he wasn't a "go-getter" when it came to casework, unlike many other Special Agents, SA Bander was by your side, offering support no matter the situation. He was the ideal candidate to manage the forensics for this case.

The forensics report didn't take SA Bander long to produce; it was only a five-and-a-quarter-inch floppy disk. At first, when I reviewed it, I was clueless. The data was disorganized. Not every value was included; certain tracks had the victim's name, while others lacked it. It was hard to make heads or tails of it. But what was recognizable were the sixteen-digit numbers. These were unmistakable. My next task was to verify whether they were legitimate and to trace their origins.

They were immediately identified and linked to a credit card processing firm called CardSystems Solutions. Over my career, I've interviewed several hackers who claim to have hacked CardSystems Solutions. They claimed that about forty million unencrypted credit card account numbers were stored on their servers. When discussing the company's security, the hackers remarked, "It was nonexistent."

We decided to make one more buy from Sone, after which it was time to arrest him. Because everything was moving smoothly, one can only figure that a complication would arise at some point. After all, it was a big case, and with big cases came big problems.

My big problem came with a phone call from Miguel. I answered, "What's up?"

Miguel replied, "Hey man, did you know Sone left the country?"

Puzzled, I replied, "How would I know? We're not watching him 24/7. When did he leave?"

"A few days ago," Miguel responded.

I asked, "A few days ago? Do you have any idea when or if he'll return?"

After a moment's pause, Miguel said, "Hmm, I'm not sure. Sorry man. I only know he left. If he comes back, I'll call you."

"Great. Talk to you later," I said before hanging up the phone.

Sone wasn't a natural-born U.S. citizen. He was Hmong and came to the United States as a refugee, as did many in the 1970s. The Hmong, mainly from Laos, Thailand, Vietnam, and China, were an ethnic minority in the region and aligned themselves with the United States during the Vietnam War. Once the United States pulled out of the war, many fled to the United States.

I initially thought that Sone had all his family in Southern California, so even though he had left the United States, I felt the odds were that he would return. A few agreed with me, while most felt Sone was in the wind, never to return.

I didn't give up hope but wanted to be alerted if Sone returned. I contacted a friend at the U.S. Customs Service and had him flagged. If it all worked when Sone reentered the United States, I'd receive an email stating as much. Now all I had to do was wait while simultaneously fearing the worst.

Chapter 8

Time to put this to bed and move on!

I was buried in work at the office when, finally, the long-awaited email arrived in my inbox. Sone had entered at the Los Angeles International Airport, but that's when everything went awry. The supposed flag escalated into a full-blown welcome-home search, with every item in in his possession scrutinized the moment he arrived in the United States. Making it worse, it wasn't just one search; there were numerous searches.

It was infuriating to learn that a simple notification had evolved into a comprehensive search that propelled Sone into the ether. As quickly as he arrived in the United States, he disappeared into its vastness. Despite my anger, I experienced a minor triumph: his return confirmed my intuition, even if he was hiding. Now, time was critical, so I initiated the final phase of the operation.

I contacted my friend at U.S. Customs and said, "So that notification was not so quiet after all?"

He replied, "I'm sorry. I don't know what went wrong. It was a bit too aggressive."

"To say the least," I replied. "New request. Can you notify me if Sone attempts to depart the United States?"

"Yes," he said. "However, this is less reliable."

I responded, "Well, it's better than zero." Given recent history, I had little confidence, but I couldn't stand by and do nothing.

Next up was to work with the San Diego Assistant District Attorney, Stan Fanning. I aimed to use the legal system to freeze Sone's bank accounts. My idea was that once Sone's assets were frozen, he'd be forced out of the shadows.

With the legal documents prepared, I served them to Sone's chosen banking establishments. The banks swiftly froze Sone's assets. Accessing them would require a further court order. All I had to do was wait, and the wait was brief. With no cash at his disposal, Sone's attorney contacted Stan Fanning and said, "My client is ready to self-surrender."

Fanning replied, "That's great news. I can get him on the court's calendar in two days. Does that work?"

"Yes," Sone's lawyer responded.

I arrived at the San Diego Superior Court early, my mind processing the questions I wished to ask. Occasionally, I wondered if Sone would get cold feet and instead run. Primarily, my thoughts centered on obtaining a straightforward assessment: Can Sone be of assistance? Does he have valuable information or insights that can advance my investigation? Or will it simply wither away, accomplishing no more than Sone's arrest?

Like clockwork, and more importantly, as promised, Sone appeared in court and voluntarily surrendered. The bailiff made the usual announcements. Sone sat in the courtroom with an emotionless, blank stare.

The clerk declared, "All Rise. Court is now in session. The Honorable Judge Jason Hughes presiding."

DOI: 10.1201/9781003680390-8

Judge Hughes states, "Good morning. Please be seated." Now reviewing the case file, he looks up and asks, "And Mr. Sayasenh, do you understand that you are here today in connection with criminal charges filed against you in this court?"

Sone replied, "Yes, your honor."

Judge Hughes asks, "How do you plead?"

Sone responded, "Not guilty, your honor."

"Your Honor," stated Sone's lawyer, "My client is here today voluntarily and of his own accord. He is a U.S. citizen living with his family in San Diego. The state has frozen his assets. We request that the court consider setting a reasonable bail so my client can manage his affairs during these difficult times."

"Your Honor," Assistant District Attorney Fanning countered, "The defendant returned from a trip to China. After learning of the government's case, he fled to Las Vegas. The defendant has a significant criminal history and an undetermined amount of concealed assets. The state argues that bail should not be granted as the defendant poses a flight risk."

After a brief pause, the District Court judge responded, saying, "The court has considered both arguments and has ruled that bail is denied. The defendant will be remanded into the custody of the San Diego Sheriff's Department and placed at the George Bailey Detention Facility."

The San Diego Sheriff's Department scheduled Sone for immediate transport to the George Bailey Detention Facility. Interviewing him was a high priority, and I wasn't the only one eager to hear his account. Headquarters was equally keen on what Sone could reveal. Knowing his transport schedule, I realized I wouldn't be far behind.

The George Bailey Detention Facility is on the outskirts of San Diego. To the south is the U.S.–Mexico International border; to the east is flat, barren land, beyond which are the Otay Mountains; and finally, to the North and West is the city of San Diego. The building is nondescript, with brown bricks, limited windows, and plain walls. Barbed-wire fences with guard towers on the corners surround it. It wasn't the ordinary resort destination Sone was accustomed to.

Inside the detention facility, they say the walls have ears. True to the saying, there were no secrets, as everyone talked and spread rumors. This wasn't just limited to the people forced to stay overnight. Even the guards were part of the problem. Of course, the information shared can be fractional. However, with a well-timed question based on a rumor, and depending on whether the answer is vague, it can contain the true answer inside. If you were an inmate, you needed to stay on your guard constantly.

I waited for him in the professional visitors' area of the detention center. Eventually, Sone was brought into the room. We quickly introduced ourselves as he entered. He was a short, thin man with a balding head. Sone didn't consume alcohol or illegal drugs—he led a clean, healthy lifestyle. Sone's lawyer assured that he would cooperate. However, there's a difference between giving minimal information to avoid trouble and genuine cooperation. My first impression left me doubtful that Sone would fully engage in this process.

Sone began by saying, "I know you. You arrested the Gonzalez sisters, searched my uncle's place, and arrested that guy who won big at the Barona Casino."

I responded, "Impressive. You seem to know quite a bit about my work in San Diego. What's the reason?"

"There aren't many good investigators in San Diego," Sone replied, "So when you find one, it stands out. You've caught my attention."

I nodded in agreement and said, "Now that I have your attention, tell me about your operation. Your lawyer mentioned you were willing to be cooperative."

"I realized when you served the warrant at my uncle's house that I would cooperate," Sone stated, "But we already knew you were coming that day. Packages don't take long to arrive; it was supposed to be delivered two days prior." Laughing, Sone added, "I told them not to sign for any FedEx package, but those idiots did anyway. I couldn't believe it! If you had come two days earlier, you would have found everything: the plastic, computers, manufacturing equipment—everything."

"Everything? What happened to it all?" I inquired.

"We moved it to my cousin's house," Sone confessed. "Hey, you know," Sone went on, "there was that time you almost arrested me."

"Arrested you? What do you mean?" I asked, confused.

"You remember that seafood restaurant?" Sone asked.

Right away, I remembered the restaurant that SA Cross had visited. I replied, "Yes, I know the place."

Sone then explained, "Yeah, two agents came in. I was working that day, and they didn't stay long. I thought I was finished. I was skimming everything I came into contact with, whether I was the server or not. I skimmed it all. Once the agents walked out, I quit. That was my last day at work."

I shook my head and asked, "What did you do next? I'm guessing that was a cash cow."

"Yeah, it was," Sone replied. "But it wasn't long after that when I wanted a new MSR505. I went to this guy, who owned uBuyWeRush. I explained what I was looking for, and he understood right away. He told me I was old school and suggested a better way. He introduced me to the forums and Slim. Once I got that contact, skimming was a thing of the past."

"Ah, got it," I said, "Why did you go to China?"

"It was a planned trip," Sone explained. "I always go to China and Thailand. This time, I visited Shenzhen and met Slimbady. Do you know Slim?"

I shook my head and replied, "No, who is Slimbady?"

"Slim, he is the man," Sone replied, now rubbing his head, and continued, "Slim knows everyone. He is old school. Been around for years. He sells me the best shit. I can introduce you to him. I'm his best client. You know, two months before he met with P0l1c3D0g, Fidel, and Leon in Shenzhen. The man knows all the old school players. And he's on all the forums. He taught me everything."

"Who is P0l1c3D0g?" I enquired.

Sone began to explain, "He owned DumpsMarket. Before his arrest, I purchased a lot from him. He referred to Leon as his Брат, which I believe means brother in Russian. Leon assisted him on the forum. It was odd that Leon seemed to vanish completely after the arrest. His items were all outdated." Reflecting further, Sone added, "I've never figured it out. P0l1c3d0g's hacker was known as 'Lifestyle' or 'LS.' He never let me speak with him. I wondered what happened to him. Anyway, afterward, all the good stuff was from Slim."

I tilted my head to the side and asked, "Is there anyone else you've worked with?"

Sone paused, then an idea struck him: "Akihikatobe. He lives in the Philippines."

"What did he do?" I inquired.

Sone squinted and scratched his head. "To be dealt in dumps and plastic. I bought a lot from him, too. He was into PlayStation 3s. Looking back, I think I sent him around ten or fifteen. Anyway, the address is in my email."

Sone was divulging information quickly. Already, he was talking about his criminal world, his connections, and their details, and in a rare interview, I wasn't the one pulling teeth. Since I was limited on time, I changed the topic, asking, "Why did you run to Las Vegas? Especially since you told me you knew you were going to cooperate."

"Aw man, that was a shit show," Sone said as he reflected on returning to the United States, "You know the Customs Agent fucked up?"

"Fucked up? What do you mean?" I asked.

"First of all," Sone explained, "they searched me twice, then sent me to the holding area for additional questioning. I couldn't believe it." Sone scratched his head and continued, "Then the guy called me to the counter. He was typing on the computer and then walked away. Since the screen was angled toward me, I leaned forward to see what he was looking at. That's when I spotted, in bold letters, 'HOLD FOR USSS INVESTIGATION.' That caught my attention. I thought fuck my next flight. I rented a car and drove to Vegas for one last gambling trip. Then you froze my shit. So, I figured the fun was over and headed back to San Diego. And here I am."

Looking at the wall, thinking about everything, I said, "What did you mean you can introduce me to Slimbady?"

"I can introduce you. It isn't a problem." Sone exclaimed.

"In person?" I inquired.

Sone explained, "You want to go with me to Shenzhen? I can take you. We can meet him together. I show you the entire operation. As I said, I knew I was going to cooperate. Let's do it."

"Well," I said hesitantly, "Let's not go too fast. I need to get a lot of approvals. But the idea is worth exploring."

During the interview, with Sone as my guide, I was still learning about the underground community. I asked my questions confidently, but inside, I felt like an observer, aware I had much to learn. I needed to familiarize myself with the community's specific slang and terminology and its key players.

After the interviews wrapped up, I would retell the story. Still, senior leaders from Headquarters, including SAIC Alan Stokes, would insist that I was wrong: the online community does not meet in person, as they claim meetings aren't necessary since all business can be conducted online. However, it was common knowledge that several prominent Russian-speaking cybercriminals did meet in person. They gathered in Odesa, Ukraine, where, like any conference of the time, they created swag specifically for the event.

This conference was less formal because it wasn't hosted in a luxury hotel. Instead, Carders from across Eastern Europe convened at a restaurant organized by Script and Abdullah. When senior leaders asserted that Carders don't meet, I pointed out the event in Odesa, Ukraine, and the more recent gathering I knew of in Shenzhen, China.

Slimbady wasn't only instrumental in the online community; he was the bridge between the East and the West. At Headquarters, the prevailing thought was that the East didn't regularly collaborate with the West. Although everyone knew a thriving online business existed in Southeast Asia, no one at the time had the evidence to support this claim. Sone shone a light on that dark picture, and it started to form.

Reflecting on Operation Firewall, it targeted Carderplanet, yet it wasn't the only illicit forum on the dark web. DumpsMarket was another well-known carding forum. Slimbady operated as a plastic vendor there, selling counterfeit credit cards and the necessary equipment for their production. Everything Sone shared was intriguing, especially the chance to meet Slimbady. I still needed to carry out my due diligence, but I recognized that I had the foundational elements for a significant investigation from the moment I left the detention center.

My relationship was also firing on all eight cylinders. Rachel and I flourished, and we spent many hours together. As we bonded, my career aspirations shifted. I realized I was no longer interested in working a full-time protection detail. The assignments were less glamorous to me. I felt like a mere pawn in the larger game, an unnoticed observer, insignificant overall. But turning away from this career path would ultimately limit my professional growth, and I welcomed it.

Since I owned a house in San Diego, Rachel and I discussed whether it made sense to live together. However, she hesitated, still haunted by past experiences and reluctant to leave her comfortable situation. While the idea took root and developed in her mind, I focused on my work.

My first task was to generate a search warrant for Sone's email account. He used Yahoo exclusively to communicate with his carding partners, and I knew these records would provide additional support for Sone's claims. While waiting for Yahoo's response, I turned to a secondary source of information, Headquarters. By this time, they had focused more on cybercrime investigations and accumulated relevant data.

The challenge was that this data was only accessible to Headquarters personnel, and I needed it to strengthen Sone's claims and validate his online activity. Lacking direct access, I had to determine what to request. I started by using the information provided by Sone, particularly regarding the arrest of P0l1c3D0g, and wondered if it was included in the data collection.

These days, meetings are the norm, where we plan and contemplate how to tackle the dilemma of the future case. I started with the idea that small cases present small problems, big cases present big problems, and significantly large investigations present significantly large problems. For this investigation, I planned an unprecedented move: I would take the digital world and move it to the real world.

Chapter 9

Breaking new ground

I knew this case was going beyond our borders and would not be played out in our backyard. If I were to be successful, then traveling outside the San Diego Field Office's assigned area of responsibility was required. But again, I needed a good argument and justification before this happened.

Step one is the operational name of the case. The case number was insufficient, as I was already dreaming big and thinking about the future. ATSAIC Carrington and I tossed operational names back and forth. The first and most liked operational name was "Operation Atlas."

The operational name had little relation to the cybercriminal underground. "Operation Atlas" failed to provide those outside the investigation with a clear link to the targeted audience.

After considerable discussion, we concluded that a name with two words would have the most meaning: one to denote the target and another to reflect the operational impact. A few hours later, I suggested an operational name that was positively received and included the investigation's targets.

Almost everyone online was identified as a "Carder," whether your role was a vendor, moderator, hacker, or community member. It made sense that the first word was "Carder," and the second word needed to convey the impact. Our goal was to create chaos in the network of carders. So now we had the beginnings of the operational name. However, I added a slight twist from my childhood to the operational name. Chaos wasn't to be spelled as one would expect the word to be spelled.

As a child, I loved the TV show "Get Smart." I looked forward to seeing "Agent 99" and "Agent 86" as they pursued operatives of the sinister organization called "Kaos." Hence, the idea was to model this investigation on creating chaos in the carding world, which parallels the fictional evil entity from the show. This threat emerged from the shadows of the underground, dramatically altering the landscape of criminal investigations. Consequently, the investigation was aptly named "Operation Carder Kaos."

After establishing the operational name, the next step was to secure approval from Headquarters. Generally, field offices don't need permission from Headquarters to initiate an investigation, but this case was different. Although the San Diego Field Office could move forward, SAIC Montaña felt unprepared to navigate this unique situation independently.

SAIC Montaña and other local supervisors often prioritized their career advancement over the investigation's actual needs, opportunities, or potential. Instead of outlining what the case required, they consistently relied on placating Headquarters by seeking their permission and approval.

An underlying concern stemmed from the question, "What if?" What if the investigation didn't yield success? What if something negative occurred during the process? What if no arrests were made? This raised further anxiety about what would happen to careers in the face of unsuccessful outcomes. It created a relentless cycle of apprehension and fear. Consequently, their support was crucial for the success of the case.

DOI: 10.1201/9781003680390-9

My opportunity arose during the upcoming annual Electronic Crimes Special Agent Program Conference, conveniently hosted in San Diego. This event would feature the senior leadership crucial for initiating the case. I was tasked with preparing a PowerPoint presentation for executive leadership.

While SAIC Montaña communicated with the executive leadership and organized the briefing, I focused on the presentation. After completing a draft, I presented it to ATSAIC Carrington and SAIC Montaña. If they approved it, I would use this material in my presentation to the executive leadership. With a successful initial run, I secured SAIC Montaña's support, laying a solid foundation for the upcoming conference.

As I awaited the conference day, I arranged a meeting with an assertive Assistant U.S. Attorney, Mickey Clifton. He was part of the San Diego U.S. Attorney's Office's proactive Computer Crime and Intellectual Property Section team and had a strong reputation in the office. Having previously worked with him, I felt confident in our collaboration. "Hey, good to see you again."

"Likewise," AUSA Clifton replied. "Take a seat. How can I help?"

I responded, "I am working on an international credit card hacking case. I have a local informant who was part of a state case. But that has run its course."

AUSA Clifton said, "I see. Are any targets local?"

"No," I replied. "The informant, Sone, has met with these people recently, in Shenzhen, China. But it doesn't end there. I aim to pursue the hackers who are in Eastern Europe."

AUSA Clifton is now looking over my shoulder. "That seems aggressive. Why do you believe we can arrest anyone?"

"Simple," I said. "Sone will be my guide. He will make the introductions, and I will become his partner. He can facilitate meetings, then we can lure the targets to extradition-friendly countries."

AUSA Clifton looked to the hallway and said, "A bit grandiose, don't you think?"

"No," I replied. "Sone met with one of the targets two months ago. Look, it won't be easy, it won't be short, but it's not impossible."

"Tell you what," AUSA Clifton replied. "This can count as one of your office's proactive cases. I will assign it to another attorney and promise to be her mentor."

Consequently, he emailed me that Operation Carder Kaos was assigned to Assistant U.S. Attorney Ayleen Peña. Mickey believed that Ayleen, being relatively new to the section and having more availability, was a more suitable candidate for the task, given his heavy workload. Ultimately, AUSA Clifton determined the case was a lost cause and preferred not to have his name linked to it.

Mickey Clifton's pledge to mentor Ayleen Peña never came to fruition. Instead, she found herself alone, facing one final stipulation: no indictments could occur without clear identification of individuals involved. Therefore, it wasn't me saying I had to work undercover, meet, and hang out with the person vending the stolen data or plastic; it was the U.S. Attorney's Office telling me I had no choice.

When the Electronic Crimes Special Agent Program Conference occurred in San Diego, SAIC Montaña informed me that I was to brief SAIC Alan Stokes from the Criminal Investigation Division and Assistant Director Darius Rookwood. The meeting was scheduled in the Office's conference room, where I waited nervously for SAIC Stokes and AD Rookwood to arrive. This meeting marked my second encounter with AD Rookwood, although he likely didn't remember our first meeting, which stood out to me.

I was in the office with other Special Agents when AD Rookwood entered and greeted us briefly. The conversation quickly turned to "What senior leadership is doing to enhance the Secret Service as a workplace." The budget became the focal point, especially since he was among the few leaders who appreciated the investigative mission.

AD Rookwood shared details about his discussions, mentioning advancements and noting that, due to his leadership, the Service would finally receive its first dedicated investigative budget this upcoming year. I couldn't help but wonder, "First ever? What has the Service been doing all these years regarding our investigative funding?"

Upon the arrival of AD Rookwood and SAIC Stokes, we quickly introduced ourselves, and they took their seats. I began my presentation by discussing previous investigations, their challenges, and how we navigated those obstacles, concluding with our successful outcomes. From those successes, I transitioned to the insights gained. I felt confident and had captured AD Rookwood's attention.

I continued by saying, "The goal of this operation, as per the U.S. Attorney's Office, is to meet in person, to put a real-world name to an online identity. They were adamant: 'They will not indict an online name.' The dark web forums are full of people pretending to be someone they are not. The last thing we needed was to indict an innocent person."

I didn't get much further before SAIC Alan Stokes stood up and began pacing back and forth around the room. Of course, this was a distraction to me. I was doing my best to stay on target, but simultaneously, I was thinking, "Who the hell stands up and begins pacing the row of chairs they just sat in?"

At first, I thought it was a bathroom break, but no, it was continuous back-and-forth pacing. Finally, the reason for his anxious behavior came out, and the question of my "why" was answered. SAIC Stokes blurted out, "They don't meet!" This is why they work online, on the Internet, and in forums; it gives them the anonymity they need to survive."

I responded respectfully, "Sir, we know in the past carders met in Ukraine..."

Interrupting and still pacing back and forth between the row of chairs, SAIC Stokes continued, "Segvec told us they don't meet; there is no reason to meet. It won't work. It isn't possible."

While striving to stay composed and respectful, I pressed on. I continued confidently, "Sir, respectfully, we are aware that carders meet. We even recovered some of the swag they made for the conference in Odesa. Sone, the informant in my investigation, has met Slimbady in Shenzhen, China. We have two confirmed instances of Carders meeting. It is reasonable to conclude they will meet again."

SAIC Stokes, unfazed, murmured, "They won't meet. Why should they? Segvec told us this. It's unreasonable for them to meet. This case is doomed to fail." Frustrated, with a grimace on his face and still not a believer, SAIC Stokes sat down.

My problem was that I was arguing against the "E.F. Hutton" of the Secret Service. Segvec had spoken, and for many, that was that. Carders don't meet. My argument was a losing argument right from the start. Well, unless you have an advocate. Luckily for me, I had such an advocate.

Throughout the entire presentation, AD Rookwood sat and listened. He was attentive and focused. He never spoke or interrupted me during the presentation. Now it was his turn to speak. AD Rookwood gazed at me, almost peering into my soul, and said, "When I presented earlier at the Electronic Crimes Special Agent Program Conference, I looked around. I saw the entire conference room, filled with the normal copy-paste of the typical agent. Then there was you. I noticed you. You were different. You stood out. You didn't 'fit in'."

AD Rookwood looked at SAIC Stokes, then SAIC Montaña, and continued, "Every agent in that room fit the 'mold.' They are what the Service expects an agent to be, but we need someone who doesn't fit this mold. The Service needs people like you. We need people who think differently and see what we don't see. Because you are different, I believe you can be successful and accomplish this mission. I approve. Good luck."

With that vote of confidence, all my uncertainty vanished in an instant. My excitement was barely contained, and I did everything possible to avoid showing it outwardly. As SAIC Stokes heard AD Rookwood's approval, I knew he would not be pleased. I feared that my excitement would be interpreted as flippant to SAIC Stokes and could provoke a retaliatory response. Because of this, I made myself scarce and left swiftly. I had a lot to do, plan, and coordinate, and there was no time to waste.

With the investigation's approval, a sense of urgency formed deep within my soul. I had to focus on the first step: bringing Sone back from his several-month online absence. An absent Carder often translates to an arrested Carder, who can be quickly perceived as a cooperator. The longer he is offline, the higher the mountain to climb to prove otherwise.

To avoid this, I needed to be very thoughtful. Sone was a Carder who was online every day, at all hours, addicted to the rush and driven by the risk. I had to confront this topic directly. ATSAIC Carrington suggested that any excuse except being arrested would work. However, I felt that anything less than the truth wasn't believable.

With Sone back on the streets, I knew time wasn't on my side. I had to prepare for the undercover operation. My first thoughts conjured visions from a movie.

I would have an undercover apartment, travel to exotic locations to meet the bad guys, and stay in safe houses around the globe. I'd be equipped with gadgets designed for protection and anonymity, and resources would obscure my true identity and a witty counterpart to help piece it all together.

Eventually, there would be travel to exotic locations and a sexy love interest. But aside from that, everything else would be a far cry from the reality portrayed in the movies. Instead of an apartment to work from, it was the San Diego Field Office.

It was the beginning of May 2005, at about ten o'clock in the evening, when there was a knock at our office's door. It was Sone, and to the surprise of most supervisors, Sone didn't flee the country. Instead, he arrived on time at the office as promised. My partner and I escorted Sone through the back-office entrance to the farthest office in our space. The room had a window, but it was already dark; there was nothing to see but some city lights.

The room from where we worked was dull; the walls were painted off-white, a fluorescent lamp provided light, three not-so-comfortable office chairs offered us a place to sit, a typical modular office desk provided the workspace, and a middle-of-the-road computer with some tracking software installed was our transportation to the dark side of the Internet.

I initially started by observing, but this wasn't meant to be the long-term plan. I was still new to the business and urgently needed to get up to speed. I needed to become a seasoned online Carder quickly. After all, I was Sone's partner, the one funding his criminal operation, and until now, I had only remained in the background, never participating. However, as my story unfolds, the allure of the underground world drew me into it.

For Sone, the online community was just a few clicks away. Once online, Sone opened his preferred instant messaging service, ICQ. Then, magically, Sone was connected to the online underworld. Immediately, offline messages flashed before my eyes; they came to life with quirky sounds and pop-up emoticons. I was fortunate that Sone had good relationships with several carders, all of whom lived in either Eastern Europe or Southeast Asia.

Despite all the sounds and pop-ups, Sone's ICQ messenger remained quiet. Everyone was offline. I feared Sone had been in jail for too long. All his contacts disavowed him for fear that he had turned to the dark side. In their eyes, Sone was An informant now. Without proof, I pushed that thought far away. There was no need to give SAIC Stokes the ammunition he needed to close my case.

Instead, I created my online profile and used the pseudonym Surfrider; I still needed to join a forum; however, today, I was in bystander mode. Sone, not fearing anything, started sorting through his messages. He left offline messages and introduced his new partner, Surfrider. As Sone answered the messages one by one, he noticed something.

Sone, peering into the computer screen and right-hand scrolling on the mouse, says, "Rich, it seems I have some new friends."

"Friends," I said curiously, "What do you mean?"

Sone, pointing at the screen, said, "SunCredit? I don't know him. I never work with him before. Looking at chat history, seems he send me plastic."

"Remind me," I said, confused. "What is plastic?"

"Plastic," Sone explained, "is the word we use to describe a counterfeit credit card. Dump is one credit card. Usually, it has Track One, but sometimes they give you Track Two. It doesn't matter, I only need Track One. From that, I can build Track Two and insert any name I want. Then I use the hitting and bang out cards. Then there is Ripper. A ripper is someone who steals from another Carder. Slim is funny. He never rip me, but he tell me all the time about people he rips."

"Okay, okay," I said, "Tell me about SunCredit. Who did what, and when?"

"Ah, I see," Sone said. "It was my people. SunCredit send plastic to my uncle's house. Funny, they must have logged in as me and ordered plastic. Seems I owe him $20,000."

My eyes popped wide open as I exclaimed, "What? What do you mean you owe $20,000? Who has that plastic now? I'm going to need to recover it."

Sone rubbed his chin and said, "Let me make phone call. I get it for you."

"Any other new friends?" I inquired.

Peering at the screen, Sone suddenly pops up and says, "Seems they reach out to people, but no, nothing really. Some dumps from Leon and Slim."

Curious, I asked, "And they did this all on credit?"

Sone proudly stated, "I'm best customer. They know I'm good for money."

Taking a deep breath, I said, "That's great. Two things. Get that plastic from your uncle and tell them to STOP working."

Curiously, Sone asked, "What about the money?"

I shrugged my shoulders and said, "I will talk to leadership. Apparently, we have a debt to pay. I know they aren't going to be happy."

Sone typed out additional messages to Slimbady, Leon, and SunCredit. Once he finished, we sat back and waited for the typical ICQ alert message notification sound, "KuKu." While we waited, we talked more about carding, life, and history. This was part of the rapport-building process. The better you know each other and the more they like you, the more effort they'll put into working with you.

By 0300 in the morning, with no one responding to a single ICQ message, we concluded the first night of online work. I felt let down yet optimistic. It was the first night, after all.

I headed home to contemplate my impending conversation with SAIC Montaña and ATSAIC Carrington. I can see the start of the conversation now: "Hey boss, we got several offline messages. Not too much, really. Only that while Sone was in jail, his team used his account to order plastic. The kicker, no one paid for it, now we owe $20,000."

His response, "Get the fuck out of here. Case closed."

I wasn't looking forward to the upcoming morning meeting.

Chapter 10

The ground game starts

As I drove into the office, meeting with management was my priority. Even though not one conversation happened that night, framing the hidden success was paramount. Yes, to some, our first night was a total failure, but I saw it in a different light. I understood the field of play, and as such, I saw the obviousness of success. Sone was in jail; typically, Carders disavowed themselves from those arrested during this time.

Carders stayed as far away as possible, fearing that the arrested had turned police informant. Sone's team convinced his network of trust, the other online Carders, specifically SunCredit, to send plastic without upfront payment, which was a significant victory. This trust allowed us to validate their faith in Sone, and we further achieved this by honoring the debt. SunCredit didn't contact us last night, but this was the first night and not our last night. It was only a matter of time.

Many leaders still didn't believe in the operation. Conversations were often negative. Executive leadership thought there was no way I could meet with Asian Carders. You might ask why they felt this; it was because I wasn't Asian. They assumed only Asians meet with Asians. This meant the target would have to be white for me to meet with them, if anyone at all would even meet with me.

"Good morning, sir," I said as I entered ATSAIC Carrington's office.

"Hey, how are you?" ATSAIC Carrington replied. "How did it go last night? Anything to report?"

"Well," I started with a long pause. "Let's start with the good news. Sone didn't run off to China."

ATSAIC Carrington laughed, "That's positive."

"And," I continued, "there were several offline messages. Some were not worth anything, but then there were others. Leon, Tobe, and Slim were never online. We left them messages. My hope is that they will reply soon."

ATSAIC Carrington popped a few Tums and said, "What else?"

I replied, "We met a new player: SunCredit. He sells plastic and seems to have a similar role as Slimbady. Anyhow, they used Sone's account and got SunCredit to send them two hundred plastic."

ATSAIC Carrington, eyes wide open, asked, "Where's the plastic now?"

"Already ahead of you," I replied. "I got Sone tracking it down. He'll get 'em back or what's left of them."

"Okay great," ATSAIC Carrington replied.

"Well, there's just one problem," I hesitantly said.

"I don't like that tone," ATSAIC Carrington replied.

"We owe SunCredit $20,000," I said. I know that's a lot of money."

"What the fuck," ATSAIC Carrington exclaimed. "Why do 'WE' owe $20,000? That money is Sone's responsibility."

DOI: 10.1201/9781003680390-10

"I disagree," I said confidently. "Look, I don't like it more than the next person, but Sone is our informant. He has no legitimate source of income. I can't very well tell him to go out and commit crimes to pay back SunCredit. We also can't walk away and then be labeled as a ripper. We are on shaky ground for now. I need to honor this debt and move on. We recover whatever Sone can and write in payment for two hundred counterfeit credit cards on our forms."

ATSAIC Carrington reached for another dose of Tums, leaned back, popped two more, and said, "Let me talk to the SAIC."

Briefing Headquarters wasn't only important; it was the cost of doing business. SAIC Montaña was more concerned about his career advancement. Support from Headquarters meant top cover. Without this support, the case would likely stagnate and experience investigative operational decay.

Everyone needed to understand, for example, that paying Sone's outstanding debt would solidify and boost our position. The contrary would mean becoming known as a "Ripper." This wasn't the label Surfrider or Sone needed to have spread throughout the underground community.

Talking with Headquarters was sensitive; for the most part, they understood, but the challenge lay in explicitly acknowledging the risk. I needed to choose the right moment to speak; when I did, my words had to be meaningful and impactful. I also needed to detach myself from the emotion or closeness I naturally felt toward the case. If anyone sensed that I wasn't logical in my analysis, it could become the death blow to the investigation.

Fortunately, the conversations shifted when I spoke, and my points were well received. We discussed the current scenario and agreed that my position was not ideal. I understood their point about the fear of being ripped off; it was only natural. However, I argued, "It was the cost of doing business online."

By the end of the conversation, Headquarters had agreed to spend the undercover funds. However, it was evident that their statements lacked any commitment or tangible acceptance of joint responsibility. Reading between the lines, the message was, "It is all on you, and we accept no responsibility for your failure if nothing of value was obtained."

My next move was to get back online and connect with SunCredit. I needed to establish communication and obtain the Western Union wire transfer "send to" information. I felt there weren't many people who would leave $20,000 on the table. I contacted Sone and instructed him to meet me at the office at ten.

At ten in the evening, Sone messaged, "I'm at the back door."

Right on time. I opened the door and said, "Greetings. Follow me."

Sone nodded his head and said, "Yup."

As we walked through the office, Sone said, "I got your plastic, 140 pieces."

I turned my head back toward him and said, "What happened to the other sixty?"

"They used them and then tossed them," Sone said, handing me the plastic.

"140 is better than zero," I replied. "About tonight, I got the ok to pay the $20,000 to SunCredit. Let's hope he comes online."

Once Sone got to the computer, he logged on, and like the night before, the messages appeared. Leon and Slimbady left, waving emoticons but nothing more. I was beside myself, wondering why they weren't online. It is afternoon where they are, and they must be near a computer at some point.

The clock ticked past midnight without any messages. I knew we were in it for the long haul, but I wondered how long I would need to wait. I was anxious to start conversations but didn't want to seem desperate.

Just then, SunCredit's ICQ icon turned green. I said to Sone, "What do you think?"

Sone pointed at the screen and said, "He's gotta see our messages. I bet he reply."

And like that, a message from SunCredit, "What up?"

Sone replied, "Good bro. What up with you?"

SunCredit's response was short and direct, "Fine. What happened to you?"

This was the moment of truth. I said, "Sone, tell him you got arrested, and your crew stepped in for you. Tell him I stepped in. Your business partner."

"Ok," Sone replied as he typed the message.

"Cops got me," Sone replied. "I just get out."

SunCredit quickly replied, "How is plastic? You make money?"

"Plastic was good," Sone typed to SunCredit. "Surfrider step in to help. We made good money."

SunCredit was direct and to the point, "Good. You owe me $20,000."

"Yeah, I got you, bro," Sone replied, "What are your details?"

"Send the money to Wu-Shen Wong, Hong Kong, China," SunCredit typed out.

"Ok, bro," Sone typed, "We send $5,000 tomorrow."

"Ok," SunCredit replied and then immediately went offline.

I looked at Sone and said, "That seemed weird."

"He only want his money," Sone shot back.

The next morning, I arrived early at the office. I met with ASAIC Dubois and received $5,000. Sending the money via Western Union or MoneyGram was pretty straightforward. However, it wasn't without its exciting dilemmas. Because the Secret Service didn't allow me to work from an undercover apartment and instead required me to work from the San Diego Field Office, I was forced to use various "services" near the office.

For example, my confidential bank account was just around the corner, the "drop" address, used for packages or stolen merchandise, was just down the street, and the Western Union where I sent money was two blocks from the office. It was at a grocery store near my house on busier days. I managed a lot of the undercover work, but at times, due to workload, having an agent who played the role of "my crew" was helpful and required.

In addition, I had only one undercover identity and was overwhelmed with responsibilities. When the case started, I was the undercover, case manager, informant handler, forensic investigator, and management liaison. Because of this, I needed help. Several colleagues also had confidential identities, and I leaned on them for support. However, simply having a "confidential identity" does not translate to being able to be an undercover agent.

Agents were taught from a young age to be ethical. Being asked to send "illegal" money, knowing this money was being sent for criminal activities, was no small task. I recall accompanying SA Grant Mason to a Western Union in San Diego. This Western Union was popular due to its location at the downtown bus station. Because of its location, the line moved slowly.

The amount of money sent wasn't insignificant, around $5,000, but it was being sent to an obscure location, Guangzhou, China. As we stood in line, slowly inching toward the teller window, I could see SA Mason practicing his lines. Mumbling his phonySocial Security number, 123-45-6789, followed by my name is Robert Jackson, and tapering off with his phony San Diego address.

As an undercover agent, I memorized everything as if it were mine from birth. I always relayed that same message to whoever asked. I told them that if ever challenged, they needed to be able to answer the question without pause. Don't be the guy whose response is unnatural. These responses will expose you, allow doubt to enter a person's mind, and potentially expose you. Lastly, never respond by repeating the question as a question. It's a dead giveaway.

Finally, it was our time to approach the window.

SA Grant Mason stated, "I want to send $5,000 to Bo-Yee Wai in Guangzhou, China."

The teller replied, "Okay, I'm happy to assist you with your transaction. What's your name?"

SA Mason said, "Robert Jackson."

The teller said, "Robert Jackson, nice to meet you. What's your Social Security number?"

SA Mason, now confused and looking like a deer caught in a car's headlights, cautiously asked, "What's MY Social Security number?"

The teller quizzically replied, "Yes, Robert, what's your Social Security number?"

His face showed concentration, frustration, and nervousness. It was unmistakable. In that instant, I sensed his fight-or-flight response. I tried to calm him and bring him back by saying, "Yes, Robert, your Social Security number."

Regaining his composure, SA Mason quickly replied, "Oh, my Social Security number. Got it right here. 123-45-6789."

It was a tense moment, for sure. Either the teller was wise to the issue and didn't care, or they were clueless. Either way, I'll never know, but the teller processed the transaction, handed us the receipt, and we headed back to the field office.

When I wasn't attempting to highlight the size of my operation, I used my alias, Richard Druc. I thought this approach would establish trust. Should I ever be challenged, it would be the trust I needed to help protect myself and my backstory. Once I returned to the office, I sent the transaction details to SunCredit.

Given the time difference, the odds were that he wouldn't be online. Therefore, I left an offline message. That night, I met with Sone. My goal was to determine if SunCredit had received the money or, at the very least, if he was satisfied with receiving the payment details.

Unfortunately, SunCredit wasn't an original target. In fact, Sone didn't even know him. Regardless, he was someone to speak with, and for the operation's sake, I continued talking and collaborating with him.

My reasoning is that today's unknown cybercriminal could become tomorrow's wildly successful cybercriminal. Regardless, while I played along with SunCredit, I desperately waited to speak with Slimbady and Leon. To date, there hasn't been one meaningful conversation.

Slimbady was vital because he was Sone's most significant partner and, according to him, provided quality information. As a bonus, they met in Shenzhen, China, five months ago. But before I even spoke with Slimbady, I faced challenges. Leadership had its theories about Carders from the East and the West. Information provided by Segvec led them to believe the East does not work with the West.

I knew this theory was incorrect and dedicated myself to proving it wrong. I knew Sone worked with Slimbady and Leon. Evidence of this relationship was everywhere, hiding in plain sight in his chat history and emails. However, no one in DC was interested because Segvec had spoken. Slimbady represented that connection to the West, specifically because he worked with people like Leon and P0l1ceD0g.

As a bonus, Leon and P0l1ceD0g were the driving force behind the criminal forum known as DarkMarket. From my vantage point, Slimbady was crucial in disproving the prevailing theory and becoming my entry point into the main stage of the underground cyber world. The primary issue was that the operation was still in its infancy; it was just getting off the ground.

My start was sending $5,000. But working behind the scenes were people like Jack Jones, Headquarters' secret weapon. According to him, SunCredit was a waste of resources. I disagreed. Since the online community was interconnected, I hoped SunCredit would communicate with other Carders and perhaps, if not now, eventually tell them, "Surfrider was a good guy."

On the operation's third night, all my uneasiness was put to bed. Slimbady not only answered the offline messages, but his ICQ status was green, which meant he was online. I was anxious to start having Sone take a back seat. Slowly, I planned to reduce Sone's role in the operation. Of course, Sone will always be required to be in the background, but the sooner Sone fades away, the better.

With Sone looking over my shoulder, I pinged Slimbady. "What up?"

If Slimbady was online, his ICQ indicator would be green, and any left message would be followed by that telltale signal, "KuKu." Unfortunately, none of the indicators were present. Nonetheless, I waited for his response. At first, I saw Slimbady's icon bubble, indicating he was responding. The only issue was that it wasn't always reliable.

Then my ICQ came to life: "KuKu," followed by a message, "What up?"

I quickly clicked on it, excited to start a conversation with Slimbady, but the message wasn't from him; it was from SunCredit. I was disappointed, but at least someone from the carding world was pinging me.

"Hey," I wrote, "Not much. How are you? Did you get the money?"

"Received," SunCredit replied. "When you send the next $5,000?"

I thought, "Wow, you just got $5,000 and already asked for the next payment," understanding, if it were me, I would have the identical eagerness. I typed my reply, "I can send tomorrow. Same details?"

SunCredit replied, "Yes, same details. Do you need more plastic?"

I was in no hurry to be in more debt to SunCredit. Besides, ATSAIC Carrington would have gone through the roof if I agreed to more counterfeit credit cards. "No, I'm good. Still working on the plastic you sent," I replied.

"Ok," SunCredit replied, "Ping me if need more."

"Hey," Slimbady replied, "How are you?"

Reading that message sent a jolt of energy through me. SunCredit and Slimbady were talking to me at nearly the same time. "I'm good," I replied to Slimbady. "What have you been up to?"

"Work," Slimbady replied. "I heard you got arrested. Is that true?"

I had already admitted it to SunCredit, which meant there was no point in changing the story now, so I tapped away at the keyboard to Slimbady, "Yeah, small problem. But all is good now. I just need to get back to business. I need to make money to pay the lawyers."

Slimbady quickly responded, "You need dumps?"

I needed to process the request. I had plastic, but I was still waiting for someone to offer me dumps. I started typing when a message appeared from Slimbady: twenty Track One dumps, sent just like that, followed by, "You want more?"

Not knowing the price, I replied, "Thank you. No, that should be good for now. How much do I owe you?"

"Free ☺," Slimbady replied. "Help you get back on your feet. Anything else?"

Since I had "lost" my equipment, I felt it would make sense to ask, "Do you have any Chinese embossers?"

"Yes, I can get for you," Slimbady replied, "How many you need?"

I thought, "How many do I need?" One, so I replied, "One, how much?"

"$1,500. What is address?" Slimbady replied.

"Give me a day," I said. "I'll get you the details."

That night's conversation went well; not only did Slimbady not bat an eye at Sone's absence, but he also sent stolen credit card tracks, referred to online as dumps. We quickly learned these dumps were from the CardSystems Solutions network intrusion. At this time, that database had a validity rate of fifty to sixty percent, which was okay, considering they had been hacked multiple times by different hacking groups.

In addition to possessing dumps, Slimbady had access to counterfeit credit card manufacturing equipment. Following Sone's arrest, the strategy I devised naturally meant we needed to restart the criminal operation. In other words, we urgently required plastic, dumps, and manufacturing equipment. Slimbady was the perfect ally because he had access to all these necessities, and I didn't hesitate to begin ordering the various items.

Over the following weeks of the operation, Sone and I worked together, with me handling the day-to-day conversations. However, we collaborated on the best approach to our online discussions. Additionally, as I was still learning, I occasionally misspoke, used incorrect phrases, and misused slang. Fortunately, Slimbady, SunCredit, and eventually Leon were happy to serve as online mentors. Still, this remained a business relationship.

Because the relationship was built on the criminal business, I always had to consider some kind of purchase. Although I was online discussing my personal life, sharing jokes, talking about travel, and trying to endear myself to them, I still needed to maintain the business aspect of the relationship. If the money stopped, the conversation gradually diminished.

However, the money flowed at this point in the operation, and the relationships thrived. Slimbady kept his word and sent dumps, counterfeiting equipment, and more plastic than I ever needed. An area of concern was that my business was thriving, typically a welcome result of hard work. As Slimbady and SunCredit introduced me to more online Carders, my sphere of influence grew.

My issue was that everyone had a scam requiring a trusted person in the United States to facilitate. This meant I needed more money, something ATSAIC Carrington only had a limited tolerance for. Worse than money, the risks often outweighed the rewards, which were never shared equally. I recall one such conversation.

"What up, bro?" Leon asked.

I replied, "Yo, I'm good. What up, brat?"

Leon said, "Glad to hear. I got a guy who need a drop in the United States. Can you help?"

"Depends," I said. "What do you need?"

"They need accounts," Leon explained. "Then they'll send money."

"Okay, sounds interesting," I said, pretending to be impressed. "Question. Bad or good money?"

"😉," Leon replied.

"😁," I said. "Ok, what's my cut?"

"Twenty percent," Leon stated.

I was taken aback and said, "Only twenty percent?"

Leon responded in surprise, "Is that not enough? Maybe I can increase it for you."

I replied with a smiley face, "Look, I have many expenses. I take care of my team. If someone gets arrested, I pay for their lawyer—it's all on me. I cover about eighty percent of their purchases when my team goes shopping. A twenty percent cut feels unfair. ☹"

"Oh," said Leon. "How do you get so much?"

"It's a long story, but here's the short version," I explained. "My guys shop for high-end electronics like iPads, iPhones, Samsungs, Macs, and IBMs. Then I have a contact in LA who buys all my stuff at eighty percent of the market price."

"I see," said Leon, "Do you check your dumps?"

This referred to dump-checking services like Try2Check, which I had tried before. However, they offered little investigative value since the U.S. Attorney's Office wasn't keen on pursuing these cases. Plus, I had heard on forums that these services could lead to dumps being canceled.

"Nope, they kill dumps ☺," I answered. "I have another way. I go to the gas station and fill up my tank. If they die, then they die, but at least I get the gas. 😛"

Leon replied, "Do I tell my guy, no?"

"😁," I responded, "Yes, tell him no. I'm not interested in such a small amount. If he has a real deal, then we can talk."

Online criminals logically desired all the rewards without any risks. They proposed that I open bank accounts in the United States, wait for illegal funds to be transferred into those accounts, and finally withdraw the money, keeping only twenty percent for my troubles.

My interest was nearly nonexistent, as I understood that, without being in law enforcement, I would end up with a pair of silver handcuffs instead.

Regardless of their acceptance, anyone who agrees must recruit and pay someone. If the person is unaware of the scam, they will use their Social Security number and driver's license. If they are aware and willing to take the risk, they will incur additional expenses, such as obtaining a fake Social Security number and driver's license.

At my expense, I would need these documents to obtain drop cell phones, bank accounts, and postal mailboxes. Then, the person taking the risk will want their share. At that rate, if I were lucky, I could walk away with seven dollars for every one hundred dollars deposited.

Since I worked in law enforcement, I considered other factors, such as the unfortunate individual whose money was being stolen, the paperwork I needed to complete, the costs associated with seizure, and obtaining authorization to spend the confidential funds from SAIC Montaña. This all added up to a lot of headaches.

Still, I needed a post mailbox. A two-minute walk from the San Diego Field Office was a great place. The post mailbox I purchased was the least expensive and the smallest available. The box was approximately three by five inches, perfect for letter-size mail.

I didn't get a larger box due to costs; the government was on a budget, and spending more money on something like this wasn't something I was prepared to contest. Besides, I was already spending a significant amount of money online. In fact, I was spending $5,000–$12,000 a week, divided among people like Slimbady, Leon, SunCredit, and Fidel.

To register the post mailbox, I used my fictitious business along with my fictitious name, Richard Druc, and an address that was in San Diego but didn't exist. Security procedures were improving; maybe the ZIP code or the street was checked, but drilling down to the exact address still wasn't part of the equation.

My philosophy to construct my backstory was to mix little bullshit with real life. As a result, I didn't need to recall imagined details; I just needed to remember my past. For example, I lived at 3856 Pendiente Court in one of the apartments. The apartment complex had many buildings listed alphabetically, but ended on the letter "T." I kept the physical address, added the letter "Z," and used my apartment number.

Regarding my name, I continue to use "Rich" because it was ingrained into my DNA. There's nothing worse than socializing with someone while drinking and being inattentive. I can imagine myself intoxicated, distracted, while my new friend calls out my made-up name, and I don't react. This situation is bound to end badly.

But the last name was different. Other than colleagues who work in the U.S. government, people don't refer to their friends by last name. Therefore, my last name can be whatever, and I chose to use the last name of a good friend, Nicoleta Druc.

We met in Belgium while I was on a protection assignment. Nicoleta and I hit it off and connected immediately. When time allowed, we spent every moment together. Our time was magical, but like magic, it was over in a flash. After several days, we went our separate ways and lived our lives.

Operational name aside, I focused on orchestrating my first overseas meeting. AUSA Peña wanted real-world names, not online identities, to prosecute criminal cases. By this time, only two weeks into the operation, I had criminal conduct from everyone I worked with online. The only missing item was the online Carder's real-world identity.

Chapter 11

The clock is ticking, let's get moving!

Operation Firewall just concluded, and this was a big success. All the offices took notice and now desired to make their headlines. Operations were popping up all over the place: Operation Hard Disk, Operation Trojan Horse, and, of course, there was mine, Operation Carder Kaos. The fever wasn't restricted to the Secret Service; the FBI and the Postal Inspection Service were in the mix and competed in the same space.

Headquarters began collecting data seized from carders worldwide to give the Secret Service an advantage. At the same time, I had been informing anyone who would listen that, according to Sone, P0l1c3D0g's hacker was named "Lifestyle" or "LS" for short. Upon hearing this, ATSAIC Miguel Lopez told me that in 2004, there was a house party in Belarus.

I never received the complete story, but the key point was that the Belarusian police arrested P0l1c3D0g. Most importantly, they confiscated and forensically imaged P0l1c3D0g's computer hard drive during the arrest. Even more significant, those forensic images were shared with the Secret Service and sat on a shelf at Headquarters.

Discovering that P0l1c3D0g's forensically imaged hard drive was in our possession gave me hope. I promptly requested a copy of P0l1c3D0g's hard drive to be sent to me, which ATSAIC Lopez assured me would happen. Since its inception, I maintained that Operation Carder Kaos was designed to start in the digital world, where I would build rapport, establish my persona, and create credibility. Once that was accomplished, the operation would transition from the online realm to the real world. This ideology had been approved by AD Roockwood several months ago, but it was still in principle only, and now it was time to put it to the test.

Sone and I met at the office for another late-night conversation. As many nights before, it began with a knock at the office door.

I opened the door and said, "Welcome, come on in."

"What's up, bro?" Sone said as he walked into the office.

"Not much," I sighed. "Meetings. Talking. More meetings. I still haven't gotten to the paperwork. I did get the search warrant results from Yahoo—lots of great data. Sorting through it all now."

"Ha," Sone laughed. "I'm glad I don't have to do that."

Laughing, I replied, "I should've made that part of the plea deal."

I sat down and logged into my ICQ account, Surfrider. I was becoming addicted to the "KuKu" sound; it felt like receiving a package in the mail. Upon hearing it, I opened the message without hesitation.

"Boring. Nothing special," I said. "Let's ping Slim. Seems he is online."

I typed a message to Slimbady saying, "What up, bro? ☺"

I didn't wait long; Slimbady responded, "What up, Sone? You need anything?"

Before I could respond, Slimbady was sending more dumps. The relationship had unspoken words; this was business, not a social hour. However, I wanted the social aspect of the interaction.

 DOI: 10.1201/9781003680390-11

I had engaged in small talk and purchased the plastic, dumps, and counterfeit manufacturing equipment—it was time to put up or shut up.

"☺ Thanks," I said. "I was thinking of coming to Asia soon. You wanna meet?"

"Sure," Slimbady replied. "When you come?"

I almost fell off my chair; it was so simple. I quickly said, "I haven't picked the dates yet, but soon. I'll let you know when I make the plan."

"Okay. ☺ I be here." Slimbady wrote and then went offline.

"That was simple," I said to Sone.

"I told you. Slim, meet me anytime," Sone replied.

"Okay, but I never thought it would be so simple," I said, smiling.

Pointing to the screen, I said, "Look, SunCredit is online. Let's ping him."

Sone just shook his head and said, "Yeah."

Writing to SunCredit, I said, "What's up, bro? I was thinking of coming to Asia."

I turned to Sone and said, "Since I'm on a roll, why not?"

I glanced at the screen and noticed the unmistakable signs of SunCredit's writing, followed by the eagerly anticipated message. "When?"

My eyes widened in disbelief as I replied, "Soon! I'm making plans. I need a holiday. ☺"

"Okay," SunCredit responded. "You need anything?"

I didn't want to spend the money yet, so I replied, "No, I wanted to say only about Asia."

"Cool ☺," SunCredit said. "Ping me if you need plastic. Take care."

The rest of the night passed slowly, but those replies were precisely what I needed three weeks into the operation. The following day, I entered ATSAIC Carrington's office and announced, "Good news! SunCredit and Slimbady agreed to meet me in Asia."

ATSAIC Carrington, who had been typing at his computer, turned to me and exclaimed, "What? When? Wait a minute, they agreed to meet in Asia?"

Smiling, I said, "Yeah, but no exact dates. Regardless, we need to start planning. I figure we have about three weeks."

Some hoped I would succeed in meeting an online Carder; others doubted it would ever happen. They murmured these doubts in the hallways of Headquarters. These individuals sided with SAIC Stokes and his sidekick, Segvec.

Segvec's message was "Carders, shielded by the anonymity only the Internet could offer, had no reason to meet." He argued that anything you needed—money, dumps, plastic, products—could be sent and received from the comfort of home.

Despite the discussions happening far from me, friends of mine, including ATSAIC Lopez, shared insights with me. The "talk track" was absurd because Jack Jones knew Carders had met. He reviewed their logs and learned that Script and Abdullah organized an event in Odesa, Ukraine.

Jack Jones explained, "They produced and sold swag during the event." If this isn't enough evidence to support my premise that online Carders will travel and meet one another, I am not sure what will.

As I prepared for my first in-person meeting, Headquarters decided to host the inaugural online undercover operations conference, "The Carder Alliance Project." Case agents were invited to Washington, DC, to discuss their goals and targets and coordinate efforts.

Behind closed doors, Headquarters withheld funding, even though it was readily available. They believed there was no need to fund two operations targeting the same Carders or cases that showed little promise. Operation Carder Kaos showed promise; therefore, it was prioritized, and I was invited. I was very proud of my accomplishments, as they were already materializing into a potential international face-to-face meeting.

Everyone met in the Woods Conference Room on the lower level of the Headquarters building. ATSAIC Lopez, who was part of the program, greeted the case agents. Because this was Headquarters, everyone was in their best business attire, clean-shaven, and had freshly trimmed hair.

Everyone except for me. I wasn't wearing the approved Secret Service high and tight haircut. Instead, since I was living in San Diego, I decided to grow my hair long to resemble Jeff Spicoli from Fast Times at Ridgemont High. Not to mention, my inner me wanted to rebel against the norm.

SAIC Stokes kicked off the conference with a typical welcoming speech that largely adhered to the same pattern: a brief motivational address and some information about the current state of the Secret Service. Once this concluded, Ben Woods, the lead case agent from Operation Firewall, was honored to speak first. He aimed to inspire and share lessons learned, focusing on what to avoid and how to avoid pitfalls. The secondary goal was to discuss how the clean-cut, well-dressed gentleman contributed to his case's success.

I had heard his name before, but this was the first time I met Segvec. Ben Woods described how Segvec, acting as his confidential informant, was the principal catalyst behind Operation Firewall. Segvec provided the targets and escorted the agents through the underground community's catacombs.

From this success, Segvec was crowned the E.F. Hutton of the online world. When he spoke, the Secret Service listened, and Segvec spoke a lot—so much so that Secret Service leadership blindly believed everything he said. Segvec gained so much trust that he was offered a consulting position. This meeting was his "coming out" party and introduction to us.

Once SA Woods had finished telling his success story and cementing the idea that everyone needs an "Segvec" to be successful, it was time to pivot. There was just one problem. Segvec was still sitting astutely, ready to listen, at the front of the room. It was evident that ATSAIC Lopez and SAIC Stokes were comfortable having Segvec "listen" to every case agent talk about their operation. And why wouldn't they? It was their idea to hire him.

Fortunately, not everyone who attended was ready to hand over their trust and the keys to the kingdom. Several agents and their supervisors contested and insisted that Segvec be removed from the room. ATSAIC Lopez and SAIC Stokes pushed back, stating that from their perspective, Segvec was a paid consultant. For him to be successful, he needed to understand the cases. Then, Segvec could provide the necessary advice. Didn't you hear, "Everyone NEEDS an Segvec to be successful?"

Initially, I stood in the background, but once I understood the conversation's subject, I joined in and agreed, "Segvec had to leave." The discussion took about fifteen minutes to resolve. Reluctantly, ATSAIC Lopez agreed, and Segvec was asked to leave the conference. However, it would take several more years, including Segvec's move to Florida and multiple investigations, before I would realize just how fortunate it was that Segvec was asked to leave that room.

After the conference, I returned to San Diego and focused on the case. I was paying off my debt to SunCredit and building rapport with Leon and Slimbady. In addition to settling my debt, I needed to devise a plan that involved criminal activity from both Slimbady and SunCredit, which started in San Diego and concluded in Macau. I faced one issue: when I mentioned SunCredit to Slimbady and vice versa, I quickly discovered they didn't like each other.

Each accused the other of being untrustworthy. To validate himself to me, SunCredit claimed he was a Triad. The Triads were a well-known Chinese gang that often resorted to violence. When I informed Slimbady of SunCredit's claim, he just laughed. Slimbady insisted that SunCredit wasn't a Triad.

Even so, it was difficult to confirm anything with complete certainty. However, I was planning to travel to Hong Kong, and the thought of going there with the possibility that

SunCredit could leverage the local criminal underground to access immigration records raised the stakes.

If you Googled Richard Druc, you wouldn't find much. However, searching for Richard LaTulip would reveal a more intricate history due to my involvement in the 9/11 terrorist investigations in San Diego. The search results would link me to the Secret Service and a different life. Having no online presence under the name Richard Druc would raise red flags. Online, I was Richard Druc; that's how everyone knew me.

I even sent money through Western Union, which required me to provide an ID. However, upon entering China, I used my real name, Richard LaTulip, and even checked into hotels under that name. If anyone looked a little deeper or checked at the front desk, it would have been enough to make a connection.

Around this time, ATSAIC Lopez was pushed out of the Criminal Investigative Division. He wanted a promotion but had not yet worked on a Secret Service protective detail. SAIC Stokes offered him a few options: accept a protection assignment or remain an ATSAIC. ATSAIC Lopez chose the latter, and just like that, he was out. ATSAIC Ken Sheehan eventually took his place.

Ken Sheehan was a dedicated company man, primarily focused on advancing his career. However, ATSAIC Sheehan believed strongly in the Secret Service's cyber mission. Like me, he viewed a role in cyber as a pathway to a career beyond the Secret Service. ATSAIC Sheehan developed a connection with Jack Jones, recognizing what ATSAIC Lopez saw in him. Jack Jones was well-versed in the underground community, which provided him with a significant advantage and influence.

Jack Jones studied in Russia and spoke several languages, a rarity among most Americans. More importantly, he had a solid understanding of computers, particularly programming and networking. Coupled with his knowledge of the dark web, he was truly exceptional. Once the contract was signed, a notable event unfolded: Jack Jones began working for the Secret Service.

With ATSAIC Sheehan now overseeing the section, he instructed me to "keep purchasing dumps and target fresh BIN lists." My operation was a valuable asset for intelligence. Every few weeks, because of the data I purchased, the Service could identify another network intrusion.

The online undercover investigation was progressing smoothly. I was putting in long hours, day and night, weekdays and weekends, meetings stacked upon meetings, phone calls lasted hours, and often were repetitive. Online, I was closing deals after deals, spending an average of $15,000 weekly. Reports fell behind, but I never neglected drafting the legal process to serve search warrants or subpoenas on every U.S.-based account. This data proved invaluable.

While all this was happening, I also planned the first trip to meet Slimbady and SunCredit. I needed to align with all stakeholders, including the U.S. Attorney's Office, which had multiple requirements. First, they were not interested in indicting anyone by their online name; they needed the real-world name. Second, there was a requirement related to venue: everything I did online required a connection to San Diego; otherwise, prosecution was at risk.

Therefore, I planned to purchase one hundred counterfeit credit cards. What I needed from Slimbady and SunCredit was for them to emboss the "stolen" account numbers and encode the date onto the credit cards. I would pick these up in person since I "planned" to be on holiday in Southeast Asia.

Looking at the map, Shenzhen, China, is located next to Hong Kong and Macau. Since they bordered each other, it was easy to travel between them. Moreover, Macau is the "Las Vegas" of Asia, but unlike "Las Vegas," it has almost no restrictions. Macau has quickly become the most attractive destination for SunCredit, Slimbady, and Vincent.

Regardless of the final decision on Macau or Hong Kong, I had the interest of SunCredit and Slimbady. Aligning with the U.S. Attorney's Office requirements, I started negotiating a face-to-face deal. Since the relationship was still new, I wouldn't get the best price point for the work or the products. However, the cost wasn't important; I knew this going in. The most crucial part was securing the meeting.

I can save the government money later during the operation. After a few conversations, SunCredit and I reached an agreement. He would emboss the one hundred stolen credit card numbers and the names I provided onto the counterfeit credit cards in his possession.

I would pay him $5,000 upfront and another $5,000 upon receiving the finished product in Macau. This part of the plan satisfied the U.S. Attorney's Office requirement for venue. I needed SunCredit to understand that the money originated from San Diego.

To help prevent future disputes about the venue, I ensured SunCredit understood I was traveling from San Diego and provided the credit card details while there. As a bonus, all the names I provided to SunCredit to be embossed on the credit cards were aliases of my colleagues.

To get this operation approved, I needed authorization from local leadership and Headquarters, the U.S. Attorney's Office, the U.S. Embassy in Hong Kong, and the local Police. However, I wasn't too concerned then because I knew I was getting closer to dispelling the myth that "people who work online" don't meet in person. Additionally, there is a persistent belief that individuals from Asia don't meet with those who aren't Asian. Sadly, these myths were deeply embedded in the minds of the leadership at Headquarters.

I was weeks away from meeting face to face with two crucial online Carders, which would help dispel these myths. Slimbady had invited me to Shenzhen, China. However, I had to decline this invitation, knowing that the U.S. government would not permit me to work undercover in China. Moreover, since Sone had just visited Slimbady in Shenzhen, an offer to meet in a different location wouldn't seem unusual.

Having positive news, I went to ATSAIC Carrington's office. I knocked on the door and asked, "You got a minute, Mr. Carrington?"

ATSAIC Carrington quickly popped several Tums and said, "Yeah, sure, what do you have?"

I explained, "Just talked to Slim and SunCredit. They are good to meet. Slim offered to meet me in Shenzhen, but I politely declined. I countered with Hong Kong."

"That's great," ATSAIC Carrington exclaimed. "Anything else?"

"Yup," I said. "I talked to AUSA Peña about the needed venue. To do that, I started a conversation with SunCredit. I will have him emboss one hundred credit cards with dumps and put the agents' undercover names on the counterfeit cards."

ATSAIC Carrington thought about it and said, "That's a good idea. How much?"

Feeling a bit uneasy, I responded, "It's $10,000. I send him $5,000 from San Diego and then give him the other $5,000 in Hong Kong."

"Wow, that is a lot of money for one hundred embossed counterfeit credit cards," ATSAIC Carrington said. "Let me talk to SAIC Montaña."

"Well, there is more," I explained.

"More," ATSAIC Carrington said, "What else?"

I explained, "Slim wants a laptop."

ATSAIC Carrington, surprised and taken aback, said, "What? Why does he want you to buy him a laptop? Can't he buy his own? Why would we buy him a laptop? This seems off."

"Okay," I explained, "Let's remember we are Sone's partners. Sone always bought electronics and gifted them to Tobe, Slim, Leon, and others. They expect it and aren't afraid to ask for it. Look, I'm doing what I can to meet them. I know I'm not getting the best deals, but the outcome matters most."

Thinking about it, ATSAIC Carrington said, "I get it. Okay. I will talk with SAIC Montaña. It's not going to be easy."

Later that day, I heard from ATSAIC Carrington that everything had been approved. However, there was some pushback. The pushback came not per se from ASAIC Dubois but rather because of the Secret Service reimbursement form.

The form wasn't overly complicated. You filled out a case number, those accountable, the "reason" for the expenditure, and then the "what" or the contraband received. It was the "what" that was causing the issues. SAIC Montaña was uncomfortable filling out the form without listing what contraband was received.

SAIC Montaña believed, "You don't give away money for free." Except this is the underground, where there's no bureaucracy or forms to fill out. If you want to do something, you just do it.

Because of this "quandary," the only solution was for me to return to the chat and negotiate the purchase of the computer for contraband. I needed to be the opposite of what Sone was before I got involved. No longer would I be "generous." Everything I "gave away" had to be linked to some form of contraband.

Part two of the discussion was particularly disconcerting for me. It concerned the quality of the computer I was allowed to buy for Slimbady. If it weren't bad enough that I had to go back online and negotiate the sale of a "stolen" computer, the computer would not be "top shelf."

Instead, I was permitted to get a "middle-of-the-road" computer, and according to ATSAIC Carrington, since it was "free," Slimbady should "accept it." The logic was flawed, but I had too many other issues that demanded my attention to care.

I went back and pinged Slimbady, "What up, Bro?"

Slimbady replied, "☺ Hey, Sone. I'm good. U?"

"All good," I replied. "I got you the laptop."

Slimbady replied, "☺"

Unsure how to phrase it, I typed, "Could you send me some dumps for the laptop?"

After a brief pause, the chat bubble appeared and disappeared. I wondered what Slimbady was thinking. Shortly after, the response arrived: "How many you want?"

I felt a wave of relief and quickly wrote, "40."

Slimbady replied, "Okay."

Surprisingly, Slimbady didn't object to or resist my request for forty dumps for the inadequate computer. With that matter resolved, I turned my attention to the U.S. Attorney's Office, where I needed to update AUSA Ayleen Peña.

Over the next several years, Ayleen and I collaborated closely and discussed the case frequently. Her primary concern was the Secret Service's policy on undercover operations, as it would ultimately impact how she presented the case to a jury. The specifics of the operational conduct could sway her arguments.

This prompted us to examine the Secret Service's Undercover Operations policy. AUSA Peña and I had to clarify what actions were permissible under the policy. I retrieved a paper copy stored in a three-ring binder labeled INVESTIGATIVE POLICY. Upon reviewing the undercover operations section, I was taken aback to discover that the policy lacked numerous details and restrictions.

Essentially, the policy stated, "YES, a Secret Service Agent can conduct undercover operations." At that time, it was just six pages long, double-spaced, and printed on one side.

Upon entering AUSA Ayleen Peña's office, she greeted me with, "Hello, please have a seat. How are you?"

I responded, "I'm good, thank you. How's work? Hope it's not too hectic."

"It's the border," she replied. "We deal with drugs and other crimes. It's the top priority in our office."

"Hopefully, you still have time for Operation Carder Kaos," I joked.

"Of course! Speaking of that," AUSA Peña asked, "Have you read your policy? What did it say?"

"I'm unsure if it's good or bad news," I said. "But honestly, not much. We have a policy that says we can conduct undercover operations. So, that's good news."

Laughing, AUSA Peña responded, "That's good! What does it say about drug use?"

"Nothing," I replied.

With a look of surprise, AUSA Peña asked, "Okay, what about gambling?"

"Nothing," I repeated.

"Alright," she said, "How about prostitution?"

"Again, nothing," I said. "It doesn't say much. Is that a bad thing?"

"Listen," she said, pondering the situation, "it's all about how the jury perceives things. If you have to use drugs to protect your life, no one will judge you. If you must sleep with someone to maintain your cover, nobody will condemn you. But the defense will portray you as an immoral person. I just need to know these details so I can protect you. The policy is crucial—it outlines what you can and can't do. Since it doesn't explicitly ban these actions, at least you're not violating anything. We can manage the rest."

"I'm glad to hear that," I replied. "If you need anything else, just let me know. Take care."

"Good luck and take care," AUSA Peña said as I exited her office.

We agreed that, good or bad, moral or immoral, I was allowed to take necessary actions to maintain my cover. The jury will be what it is when we cross that bridge. As an undercover agent, I needed to fit in, belong, and blend with my new friends, who were far from moral.

Approval from SAIC Montaña and the U.S. Attorney's Office meant it was time to speak with Headquarters. People like SAIC Stokes still believed no one would meet, saw it as a waste of money, and were skeptical there would ever be any "real" success. However, because SAIC Montaña supported my operation, SAIC Stokes had little choice but to placate us. He agreed to proceed with the operation.

To the investigation's detriment, with their support also came their limitations. The rules of the road were outlined as follows:

- The meeting must be in a public location.
- The U.S. Embassy and local government must support the operation.
- I could only meet one target per day.
- I wasn't allowed to move from the meeting location.

I protested, indicating that some requirements were not "normal" for personal interaction. It was strange to travel halfway around the world to meet with someone you did business with for several hours and not leave or even go outside the original meeting location. Nonetheless, I received no support from SAIC Montaña, so I reluctantly agreed to the requirements.

The last step was establishing the operation, which involved traveling to and collaborating with the U.S. Embassy in Hong Kong alongside Sone. Since he was on bail, there was a lengthy discussion about his travel permissions. I contacted the local Prosecutor's office in San Diego, which quickly referred the decision to the U.S. Attorney's Office.

During my conversation with AUSA Peña, she inquired about our policy. I reviewed it, and unsurprisingly, the Secret Service didn't specifically address this matter. Thus, no mandatory actions were required to prevent Sone from fleeing to mainland China. Moreover, I wasn't particularly concerned, as Sone had three months to escape to Mexico and chose not to; therefore, it seemed reasonable to conclude he wouldn't flee to China either.

Above all, I adopted a strategy that involved treating Sone with respect and seeing him as a person rather than merely a convicted criminal. This approach allowed me to build rapport and, importantly, trust.

Next, I was scheduled to meet with officials from the U.S. Embassy and Secret Service Agents assigned to the Embassy in Hong Kong. The meeting felt more like a formality than a necessity. After everyone was briefed, they gave us the green light to proceed, with one stipulation. The local police must also approve.

To facilitate the operation, RAIC William Stone from the Hong Kong Resident Office appointed Agent John Butters to work alongside me. SA Butters coordinated the meeting with the local police. However, it quickly became apparent that he lacked experience in casework; his primary focus was solely on protection activities. I appeared to be more of a distraction, yet he eventually succeeded in arranging the meeting with the police.

SA Butters said, "Senior Inspector Mei Wong, meet Agent Richard LaTulip from our San Diego office. He is the undercover agent for this case."

I responded, "Senior Inspector Wong, it's a pleasure to meet you."

Senior Inspector Wong replied, "The pleasure is mine. Please, have a seat. Would you like something to drink? Tea or coffee?"

"Tea, if that's alright," I answered.

"Absolutely," Senior Inspector Wong said. "While we wait, I'm aware you're handling a case involving local online criminals. We're keen on assisting you. Can you update us on its status?"

"Yes," I confirmed, "I've been conducting online discussions with SunCredit and Slimbady. I don't know their real names, but SunCredit asserts he's linked to the Triads. Both individuals are involved in selling counterfeit credit cards online. Over the past month, I've been purchasing counterfeit cards from them, which they ship from Shenzhen to a drop address of mine in San Diego. We've arranged to meet, and I hope that will be in Hong Kong with your help."

"Interesting," Senior Inspector Wong remarked. "How long do you plan to meet with them?"

"For now," I replied, "I aim to meet each of them for one day. I've been in touch with them online. They're supposed to provide me with a hundred counterfeit credit cards in exchange for $5,000. Additionally, I have a laptop to give to Slimbady."

"Ah, I see. So, SunCredit is the one making the cards?" Senior Inspector Wong inquired.

"I'm not sure," I replied. "I asked them to create these cards with names of Secret Service Agents embossed on them. I initiated the transaction in San Diego, even paying SunCredit $5,000 to kick things off."

"I understand," Senior Inspector Wong said.

SA Butters interjected, "We simply need your support and approval for this operation to move forward."

"What other criminal activities are planned?" Senior Inspector Wong questioned.

"None," SA Butters quickly responded.

Extending my hand toward SA Butters, I added, "We don't have further plans, but I cannot guarantee that nothing else may arise. They are my online business associates, and we'll discuss. They might have something to offer me; I just don't know what."

"I understand," Senior Inspector Wong said. "Thank you for the details. Do you have any additional information?"

SA Butters said, "No. We just need to know if your team can support this operation."

Senior Inspector Wong replied, "We are eager to support your operations. We are very interested in SunCredit and Slimbady. However, we'll need to prepare for the operation. A letter will be meticulously crafted for the Prosecutor's office, and once they consent, we can proceed. Keep in mind, this process will require some time."

"We understand," SA Butters agreed. "How long do you estimate?"

"A few weeks," Senior Inspector Wong said. "But there's one more thing. As a U.S. citizen, you aren't recognized as law enforcement in China and will be treated accordingly. The letter will authorize all actions stated within it." He then looked at me and winked, adding, "Anything not written in the letter will be beyond your authority."

Noting the wink and nod, I interpreted it to mean that more could be done, but I needed clarification. "I'm not sure I grasp that fully. Could you clarify?"

"Certainly," Senior Inspector Wong replied. "We aren't the only agency monitoring SunCredit and Slimbady. Other agencies in Hong Kong may also be involved in this case. If you act outside of what's outlined in the letter, other agencies could arrest you. But don't worry."

Interjecting, I asked, "If Slimbady were to hand me a disk with dumps on it, you're saying I will be arrested?"

"Technically, yes, you can, but we would not arrest you," Senior Inspector Wong assured me.

"You just said 'I would be arrested' if it wasn't in the letter," I responded. "This is a little concerning."

Senior Inspector Wong, attempting to calm me, said, "It is only if another agency were investigating this case. You don't need to worry about us."

Looking at SA Butters, I said, "I think we need to discuss this with the U.S. Embassy."

Senior Inspector Wong shook her head and said, "Yes, of course; in the meantime, we'll prepare the letter."

"Thank you. And thank you for your time today," I said as the meeting concluded.

As SA Butters and I departed the police station, I asked, "Do we have any other options?"

"Let me call our contacts in Macau," SA Butters replied.

After the meeting with the local police, I was disappointed, but ultimately, they approved. Unfortunately, this approval came with an uneasy feeling. If we are going to work in an undercover capacity, there are some unknowns and uncontrollable factors. In regrouping, the only other option was Macau. Macau offered gambling, spa treatments, excellent cuisine, a diverse atmosphere, and women.

After several phone calls, SA Butters arranged a meeting with the police across the bay. We immediately made reservations for the TurboJET to go to Macau, which would take fifty-five minutes from Hong Kong. When we arrived in Macau, we were greeted by Chief Superintendent Weng-Hou Chen and several of his colleagues from the police. Once the introductions were complete, we were transported to the police station.

At the station, I outlined the operation, our objectives, and our aim of identifying SunCredit and Slimbady. We intended to meet with both online Carders to establish rapport and conclude the deals we initiated in San Diego. Chief Superintendent Weng-Hou Chen listened and committed to collaborating on the operation without reservations or hidden agendas. I was empowered to take any necessary action without fearing arrest, and my safety was their utmost priority.

With this news, the meeting location was chosen, and to celebrate, the police treated us to dinner at a local Portuguese restaurant.

Chapter 12

With a small bang the show begins

It was August 2005, and a once-in-a-lifetime opportunity was approaching. If successful, I would join an elite group of individuals who had served as long-term undercover agents. My adventure would take me across the globe. Questions would arise later in my career about what the U.S. government had done to help prepare me for this journey. Strangely enough, the only guidance I received was an introduction to a former KGB officer now working for a private company.

SA Sarah Moore called me and asked, "Hey, how's it going?"

I replied, "I'm well. Thanks. What's up?"

SA Moore responded, "A while back, I met a former KGB Agent. His name is Sergey Kuznetsov. He's attending a conference in Sacramento. I think that if you met him, you would gain a valuable insider perspective on Russian cybercriminals. What are your thoughts?"

Delighted, I replied, "I would love to meet him."

SA Moore responded, "Great. Let me arrange it. While I do that, book your flight. The conference is in two days."

With Kuznetsov's guidance, I could be better prepared to navigate the challenges of working undercover while targeting Russian-speaking criminals. Still, I was uncertain about how the meeting would unfold, but I embraced it. When I arrived, I planned to play it cool. I needed to avoid appearing "too green" or overly anxious. So, I found a seat near him and initiated small talk. As with many gatherings, the discussion was pleasant, the food was delicious, and the wine flowed freely.

Sitting next to Kuznetsov, we chatted about our jobs and personal lives. We connected right away, and our conversation flowed effortlessly. Our icebreaker was World War II history, a subject I was passionate about and had extensively read, making me well-equipped for an engaging discussion. It was after dinner that the conversation indeed became intriguing.

Kuznetsov looked at me intently, stating, "The Russian mindset is complex. How do you intend to connect with Russian carders?"

I replied, "That's precisely why I'm here. I need your insights. What should I consider? How should I get ready?"

"You mentioned having an informant," Kuznetsov inquired. "Where is he currently located?"

"He resides in San Diego," I answered. "We're working together late at night."

Kuznetsov appeared perplexed. "He's free? You don't have him under control?"

I clarified, "He is on probation. I need him to be available to assist me. Moreover, I need him to introduce me to Slimbady."

Deep in thought, Kuznetsov responded, "That approach won't work. You need to have control over him. He should be in prison."

While I grasped his reasoning, I countered, "That's not how it functions in the United States. I can't imprison people merely for my convenience."

DOI: 10.1201/9781003680390-12

Kuznetsov, taken aback, replied, "It's not about your convenience. It's about your safety. You must have him incarcerated."

"It's a risk," I told him. "Sadly, locking my informant up isn't a solution."

"This is where you're vulnerable," Kuznetsov noted. "You need to establish a way to control him."

"Again, I understand, and for the last time," I stated, "This is the best I can do. Unfortunately, this risk is mitigated to the furthest extent possible."

With the alcohol affecting him, Kuznetsov shifts his perspective and remarks, "The Russian criminal mind is a fortress, Richard. Paranoia and loyalty form its walls. They trust no one beyond their circle. Every smile, every handshake—it's a test."

Nodding and listening closely, I inquired, "So, how do I pass their tests? How do I earn their trust?"

With a smirk, Kuznetsov replied, "Not by pretending to be like them; that's the first error Americans make. Russians can detect pretense as keenly as wolves sense fear. Instead, you must demonstrate what they value: strength and utility."

"I think I get it," I said. "You mean by proving I can be useful?"

Kuznetsov tapped the table for emphasis, confirming, "Exactly. In their realm, every man serves a function—be it as a partner, a pawn, or a scapegoat. You need to show them you possess something they need, something they can exploit. But don't give too much away. Make yourself essential but not irreplaceable. If they believe you're too significant to control, you'll face elimination."

Seeking further clarification, I asked, "And what does strength look like to them?"

Kuznetsov leaned back, sipped red wine, and stated, "It's not just about physicality or aggression. It's about resolve. Russians admire a man who keeps his promise, no matter how grim. You must exhibit that you're unafraid of consequences and willing to get your hands dirty without flinching. At the first hint of hesitation, they will turn against you."

I paused to reflect on this and then asked, "But won't that raise questions about my background? I'm not exactly one of them."

Kuznetsov chuckled, responding, "That's the beauty of it. You don't need to be Russian, but you must embody their principles, their code. Speak less, observe more. A man who listens and acts is far more dangerous than one who talks. And one last thing, don't overextend yourself."

I was slightly puzzled and asked, "What do you mean?"

Kuznetsov leaned in, locking eyes with me, explaining, "Don't appear too eager. They'll interpret desperation as a weakness. Let them invite you in. Reveal enough to spark their interest, but keep the rest mysterious. Russians love puzzles, but only those they think they can master."

Nodding, a smirk creeping onto my face, I said, "So I'm to be the puzzle they think they can solve?"

Kuznetsov grinned broadly, proclaiming, "Da, my friend. But remember—if they ever figure you out, you lose your value. Always stay one step ahead. That is how you survive in their circle."

Reflecting on our time together, I sensed that Kuznetsov was evaluating my trustworthiness. However, by the end of the evening, we had forged a solid foundation for a long-term relationship and friendship. As our meeting came to a close, so too did my undercover training. My next assignment centered on backstopping my new persona.

To accomplish this, I sought help in creating a backstory for the person I was becoming. I began by detailing an identity, drawing from my past to weave together a narrative. I envisioned a place I hailed from, the addresses I lived at, and my parents' history, all with roots leading back to Moldova. I understood the significance of connecting to a "Russian-speaking" area for someone engaged in online carding.

This new life story was something I needed to embed in my memory. It had to feel authentic, as if it were real, allowing me to recall it seamlessly if questioned, just like my actual details. Yet, what would show up if an online Carder searched my name? What would they uncover? The truth was nothing. I wanted to alter that narrative.

Backstopping is a detailed practice that shields the undercover agent from being traced, identified, or connected to their real identities. This process involves carefully crafting an altered identity along with the associated documentation. It requires skillful manipulation of personal information, including various records, personally and financially. The goal is to fabricate a narrative to obscure one's tracks systematically, ensuring no digital breadcrumbs or traces remain that could reveal my true identity.

Regrettably, all attempts to secure my new undercover identity with support from the U.S. government were unsuccessful. I would not receive additional aid or resources for this purpose. Nevertheless, to establish some support, I requested an apartment where I could work, meet with informants, and receive packages.

ATSAIC Carrington considered a local apartment, but the costs were quickly rejected. However, to his credit, ATSAIC Carrington did authorize a Wi-Fi hotspot, a cell phone, a mail drop, and a bank account. The main issue was that the mail drop would serve as my apartment. A quick Google search revealed that the San Diego Field Office was just two blocks away, and if one continued to search, they would find a Western Union outlet three blocks away.

Notwithstanding any real backstopping, I prepared for the upcoming meetings with SunCredit and Slimbady. I had all the necessary travel documents, including my passport and the newly acquired undercover credit cards. However, coordinating the precise dates and times proved to be a logistical nightmare for Sone and me.

Headquarters mandated that Sone and I stay in Hong Kong rather than Macau. Consequently, we had to take the TurboJET to Macau each morning and return in the evening. Another layer of complexity was that each meeting was scheduled on consecutive days. Because of this, I had to justify why Sone and I could only meet on specific days at specific times.

Meeting SunCredit presented no issues, as it was our first encounter. However, dealing with Slimbady proved to be more challenging, given his prior meeting with Sone several months ago. During that meeting, they explored the city together and enjoyed various activities, including massages. This was going to be different, as massages were off the table. I was uncertain about how Slimbady would react to this new "style" meeting.

Ultimately, the meetings were scheduled to take place at the same casino. SunCredit's meeting was on the first day, followed by Slimbady's on the second. Once we all arrived in Macau, we briefly gathered at the police station before the meetings began. This was our chance to introduce Sone and take some photos. The photos would be provided to the surveillance teams so they would know whom to "protect." The meeting started as SAIC Stokes and others had speculated.

I extended my hand, bowed slightly, and greeted Chief Superintendent Weng-Hou Chen, saying, "Hello, it's a pleasure to see you again. I'd like to introduce my partner, Sone. We'll be the ones meeting with SunCredit and Slimbady over the next two days."

Weng-Hou, unaware that I was one of the two undercovers, promptly remarked, "You aren't Asian." He continued, pointing at me, "You are going to meet with SunCredit?"

Acknowledging my lack of clarity in our previous meetings, I replied, "Yes. Sone and I will meet with SunCredit and Slimbady. I won't worry about being an American; they are aware. I have sent them Western Union using my undercover name."

Shaking his head, Weng-Hou said, "Okay, it is your operation. What's your plan?"

I explained, "We'll meet SunCredit soon, it's the place we discussed during our last visit. I imagine we'll have the usual 'get to know you' chit-chat. Then, at some point, we'll exchange $5,000 for one hundred embossed counterfeit credit cards."

Weng-Hou said, "Anything else? Should we expect you to move from the casino?"

"No," I said. "We are only authorized to meet at that place. Now, if he wants to gamble, eat, or drink, we can, but again, we aren't leaving the premises."

Weng-Hou shook his head, contemplating the plan, and added, "You know Asians love gambling. How much money did you bring to gamble?"

I replied, "The Secret Service authorized me to gamble one thousand dollars."

Weng-Hou stated firmly, "WHAT? You need to listen. You MUST NOT GAMBLE with any suspects. Gambling is deeply rooted in Asian culture and is linked to one's luck and fortune. We have no less than $10,000 when we operate in the field."

I responded, "It's fine. I already have a strategy. I've told them online that casino gambling is purely based on luck, and since I don't have luck, I avoid those games. Instead, they know that I bet on college sports. They understand that when I wager here, it's for thousands of dollars."

Still skeptical, Weng-Hou replied, "I still advise you not to do it."

I realized it was too late; I would gamble if SunCredit or Slimbady decided to gamble. Moreover, I was confident in my plan and backstory. I replied, "I appreciate your advice and suggestions. I know you mean this for my safety."

Once the briefing concluded, Sone and I were escorted to the meet location, a short walk from the police station. Thanks to the police's connections, we bypassed the external security measures. My colleagues were stationed in the surveillance room. The room had multiple screens connected to the many "eyes in the sky."

Sone and I found a table near the bar where we could sit. After we settled in, I texted SA Butters, "In place, seated near the bar."

SA Butters quickly replied, "Got you on the big screen. Good luck."

While we waited for SunCredit, I ordered a drink from the waitress and sent a message to SunCredit: "Greetings. Waiting for you at the bar."

Instantly, my phone lit up with SunCredit's reply: "Five minutes."

I hurriedly messaged SA Butters, "SunCredit will be here in five minutes. Let me know if you see him." Now, the waiting game has commenced.

I glanced at Sone and stated, "Everything is set. The team is watching. The police are nearby, and SunCredit will arrive in about five minutes, or maybe just three."

"What's your take?" Sone inquired, "Will he have the plastic on him?"

"Your guess is as good as mine," I replied, "But if he's carrying it, then perhaps he's not with the Triads. Perhaps he is just a regular old SunCredit."

Sone chuckled and said, "Yeah, I suppose so. By the way, thanks."

"Thanks for what?" I asked.

"For treating me like a person," Sone responded.

Just as I was about to answer, my phone buzzed. I glanced down and read, "Looking for you."

Scanning the area, I spotted a man in wire-rimmed glasses and a leather jacket. I figured this was SunCredit, so I waved and asked, "SunCredit?"

Upon hearing this, he turned toward me and Sone and waved back. I stood up and reached out my hand, saying, "Surfrider, but feel free to call me Rich. This here is Sean."

"Pleasure to meet you," SunCredit said.

"Please, have a seat. Would you like a beer?" I offered.

"No, thank you. I'm hungry. Do you like Chinese? Care to join me?" SunCredit replied.

I glanced at Sone and shrugged, replying, "Yeah, definitely. I like Chinese, and it's time for lunch. Lead the way."

Inside, I still felt nervous and uncertain about how hungry I would be, but skipping a meal wasn't an option. As we walked, I quickly typed to the surveillance team, "Moving to restaurant."

I held the phone face down to ensure that if a message arrived, no one else would accidentally see it. It didn't take long for a reply to come through: "Got you."

Once we arrived at the restaurant and were seated, SunCredit asked, "I'm curious. How do you work in the United States? I wonder if we can work together."

This was precisely the situation I aimed to avoid. I had no intention of working directly with carders, so I needed to devise a plan, and the first thing that came to mind was Sone's operation. It was already set up and straightforward for me to replicate.

I explained, "It's simple. The first rule is that we never card in our city. Instead, I target nearby cities. I map out all the major retail stores, like Best Buy, Wal-Mart, Circuit City, and others. After that, I send the team to execute the plan. One person rents and stays with the van while the others hit the stores. They work in pairs: one scouts while the other makes the purchase. They focus on big-name electronics like Apple, IBM, or Dell."

SunCredit, listening closely, asks, "What do you do with it? Sell it on eBay?"

"No," I replied. "The team drives back to San Diego, and then I connect with my contacts in Los Angeles. They usually purchase everything for eighty percent of the value. About eBay, it puts me too close. I know too many people who get busted for selling stolen shit on eBay. I stay away from it."

SunCredit, looking confused, asked, "What about the dumps? Do you use checker, you know like Try2Check?"

Many carders utilize Try2Check, a service that verifies credit cards and dumps. The operation of such a dump-checking service was straightforward. The team behind it hacked into a credit card processing terminal. Carders would purchase checks in large quantities and upload the credit card track data. The service would then carry out a preauthorization transaction with the credit cards.

The preauthorization amount was set at a minimal fee ranging from one to five cents, based on the assumption that such a small amount would not trigger issues with the credit card. However, checking the credit card could activate alarms, leading to the card's cancellation. When it was used at the register, the transaction would be declined.

With this in mind, I replied simply, "I'm not a fan of Try2Check as it kills dumps. Instead, I'll stop for gas, grab coffee, or pick up a candy bar at the store. We prefer making small purchases at locations we plan to hit. This approach works well for us."

Nodding in agreement, SunCredit said, "You're correct. Dump checkers kill cards, but I use them." Turning his head to glance at the floor, SunCredit adds, "I must be cautious. I'm with the Triads. I have a surveillance team." He then gestures toward the floor and adds, "They are out there. All I need to do is send text."

Sone and I gazed at the establishment's floor. While nothing seemed out of place, my mind raced with movie images, prompting questions: Did they carry guns or knives? Were there any martial arts experts present, or a mix of everything? Turning to SunCredit, I remarked, "You can never be too careful. Hopefully, you won't need to use them." Shifting gears, I inquired, "How's your lunch?"

"It okay," SunCredit said. "I'm not like this place. Restaurant lack authenticity; better ones are downtown in Macau. How long will you be in China?"

"Just a few days," I answered. "We have other friends to see before returning to San Diego."

"Good, it is good to see other places," SunCredit remarked. "I want travel more, but my wife, she no like to."

As I listened to him discuss his wife, I sent SA Butters a message under the table, "Target has Countersurveillance Team in Casino."

"Roger," SA Butters replied.

Returning to business, I inquired, "How should we proceed? I have the 5K with me. Do you have the plastic?"

"I no have plastic," SunCredit retorted. "My team has. They bring once I get the cash. But I like you. Give me moment."

SunCredit then pulled out his phone and contacted his surveillance team, conversing in Mandarin. After a brief discussion, he looked at me and said, "Two minutes."

Sure enough, two minutes later, a young man and a woman came to the table. SunCredit conversed with the man in Mandarin. After their conversation, the young man took a pack of cigarettes and placed it on the table. The pair then turned and walked away. SunCredit picked up the cigarettes, handed them to me, and said, "Your order."

I reached into my pocket, gave SunCredit the money, and replied, "Your money." Sone and I stood up, exchanged goodbyes, and walked away. Sone and I headed straight toward the taxi stand. Once we arrived, we got into a taxi, and I instructed the person to take us to the Macau Tower. I thought that just in case SunCredit's surveillance team followed us, they would only see us going to the Macau Tower. After all, we are still tourists who have not visited Macau.

While Sone and I were in the back of the taxi heading toward the Macau Tower, I messaged SA Butters, "Sone and I departed with the plastic."

SA Butters replied, "Copy. We have eyes on SunCredit and his surveillance team. We'll watch them until they leave the casino."

After approximately two minutes, SA Butters sent another message: "Targets departed. They didn't follow you."

Realizing that Sone and I weren't being tracked, I recognized the meeting was an adrenaline-high letdown. I had envisioned something more akin to Mission Impossible, but instead, we met, discussed, finalized our business, and departed—nothing extravagant or fast-paced.

After we arrived at the Macau Tower, we quickly pivoted, hailed a new taxi, and instructed the driver to take us to the police station. There, we met the core team.

I entered the briefing room, and Weng-Hou was waiting for me. "You made it. Congratulations! I never thought an American could meet a Chinese Triad without being Chinese," he remarked.

I chuckled softly and remarked, "Thank you. Initially, I felt a bit anxious. But as we conversed, my comfort grew. Honestly, it ended up being underwhelming. I anticipated that the credit cards would be stored in a locker at the bus terminal. To be handed a key and softly be told the locker number. Instead, two teenagers, supposed to be Triad countersurveillance, merely handed the package to SunCredit. It was so straightforward that it felt disappointing. My perspective on movies has changed forever."

Weng-Hou gave me a reassuring pat on the back and asked, "Do you have the plastic? I'd like to take a look at it."

"Of course," I replied, "I have it right here."

I took out the pack of cigarettes and laid out the plastic. Each was embossed with the names I had provided over ICQ to SunCredit. Weng-Hou and his team examined the counterfeit credit cards and commented, "These are impressive. They include all the security features."

"Yeah, these are some of the best counterfeit cards I've seen," I replied. "Look, it even has the microprinting."

"Very detailed," Weng-Hou remarked. "Excellent work."

"Thank you," I replied. "Now we need to go catch the boat back to Hong Kong. We will be back tomorrow morning."

Next up was the meeting with Slimbady.

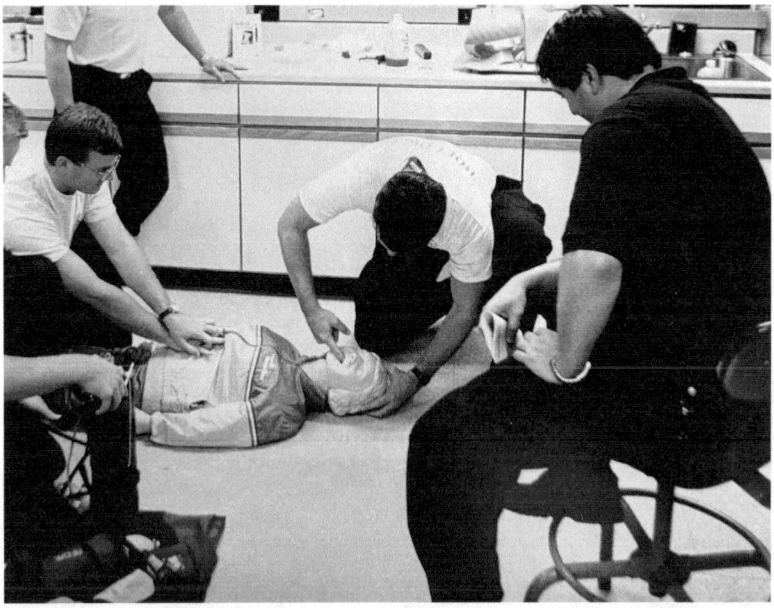

Photo 1 Learning life-saving skills during CPR training at the U.S. Secret Service Academy. An instructor observes as we apply the techniques covered in class, reinforcing precision, readiness, and the significance of hands-on preparation.

Photo 2 Navigating the obstacle course at the U.S. Secret Service academy is part of the intense physical training designed to test endurance, agility, and determination. This is one of the few rare photos taken during our time at the academy, capturing a moment of challenge and commitment.

Photo 3 Certificate of graduation from the James J. Rowley Training Center, awarded on February 10, 1999, upon successful completion of Special Agent Course No. 163. Shown here with my first badge, issued under the Department of the Treasury, which was later replaced when the U.S. Secret Service transitioned to the Department of Homeland Security. A proud milestone marking the beginning of my career as a Special Agent.

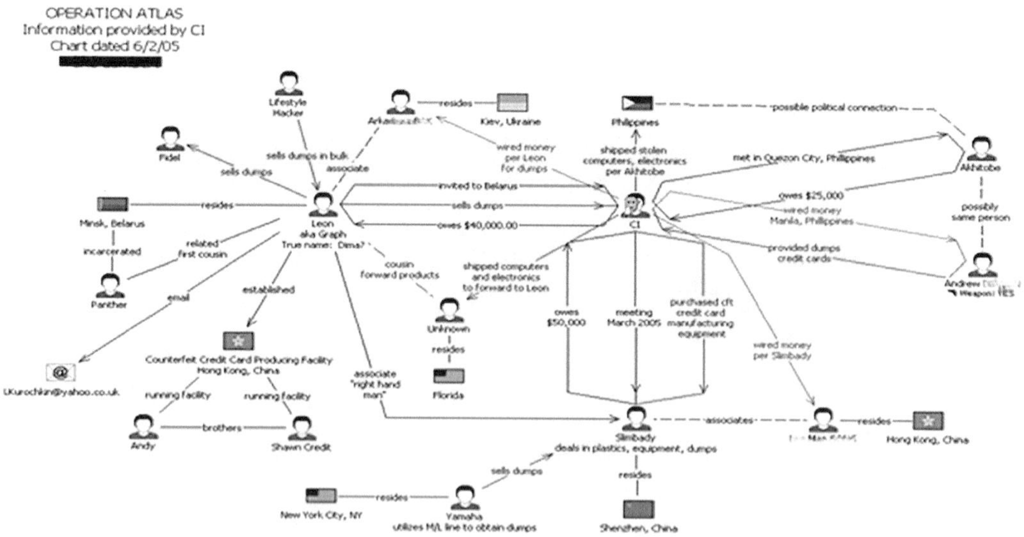

Photo 4 First generation link analysis chart displaying suspects' ICQ nicknames (NICs) and their purported geographic locations. This early visual map served as a foundational tool in identifying key players within the carding network and tracking their digital footprints across international borders.

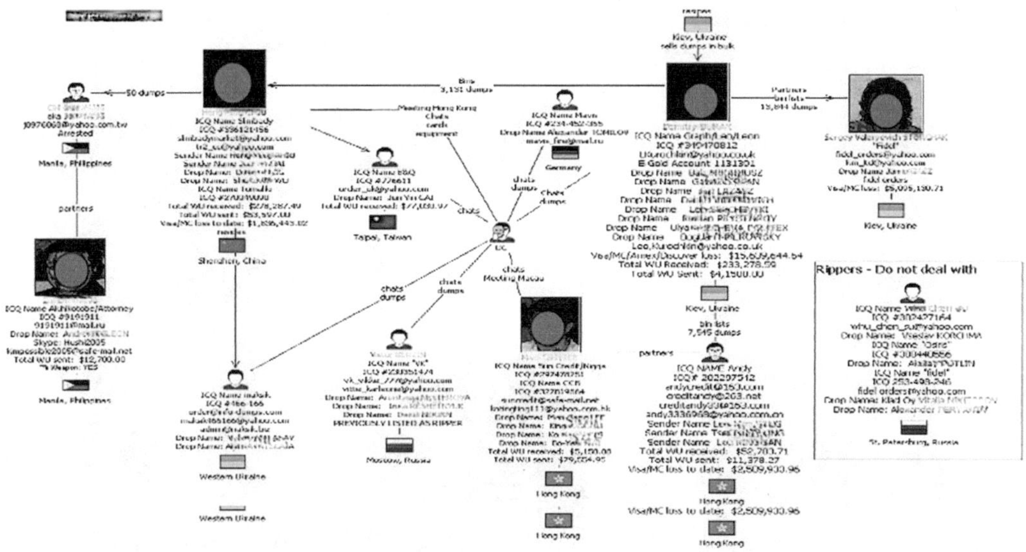

Photo 5 Second-generation link analysis chart created following in-person meetings with key targets such as Slimbady and SunCredit. The diagram illustrates the evolving structure of the criminal network, mapping critical connections and shedding light on previously obscured relationships within the carding ecosystem.

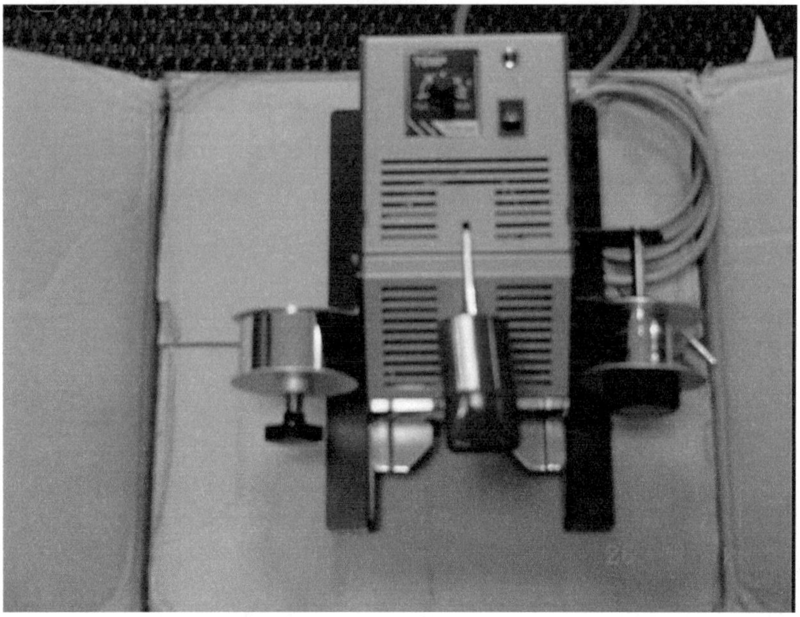

Photo 6 A counterfeit credit card tipping machine accompanied by silver tipping foil—shipped from Shenzhen, China by Slimbady. When unrolled, the foil revealed traces of prior use, bearing impressions from multiple counterfeit cards. This device was a crucial tool in replicating the metallic finish typically found on genuine credit cards, further enabling the production of high-quality counterfeit cards.

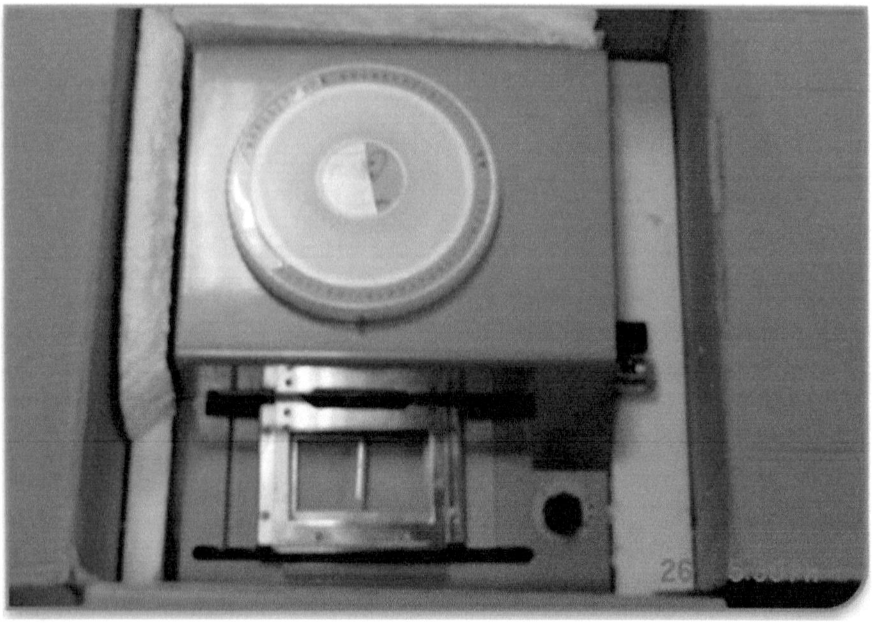

Photo 7 Embossing machine bearing the stylized "MC" and flying "V" logos—symbols often used to mimic legitimate branding. Shipped from Shenzhen, China by Slimbady, the device played a key role in producing high-quality counterfeit cards central to the fraud operation.

0MB 3MB
3MB free

Reply | Mark | Move To | Options | Delete | <-- Prev | ^ | Next -->

Folders [new - edit]
Inbox
Notices
Sent
Drafts
Junk
Trash
Last search

Search mail(from/to) Go
Advanced Search

Subject: Re: order
Date: Saturday, 7 Jun 2008 04:39
From: SS <lkurochkin>
To: mrtowelie

[redacted]
Ukraine

yes. u calculated right)
-------- Original Message --------
From: [redacted]>
To: lkurochkin
Subject: order
Date: Fri, 6 Jun 2008 19:03:22 -0400

\> Never mind I figured it out brat.
\>
\> here is the order
\>
\> 400927 x 20
\> 401135 x 30
\> 412185 x 20
\> 424617 x 20
\> 425330 x 10
\> 435114 x 10
\> 435336 x 10
\>
\> I think total is like $1.9k So I will send $2k
\>
\> give me WU details

Photo 8 In the early days of carding, email was the primary conduit for delivering stolen credit card data. This message from Leon, sent to one of my undercover accounts, followed a small intentional overpayment, designed to build goodwill and subtly reinforce a sense of collaboration. It was a calculated move to establish trust and deepen the operational relationship.

Photo 9 A package shipped by Slimbady containing Chinese-manufactured desk telephones. On the surface, the shipment appeared innocuous, but it would soon reveal itself as part of a sophisticated concealment method used to traffic counterfeit credit cards across international borders.

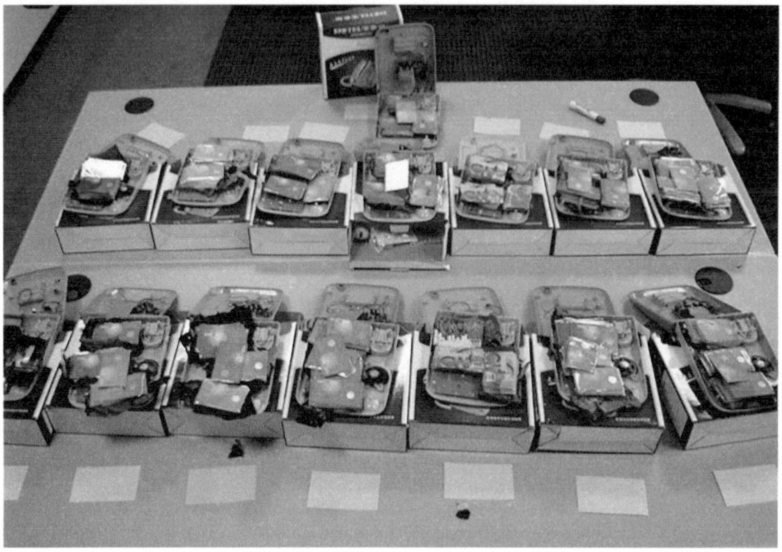

Photo 10 Upon closer inspection, the Chinese-manufactured desk telephones were found to be packed with counterfeit credit cards, each carefully wrapped in carbon paper. Curious about the purpose of the wrapping, I examined the devices using current X-ray technology, which revealed the concealed illicit contents. The carbon paper not only protected the cards but helped obscure them from casual inspection, demonstrating the operation's evolving tradecraft.

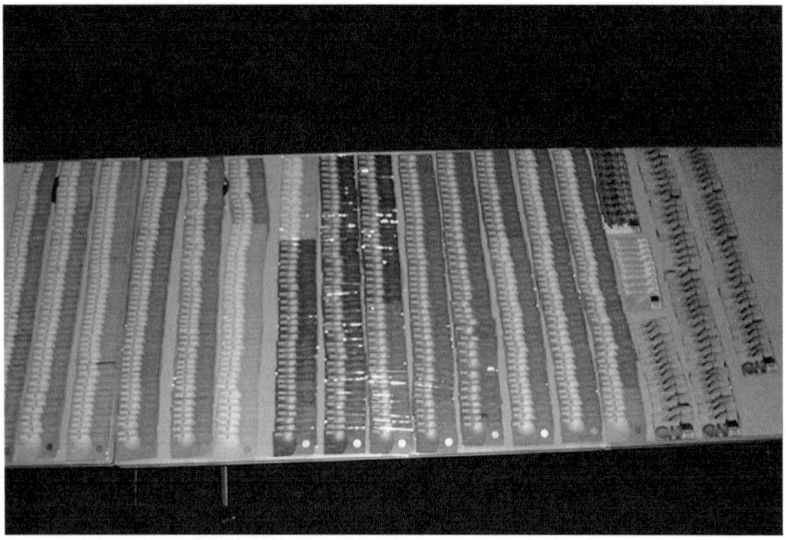

Photo 11 The contents hidden within the Chinese-manufactured desk phones—approximately 1,000 counterfeit credit cards, including Visa, Discover, and MasterCard. Ingeniously concealed, the shipment exemplified the lengths to which the operation went to evade detection and move illicit goods across borders.

Photo 12 Close-up images of unembossed counterfeit credit cards highlight the meticulous craftsmanship. Each card incorporated microprinting, UV security features, counterfeit foil, and other advanced anti-counterfeiting elements—professionally replicated and defeated. The result: near-flawless fakes that allowed carders to operate undetected and conduct fraudulent transactions with alarming ease.

Photos 13.1–13.4 Photographs of my official and personal passports, bearing entry and exit stamps from Macau and Thailand—evidence of multiple undercover operations. These pages reflect not only the scope of international engagement but also the inherent risk of traveling under my real identity while meeting high-level targets, such as Maksik, Slimbady, and SunCredit. The use of original passports underscored both the trust placed in the operation and the personal danger faced throughout.

Chapter 13

His name was Slimbady

The TurboJET to Hong Kong was swift, taking approximately fifty-five minutes. Once the boat left the bay, the captain accelerated, lifting the jet boat elegantly above the South China Sea to glide over the waves. The only components in contact with the water were the hydrofoils and the slim fiberglass piece linking them together.

Sone referred to Slimbady as "The Man." He embodied everything good, albeit in a morally questionable sense. Slimbady possessed top-tier plastic, dumps, and counterfeiting equipment, but most importantly, he had connections. Whenever Sone required anything, all he had to do was reach out to Slimbady. Within hours of sending a message, Sone would receive what he needed. I witnessed this personally and understood that Slimbady was the key to the underground community.

On the return trip to Hong Kong, I seized the chance to ride the wave of success and start a conversation. I approached ATSAIC Carrington and said, "This isn't going to work."

Confused, ATSAIC Carrington replied, "What isn't going to work?"

"Look," I began to explain. "Slimbady knows Sone. He remembers what they did last time he was in Shenzhen. If we are too rigid about this plan, and only stay in that casino, and aren't able to move outside. He's going to realize something is off."

"What do you suggest?" ATSAIC Carrington asked.

"If Slimbady offers to go to dinner, we should accept, even if it's outside the casino," I said.

"So, you want to leave the casino?" ATSAIC Carrington questioned.

I emphatically replied, "We can't be tied to a single place. Plus, we're talking about safety. Slimbady will have to go through the magnetometer, so we'll know he isn't armed."

"Okay," ATSAIC Carrington conceded. "If he wants to go out for food, we can go to the Portuguese restaurant we visited the other night."

I recognized it wasn't perfect but accepted the minor victory, saying, "Deal."

The plan remained essentially unchanged. However, according to SAIC Stokes' regulations, my options were restricted. Visiting massage parlors was prohibited. The only modification was that I could recommend a Portuguese restaurant for dinner. This wasn't a favorable adjustment for those familiar with Chinese culture, but it was an option.

What was overlooked was that Slimbady wasn't SunCredit. Sone was familiar with Slimbady and understood his preferences for saunas and massage parlors. It was my responsibility to navigate us away from these vices. After the briefing, Chief Superintendent Weng-Hou, Sone, and I walked to the casino and were greeted by the casino's Head of Security. As we entered, he waved us past the magnetometers.

Like the previous day, Sone and I meandered to the same bar, settled in, and ordered a beer. I set Slimbady's laptop on the empty seat beside me. Once we were comfortable, I messaged SA Butters, "Same place. Contacting Slim."

SA Butters responded promptly, "Roger. We have eyes."

I quickly texted Slimbady: "At the bar. ☺"

DOI: 10.1201/9781003680390-13

Slimbady answered, "Just landed. About ten minutes away."

"That's interesting," I remarked, glancing at Sone. "Slimbady said he just landed. Did he fly here?"

Sone pondered for a moment and replied, "Oh, right. He's in Shenzhen. The best option for him is to take a helicopter."

"I guess carding is doing well these days," I noted.

Sone laughed, saying, "Yeah, I suppose so. Slim got a big operation. He makes a lot of money and has expensive tastes."

Jokingly, I said, "Like your obsession with Coach bags?"

Sone explained, "Man, you've got to keep your lady happy."

I chuckled, "It certainly helps when it's free."

"Hey," Sone replied, "the DEA didn't find all my cash."

"That's great to hear," I said.

"You'll never track it down," Sone asserted.

I understood his concern and said, "I'm not searching for it. Besides, that case is closed. The government lost its chance, so you're welcome."

My phone lit up, prompting me to check it. "We have a problem! Call me."

Confused, I glanced at Sone and said, "It seems there's an issue. I need to contact Carrington."

"What does he want?" Sone asked.

"No idea, but I'll find out," I replied.

I dialed ATSAIC Carrington's number. The phone rang a couple of times before he answered, "What's up?"

ATSAIC Carrington explained, "I spoke with the head of security."

"And?" I prompted.

"And," ATSAIC Carrington replied urgently. "You need to get rid of the computer."

"Get rid of the computer? How am I supposed to do that? Plus, I already told Slim I have it," I said.

"Security doesn't allow bags inside the casino. Having a bag is problematic." ATSAIC Carrington insisted. "You gotta try to get rid of the computer!"

While conversing with ATSAIC Carrington, I heard a beep indicating a new message. It was from Slimbady, saying, "Pass security, be right there."

I rubbed the back of my neck and replied, "Look, this isn't my problem. Slim is here, and I'm not getting rid of the computer. It's not my fault security informed you at the last minute. As far as I'm concerned, they fucked up and allowed me into the casino."

After hanging up the phone, I turned to Sone and said, "Slim is here."

Sone raised his head and scanned the area, quickly spotting Slimbady. Upon seeing Sone, Slimbady made his way over to our table. Sone greeted him with, "Slim, it's great to see you again! This is my partner, Surfrider."

I extended my hand to Slimbady, saying, "Good to meet you, Slim."

"Same," he replied.

"Please, take a seat," I invited. "Can I get you a beer?"

Slimbady, showing no hesitation, bowed his head, and responded, "Yes, Tsingtao."

I signaled to the waitress and ordered two Tsingtao beers for Slimbady and me. The challenge with Slimbady was his English. Unlike SunCredit, who spoke well, Slimbady struggled significantly with the language. This made the conversation difficult, but he was engaged and asked, "How was business?"

"Busy," I replied. "The dumps you provide are good."

Slimbady shook his head and said, "Yes, good."

Taking the chance, I pointed to the laptop, "Here's your laptop."

"Thank you," Slimbady responded, promptly taking it from the bag to inspect it. After a moment, he looked at me and asked, "Why so bad?"

Under my breath, I cursed SAIC Montaña for refusing to approve a quality computer. I realized this would be a problem when I purchased the laptop. I was aware it wasn't up to standard, which is why I had my explanation prepared. I grimaced slightly and replied, "I know; it's not the best. I sold the rest to my contacts in LA, and this was my last one. If it doesn't work, I can find you another."

"No," Slimbady replied, "It okay. I can use."

My excuse seemed practical, but it felt like Surfrider minus one when it came to building rapport. It wasn't a great start, but it would only get worse from here. Having had enough beers and ready for something else, Slimbady said to Sone, "Let's get massage."

Before Sone could reply, I cut in, saying, "You know, I'm hungry. How about we grab some food?"

Slimbady shrugged and responded, "I can eat. I know good Chinese restaurant."

"Chinese, huh?" I said. "That sounds nice, but I heard about a great Portuguese restaurant. After all, we're in a Portuguese area of China, and they say this place is delicious." I desperately tried to pitch this idea, but Slimbady's expression showed he wasn't thrilled.

Nevertheless, Slimbady said, "Okay, we go here. Where is?"

"Yes," I answered. "I just need to use the restroom first. After that, we can take a taxi there. It's only about five to eight minutes away."

Using the bathroom became my chance to send a message without worrying about Slimbady or anyone else seeing what I was writing or asking, "Who are you texting?" Walking to the bathroom, I messaged SA Butters, "Drinks done. Heading to the Portuguese restaurant."

SA Butters quickly replied, "Roger."

The dinner was relatively uneventful. Although we avoided the expected topic during our conversation, once dinner ended and we stood at the restaurant's entrance, Slimbady asked one last question: "We go now to get massage?"

Despite how difficult it was to decline, I responded, "Thank you for the offer, but we have an early flight tomorrow and need to return to San Diego. Perhaps next time."

I had already lost a point due to an earlier slip-up, and now my score dropped from minus one to minus three. Despite this, Sone and I took a taxi straight to the police station. Upon arrival, we conducted the debriefing session.

Chief Superintendent Weng-Hou began, "Welcome back. How did the night go?"

"I think everything went smoothly," I responded.

Weng-Hou continued, "That's good to hear. We noticed you drinking at the bar. I instructed my team to recover the glass Slimbady was using to test for fingerprints."

"That's fantastic," I replied. "Were you able to identify him?"

Weng-Hou replied enthusiastically, "Not only did we identify him, but we also obtained his immigration records and passport. I will send this information to your embassy. You will receive his passport details and photographs in two weeks."

"That's incredible," I said with enthusiasm. "Anything else?"

"No," Weng-Hou replied. "Slim took a taxi directly to the heliport. I assume he returned to Shenzhen."

As Weng-Hou concluded his narrative, my phone buzzed with a message from SunCredit: "Hey, I wanted to invite you and Sone to dinner."

I looked up at ATSAIC Carrington and said, "I just received a message from SunCredit inviting Sone and me to dinner. What do you think? We should meet him."

ATSAIC Carrington hesitated, and before he could respond, SA Butters interjected, "I think we won here. What's the point of meeting him? We hit a home run."

ATSAIC Carrington pondered deeply as I stated, "The objective? It remains unchanged. It's about building rapport."

Weng-Hou stepped back, listening to our discussion. Ignoring him, SA Butters commented, "You've already done that. We're winners here. It's better this way. Besides, we don't know his true intentions. What if he's planning to kill you? Or if it's a trap?"

With each word from SA Butters, my frustration mounted, and I retorted, "Kill me? Set a trap? After we've just done a deal for 10K? That seems far-fetched. I didn't fly all this way not to take risks. Building rapport is the key objective. Turning down the invitation is like saying, 'Fuck off.' I say we meet him."

ATSAIC Carrington raised his hand and responded, "I'm inclined to side with SA Butters. We've won this round. Let's take it and regroup in San Diego."

I turned to Weng-Hou and asked, "What do you think? Can you support this?"

Weng-Hou grimaced, aware of the leadership's stance, and replied, "We view this as non-threatening since there's no indication of criminal activities. You're free to have dinner with him, but if you do, you go alone."

With that, the final nail was driven in. ATSAIC Carrington agreed, saying, "Then it's settled. We won't be going to dinner. Inform him that you and Sone are unavailable."

Deep down, I felt this was a mistake, but I texted SunCredit as instructed, saying, "Sorry, I'm already settled in for the night. Next time."

Sending that text message caused my score to drop by another two points. For ATSAIC Carrington and SA Butters, success is defined differently. I relied on SunCredit and Slimbady to help me ascend the Carding ladder. Ultimately, I achieved what some leaders at Headquarters believed was unattainable. I would later hear someone say, "I got lucky." Additionally, SAIC Stokes remained convinced that Russian speaking Carders would not agree to meet with me.

Nonetheless, I did connect with Asian Carders and formed some rapport, but those successes came at a cost. I failed to be "normal." I didn't fit the typical persona of an online Carder. I aspired to be someone who defied expectations. Instead, I found myself rigid, constrained, and ultimately BORING. My experiences taught me that choir boys stayed home, missing out on social invitations.

Those who chose a different path, one of rule-breaking, were the ones who received the invitations. They defy social norms. This insight will shape my future discussions regarding the next undercover operation. To be truly impactful, I will need assistance from an unsuspecting new friend.

Chapter 14

Kutsenov comes through again

During the flight from Hong Kong, I contemplated how I would advocate for a change in tactics, which weighed heavily on my mind. I realized I wouldn't be successful for long if I only traveled, met for a few hours, didn't do anything but have dinner or a drink, and then left. Boring people don't get invitations to the fun parties, and I needed to be invited back.

Upon arriving at my next destination, I found myself transiting a unfamiliar airport in a foreign country. The flight was slightly delayed, but I was in the international terminal, so I thought I didn't need to pass through security. Unfortunately, I was mistaken. After 9/11, additional security measures were implemented for international flights returning to the United States. Since I was on time for my flight, I didn't rush, but boarding was imminent.

I approached the airport screening staff and handed my passport to her. She meticulously examined it. After confirming everything was in order, she directed me to place my luggage on the X-ray machine's conveyor belt. I set my bag on the belt for scanning and then walked through the magnetometer. Fortunately, there were no alerts, which is always a comforting sign, there was no need to return to remove my shoes for additional scanning.

While I waited for my bag, I noticed the operator pointing to something on the screen. At first, I thought I hadn't packed or bought any water. Or was I mistaken? It was early in the morning when I left Hong Kong. As my luggage exited the X-ray machine, the security lady picked it up and asked, "Whose bag?"

I answered, "That one was mine."

I was curious about what had attracted their attention. I observed the security guard sifting through my luggage. Suddenly, I realized that the fake credit cards I had obtained from SunCredit were in my carry-on. Instantly, my blood pressure surged, and all my fatigue vanished; I was now completely alert.

I felt anxious, hoping she would overlook the fake credit cards. However, she reached in and extracted the bundle. She examined them thoroughly, turning them from left to right and flipping them from bottom to top. My mind raced, and I thought, "Great, I am going to get arrested."

This was an undercover operation, so I wasn't carrying my official government passport or Secret Service credentials. My concern was how I would explain to the security lady that what you have in your hands is evidence and that I'm an agent working for the U.S. Government. I imagined my new accommodations would be courtesy of the local police.

But much to my surprise, this isn't how it ended. Once her inspection was complete, the security guard returned the counterfeit credit cards in my luggage and closed the bag. She then looked at me and said, "Have a nice flight."

I quickly took back my luggage and said, "Thank you. Enjoy your day."

That day, I was fortunate that airport security was only on the lookout for bombs or bomb-making materials. What she held in her hands wasn't a bomb and, thus, wasn't the threat she sought at that moment.

DOI: 10.1201/9781003680390-14

Upon returning to the office, one might expect a celebration to ensue. However, despite our successes, a sense of emptiness lingered amid these accomplishments. The team convened at the San Diego Field Office, quickly engaging in discussions about our successes and shortcomings. Ultimately, I contended that to enhance my network and strengthen relationships with those working online, we need to adopt a more flexible approach to our undercover operations.

I emphasized that when invited to dinner, we can seize the opportunity or let it pass us by. Two days ago, we potentially missed our chance, or perhaps we boarded the boat and dozed off, failing to leave a meaningful impression on anyone we encountered. When SunCredit extended an invitation on the second night, we declined, missing the opportunity.

The discussions may have shifted things slightly in my favor, but it was time to concentrate on business and relationship-building. I focused on the sole positive element of the case: the acquisition of stolen credit card data from Graph, who was now operating under the ICQ alias Leon. He was linked to P0l1c3D0g, who, due to his imprisonment in Belarus, was using the ICQ name Diplomaticos. Leon had become less relevant; engaging with him provided a channel to reach Diplomaticos, who communicated with the outside world through an illegal cell phone from within the Belarusian prison.

Alongside Leon and Diplomaticos, I conversed with Fidel, Tron, and Kaiser. Each had a unique appeal. Tron and Kaiser were seasoned players, having been online for many years, which drew my attention due to their extensive track record without any arrests. Conversely, Fidel proved unreliable for acquiring stolen credit card information, as all transactions stemmed from outdated database breaches, such as CardSystems Solutions.

When I told ATSAIC Sheehan about the conversations, he showed no interest. He considered them trivial and discouraged me from engaging with them. Nonetheless, I persisted in these discussions. I recognized that building a broader network would create more opportunities to earn trust and encourage others to advocate for me. Despite having limited support and resources, I made every effort to nurture these relationships.

Another goal was to connect with Lifestyle, who also went by the online alias Jonnyhell. He was Diplomaticos' hacker. The lingering mystery was with whom he was collaborating now. I would naturally expect Leon, but the data he sold was outdated. With no leads available, I contacted my new best friend, Slimbady. Unfortunately, my latest issue arose from the management of the Secret Service.

SAIC Montaña expressed concerns about the optics of my online spending. He argued that I had met Slimbady and SunCredit in Macau, conducted several undercover buys, and learned their real-world identities. This was enough for the government to pursue criminal indictments. SAIC Montaña concluded that undercover purchases from them were no longer necessary.

However, Slimbady and SunCredit were part of a broader strategy. My aim wasn't just to arrest a few Carders but to take down hackers. Regardless, SAIC Montaña's reasoning would plague the investigation throughout the entire operation. I often reminded ATSAICs Sheehan and Carrington that, although I may be stimulating to speak with, it was business, not my personality, that kept everyone coming back.

I frequently demonstrated that my personality wasn't what only attracted Slimbady or SunCredit to me. Although we communicated regularly, our conversations became superficial over time without any business being conducted. I found myself receiving only brief replies. Two or three replies and then nothing. They ended without even a goodbye.

Since the issue involved confidential funds, I proposed a solution to ATSAIC Carrington and SAIC Montaña. We should work together with the FBI. If the Secret Service lacked the confidential funds, partnering with the FBI would benefit both parties. We would provide the undercover agent and access, while the FBI would supply the funding. The mutual benefit is that the FBI and the Secret Service share the glory.

When I suggested collaborating with the FBI, the idea was rejected, and SAIC Montaña approved the undercover expenses, enabling me to further develop relationships. As a result, I was tasked with reviewing stolen credit card accounts, which meant I had to assess their validity.

Our intelligence indicated that the Russian-speaking Carder supplied the freshest stolen data. Therefore, I anticipated Leon would be the most dependable and productive source. I was mistaken, or at least I was mistaken, regarding this Russian-speaking Carder. Contrary to the intelligence, Slimbady provided the highest quality dumps. Oddly, the results from Leon's Yahoo email search warrant revealed the answers.

After our Criminal Research Specialist analyzed the data, I realized Leon was linked to more than 150 distinct emails. These Carders originated from over thirty-four different nations and bought or sold more than 14,000 dumps. Due to fraudulent activities, total losses surpassed twenty-three million dollars. When we mapped the communications, it became clear how many resellers were active online.

Interestingly, Slimbady was quite similar. He was also a reseller, selling to me, but we both agreed that Leon's dumps were subpar. When I shared my frustration with Slimbady about the poor quality of the available dumps online, he made a suggestion. Slimbady offered to connect me with his source, Maksik, and I happily accepted.

I hadn't previously come across the alias Maksik. He was off Headquarters' radar, and my conversation with them yielded limited information about him. His ICQ number, 466-166, stood out as noteworthy. Low ICQ numbers are rare; my own is nine digits, which typically indicates the user is a newbie.

Maksik quickly gained prominence. The first order of business was to obtain a BIN list. The BIN list, or Bank Identification Number list, consists of the first six digits of a credit card. These digits identify the issuing bank and the card type, including options like classic, gold, or platinum, and distinguishing between European and American cards.

This information helps establish pricing. Classic credit cards from the United States are the least expensive and usually come with the lowest available credit. Prices increase from there, with European dumps being the costliest.

I texted Maksik first, saying, "What up? My friend Slim gave me your contact. 😀"

Maksik replied quickly, asking, "How do you know Slim?"

His prompt response surprised me; perhaps it was because Slimbady had a strong rapport with him, or they were already conversing. I said, "Slim and I go way back. We worked together for years. Slim mentioned you have the best dumps. ☺"

Maksik responded with a smiley: "😀"

I inquired, "Do you have a BIN list? Can you send it?"

Maksik asked, "What's your email?"

"rmdruc@yahoo.com," I wrote, and moments later, he replied, "Sent."

When I checked my inbox, I saw an email from maksik466166@yahoo.com with the subject line "BIN list." Immediately, I responded, "Got it. ☺ BRB."

I took my time and reviewed the list. I was looking for specific BINs linked to my reliable banking contacts. After identifying several suitable accounts, I ordered one hundred classic U.S. credit cards. I then messaged Maksik, "Order sent."

Maksik said, "1 sec."

Moments later, Maksik replied, "$1.5k send WU to First Name: Valery Last name: Kayatskaya City: Kharkiv Country: Ukraine."

With the Western Union details, I went to the local storefront to send the wire transfer. Shortly after he confirmed receipt, he sent me my order, which arrived via Maksik's email, maksik466166@yahoo.com. It was time to obtain another search warrant to gather more intelligence and evidence against him.

While I anticipated the search warrant results from Yahoo, I forwarded the credit card information to my banking contacts. The validity rate was the highest we observed, and the data indicated that the dumps were tied to a new business. This suggested the presence of a business with an undiscovered network intrusion. These were the results I had been seeking.

Due to this recent development, I contacted ATSAIC Sheehan and Jack Jones to inform them about Maksik.

"Hey," I said, "How is DC these days?"

"Good," ATSAIC Sheehan responded, "How can I help you?"

I answered, "I have some news to share. Recently, Slimbady introduced me to Maksik. His ICQ number is 466-166, and his email is maksik466166@yahoo.com. Anyway, I ordered one hundred dumps, and my banking contact mentioned the validity rate was around ninety-five percent, linked to a newly hacked business."

"Hmmm, alright," ATSAIC Sheehan said, "Give me a moment to get Jack Jones. I'm curious if he knows about Maksik."

"I shared the details with him recently," I replied.

"Hey Jack," ATSAIC Sheehan called, "I have Rich on the line. Are you familiar with Maksik?"

Jack responded, "Rich provided me with his details yesterday. I checked our databases and there wasn't much available. He seems to be a low-level Carder, with some presence on the boards but limited activity."

"That's odd," I remarked. "The dumps are priced to sell. So, I know he can't be a reseller. I'm waiting on Yahoo for his emails; once I have them, I can determine if he's a reseller or the source."

Jack replied, "Once you receive the results, could you forward them to us?"

"Of course," I said, "But only after you send me P0l1c3D0g's hard disk drive."

ATSAIC Sheehan grimaced and said, "I apologize, I keep forgetting. We'll mail that today."

Jokingly, I said, "I won't hold my breath. One more thing, you need to speak with SAIC Stokes. The operation in Macau was one of the most bizarre experiences I've ever had. I traveled across the globe to meet with two Carders for several hours. I was unable to move or do anything. If we expect them or anyone else to meet with me, we need more than a few hours; we need days."

ATSAIC Sheehan pondered for a moment before replying, "I understand. I'll discuss this with him and convey your concerns. Anything else?"

"Yeah," I said. "Are we having issues with confidential funds? I feel like we might be running low."

ATSAIC Sheehan replied, "Not to my knowledge. We spend as necessary."

"Hmmm," I said, "Maybe it's just a local matter. Anyway, please update me about the drive and speak with SAIC Stokes. This situation can't continue."

"Understood," ATSAIC Sheehan stated, "Talk to you later."

After my conversation with ATSAIC Sheehan, I focused on the investigation's business development and social elements. In addition to discussing business matters, I shared tales of exotic locations, pursuing women, adult entertainment, and drinking adventures. These anecdotes always captured their interest, and thanks to the Secret Service, I had a wealth of stories to tell.

With minimal undercover training, I had to create my narrative, blending my real life with my undercover persona. I purposely omitted any mention of dating Rachel. At the same time, I doubt anyone would be concerned about whether I was married or in a relationship; I wanted to avoid potential complications during operations. Furthermore, one could never predict if someone held strong moral views that might lead to judgment against me.

I quickly realized that American humor didn't necessarily translate well in China, although it resonated in the United States. For instance, around November, coinciding with Thanksgiving, I spoke with Slimbady and made a joke about the holiday.

I wrote, "Too bad the Pilgrims didn't eat cat for Thanksgiving, because I could be eating pussy right now. 🤪"

Slimbady replied, "We don't eat cats in China."

Noticing Slimbady's confusion, I clarified, "I'm not suggesting you eat cats in China, ☺ I'm just saying we all could be eating pussy right now. 😆"

Slimbady, now even more confused, responded, "I don't understand. Do you eat cat?"

I realized my joke didn't land well, so I tried to explain, "NO, we don't eat cat! It's a play on words. It's not really about the cat. It's that a cat is called a "Pussycat," and I'm just using the term "pussy," which is also slang for a girl's vagina."

Slimbady, being polite, responded, "😛."

Slimbady "laughed" during our online chat, but I doubt he understood the joke; nonetheless, that conversation was significant. Discussing travel encouraged people to consider trips. I aimed to plant these thoughts in everyone's minds, especially Maksik's. While doing so, I also heard gossip from Headquarters. To avoid being wrong about his speculation, SAIC Stokes and his allies admitted, "Yes, it's true that Carders from Asia meet, but Russian-speaking Carders don't. This much is a fact."

My conversations with Maksik were going well, and he expressed interest in traveling. However, he mentioned that he was too busy for that. He assured me he would soon be ready for a trip and promised to let me know when he was available.

Interest in Maksik and his data quality grew, leading SA Moore to contact me again. This time, she wanted to introduce me to Boris and Natasha, two Eastern European investigators investigating Russian-speaking cybercriminals. I couldn't help but chuckle at the names; they struck me as amusing. "Boris and Natasha, two investigators targeting cybercriminals; unlike the characters from Rocky and Bullwinkle, they're the good guys."

SA Moore knew Boris and Natasha were attending training at the International Law Enforcement Academy in Budapest. Coincidentally, Sergey Kuznetsov was also in Budapest for business and was familiar with Boris and Natasha. He kindly agreed to introduce us.

When I received the news, I flew to Budapest to meet Kuznetsov. Uncertain about how the meeting would unfold, I didn't schedule excessive time in the city. According to protocol, the U.S. Embassy in Hungary arranged accommodations at the Marriott Hotel right next to the Danube River.

When I arrived in Hungary, it was morning. I was exhausted from the journey, but I contacted Kuznetsov as instructed. Unfortunately, I reached his voicemail, which asked me to leave a message. Unsure I would hear back, I decided to shower and rest my eyes. However, as I lay down, my phone rang—it was Kuznetsov.

"Hello," I replied when I picked up the phone.

Kuznetsov spoke with a thick Russian accent, saying, "I'm in hotel lobby. Come down."

I shook off the sleepiness and responded, "I'll be down shortly. Give me ten minutes."

"Kuznetsov pressed, "See you at bar."

When the elevator door opened, I spotted Kuznetsov sitting at a table by the bar. I walked directly to him and said, "It's wonderful to see you again."

Kuznetsov smiled, responding, "Please, sit."

He then picked up his phone and began speaking in Russian with a colleague. While he was on the phone, the waitress approached and asked, "Can I get you anything?"

Chaos erupted in my mind; I was eager for a drink after a long flight. I had I worked my shift despite it being normal working hours. Still I felt uneasy about drinking and I had to remind myself that this wasn't a typical assignment. Unsure of what to do, I decided to wait for Kuznetsov to order first.

Kuznetsov glanced up and politely said, "I'll have your pinot noir."

Hearing his order, I replied, "I'll have the same."

"I'll be right back," the waitress said.

While waiting for our order, I asked, "Will Boris and Natasha be joining us?"

Kuznetsov shook his head. "No! Natasha not here. Boris at academy. He'll join us soon."

"Oh," I replied. "I thought Natasha was here as well."

"No, she couldn't make trip. Too much work back home" Kuznetsov explained.

At that moment, the waitress arrived with our drinks. "Here you go. Will you need anything else?"

Kuznetsov quickly responded, "No, please bring me the bill."

I had only met him once before, mostly over drinks, and curiosity got the better of me. Since Boris wouldn't be joining us until later, I asked, "What's the plan?"

Kuznetsov looked at me and said, "Finish your drink. We go now to lounge and wait."

Kuznetsov and I spent the next several hours in the lounge, drinking and discussing World War II and Operation Carder Kaos. Boris arrived at five in the afternoon, and since he didn't speak English, I depended on Kuznetsov for translation.

Upon Boris's arrival, I stood and introduced myself: "Greetings, my name is Richard LaTulip, and I work for the Secret Service. It's a pleasure to meet you, Boris."

Kuznetsov raised his hand, motioned for me to sit, and spoke to Boris in Russian. Once he finished, Kuznetsov turned to me and said, "He is pleased to meet you."

I couldn't understand the conversation due to my lack of understanding Russian, but it was clear that Kuznetsov and Boris were engaged in quite a discussion. So, when Kuznetsov spoke only six words to me in English, I was taken aback. Nonetheless, I explained my case, concluding with, "How well do you know a Carder named Maksik?"

This led to another lengthy Russian conversation between Kuznetsov and Boris. Eventually, Kuznetsov clarified that Boris was acquainted with Maksik. However, due to rampant corruption in the region, Boris found it difficult to perform his duties, as he faced constant attempts at bribery. Boris reassured me of his commitment to working honestly despite his limited options.

Boris glanced at his watch and said, "I'll return to home soon. When I do, I send you investigative notes on Maksik through the U.S. Embassy." After that, he said his goodbyes.

Kuznetsov then suggested, "Let's go to dinner. There are more people we need to meet."

"Absolutely, let's go!" I replied eagerly.

We encountered some familiar faces, colleagues of Kuznetsov whom I had previously met in Sacramento. The gathering stretched into the evening as we enjoyed our discussions and indulged in drinks. Suddenly, Kuznetsov broke in, saying, "You have important work. It's time for you to go to bed." I hesitated briefly, but it was evident that I needed to leave. Maksik was waiting for me.

Chapter 15

Can you buy a database?

While traveling to different locations, I met diverse people and learned about unique cultures, which broadened my perspective. I began to see the world differently. Gradually, my clothing choices, worldview, and thought processes evolved. At the time, I didn't realize these changes resonated with people beyond the United States. I chose to leverage this, although not all my colleagues shared my views.

Upon returning from Budapest, I aimed to share my experiences with Slimbady, SunCredit, and Maksik. I intended to evoke a sense of jealousy while also motivating others to join me on these adventures. Additionally, I sought to organize more meetings with SunCredit and Slimbady, but my main goal was to connect with an Eastern European Carder, specifically Maksik.

While prepping for another in-person meeting, ATSAIC Sheehan contacted me, asking, "Can you buy a database of stolen credit card numbers from Maksik?"

Intrigued, I responded, "Why?"

ATSAIC Sheehan replied hesitantly, "Other operations have claimed they can obtain a database, but none have been successful. We're interested in purchasing one, and since you have a relationship with Maksik, I thought maybe you could help."

I paused for a moment before replying, "How big?"

"I'm not sure," ATSAIC Sheehan admitted. "What size can you buy?"

"How much are you willing to spend?" I inquired.

Once again, ATSAIC Sheehan replied, "I don't know."

I shook my head and said, "Alright. I'm unsure if I can buy one, but let's find out. I'll speak with Maksik and let you know."

"That's all I'm asking for," ATSAIC Sheehan responded cheerfully.

With guidance from Headquarters and an understanding that purchasing a database from Maksik could enhance my online credibility, I focused on my task.

I messaged Maksik, saying, "Hey, Bro! Quick question. ☺"

Maksik promptly responded, "Hey, what's your question?"

"I'm looking to buy a database. Are you selling?" I inquired.

"Hmmm," Maksik thought. "How big of a database are you considering?"

"Not sure, let's start with 500k. ☺" I responded.

"😀 Give me a moment," Maksik replied.

While I waited, I received a message from Slimbady, "Hey."

I quickly answered, "Hey, how's it going?"

"Working," Slimbady replied. "You?"

"☺ Same here," I typed back.

"Need anything?" Slimbady asked.

"I'm in touch with Maksik," I responded. "I just returned from Budapest, and I'm thinking of heading to Thailand soon. Want to meet up?"

DOI: 10.1201/9781003680390-15

"You travel a lot," Slimbady commented. "How much do you work?"

Just then, a response from Maksik popped up, "I have a fresh database. 50k."

"50k dumps? Or dollars?" I quickly typed.

"I don't work. 🙂" I told Slimbady. "My team does the work. Besides, I can't take my money with me. 😅"

"Yeah, 😁 50k dumps," Maksik replied, "$1.2 million."

Using that figure, I calculated that my average price per credit card was twenty dollars. Usually, a standard U.S. credit card sells for ten to fifteen dollars. However, a new database with high validity is significantly more expensive. To rationalize the expenses, I considered the possible loss.

At that moment, the lost value for each credit card was $500. The estimated loss would amount to $25,000,000 if I purchased 50,000 stolen, unused credit cards. That was an impressive number. Unfortunately, there was one problem: $1,200,000 wasn't an amount I would get approved.

I replied to Maksik, "That's too much for me. ☹ Are there any other options?"

"🤣 You're doing it right, Sone," Slimbady responded. "Keep me posted about Thailand. I'm thinking of joining you."

"😎 I'll keep you updated," I told Slimbady.

Maksik asked, "🤔 How much do you want to spend?"

"What can I purchase for $500k?" I inquired.

"You can buy older database. About 50–75K pieces," Maksik informed me.

I understood that U.S. courts wouldn't question the validity or freshness of the credit card; they focus on the amount, the estimated loss, and the community damage. I aimed to highlight the scale of the operation and its adverse effect on society. I didn't want a flimsy indictment, but I recognized that $500,000 was still too high, leading me to ask Maksik, "What about an old database?"

Following extensive discussions, we reached a preliminary agreement. Maksik stated, "I have a database containing 165k dumps that I can sell for $75k. 🙂"

I replied, "Alright. 😊 Give me time to get the money."

"🙂" Maksik wrote.

Next, I focused on constructing my argument and rationale for the purchase. I estimated my cost per piece at around forty-eight cents for each credit card. On the open market, the average price was fifteen dollars, implying my expenses would total $2,400,000 under normal circumstances. Notably, the overall estimated loss was about $80,000,000.

By acquiring this database, I mitigated potential damages to the community, helped the U.S. government save approximately $2,325,000 in confidential fund expenditures, and validated my ability to procure a database. It was a win-win scenario.

Just before I logged off my undercover computer, Maksik messaged me, "One sec, I have more for you."

"🙂 Sure," I said.

"I have dump+PINS," Maksik typed. "I can sell you 10 for $3k."

"Dumps+PINS?" I asked.

"D+P includes the PIN. 100% valid," Maksik replied. "My team decrypted a batch. You can take money from ATM. 🙂"

"Let me think about it," I replied.

"Okay," Maksik responded. "Just make it quick, they sell out fast, and I'm not sure how many more I can obtain."

I recognized the offer's value, but as with all deals, I had to postpone my decision. I might have quickly said yes in some situations, but this was something new. I required time to discuss its benefits and secure authorization for the purchase. Interestingly, no other credit card vendors on any carding forum were providing dumps with PINs at the time of this offer. The combination of dumps and PINs was unexpected and new to the market.

Maksik's decision to make this offer to me signified his trust. This opportunity was akin to receiving an insider tip about the next big stock. However, I was aware that my chances of approval were slim. Still, I needed to speak with ATSAIC Carrington about the various developments.

As I had done numerous times, I peeked into ATSAIC Carrington's office and asked, "Do you have a moment?"

ATSAIC Carrington, munching on a few Tums, replied, "Sure, come in. What's on your mind?"

"I spoke with Maksik," I replied. "There are two key points. First, he agreed to sell me a database."

Interrupting, Carrington asked, "That's fantastic. How much is it?"

I explained carefully, "Hear me out. Maksik is willing to sell me 165k dumps. It's an older database, and honestly, Headquarters didn't specify whether it should be new or old. However, a new database of 50k dumps costs $1 million."

Suddenly choking on a Tums, ATSAIC exclaimed, "What? One million dollars? Did you agree to that?"

"NO!" I answered emphatically. "Absolutely not. I realized that was far too much money. Instead, I got 165k dumps for $75,000."

Skeptically, ATSAIC Carrington asked, "$75,000? Did Headquarters approve this?"

"Not really," I responded. "But they never indicated how much to spend or the quantity to buy. ATSAIC Sheehan only inquired if I could purchase a database. If they want a database, it will be $75,000."

"I'm not sure if it will get approved," ATSAIC Carrington said frankly.

"Well, in that case, they won't receive a database," I replied dismissively.

"Alright," ATSAIC Carrington said. "What else? What was the second thing?"

"Maksik is offering to sell me ten dumps, with PIN, for $3,000," I said.

"What?" ATSAIC Carrington responded in disbelief. "Why on earth would we purchase ten dumps for $3,000? That's $300 for each credit card. What do we usually get for that amount?"

Once again, I warned ATSAIC Carrington, stating, "At the moment, I get around 200 credit cards for that amount; however, it varies depending on whether it's classic, gold, or another type. Ultimately, this is a good opportunity for me. There are no online vendors for these cards. It's like cash from ATMs. The risk is minimal for a Carder: there's no need to enter a store and no hassle in selling stolen items on eBay. It's an excellent deal but comes at a high cost."

ATSAIC Carrington reclined in his chair, pondering for ten seconds before saying, "No, it's not worth it. However, let's contact Headquarters to discuss the database."

Feeling frustrated, I left his office and approached ATSAIC Sheehan with the same proposal. I believed that if I could secure support from Headquarters, San Diego would be obligated to agree. I was aware that ATSAIC Carrington and SAIC Montaña disliked the political aspects of this investigation, and I knew I needed to leverage that to obtain the necessary approvals.

Unfortunately, ATSAIC Sheehan concurred with ATSAIC Carrington, contending that the ten dumps with PINs were excessively costly. He also pointed out that this approach had no significant prosecutorial value and urged me to opt for the standard, cheaper dumps.

Strike two; however, it was unclear whether anyone trusted Maksik. I concurred that the notion was unprecedented, as no forum offered dumps and PINs. Additionally, breaking PIN encryption appeared implausible, and we hadn't received any updates from our industry connections. This culminated in a typical dead-before-arrival proposition, yet I still knew an opportunity was missed.

For now, I set this aside. It was time to persuade ATSAIC Sheehan that I had a solid strategy for acquiring their requested database. My position was that the U.S. government was getting a good deal, and if executed properly, the database purchase would emphasize the scale of Maksik's operation.

After the greetings, I began the conference by stating, "I spoke with Maksik regarding purchasing a database. Without detailing the entire conversation, he offered to sell me 160,000 stolen credit card numbers for $75,000."

The phone fell silent, leaving me with the impression that my words had gone unnoticed. At that moment, ATSAIC Sheehan inquired, "What led you to negotiate the purchase of 160,000 stolen credit card numbers for $75,000?"

Taken aback, I responded, "This wasn't my deal; it was yours. I was the only one who could bring it to the table. Furthermore, no one informed me what to buy or how much to spend. By the way, the first database offered was for one million dollars. I knew that was too high, so I negotiated to a more reasonable number: $75,000 for 160,000. It's a good deal."

Once more, there was silence. After approximately thirty seconds, ATSAIC Sheehan instructed, "Go back to Maksik and request 100,000 stolen credit cards for $50,000."

I quickly responded, "What? Are you kidding me? I spent over an hour with him on this deal. Going back to negotiate further is ridiculous. I'm in the big leagues, working with the elite Carders with direct access to hackers. If you want to compete at this level, you must spend money."

Going back and nitpicking felt cheap, so I added, "Besides these offers, I'm receiving positive feedback from Maksik about his willingness to travel and meet me in Thailand. If this deal happens, my chances of meeting Maksik also increase."

"Okay," ATSAIC Sheehan said. "I will talk to SAIC Stokes and get his authorization for the deal. Anything else?"

I glanced at ATSAIC Carrington, sensing I had nothing further to contribute, and replied, "No. Thanks."

Ultimately, as ATSAIC Sheehan pursues authorization for the deal, I decided to hold off mentioning anything to Maksik. I anticipated that if I spoke too early, considering all the ongoing issues with this investigation, agreeing too quickly and later backtracking would result in disaster.

I waited two weeks, holding off Maksik until I finally heard from ATSAIC Sheehan. I presented the proposal to AD Dubois, who concurred that it was a sound idea. To bolster my operation, AD Dubois recognized that transactions like this must occur for the Secret Service to compete at a higher level.

I finally felt comfortable telling Maksik I agreed to buy the database while gathering the funds. I kept talking online about my desire to visit Thailand, specifically Phuket Island. This was one of the better places to visit in Thailand. It had beaches, good food, and most importantly, women eager to meet a man.

While conversing with Maksik, I also spoke with Slimbady and SunCredit, who expressed interest in meeting with me in Phuket. Though Slimbady and SunCredit were additional opportunities, my primary focus remained on Maksik. I knew I needed support from others like Slimbady to encourage his travel.

Since Slimbady had previously met me and had recommended that I connect with Maksik, I thought he might reach out to Maksik on my behalf. To facilitate this, I ensured that Maksik knew about our meeting in Macau.

In our discussions, Maksik fluctuated between a firm "yes," to a casual "I will go," and ultimately to a hesitant "maybe I will meet you." Even though his commitment varied, I sensed I was nearing a breakthrough in brokering a face-to-face meeting with a Russian-speaking cybercriminal who, as SAIC Stokes believed, does not meet with Americans. While promoting

Phuket, I failed to consider one crucial detail: the island had suffered a catastrophic tsunami that devastated its coastline, destroyed boats and homes, and completely altered its landscape.

Maksik felt Phuket had not yet recovered from the tsunami's effects. As a result, I swiftly adjusted my approach, researched the situation, contacted the U.S. Embassy in Thailand, and discovered that Phuket was undergoing significant renovations and that the beachfront resorts were restored to their former glory.

I shared this information with Maksik, explaining that while Phuket was affected, it is being redeveloped and will improve beyond its pre-tsunami state. Although I'm uncertain if Maksik accepted my perspective, I suggested that he could verify this through Google.

During my discussions with Maksik, Slimbady, and SunCredit, I encountered a new Carder named Vincent. He was from China but lived in Bangkok. Since Maksik was uncertain and I wasn't entirely sure about his trip to Phuket, I began inviting Slimbady, SunCredit, and Vincent. I aimed to do everything possible to support the travel I was promoting, as I wanted to prevent the next operation from becoming a complete loss.

Furthermore, I was granted permission to spend more time out, allowing for a more normal experience. Headquarters and SAIC Montaña recognized that the limitations imposed on me in Macau were excessive. As a result, they eased these restrictions. With fewer limitations, I could change locations freely and was no longer prohibited from visiting massage parlors, bars, or restaurants, nor was I restricted by time. When this was told to me, I felt progress toward a more real-life interaction in front of me, or so I thought.

After several days of online discussions, Slimbady, SunCredit, and Vincent agreed to meet me in Phuket. I informed them that I was staying at a hotel on Patong Beach. Meanwhile, Maksik was still undecided; I figured if he attended, it would be the icing on the cake.

I briefed ATSAICs Carrington and Sheehan on the operational plan. I would spend at least two weeks in Phuket, Thailand. The plan was to meet, with a day's separation, in the order of Maksik, SunCredit, and finally Slimbady and Vincent. I scheduled each meeting for two to three days, except for the meeting with Maksik, which would last for his visit.

Building on my previous topic, I wanted to initiate a criminal scheme that started in San Diego and ended in Thailand. This time, I focused on Vincent, engaging him in conversation to ask him to produce one hundred counterfeit credit cards. As with SunCredit, I would provide the credit card account numbers and the "names" to emboss the physical credit card. Vincent agreed to handle this and have them for me when I visited him in Phuket.

With the deal finalized, I went to the local Western Union storefront and sent him $5,000. This amount represented half of the total, with the other half to be given to him in Phuket. The face-to-face transaction poses a challenging defense for Vincent if he is arrested and extradited to the United States.

Several months had passed since the August 2005 meeting with SunCredit and Slimbady, along with numerous discussions with Headquarters. As is often the case with the Secret Service, if you wait long enough, the current situation will change, sometimes for the better, and at other times for the worse. Unfortunately, this instance fell into the latter category.

SAIC Stokes still allowed me to meet for multiple days; however, the duration of those days became a contentious issue. SAIC Stokes and others felt I could control everything—literally everything. They directed me to inform everyone about their travel details and, almost as if I were their parents, when to return home. This reasoning was flawed and, more importantly, put me in a precarious situation.

To complicate matters further, ATSAIC Sheehan and others at Headquarters, sticking with their isolated approach, were given only limited information. Jack Jones concluded that we lacked sufficient detail on SunCredit, branding him as low-value and not worth investing time and resources in. Consequently, I was told to uninvite SunCredit.

Fortunately, ATSAIC Sheehan still saw value in meeting with Slimbady. Vincent was another story. He was an unknown entity, just like SunCredit. Everyone agreed that it was fine for this operation if Vincent traveled with Slimbady; I could meet with both simultaneously. However, I wasn't encouraged to urge him to travel.

ATSAIC Sheehan has now mandated that my meeting with Slimbady and Vincent can only last two days. Moreover, irrespective of any developments with Slimbady and Vincent, I was instructed to sever ties after this period. I was advised to inform them of my return flight to the United States, and that would be the end of it.

Compounding my stress, ATSAIC Sheehan also wanted me to mislead everyone. I was to give Slimbady, Vincent, SunCredit, or Maksik the impression that I was meeting with them individually, despite the likely reality that they were already aware of my actions, as they had all communicated with one another.

Regardless of how you viewed it, Headquarters' demand placed me on a slippery slope. Patong Beach was a small community with only a few main roads, in contrast to Bangkok's numerous routes. Several unforeseen scenarios could arise. For instance, Maksik and I might be out drinking and unexpectedly bump into Slimbady and Vincent. What then? I can almost anticipate the question.

Slimbady, with a look of surprise, asked, "I thought you left?" Being caught off guard, I replied, "Nope, I chose to stay and hang out with my friend Maksik. You remember him; you introduced us two months ago."

A phrase that will echo throughout the investigation is, "Your safety is our only concern." However, whether deliberate or not, SAIC Montaña and SAIC Stokes took every measure to put me in a precarious situation. I feel that SAIC Montaña's actions were taken because he didn't know better, and let's be honest, most leaders weren't promoted because of their investigative prowess.

Upon receiving the green light, I updated Resident Agent in Charge (RAIC) Duc Tran and Foreign Service National Investigator (FSNI) Anchalee "Lea" Boonme about our operational objectives and anticipated outcomes. RAIC Tran, born in Vietnam, was an ideal match for the area due to his cultural insights, making him a valuable information source. Notably, he grasped the nation's dynamics and carried a relaxed demeanor.

FSNI Anchalee "Lea" Boonme previously served as a Police Major in the local police force. During her time in law enforcement, she gained experience not just on the streets of Bangkok but across Thailand. FSNI Boonme's extensive connections within the various police departments were an additional advantage; she could reach out and mobilize resources swiftly, often within an hour.

Due to local politics, even with this information and before the commencement of any operation, RAIC Tran requested that I travel to Bangkok for an in-person brief. ATSAIC Sheehan initially opposed this idea and of me flying to Bangkok to conduct an in-person brief. When word reached RAIC Tran, he pushed back, stating this wasn't an ask but a requirement. ATSAIC Sheehan pulled back and relented.

ATSAIC Sheehan either lacked the determination to resist or considered this decision not worth contesting. Regardless, it was January 2006 when Sone and I boarded our flights to Thailand.

Chapter 16

A club, a chance encounter, and a room

The flight was long, and I struggled to get quality sleep. The airport was enormous yet impressively clean, surpassing what I had anticipated. Our group made its way to baggage claim, navigating through customs smoothly, and thankfully, there were no lost bags. After retrieving our luggage, I was eager to rest, especially since it was already quite late.

When we arrived, the hotel staff greeted us warmly and offered their assistance. Stepping into the hotel lobby for the first time, I was mesmerized. The lobby was a vast display of luxury, embodying a perfect blend of elegance and opulence. Every element appeared thoughtfully selected, from the stunning chandeliers that emitted a cozy, welcoming light to the carefully positioned greenery, each reflecting the hotel's bond with its surroundings.

During our interactions with the courteous staff, the lobby elevator doors slid open with a gentle hiss. The air was instantly infused with a cascade of musical notes, each chord vibrating with pulsating energy. The music carried with it an undeniable sense of vitality, and each beat pushed me away from the sleep I so much desired to a newfound sense of energy.

As the elevator doors gracefully closed, the auditory tapestry that had briefly enveloped us began to recede, leaving behind a muted sense of longing. Once robust and vibrant, the sound turned into a distant murmur, gradually fading into the background. It felt as if the music had offered us a fleeting glimpse into a world where time stood still, only to be gently whisked away as the doors shut.

As we finished our check-in, ASAIC DuBois turned to me and asked, "Any interest in following that sound?"

I replied without hesitation, "Absolutely. Just give me five minutes to change my clothes and brush my teeth."

With a grin, ASAIC DuBois said, "I'll see you in five."

New energy pulsed through my body. Uncertain of how long the music would continue, I felt an urge to quickly turn around and meet ASAIC DuBois. In no time, I found myself back in the lobby. Not far behind me was ASAIC DuBois. We met with a silent nod and set out to find the source of the music.

The pulse of the music thrummed beneath our feet like a steady, alluring invitation. It beckoned us downward, down the rabbit hole. As we stepped into the elevator, the music's bass surged, its vibrations becoming almost tactile, as if the very air was charged with anticipation. The bass grew more insistent as we descended each floor, seductively tugging at our senses.

As the elevator doors parted, they revealed a world of sensory indulgence. The music directed us toward our goal, compelling us to move toward the bar. It was as if the walls were alive, throbbing in time and guiding us in the right direction. Just around the corner, the source of our draw revealed itself—a bar, an oasis of luminescence amidst the shadowy hall.

As we approached the bar's entrance, the doorman looked at us and gave a subtle nod of recognition, simultaneously stepping aside to allow our arrival. The lights scattered across the bar, dancing in hypnotic patterns, casting their spell on every surface they touched. A disco

DOI: 10.1201/9781003680390-16

ball hung like a luminary deity, casting fragmented constellations across the room, guiding us toward the heart of the spectacle.

The bar, a well-choreographed stage for the evening's performances, presented itself in layers. To the left, a circular bar exuded a warm, inviting glow, where bartenders displayed their skilled craft, mixing the perfect drink. Like islands in a sea of movement, tables punctuated the dance floor's expanse, each strategically positioned to offer refuge and vantage. And amidst this orchestrated symphony of light and sound, figures moved with deliberate grace, a harmony of bodies and music.

Among them, a tapestry of elegance painted in ebony hues. Asian women, draped in attire that sculpted allure, donned the night like a second skin. They wore a symphony of blacks, flirtatiously short leather skirts, and cropped tops that bared hints of vulnerability. The play of light across their artfully applied makeup revealed the precision of their allure, with red accents igniting the darkness like embers of passion. Cascades of raven-black locks framed their faces, cascading like silken waterfalls over their shoulders.

ASAIC DuBois and I ventured deeper into the bar, the women's collective gaze swiveled in unison, acknowledging newcomers to their party. The air hummed with intrigue, curiosity mingling with desire. The bar offered its pleasures but was divided by tables, where companions engaged in intimate conversations, sipping from glasses of intoxicating creations and the smooth depths of Johnny Walker Black Label—two distinct worlds.

Set against the skillfully arranged tables, the bar pulsed with its unique form of communication. Ladies surrounded this island, seemingly propping up the bar, holding it steady. As they caught your gaze, they offered a subtle tilt of the head, a glance filled with unspoken intention, a playful nibble of the lower lip—these were the signals exchanged in the dance of attraction. Bodies drew nearer, almost magnetically, secrets shared through the brush of fingertips against skin, journeying from hair to shoulder to the delicate curve of a lower back.

Stepping toward the bar, I caught the bartender's attention and ordered two Red Bulls and vodkas. In that space, the backdrop to my purpose, I felt a touch, ever so slightly, against my arm, a hint that carried an undercurrent of an invitation. Before I could speak, the bartender presented me with our drinks, a slight interruption that paused the beginnings of a conversation.

As I passed the drink to my companion, he recognized the unfolding events and retreated to the other invitations the rest of the club offered. Once ASAIC DuBois departed, I was able to explore my spontaneous connection. The lights from the disco ball cascaded through gentle shadows and bright lights that only served to accentuate her features. Her petite form and the graceful curve of her neck echoed old-world charm, seamlessly juxtaposed against the modernity surrounding us.

I was captivated, unable to look away from the gentle light dancing off her silken hair, the subtle movement of her lips as she laughed with her friends nearby, the enigmatic depth of her almond-shaped eyes, the graceful curves of her body, the firmness of her backside. As I moved closer, I took a deep breath to collect my thoughts. The last thing I wanted was to stumble over my words, especially since they were fueled by such sincere admiration.

Looking deeply into her eyes, I said, "My name is Rich. Can I buy you a drink?"

She gazed back at me, her dark eyes meeting mine, perhaps searching for the truth in my words. A slow smile appeared on her lips, and she nodded in acceptance, saying, "My name is Yu Mei. You can call me Cindy. And yes, I would love a drink."

Curious, I responded, "Cindy? That sounds very American. If you don't mind, I prefer Yu Mei. What would you like to drink?"

Yu Mei leaned closer and whispered, "I'd like a Singapore Sling."

As our bond grew, I touched her arm and remarked, "A local drink. I like that."

Energized, I turned back to the bartender and ordered, "One Singapore Sling and a Johnny Walker Black Label on the rocks."

As our conversation became more intimate, we engaged in a playful dance, laughing together. Time felt suspended, yet it continued its relentless march. The dim lighting and the gleam from the disco ball faded. It was two in the morning, and the bar was closing. Eager to prolong our evening, brimming with energy and desire, I inquired, "This spot is closing soon. Do you know another place where we could enjoy a drink?"

Yu Mei nodded without a moment's pause and replied, "I know a spot."

Smiling, I responded, "Great. Let's go."

Yu Mei turned, glanced back at me, and said, "Follow me."

"With pleasure," I answered.

Yu Mei guided me to her favorite mode of transport: a moped. She donned her helmet, hopped onto the moped, turned to me, and said, "Get on."

"Alright," I replied, swiftly climbing aboard.

Yu Mei glanced back and winked, saying, "Ready? Hold on tight."

Before I could answer, she sped off. As I looked around, I realized that despite the late hour, the city buzzed with life, its nighttime energy palpable in the distant murmur of voices, glowing lights, and the sporadic honk of a taxi. The moon cast a silvery sheen, enhancing Yu Mei's features and making her shine even more brightly than she had inside the sparkling bar.

The journey was brief but full of twists, highlighting the city's vastness. Without Yu Mei, I'd be lost. As we sped through the streets, she suddenly turned into a dark alley and stopped. I dismounted and observed my surroundings. Tall buildings loomed over us, their shadows merging with the night. Before us stood an abandoned building, its façade weathered by time.

I asked, puzzled, "Is this a bar?"

Yu Mei giggled and replied, "Absolutely! Come on."

She gestured for me to follow, and I couldn't help but say, "Sure."

As we stepped into the building, my Secret Service training kicked in. I quickly assessed the interior, trying to map out the layout. Dim, flickering fluorescent lights created eerie patterns on the walls, just enough to light our path. A deserted elevator stood beside the unfinished staircase with its doors slightly open, hinting at its broken condition.

I wondered about our destination, but before I could ponder further, a towering Western man interrupted my thoughts. His commanding presence struck me, and with a quick nod and a pointed gesture, he directed us up the unfinished staircase. When we reached the second floor, another sharply dressed man awaited us. The routine check of Yu Mei's ID and a swift pat-down of me felt strangely formal against the surreal backdrop.

Once satisfied, the doorman flung open the heavy doors, unveiling an unexpected scene. The room buzzed with energy, with a vast crowd from diverse backgrounds swaying to the latest music. The vibrant bar contrasted starkly with the building's run-down exterior, creating a mesmerizing image.

As we navigated the bustling crowd, our fingers lightly intertwined, Yu Mei and I headed toward the bar. I ordered a Johnny Walker, and Yu Mei continued her quest for a Singapore Sling. As the music's rhythmic beats engulfed the room, a sultry bass melded with a haunting melody, prompting Yu Mei to pull me onto the dance floor.

On the bustling dance floor, Yu Mei turned and pulled me closer, her eyes conveying an alluring promise. Our bodies swayed together, perfectly in sync with the song's rhythm. The space between us vanished, and I could feel her warmth, each heartbeat resonating with mine. Yu Mei's delicate fingers traced soft patterns on the back of my neck, sending tingles down my spine. We became one on the dance floor, our movements creating a passionate exchange.

Feeling the escalating desire, I reciprocated, my hands gently exploring Yu Mei's body, caressing her curves while steadying her slender form. As my fingers roamed, the flow of her body invited a deeper exploration. Starting at the nape of her neck, an area often overlooked, my fingertips danced lightly across her skin. The gentle slope of her collarbones guided my hand to the tender curve of her shoulders.

As I followed her outline, I admired her unique figure—a beautiful blend of delicate femininity and hidden strength, with deliberate, graceful movements. The subtle muscular definition in her arms revealed her discipline and resilience, a quiet power wrapped in elegance. My fingers drifted down Yu Mei's back, tracing the gentle contours of her spine, and I marveled at her strength and, at that moment, the vulnerability it displayed.

Venturing to Yu Mei's waist, my hands discovered the gentle flare of her hips, the curve speaking tales of her agility and rhythm. I felt the subtle tension in her slightly muscular thighs, resulting from countless hours of dedication and perseverance, indicating a hunger for life and its myriad activities.

Every curve, every muscle, every nuance of her form told a story. In their journey, my hands sought to understand and appreciate these tales, celebrating the beauty and strength of a woman as tenacious as she was delicate. The act wasn't just a touch; it was a silent ode to the masterpiece that was her body.

The firmness of Yu Mei's body, our body, and my hands appreciating our closeness, the world beyond the pulsating lights and the music faded into oblivion. The intensity of our dance lasted until the first soft hues of dawn at five a.m. With the club's patrons thinning out, I offered an alternative.

I leaned in and whispered in Yu Mei's ear, "Would you like to stay with me at my hotel?"

Yu Mei looked at me, clearly enjoying her evening, nodded, and said, "I would."

She reached out, taking my hand, and led me out of the club. Waiting outside was Yu Mei's moped. After putting on her helmet, she climbed on, started the engine, and nodded to me, signaling she was ready. I quickly jumped behind her, wrapping my arms around her waist, eager for our night to unfold.

The streets of Bangkok stretched out before us, an untouched canvas beneath the serene cityscape. We wove through alleys and main thoroughfares, the wind rushing past, mingling excitement with anticipation. As we approached the impressive luxury hotel, Yu Mei effortlessly parked the moped.

The hotel lobby's grandeur contrasted sharply with the vibrant club behind a run-down building. Hand in hand, we walked over the echoing marble floors. The elevator doors opened like a long-awaited play, and the outside world faded as we stepped inside. A soft chime announced our ascent, and I took Yu Mei's hand, guiding her through the velvet silence to my suite.

Crossing the threshold, the room welcomed us with serenity. The city's heartbeat faded, as if the world dared not intrude on this moment. The dim lights cast a warm glow, enveloping us in intimacy. Our eyes locked in a silent conversation, each glance a word, each blink a sentence of longing.

As the door clicked shut behind us, we immediately embraced. Our kisses were strokes of desire, creating a masterpiece on the canvas of the night. Hands explored with purposeful tenderness, urged on by the silent cravings of our skin, eager to trace one another's curves and contours.

We honored the raw reality of one another's bodies, balancing reverence with urgency. Our clothes fell away as if they had never been there. Cradling her gently, we surrendered to the bed's embrace. The urgency of our connection surged like an unstoppable tide, filling the room with the music of our union.

As the flames of passion softened to glowing embers, I lay next to Yu Mei, feeling the rhythm of her breath and the warmth of our skin, a gentle echo of the night's intensity. Side by side, we basked in the afterglow, the sanctuary of the bed cradling us in a tender lull.

But as the dawn's golden light began to fill the room, a quiet alarm within me hinted at the hours slipping away. The sun rose, not just a celestial body but a timeless witness to the ethereal dance of love and connection. In that tranquil morning, I realized I could neither rest nor relent.

The call of duty was like a siren's song, drawing me away from her warm embrace. Although I found comfort in Yu Mei's arms, I rose with quiet determination, each action a soft goodbye to the night and its memories. After preparing myself, my singular focus returned to the reason for my presence here—the undercover mission. I leaned down to kiss Yu Mei one last time as she slept peacefully in my bed, silently signaling my farewell.

In the lobby, I found Sone alongside my colleagues from San Diego, RAIC Tran and FSNI Boonme. FSNI Boonme guided us to their office, where we would brief our various counterparts. Still feeling tired and my mind clouded with exhaustion, I immediately sought out coffee.

FSNI Boonme introduced me to Lieutenant Colonel Somsak Chaiwat, the head of the specialized unit I would collaborate with during the operation in Phuket. His lean and chiseled physique indicated that his ascent through the ranks had been challenging and well-earned.

As the meeting began, Lieutenant Colonel Chaiwat stated firmly, "You and Sone are visitors to my country. Although you hold a position as a police officer in your home country, here you have no authority. However, you are allowed to work undercover to complete your mission."

I nodded and replied, "Yes, I understand. Thank you."

Lieutenant Colonel Chaiwat continued without altering his tone, "My team and I will monitor and provide cover for you and Sone. We will not interfere unless either of you is in trouble. Do you understand?"

"Of course," I assured him. "We understand."

Lieutenant Colonel Chaiwat gave a slight nod and said, "Good. We'll see you in Phuket."

After the meeting, the team headed to the airport to travel to Phuket. Sleep overwhelmed me, and I only awoke when the airplane wheels touched down with a gentle thud on the beachfront tarmac of the Phuket International Airport. The day's sweltering heat caused the horizon to waver, giving the distant palm trees a mirage-like quality.

Once the plane was in position, the cabin doors opened, and a gust of tropical air swept into the aircraft, enveloping the passengers and bringing with it the scent of the sea. As I exited the plane, I was greeted by a symphony of sounds: the distant calls of exotic birds, the soft hum of airport activity, and the occasional roar of another plane taking off or landing. Although the airport was modern, it had an unmistakable island charm.

As I walked through the terminal, Sone and I distanced ourselves from my colleagues. From this point onward, Sone and I would be two friends on holiday. I looked around and noticed a colorful array of advertisements showcasing idyllic beaches, vibrant underwater scenes, and serene Buddhist temples. Once we had collected our bags, we looked for a taxi.

Since it was my first time in Phuket, I didn't barter or haggle with the taxi stand attendant. Instead, I explained our destination, listened to the offer, and accepted the first proposal. From my previous international travels, I knew that a tourist's chances of getting the best rate were slim. We began our journey, weaving through the island's lush interior.

The scenery was an ever-changing tapestry of dense tropical forests interspersed with glimpses of azure waters. The taxi's open windows let the scent of the vegetation, rich with an earthy undertone, permeate the car's interior. As we drove along the route to Patong Beach, our driver told us about the local festivals, parties, hidden temples, and legendary sunsets.

As we neared Patong, the energy shifted. The taxi finished making its way through the winding roads of Phuket. I looked out the window to get a better view of the glimmering sea that painted a picture of serenity. Sensing my curiosity, the driver explained the island's uniqueness, "During the day, Patong Beach is calm. Most people are resting up, you see, recovering from the previous night's festivities."

I raised an eyebrow in intrigue. "Hmmm? Interesting. Anything more you can share?"

The driver chuckled softly, "Patong Beach transforms as the sun sets. It's like the whole place comes alive. Especially around the beach areas, the streets are abuzz with activity."

The taxi drove along the main road near the seafront. As we went by, the remnants of the recent tsunami were ever-present. Walkways were being repaired or replaced brick by brick. The scene was a mix of construction and beauty. I immediately reflected on my conversations with Maksik. I knew he was concerned about the beach's condition, but thought he'd be happy once he saw this rebuilding progress.

My thoughts were disrupted, and the driver added, "To the left is Bangla Road. When the sun goes down, people seem to appear from nowhere. They fill the streets, bars, and discos, turning the night into a wonderland."

I smiled, "I can't wait for the night."

At last, the taxi arrived at our hotel. Situated on a high point, the hotel provided sweeping views of the crescent-shaped Patong Beach. As the sun dipped below the horizon, I could hear the distant sounds of music, laughter, and chatter echoing in the air. I immediately felt like I was missing out on the essence of this place. The excitement of Patong Beach's nightlife felt so close, yet I was far removed from it here.

Though picturesque, the hotel's seclusion wasn't ideal for my covert operation. As I approached the reception, I hoped for a smooth check-in, but in the back of my mind, I knew this would be my last time at this hotel. It was just too far from the fun.

I walked up to the front desk, where the attendant greeted me with a smile and said, "Welcome, I'm Noi, here to assist you with your registration. Could I please have your passport?"

"Of course," I said while handing her my U.S. passport.

She flipped through the passport pages, checked the computer, and said, "Yes, I see your details here. Thank you for choosing our hotel. Your accommodations are secured, and we've applied the U.S. Embassy rate to your room. Could I have your payment method?"

My heart skipped a beat. Despite my explicit instructions, the U.S. Embassy registered the rooms at a government rate. I attempted to maintain composure and responded, "There must be a mistake. I have no connection with the U.S. Embassy."

Noi appeared slightly flustered, yet she scanned the system again and remarked, "I apologize, sir, but it's indicated here. You are part of the U.S. Embassy."

Swallowing my frustration, I accepted the key from Noi and said, "Thank you."

Frustrated and with a whirlwind of thoughts, I went to my room and called ASAIC DuBois's number.

ASAIC DuBois picked up the phone and said, "Hey Rich, what's going on?"

I didn't hold back, saying, "Are they intentionally trying to get me killed? Do they want to blow my cover? The Embassy booked Sone's and my rooms at the government rate. Plus, who picked this hotel? It's isolated and far from the beach. Who would believe for a moment that I'm here for a fun weekend?"

A silence hung in the air before ASAIC DuBois grumbled, "Hmmm, so you think you need to relocate? Where do you plan to go? I can contact local agents; they can find you another hotel."

"No! They were the ones who caused this trouble. I can't handle any more errors. I've already discovered a place," I said, "It's a resort that offers suites with pool access, located in the center of the entertainment district, just steps from the beach and Bangla Road. It's perfect."

"Alright, go ahead and make the arrangements; I'll update the team," ASAIC DuBois responded.

After hanging up, I felt the gravity of the situation. But there was no time to dwell; I needed to act fast, ensuring my identity remained hidden and that I was as far away from this hotel as possible.

Chapter 17

Maksik goes to Egypt

Under stress, I concentrated on my mission. Knowing Maksik wouldn't arrive until the second day gave me the chance to leave the first hotel. Rather than heading to Bangla Road, I opened my laptop and checked my ICQ messenger for any messages.

I gazed at the screen, anticipating it to load and spring to life. After a moment, as the connection was established, several "kuku" sounds echoed around me. Unfortunately, none of them came from Maksik; instead, they were from SunCredit, Slimbady, Vincent, and Leon. I held off from replying, wanting to wait for more information from Maksik.

I realized that if I revealed to Slimbady and Vincent that I was in Phuket, they would likely rush to meet me there. It was wiser to remain silent tonight. Additionally, I was still seething from my check-in ordeal. I'd let it go and transition to the new resort in the morning, happily leaving this experience behind.

Morning couldn't arrive quickly enough. Sone and I met in the lobby, where I noticed Noi at the counter. I asked her, "Could you please call a taxi for us? Sone and I are checking out this morning."

With a sorrowful expression, Noi responded, "Is there a problem with the room? What can we do to fix this?"

I gestured dismissively and replied, "The room is fine, I just prefer a hotel closer to the beach."

"Understood. I'll arrange for a taxi," Noi said.

Sone and I lingered in the hotel lobby, soaking in the stunning view one last time. When our taxi arrived, we headed toward the our new resort. As we sped along, I gazed out the window, feeling both excitement and nervousness. The taxi veered past a bar, designed to resemble an 18th-century ship, and I mused about what an ideal meeting spot it would be.

Close to that bar stood the our new accommodations, where its impressive grandeur was immediately noticeable. Traditional Thai architecture harmoniously mingled with contemporary designs, resulting in a luxurious yet inviting exterior. As Sone and I stepped outside, we were welcomed by the soothing sounds of water features and the gentle strains of traditional Thai music in the background.

As Sone and I approached the check-in counter, the hotel attendant, a young and attractive woman in traditional Thai dress, greeted us with a traditional greeting—a Wai, which is considered a gesture of respect. She directed us to sit and kindly asked for our travel documents, which she needed to proceed with the check-in process. Flipping through my passport, her brow furrowed as she noted the absence of an entry stamp. "Excuse me, do you have another passport? There's no stamp here."

I responded, "I believed they stamped my passport. Could you please check again?"

She examined the document again, looking at me as she said, "I'm sorry, but I don't see any stamps."

DOI: 10.1201/9781003680390-17

I maintained my composure and feigned surprise, saying, "I didn't know. I'm not employed by Thai Customs; I merely followed the crowd. The official gave me my travel document and let me through."

The attendant lifted an eyebrow but shrugged, showing no interest in continuing the discussion. Once formalities were done, the attendant guided me to my suite. It was a brief stroll through the resort, past the pool and a quaint tropical oasis. Palm trees danced lightly in the breeze, and the air was fragrant with blooming orchids and jasmine.

As I entered the suite, I couldn't help but feel awe. A sliding door revealed a private pool, glimmering softly in the ambient light, alongside a cozy deck featuring loungers. Lush tropical plants surrounded the pool, creating a tranquil environment that enhanced the sense of privacy and opulence.

The attendant flashed a smile and remarked, "We hope you enjoy your stay, sir. Don't hesitate to call if you need anything."

With a nod of appreciation, I closed the door to my suite, the weight of my mission momentarily forgotten amidst the beauty and tranquility of the resort. But as the door closed, I quickly pulled out my laptop and checked for online messages. I thought, indeed, Maksik had arrived. But to my surprise, there were no messages.

I reflected on my situation and realized it could be a while if there were no messages today. So, why not begin exploring the area? After all, I was on a mission to be a tourist, and this was my opportunity. I strolled down the road toward the beach. As I passed the Port Bar, it struck me as an ideal spot for a quick drink.

At the bar, I ordered the local beer, Singha, and engaged in a brief chat with the bartender. I sought recommendations for places to visit on Bangla Road, but the bartender seemed disinterested in the conversation. It was likely that every tourist posed the same questions. His only response was that all places on Bangla Road were good.

After finishing my drink, I made my way toward the famous road. To my surprise, as I strolled around, the area was unusually quiet, with only a handful of people wandering about. I found myself wondering where everyone had gone during the day. Not dwelling on it too long, I returned to my room to check online.

Once again, I hadn't heard from Maksik. The only messages I received were from SunCredit, Slimbady, and Vincent. I considered responding and decided to keep the conversation brief with SunCredit, as I didn't want him to ask too many questions. Then it occurred to me, "What if Maksik doesn't show up?" I didn't want this trip to end in failure, so I reached out to Slimbady and Vincent.

At 6 p.m., with no word from Maksik, a wave of sadness washed over me. I checked every potential flight from Ukraine to Thailand, realizing he should have arrived by now. The truth hit me: Maksik wasn't coming. As I contemplated my next step, my phone buzzed with a message from ASAIC DuBois, inviting me to his room at the Baan Lai Mai resort.

Upon my arrival, the whole team was gathered. I greeted everyone, saying, "I haven't heard from Maksik. He should have arrived by now, based on the flights I looked up. I did leave Slimbady a message offline. Additionally, I talked to Vincent, who assured me he would arrive in five days."

ASAIC DuBois responded, "Understood. What shall we do in the interim?"

"Outside of what I've already mentioned," I explained, "I have just one option left. I will keep the line open, and if I receive any updates from Maksik, I will inform the team."

ASAIC DuBois contacted ATSAIC Sheehan and explained our current situation. While he didn't share specifics with me, his expression indicated that Russian-speaking Carders don't meet with Americans. At the same time, ATSAIC Sheehan didn't request that we cancel the operation, suggesting I was being afforded some trust. I didn't feel that all hope was lost.

After the meeting concluded and everyone departed, ASAIC DuBois turned to me and suggested, "How about we meet at Rock Hard on Bangla Road later tonight? Let's say around 9?"

Wanting to refresh my mind and find out what made Patong Beach renowned, I eagerly responded, "Definitely. I'll message you once I arrive."

With a friendly pat on my shoulder, ASAIC DuBois said, "Copy that."

From that moment on, the evening took on a life of its own, the ambient oranges and purples of twilight blending into the neon hues of Patong Beach's nightlife. As I finished dinner, a noticeable change was occurring. The quietness disappeared. The streets were alive, Tuk-Tuks buzzed around like flies, and men and women filed toward Bangla Road.

Bangla Road was a riot of sensations. The air was thick with competing melodies—Thai pop music clashing with Western hits. Bars and nightclubs lined both sides of the street, their entrances marked by women in vibrant attire, who aimed to catch the attention of passersby with their playful gestures and inviting smiles.

Overlooked by casual tourists, hidden alleyways invited curiosity with their secrets. Inside these venues, the atmosphere was distinctly different. Drinks flowed generously, and in every nook, women were seen engaging men in lively conversation or playful games. This was all part of the evening's entertainment, featuring games like Connect Four, Jenga, and the nail game.

Time flew by as I observed the scene of men and women unfolding before me, when a text message came through: "Where were you?"

After reading the message, I thought, "What time is it?" I then realized I was running late, so I quickly replied, "On my way now, five minutes."

I walked up the street for about one hundred meters. When I looked up, I found myself outside a bar that reminded me of the Hard Rock Cafe. The place was unmistakably unique. Inside, the atmosphere was reminiscent of Western bars, infused with distinct Thai elements. Women danced freely on gleaming poles, dressed in alluring lingerie, and wore a noticeable number pinned to their clothing.

I noticed ASAIC DuBois seated at a table and joined him, saying, "Sorry, I got distracted watching the women at the bar down the street."

ASAIC DuBois chuckled and replied, "No problem. Look at this." He gestured toward some men tossing ping-pong balls on the ground.

I noticed a few men relaxing on plush chairs, with drinks in hand and a bucket of ping-pong balls between their legs. They took turns tossing balls onto the stage, onto the floor, or straight at the dancers. I flagged down the waitress and inquired, "What are they doing?"

The waitress replied, "Each ping-pong ten Baht. Girls chase them. Get money."

The playful scene was intended to entertain the men, eliciting laughter or cheers from the patrons. However, I wasn't a fan of the activity. Women scrambling about to collect a few ping-pong balls felt belittling. But this was Thailand, and unfortunately, these ladies needed the money.

As we chatted, women purposefully approached our table, initiating conversations with us. A few adopted a more direct approach by sitting down and explicitly asking for a lady drink. I chose not to rush, opting instead for patience. The night was still young.

Just then, I noticed her in the heart of the club, amid the pulsating beats and mesmerizing lights. She was a petite woman who captured the attention of many. Standing at around five feet five inches tall, her stature was accentuated by a pair of shimmering silver high heels that added grace to every step she took.

Her medium-length black hair cascaded like a silken waterfall, sometimes catching the club's lights and forming a halo effect around her. Dressed in sleek black lingerie, her outfit accentuated her lean, toned body. She likely weighed just forty-six kilos, with a gently curved waist that complemented her perfectly proportioned breasts, creating a harmonious balance to her figure.

Watching her dance was a one-of-a-kind experience. The combination of her physical features and captivating movements created a magnetic presence on the dance floor, drawing the attention and admiration of everyone in the club. I felt an irresistible attraction to her. I quickly caught the waitress's attention and asked, "I'm not sure of her name, but could you ask her to come over and talk with me?"

The waitress replied, "Yeah, sure."

After a few minutes, she approached our table. Without much thought, I asked, "What's your name?"

She responded, "Roxy, why you want to know?"

I doubted that was her name, so I remarked, "Roxy? That's quite an unusual name. I just don't believe it's your real name."

Roxy looked at me and said, "What you care?"

Her spirit reflected her dancing style. I could feel the vitality in her, so I said, "This morning, I went SCUBA diving in the Andaman Sea. We visited a stunning island that the locals call Dok Mai, which means 'beautiful flower.'"

Roxy interrupted, saying, "I know what it mean."

I chuckled and continued, "Since I know Roxy isn't your name, and you are as lovely as that island, may I call you Dok Mai?"

She blinked and tilted her head, blushing. When she faced me again, she replied, "I like Dok Mai."

Dok Mai's real name was Anong Supasri. It wasn't merely her beauty or her fractured English but her spirited personality and playfulness that captured my attention. As we engaged in deeper conversation, a sense of comfort emerged, with the obstacles of language and intention briefly fading away. Time was filled with laughter, the clinking of glasses, and shared stories.

As the night progressed, I felt a genuine connection with Dok Mai. Not wanting it to end and eager to prolong the evening, I looked for an alternative location. I wanted Dok Mai to accompany me, so I respectfully asked her, "Would you join me tonight? We can head to another bar and dance."

Nodding, Dok Mai responded, "I like. I go with you."

ASAIC DuBois also met a woman, and before long, Dok Mai and I were strolling hand in hand, immersing ourselves in the energetic musical atmosphere of Patong Beach. We settled at an electric discotec, where the pulsing electronic dance music drew us to the dance floor, surrounded by dazzling lights and a vibrant crowd.

As dawn approached, the cumulative effects of a night of heavy drinking began to show. Once teeming with energy, the streets of Bangla Road started winding down, with only a few die-hard revelers and early-morning vendors setting up. I looked toward ASAIC DuBois and said, "Thoughts?"

With a smirk, ASAIC DuBois remarked, "We should bring these ladies to your room. After all, yours is the best."

I chuckled and replied, "You're right."

Turning to Dok Mai, I said, "My hotel is just around the corner, care to join me?"

Clearly under the influence of alcohol, Dok Mai slurred, "I go with you."

I glanced at ASAIC DuBois and said, "Let's go."

Once inside my suite, I opened the mini bar and poured drinks for everyone. Dok Mai wasn't so interested in drinks, overwhelmed by fatigue and alcohol, but determined to pursue intimate pleasures, started undressing. Then she lunged toward me, quickly unbuckling my belt and starting to unclothe me. Seeing Dok Mai's intentions, ASAIC DuBois looked at me and said, "I think I should go."

I laughed and replied, "You think? Cuz she isn't accepting 'NO' as an answer."

"I hear ya." ASAIC DuBois responded, "Have fun."

I turned around just in time to see Dok Mai lose consciousness where she lay. To ensure her comfort, I set a bottle of water beside her and watched as she drifted into a deep sleep. For me, the night had been an unexpected blend of scouting the area and a genuine human connection. Watching her sleep, I hoped she'd be okay when she woke.

It had been five days of waiting. I continued the nights of partying, lounging on the beaches, sightseeing, riding elephants, gathering intelligence, and hoping for a message from Maksik. I thought Slimbady and Vincent would arrive tomorrow, and there was no word from Maksik. My only hope was that I would get some information from him and that his delay would not overlap with Slimbady and Vincent. It was on the fifth day that he finally answered.

My ICQ account buzzed with that unmistakable "KuKu" sound. I checked and realized the message was from Maksik.

Maksik messaged, "Hello, Surfrider. How are you?"

I was shocked and quickly replied, "What's up, bro? I'm in Phuket, waiting for you. ☺"

Maksik replied, "I know. I didn't come to Phuket. I went to Egypt."

I thought, "What on earth? Egypt? Didn't we agree on Thailand?" I wrote, "☹ I don't get it. Why did you go to Egypt?"

Maksik answered, "I spoke with my friends, and they told me NOT to meet you. They don't trust Americans. Plus, we agreed on a database of stolen credit card numbers. You haven't paid yet. Once you pay me, we can discuss celebrating in Thailand."

I didn't expect or want to hear this answer. In my mind, I knew ATSAIC Sheehan and SAIC Stokes would celebrate when they learned this news. I could hear them saying, "See, I told them Russian-speaking Carders don't meet."

After five days of waiting in Thailand, my hope for redemption rested on Slimbady and Vincent's arrival.

Chapter 18

A man called Vincent

As the mid-afternoon sun softly illuminated my room, my ICQ messenger buzzed to life. A message from Vincent appeared, announcing his arrival in Phuket. I recalled that driving from the airport to Patong Beach took about forty-five minutes.

The following message, typed by Vincent, asked, "Where can I meet you? ☺"

I replied, "A bar. ☺ It's designed like a pirate ship and is located across from the beach on Thawi Wong Road."

I quickly contacted ASAIC DuBois, informing him, "Vincent has arrived. I've asked him to meet me at the bar near my hotel. He'll arrive in about forty minutes."

ASAIC DuBois replied without delay, "I'll get the team ready. Any news from Slim?"

"No word from Slim," I replied.

ASAIC DuBois curiously asked, "Is Sone with you?"

"Sone is sick. He is out," I replied candidly.

"Roger," ASAIC DuBois responded.

After texting ASAIC DuBois, I headed to the bar, assessed the scene, and chose a seat that offered a view of Thawi Wong Road. Satisfied, I signaled the bartender and ordered a cold Singha beer.

While sitting there, I struggled to keep my thoughts in check, my eyes firmly fixed on the main road. I balanced two tasks: enjoying the stunning sunset over Patong Beach and staying alert for any sign of Vincent's arrival. The last thing I wanted was for him to catch me off guard, whether he knew who I was or not.

Time flew by quickly, and as I enjoyed my second Singha beer, I noticed an airport taxi pull up across the road. A man, around five feet ten and slender, got out. With ordinary features and glasses, he scanned the area briefly before heading straight to bar. His focused expression revealed his purpose—he was looking for someone.

As he neared me, I took a gamble and called out, "Vincent?"

He pivoted toward my voice, a glint of recognition in his eyes. "Surfrider?" he inquired, extending his hand.

I reciprocated the gesture, extending my hand and saying, "I'm Surfrider, but feel free to call me Rich." I motioned to the chair across from me and said, "Sit. Would you like a drink?"

He glanced at my beer and said, "What you drinking? Singha? I have."

I signaled the bartender for another round. As we waited, our conversation drifted into typical, casual banter—light-hearted and rapport-building. When the beers arrived at our table, I lifted mine. "To new friends gathering in unforgettable places."

We raised our glasses, the sound marking the start of our growing friendship. However, while engaging in light conversation, a persistent thought urged me to message ASAIC DuBois. With purpose, but without drawing attention, I typed: "Made contact. At bar. Moving to dinner."

DOI: 10.1201/9781003680390-18

I wasn't concerned about proper English. All I needed was for him to be aware of the current situation. Albeit my actions were intentional, I knew if Vincent challenged me, inquiring who I messaged, what my response would be. I had this part played out in my mind, a rehearsed answer. But I was never challenged, and, in this game, volunteering information was never a wise idea.

After our drinks, I led Vincent to a nearby Thai restaurant I had visited before. He appeared to enjoy the ambiance. Once we were seated, he chuckled and commented on my skill with chopsticks. "I expect you want burgers and hot dogs. Go-to food for Americans," he joked.

Chuckling, I replied, "Not all Americans are the same. I enjoy the local food experience. Plus, I'll be back in the States soon enough. Then I can have as many hot dogs as I want."

As we enjoyed our meal, the discussion naturally shifted to work. Vincent's interest in my operations was evident; he sought more information about them. I explained that my contacts in LA provided me with "shopping lists." My team would acquire the stolen items, which I then sold to buyers in LA, typically at around eighty percent of their value.

What I shared was quite captivating for Vincent, yet it also provided me with an escape from direct collaboration. Few Carders could secure eighty percent of the value of stolen items. Vincent understood that I would not engage directly with him unless he presented me with a more compelling offer.

"Our approach is methodical," I explained. "We survey the city, tagging stores and visiting them one after another until we've checked off our shopping list. Occasionally, the collection is so large that we must hire vans for the return trip to San Diego."

As he sipped his drink, Vincent asked, "How you know cards will work?"

With a sly grin, I responded, "Gas stations are my litmus test. Filling up my tank doubles as a validity check for the cards."

The truth is, I used my banking contacts to give me the card's secrets. They provided me with the validity rates. However, Vincent didn't need to know that truth.

I continued, "I rely heavily on my most trusted associate to lead the team. He preps the cards and oversees the operations. If he senses anything off, he signals the crew. This ensures an immediate abort and retreat."

Eager to steer the conversation away from the intricacies of my operations, I pivoted, "What happened to Slim? I thought he was coming with you?"

Vincent reclined, a grimace appearing on his face. "Slim don't see appeal. Say your time in Macau was ... boring. Honestly, I almost not come. Why fly to Phuket for drink?"

His words stung, underscoring my earlier apprehensions. Our standoffish conduct in Macau wasn't typical, and I knew it could jeopardize future endeavors. Instead of championing my likeability, Slimbady seemed to be doing quite the opposite.

My only saving grace was that, contrary to ATSAIC Carrington's frugalness, I spent "somewhat lavishly" while conducting business online, which I'm sure helped maintain my carding credibility. However, the very essence of my mission—to connect online personas to real identities as required by the U.S. Attorney's Office—was now at risk.

Thoughts raced. Had SunCredit, whom I was ordered to snub earlier, expressed similar sentiments online? Did Slimbady's less-than-glowing review sway Maksik's decision to reroute to Egypt instead? These uncertainties clouded my mind, but Vincent's presence was a clear reminder: I needed to recalibrate and make the most of this encounter.

Mustering a smile, I retorted, "Macau with Slimbady was a first-time meet, so I kept it low-key. But this is Phuket, Vincent. The night's young, and I know where to go for some fun. Interested?"

Ever the opportunist, Vincent nodded enthusiastically, "Lead the way."

Leading Vincent toward the pulsating heart of Phuket, Bangla Road, I could feel the energy shift; the street was coming alive. The lively chatter of tourists and locals grew louder while the dazzling neon lights painted a vibrant tapestry on the street.

Curiosity piqued, I asked, "Where have you booked your hotel?"

Vincent shrugged casually and said, "I no make reservation. I figure now I go back to airport."

I looked at him, incredulous. "Heading to the airport? Come on. I'll get you a hotel. Didn't book anything!"

Chuckling, he retorted, "Well, Slim might be right. Maybe you boring. But you make it interesting, so I stay."

His candid admission surprised and flattered me. Although his lack of planning reaffirmed my previous missteps in Macau, his evident enjoyment now was a comforting antidote.

As we walked down Bangla Road a neon sign caught my attention, its glow illuminating the billiards tables inside, I suggested, "How about a few rounds of pool?" Glancing at my watch, I continued, "It's a tad early for the girls."

His eyes lit up, and Vincent enthused, "Billiards? Absolutely, yes, let's play!"

When Vincent and I walked into the establishment, I was instantly impressed by the detailed layout. A quick look showed a design that thoughtfully caters to guests. The main bar, positioned at the back and slightly to the left, commanded the room's attention. The front area featured billiard tables strategically arranged to engage visitors.

Among the billiard tables were high-top tables, perfect for guests to enjoy their favorite drinks. Walls adorned with football memorabilia—or, as Americans would call it, soccer—surrounded the high-tops and billiard tables. Given its sports theme, televisions were mounted everywhere, each tuned to a different game, casting dynamic shadows over the place.

Vincent and I chose a table near the center, our spot for now. The ambiance was still subdued, and the evening was just beginning. A petite waitress with a playful twinkle in her eyes approached, her crisp white shirt bearing the name tag "Lila." She greeted us, her eyes questioning our drink preferences.

I knew the night was still young, and there was no rush to become inebriated. I ordered the local beer, Singha, and Vincent joined me. As we waited for our drinks, we immersed ourselves in a game of pool. Since I had a mission, I didn't mind talking shop with Vincent. However, the recent news regarding Slimbady's changed travel plans heavily influenced my thoughts.

I was determined to extract as much information as possible from Vincent. With this knowledge, I aimed to sound the alarms to ATSAIC's Carrington and Sheehan. I would use Vincent's words to prove my point.

These words would reinforce and validate my objections to the oppressive conditions I faced while working in Macau. I also knew that despite Slimbady's and SunCredit's criticisms, I could turn things around and regain their support. This led me to start mentally planning my return visit to Macau—a trip to rectify the situation.

I pressed further, asking, "Did you get the money?"

Vincent understood perfectly and replied, "Yes. My guys pick up the $5k few days ago."

"Excellent," I responded. "Do you have the plastic?"

He paused briefly before saying, "I forget. They in Bangkok. We must go there."

I was slightly taken aback but concealed my disappointment as I nodded and replied, "Alright."

At this point, the bar was buzzing with activity. The increasing crowd indicated that it was time for a change of scenery. Just as we were leaving, Vincent noticed something and exclaimed, "What that?" He pointed toward the back of the bar, captivated by the flashing lights and the entrancing music coming from the previously hidden back bar area.

I was already aware of what was happening in the back room. It was typical for this place, something I pieced together during the six nights I spent waiting for Maksik. I recognized Vincent's curiosity and said, "If you're interested, we can check it out. But I have a better location in mind."

Vincent considered momentarily before agreeing, "Alright, let's try your place."

Before our departure, I needed a discreet moment to update ASAIC DuBois. Throughout my life, I have known that "the boys" heading to the restroom together wasn't a thing. I also appreciated that the restroom offered the privacy I needed to send my update.

I turned to Vincent and said, "I need to use the restroom before we go."

Vincent nodded and replied, "I wait you outside."

Once I knew Vincent wasn't watching, I reached into my pocket and quickly pulled out my phone. I already set up the group text message and promptly sent a message, "All well. Done pool. Head to next location."

Upon leaving the bar, I spotted Vincent and waved, saying, "This way."

Bangla Road transformed from a desolate alley to a bustling thoroughfare. Neon lights beckoned visitors into myriad establishments, where enchanting hostesses spun tales of beauty, companionship, and irresistible drink deals. With experience guiding my steps, I avoided many traps, and soon we found ourselves ascending the stairs to a bar I grew fond off during my time in Phuket.

Inside, the electrifying atmosphere was palpable. The ambient lighting cast a warm, golden hue, revealing a stage alive with dancers. Each performer, clad in shimmering outfits, moved with a grace and allure that captivated onlookers.

Once we entered, I scanned the room, searching for Dok Mai. It had been several days since we last met. Part of why I suggested this place to Vincent was twofold: I knew the ladies were beautiful and that Dok Mai frequented this place and I hoped that she would be here tonight.

At first glance, I didn't notice her, but I pointed to a prominent table and said to Vincent, "Let's sit there."

"Okay," Vincent replied, unaware of my reasoning.

Once seated, we had an unparalleled view of the dancers, who bewitched the crowd with their allure. The waitress approached us and asked, "You want drink?"

Sensing the time was ripe, I said, "Yes, two Johnny Walker Black Labels with ice."

Vincent nodded in agreement and said, "Good choice."

We turned our attention from business to revelry. Although I didn't spot Dok Mai upon entering with Vincent, she certainly noticed us. My vibrant beauty, Dok Mai, with her jet-black hair and love for spirited nights, had been observing me from a shadowy corner of the bar.

As we waited for our drinks, the bar's ambient lighting highlighted the captivating scene before us. Dancers dressed in sparkling, fitted costumes moved gracefully from the stage to the floor, then into the room's hidden corners. With each step, they created a seductive blend of elegance and charm. Their performance on stage was more than just a display; it was an invitation, a promise of mystique and enchantment.

I wisely chose to sit back and wait for Vincent. I was in no hurry. Vincent was my guest, and I intended to do everything possible to entertain him. I knew that if he had a good night, he would eventually go online and leave a glowing review. I already knew Slimbady had left a one-star review for me, and I needed Vincent's support to balance it out with a five-star critique.

When the waitress brought our drinks, I was lost in thought, planning my next move. I was too preoccupied to notice that she was accompanied by two women. As the waitress placed the drinks on the table, the two women stepped out from her shadow, and I immediately recognized one of them as Dok Mai.

Dok Mai's sudden presence filled me with excitement and energy. Phuket was home to countless enchanting souls, yet hers stood out like a luminescent pearl amidst its myriad faces. I had convinced myself that our serendipitous encounter that night was a fleeting stroke of fate, a momentary dazzle in an expanse of opportunities. Yet, the memories we wove that night shimmered too brilliantly to be forgotten.

And there she stood, a luminous sight, her spirit as vibrant as ever, her eyes reflecting the gentle curiosity of our brief but unvoiced history. I opened my arms and embraced her, saying, "Dok Mai, where have you been hiding?"

Dok Mai withdrew slightly, a frown on her face, and replied, "Where you been? I am wait here for you. Why you not come back?"

"What?" I gasped in disbelief. "What do you believe I'm doing here? I returned for you."

"I am sad," Dok Mai said while hitting me. "I wait Rich to come back. He no come back for me."

With a bittersweet yet playful expression, I said, "Dok Mai, I have returned. I'm here for you. Look, this is my friend Vincent; we came searching for you and a new friend for him."

Vincent's surprise was evident. He wondered silently about the connection I shared with this lady. After all, we had just walked into the bar. Yet he took it in stride, saying, "Hi, my name is Vincent. Who is your friend?"

Dok Mai looked at her friend and said, "Her name is Sandy. She here for you."

Rather than extending the conversation with Dok Mai, I redirected my attention to the pressing matter at hand. Vincent and I had two beautiful women at our table, and they were without drinks. I pulled Dok Mai to me and asked, "What can Vincent and I get for you and Sandy?"

Dok Mai responded, "Two Mai Thai."

"Done," I exclaimed.

After introductions, Dok Mai and I reminisced about our previous adventures. During this time, it was evident that Vincent and Sandy lacked chemistry, and she exited gracefully. It was apparent that Dok Mai was torn between genuine affection and professional obligations. While we may have shared a connection, the allure of money remained ever-present.

To solve the issue, I quickly pivoted and recommended moving to a more enchanting venue, the discotic, which was among the most frequented places on Patong Beach. After everyone consented, I gestured for Dok Mai to change. Her smile radiated joy as she hurried toward the back room, excited to get ready.

Dok Mai disappeared for only a moment and then reemerged in a stunningly seductive, form-fitting halter top and mini-skirt. My gaze instinctively shifted toward her, but I quickly looked away, not wishing to be impolite. Instead, I faced Vincent and said, "Let's go."

As we hurried toward the discotic, an unexpected sight caught my eye. Dok Mai and Vincent were deeply engaged in a lively conversation, conversing fluently in Thai. This astonished me since I had always thought of Vincent as Chinese.

As they continued their conversation, a growing sense of unease began to settle within me. I had been cautious when I first met Dok Mai, ensuring I never revealed my real-world identity or that I was an agent working undercover in Phuket. However, Dok Mai's familiarity with me could complicate matters in ways I hadn't anticipated.

Dok Mai knew I had been in Phuket for several days, which contradicted what I had told Vincent when we first met, claiming I had only arrived a day ago. If Vincent were to start probing deeper into our connection, it could pose a significant risk to me. Feeling the pressure, I quickened my pace and strategically interrupted their conversation.

I steered Vincent's attention elsewhere, hoping to redirect the conversation's course. My tactic worked, albeit momentarily, until Vincent abruptly shifted the topic, as if to intensify the discussion.

Suddenly, they stopped talking; Vincent tapped my arm and said, "Dok Mai and I are talking Thai."

Quizzically, I replied, "I didn't know you spoke Thai."

Vincent laughed and replied, "Yeah, of course. I've traveled here a lot, and my wife is Thai."

I was a bit surprised. Jokingly, I said, "Then you must speak Thai very well. I think it's great to have someone with me who can talk to the locals."

Vincent smirked and said, "I talk to Dok Mai about Patong Beach and how you met. She likes you a lot. She says you're a good man."

Hearing that comment eased some of my pressure. While it didn't clarify everything, it certainly calmed my mind. I sought comfort in familiar places, knowing we were just moments away from the next destination. Vincent was already inebriated; his chances of recalling his conversation with Dok Mai would diminish significantly with a few more drinks.

As my mind eased, I caught a glimpse of a familiar face. ASAIC DuBois was strolling hand-in-hand with a woman, just an arm's length away. I quickly looked away, aware that eye contact could spark our instincts and create an uncomfortable situation.

Fortunately, Westerners are frequently seen in Phuket, so my pre-planned excuse was, "We already crossed paths." Fortunately, ASAIC DuBois never noticed us, and Vincent never noticed him.

Once we entered the bar, we climbed the stairs and headed toward the dance floor.

I looked at Dok Mai and said, "Be right back."

I stepped into the restroom to give the surveillance team a quick update. While there, I pulled out my phone and sent a brief message: "All good, target and I at the disco." With that said, I made my way directly to the bar.

"Vincent," I said, "What do you want?"

"Same," Vincent responded.

I turned to the bartender and ordered three Johnny Walker Black Labels. Once we had our drinks, I wrapped my arm around Dok Mai, raised my glass, and proclaimed, "To new friends meeting in new places!"

Vincent responded, "To new friends."

I tried to talk to Vincent as the night progressed, but Dok Mai became aggressive. She wanted me to pay attention to her, so she pulled at me, wrapped her arms around my neck, and hung. Dok Mai whispered, "We had unfinished business from the other night."

Enticed by her statements, I could see Vincent was alone, not talking to or engaging with any of the ladies. I had to resist the temptation of focusing on Dok Mai for the moment. As challenging as it was with Dok Mai's seductive looks, soft kisses on my neck, sexually explicit demeanor, and the movements of her body, I had to resist temptation.

My first mission was to ensure Vincent had a good time. I knew there were many ladies, so pointing into the crowd, I asked Vincent, "Do you like the bar?"

Vincent drunkenly replied, his speech slurred, "Yeah, love it, thank you."

The night continued to heat up. The pulsating music seemed to reverberate through my very core as the atmosphere turned electric. The dance floor was a riot of colors and bodies, moving in sync with the music's hypnotic beats. Dok Mai's seductive advances grew more intense, her intentions becoming more apparent with each passing moment.

Dok Mai's undeniable beauty was a powerful distraction, but I had to address Vincent's issue. He lacked a lady of his own. Dok Mai's lips brushed against my ear as she whispered promises of passion and secrecy. Finally unable to hold back, I pulled Dok Mai toward me by her waist and said, "Find a lady for Vincent, and then we can be alone." Without another word, she turned and vanished into the crowd.

As Dok Mai left, Vincent looked at me confusedly and asked, "Where did she go so focused?"

I replied, "Dok Mai is finding you a lady, and you can't say no."

Vincent then patted my shoulder and exclaimed, "I'm so glad I didn't pass and stay in Bangkok!"

Vincent and I toasted just as Dok Mai returned, lady in hand. Dok Mai looked at Vincent and said, "This Kanchana. Kanchana, this Vincent."

I looked at Dok Mai and said, "Thank you."

Most importantly, Vincent and Kanchana clicked right away. Dok Mai instinctively understood what he desired and retrieved her from the dressing room like a product off a shelf. With this matter settled, I could focus on Dok Mai.

As the night wore on, Vincent's drunken state became more apparent. He stumbled toward me, his words slurred, eyes glazed over, and mumbled incoherently. Kanchana did everything she could to keep him upright.

Dok Mai, confused but curious, asked me, "What he say?"

I laughed and replied, "I have no clue, Dok Mai."

Regardless, it was the perfect opportunity for me. I knew Vincent was about to fall over, consumed by alcohol. Sensing that his party would soon end, I handed Dok Mai four thousand Thai Baht and said, "Tell Kanchana to take care of Vincent tonight and give her that money."

Dok Mai looked at me and dutifully talked to Kanchana. When she returned, she said, "Done. She know what to do."

Kanchana waved goodbye and pulled Vincent toward the bar's exit. "Oh, before I forget," I yelled to Vincent. "You're all set. Kanchana will take care of you tonight."

He looked at me and then at her, and together they made their way across the dance floor toward the stairs, slowly fading from sight. I wondered if Vincent grasped it. But it didn't matter; it was too late. Vincent was gone. It was now time to send a final message: "Vincent in for the night."

The response arrived swiftly: "Copy. Shutting it down."

As the evening wound down, the dance floor started to empty. Although Dok Mai and I had been energetic, we were now beginning to show signs of fatigue. Our previously dry clothes were now dampened with sweat and wrinkled from hours of dancing. I leaned in close to Dok Mai and whispered in her ear, "Would you like to join me in my suite?"

The promise of intimacy and the allure of the Baan Thai Resort's luxury beckoned us. Dok Mai took my hand and said, "Yes," as she led me away from the disco.

We stepped out of the club and onto the empty streets of Phuket. Once vibrant and filled with people, now all that remained were the city's neon lights dancing before our eyes, blurring into a kaleidoscope of colors. With Dok Mai by my side, we strolled toward my hotel, the night's silence broken only by our laughter and the occasional passing Tuk-Tuk.

As Dok Mai and I approached my suite, our yearning intensified, resembling an unseen force pulling us closer. Once we entered, I realized we were free from prying eyes; it was just Dok Mai and me. We embraced tightly, our lips meeting, our hands exploring and swiftly discovering their destinations.

Slowly, we removed each other's garments, the sole threads that concealed the essence of souls. Piece by piece, each layer fell away, and the anticipation grew, unveiling the raw desire that had simmered beneath the surface. Every touch and every kiss stoked the flames of passion that burned between us, igniting an unquenchable fire.

As I pressed my lips against her quivering abdomen, a surge of desire coursed through me. My fingertips, filled with a rare urgency, grazed her heated skin, caressing her small but ample breasts. Her nipples were erect, accentuating her excitement, the inner desire, longing for her sexual needs to be fulfilled. Slowly, I traced a path down her legs, exploring the depths of her forbidden realms with a hunger that only the chosen could comprehend.

The room became a haven for our passions, the air thick with the intoxicating scent of our desire. Moans of pleasure mingled with whispered invitations, urging us to surrender to our primal instincts. At that moment, there was no room for hesitation or restraint. Our bodies merged, entwined in a dance that defied explanation. It was a symphony of ecstasy, each touch and caress building toward a crescendo of pleasure that shattered all inhibitions.

The world around us disappeared as we fully immersed ourselves in the pure intensity of our bond. In the quiet aftermath, our bodies were intertwined, exhausted yet fulfilled. We shared gentle kisses, relishing the echo of our mutual desire. It was a moment of genuine intimacy where time paused, leaving only our love behind.

Exhaustion overtook us, and we surrendered to the embrace of sleep, still entwined in the aftermath of our lovemaking. The night's events faded away in the blissful haze of our intimacy. As the sun rose, revealing a stunning blue sky, a beam of sunlight brightly illuminated the room. The warmth enveloped the space, gradually pulling me back to reality. Duty called, interrupting our blissful repose.

Reluctantly, I tore myself away from the warmth of Dok Mai's embrace, knowing that a meeting with my supervisor awaited me at the local Starbucks. As I stepped out of the room, the sun's warmth enveloped me, its rays casting a golden glow on the surroundings. The sky stretched above me, a vibrant blue canvas adorned with fluffy white clouds that floated effortlessly. It was a picturesque scene, a moment of tranquility amidst the bustling city.

As I approached Starbucks, I quickly realized that, despite being in Phuket, Thailand, it bore a striking resemblance to any Starbucks I had visited before. Upon entering through the front door, I spotted a figure seated against the wall. ASAIC DuBois attempted to blend in, donning a baseball cap, a plain t-shirt, shorts, and gym shoes—the typical American uniform. The good news was that, in this part of the world where Western tourists were common, he didn't stand out, as many others were also typical Western tourists.

As I focused on the crowd of Westerners, I couldn't help but laugh, realizing they were nursing hangovers like me, looking for coffee and eagerly awaiting the evening's events to resume. With one exception, I was on a secret mission tasked with tracking cyber criminals. My goal was to blend in with the unsuspecting crowd, unaware of the intelligence operation happening around them. This notion fueled and motivated me.

Coffee in hand, I casually seated myself near ASAIC DuBois. I stole a glance at him, then looked away a bit before saying, "Good morning."

In a discreet manner, ASAIC DuBois responded, "Good morning. How was your night?"

It was the invitation I had been waiting for, and I replied, "Not good."

"How so?" ASAIC DuBois responded.

Disappointedly, I remarked, "Vincent came alone. Slim isn't coming. SunCredit isn't coming. Maksik went to Egypt. In fact, Vincent almost decided not to come at all. Do you know why?"

With caution, ASAIC DuBois replied, "Why?"

"Because I'm boring," I said sadly. "Vincent said that Slim told him there was no point in going to Phuket for just one or two drinks. He didn't even bother to book a room. After dinner, he planned to take a taxi back to the airport and return to Bangkok."

"That's not good," ASAIC DuBois said sternly. "Where is Vincent now?"

"He was wasted last night," I said triumphantly. "By the end of the evening, Vincent was my best friend. He often said how glad he was that he ignored Slim's advice. But I have no idea where he is now. I arranged for a girl to look after him. I guess he's currently nursing a hangover nearby."

Contemplating the scenario, ASAIC DuBois said, "What do you think went wrong in Macau?"

"What went wrong?" I said emphatically, "I traveled halfway around the world and didn't DO ANYTHING. Sone and I had dinner and then basically went to bed. We refused an invitation and stayed for hours instead of days. That is what went wrong."

ASAIC DuBois said shyly, "I see. What do you propose we do next?"

"Once we're done here," I said firmly, "we'll return to Macau and address this issue. Sone and I must have the freedom to go wherever and for as long as necessary."

"I agree," ASAIC DuBois concurred. "By the way, what time did you turn in last night?"

I found it to be a strange question, and our rendezvous became even more intriguing as a result. I replied, "When I texted you. I'm sure you saw me."

Sheepishly, ASAIC DuBois replied, "No, the team turned in for the night early."

My mind raced, and thoughts passed quickly, culminating in the realization that the surveillance team had gone to bed. The team I believed was diligently shadowing me instead retired to their hotel rooms. Magically, like Cindarella who at the stroke of midnight disappeared, they just got up and went to bed, their mission of safeguarding me shelved for the night.

I forced a half smile and said, "What, they couldn't keep up?"

"You stay out too late," ASAIC DuBois laughed. "Besides, the guys are getting old. They need their rest."

Mixed emotions surged within me. On one hand, the less they observed the late-night activities, the better. External eyes scrutinizing actions they couldn't comprehend, or worse, actions they saw that they disapproved of, was a liability—something I could do without.

ASAIC DuBois continued, "Anything else to report?"

I responded, almost forgetting, "Yeah, Vincent forgot the plastic in Bangkok. I will need to go to Bangkok with Vincent to get them."

With surprise, ASAIC DuBois gazed at me and asked, "What do you mean you have to go with him?"

"If I want my plastic, I have to go to Bangkok," I stated firmly.

"I need to update Headquarters," ASAIC DuBois responded. "What's today's agenda?"

"I don't know. Let me text him," I said.

I sent Vincent a discreet message, aware of the early hour but reluctant to risk an encounter with him during my conversation with ASAIC DuBois. Although such a meeting wouldn't be conspicuous, I saw no reason to invite unnecessary scrutiny.

I turned and replied, "Message sent. Once I hear from him, I will let you know."

"Copy," ASAIC DuBois responded. "I will update SAIC Montaña and Headquarters. Meanwhile, hold off on any agreements for now."

"Understood," I replied. "Be safe."

After last night, I managed to get Dok Mai's contact info so now, I could freely contact her. With no response from Vincent on my phone, I headed to my usual refuge—Patong Beach. Even with the coffee, the fatigue from last night's adventures lingered. I remembered the beach had inviting lounge chairs, the ideal spot to relax and rejuvenate.

The soft sands of Patong Beach welcomed me, offering a haven of tranquility amidst the city's cacophony. I settled into a comfortable chair; I couldn't help but ponder the challenges ahead. The uncertainties, the risks, and the delicate balance between my personal life and the mission.

I gazed out at the turquoise waters that stretched infinitely before me. The rhythmic melody of gentle waves lapping at the shore washed away the residue of fatigue. My phone remained within reach, and I dispatched updates to the team, keeping them informed of my ongoing efforts to establish contact. Simultaneously, I patiently awaited Vincent's response.

Chapter 19

Vincent's last night in Phuket

Soaking up the sun's warmth, I savored this fleeting moment of peace. I knew it wouldn't be long before I dove back into the shadows of my secret life. Yet, a wave of calm enveloped me as the day went on. In the distance, I noticed young Thai girls offering foot massages, hand massages, manicures, and chilled Singha beers. Drawn in by their affordable prices, I treated myself to a cold beer and a manicure.

As time ticked by, I grew increasingly anxious about Vincent's silence when, almost miraculously, my phone buzzed to life with his message: "Where are you?"

I wasted no time replying, "Just in front of the resort on the beach, having a beer. Come join me."

Vincent's response came quickly, "Okay."

With Vincent's confirmation, I promptly notified the team of my location and announced, "Target en route."

A familiar voice called out from behind me, "What up, bro?"

It was Sone, and I quickly replied, "Hey, how are you feeling? Feeling better?"

"Honestly, I'm not sure what happened, but I feel better," Sone said.

As Sone and I discussed the previous night, a hungover Vincent showed up. He looked surprised to see me with a beer and asked, "You drinking?"

The smell made him nauseous, so I kept the bottle away from him, letting him enjoy the cool sea breeze as I said, "I'm on holiday. By the way, this is my partner, Sone. Sone, this is Vincent."

Sone and Vincent exchanged handshakes, saying, "Nice to meet you."

Vincent settled into the beach chair, cradling his head in his hand. He asked, "What happen last night? I woke up next to girl. I think name was Kantana?"

Laughing, I replied, "You don't remember anything?"

"The last thing I remember is dancing," Vincent said with a smirk. "How I meet that girl?"

"That's hilarious," I said, grinning. "Dok Mai found her, and her name was Kanchana."

"Okay," Vincent remarked. "Well, we both naked, so I think we have sex. But I don't remember. Anyhow, I gave her money and then leave."

"Wait!" I exclaimed with excitement. "You gave her money?"

"Yeah, why?" Vincent answered.

"I gave her money," I said, laughing. "What a night for Kanchana! She may or may not have had sex, but she walked away with extra cash. That's amazing!"

Vincent squinted against the sun and said, "I don't care. That was best night of my life. I'm so glad I come to Phuket. Where you stay?"

I pointed across the road and said, "It's a wonderful place. Can I get you a room there?"

Vincent shook his head and added, "Can we check it out?"

I replied, "Yeah."

DOI: 10.1201/9781003680390-19

"Okay," Vincent said. "But, first, check out of other hotel. Then book me room?"

Recognizing this as a chance to learn more about Vincent, I eagerly agreed. "Of course, let's go."

We crossed the street together and entered the hotel lobby. Vincent seemed taken by its charm and expressed his appreciation. He handed me his passport and said, "Get me room." Then, turning to walk away, he said, "I be back."

I did my best to hide my astonishment and replied, "Okay. See you soon."

As soon as Vincent was out of sight, I took the opportunity to photograph his passport and sent it to ASAIC DuBois with the message, "Check out what Vincent just gave me. ☺"

Afterward, I approached the front desk to secure a hotel room for Vincent. Just as I finished the paperwork and made the payment, my phone rang—it was ASAIC DuBois.

I picked up and said, "What's up?"

"How did you get a picture of Vincent's passport?" ASAIC DuBois asked.

"He gave it to me," I replied.

ASAIC DuBois exclaimed, "Why did he give you his passport?"

"Vincent asked me to book him a hotel room," I clarified.

"Wait, you booked a room for him?" ASAIC DuBois queried.

"Yes, I did," I replied proudly.

"How much did it cost?" ASAIC DuBois pressed.

Noticing the worry in ASAIC DuBois's tone, I said, "Four hundred dollars, why?"

"I just don't get it," ASAIC DuBois reprimanded. "Why would you book him a hotel room?"

I defiantly stated, "I am working undercover. My mission is to gather intelligence. It's about connecting an online alias to a real-world identity. I've just achieved that, and for how much? Four hundred dollars. I'd say it's a bargain."

ASAIC DuBois, frustrated, snapped, "We'll discuss this back in San Diego. What's the plan for tonight?"

"Vincent is coming back," I quickly interjected. "I'll update you shortly."

"Vincent, what's up, bro?" I cheerfully called out.

Vincent, still noticeably hungover, replied flatly, "Hey."

"You don't look so hot," I chuckled. "Here are your keys."

Vincent took the keys and said, "Thanks, man."

"Listen, clean yourself up," I suggested. "Let's meet in a few hours."

With a hint of embarrassment, Vincent managed a soft, "Okay. See you soon."

Once I arranged Vincent's room and returned his passport and key, I headed back to my suite. As I entered my room, the subtle scent of Dok Mai's perfume still hung in the air, reminding me of the previous night's events. Memories rushed back, but I immediately set them aside, realizing that focusing on them would only divert me from the task before me.

I promptly updated the team on our progress with a quick text: "Meeting in an hour for dinner." With about an hour to spare, I opted to take a refreshing shower before meeting in the lobby.

After getting ready, I sent a last message to the team: "Heading to the lobby."

Their reply was concise yet clear, signaling they were ready for the mission: "Copy."

My clandestine meeting was just moments away, and as an undercover agent, I was aware of the seriousness of the situation. Each interaction felt like a carefully crafted act, with the stakes high and potentially life-threatening, and this night promised to be particularly captivating.

Upon entering the lobby, I immediately spotted Vincent, who was waiting there. Although he looked somewhat better, signs of his suffering still lingered on his face. Sone, Vincent, and I headed toward the busy main street, my mind already set on the restaurant. It was a familiar spot, a refuge where the fragrant aroma of Thai spices filled the air, harmonizing with the soft murmurs of regular patrons.

This would mark the first of many dinners, each evolving into a venue for sharing hushed secrets and engaging in illicit online activities. Inside this local haunt, the atmosphere buzzed with anticipation, as if the air itself contained secrets yearning to be revealed. Sitting across from each other in the dimly lit room, Vincent captivated us with his tale, his words crafting a narrative rich with betrayal and ambition, each detail uncovering a concealed truth.

He reminisced about his beginnings as a junior "runner" for the notorious SunCredit and AndyCredit, the masterminds behind the illicit carding schemes in Hong Kong. AndyCredit, the key player in the city, wielded influence, whereas SunCredit acted as his loyal lieutenant.

Together, SunCredit and AndyCredit controlled the city's underbelly, their empire growing with each stolen credit card account. From their perspective, perched atop the criminal hierarchy, the rewards were high and the risks seemingly low. But beneath their expanding empire lay an ambitious employee dedicated to crafting his narrative.

Vincent meticulously detailed his plan to bite the hands that fed him and rise above the scraps he had been dealt. He hungered for more, eager to carve out his niche in the criminal underworld. As his story unfolded, I couldn't help but feel drawn into the dangerous web he was weaving. I was forming a relationship with Vincent and the enigmatic SunCredit, and I knew that the more information I had, the more I could cultivate that connection.

Vincent offered me a glimpse into the dark heart of a world where trust was a luxury and loyalty a mere commodity. His story wasn't only about revenge and ambition. As he dove in, he painted a vivid picture of the treacherous path he was willing to tread, a path that would test his cunning and resilience. And as I listened, I realized the lines between right and wrong, justice and betrayal blurred in ways I couldn't yet comprehend.

Vincent leaned in and pointed at me, explaining, "I work for many years but got only pennies." He leaned back and continued, "They treat me like servant. Like I'm nothing, even stupid. But I understand Andy and Sun's game. I have only one problem... contacts."

"So, what did you do? How did you get the contacts?" I asked.

Vincent loved the spotlight, and he regaled me with the intricacies of his plan to bite the hands that fed him, saying, "They trust me. I use this against them. I watch as they logged on to ICQ. It was like days when I shoulder-surf unsuspecting ATM user and steal the PIN. But this time, I need Andy's supplier. I need good dump vendor."

I played the role of the captivated audience, hanging on to every word, giving Vincent the spotlight he so desperately sought, asking, "Who was it?"

Vincent leaned back in his chair, winked, and proudly continued his story, "That how I found Leon and P0l1ceD0g. They supply Andy with dumps."

As I listened to Vincent, deep in the back of my mind, the weight of my clandestine mission weighed on me. Vincent had no clue about my true mission, my true self, the ultimate goals I sought to achieve. My heart hammered with the knowledge that his words were not just confessions but the keys to dismantling the network he and others had built.

As thoughts of arresting him entered my mind, they were gently whisked away. Now was my time to put aside my morals. In this role, I wasn't Richard LaTulip, the Secret Service Agent, but Richard Druc, the Carder. Vincent and I were brothers on the same side, rallying against oppressors. The people who held us down were those who sat on top of the system, and those who enforced their will, like the police.

My thoughts were interrupted by a simple statement and question. Vincent, with a stern look, stated, "You know, P0l1c3D0g arrested." Then he asked, "What you think? Can police find me?"

I knew what he sought, my reassurance that the police would not arrest him. His question reminded me of a broken promise. A hard drive yet to be received from Headquarters, and the knowledge that on that hard drive were his deals with P0l1c3D0g. Brushing this aside temporarily, I replied, "Depends. Did you give him your name? Address? Anything that links to your NIC?"

"No," Vincent confidently confessed. "I only use drops in China."

"Then you should be good," I nonchalantly replied.

While rubbing his chin, Vincent asked, "You know them?"

Laughing, I said, "Yeah. Of course. Sone and I bought dumps from them."

"What you think of Leon's dumps?" Vincent inquired.

"They are shit," I replied.

Vincent looked up, clearly thinking about his next question. He then said, "I agree. They bad. His dumps cost me money."

"Why do you still buy from Leon?" I questioned.

Vincent, sensing an opportunity, asked, "Who else sells?"

"I get my dumps from Maksik. Do you know him?" I asked.

Vincent shook his head, indicating he didn't know Maksik. Seizing the acknowledgment, I said, "I will introduce you."

Excitedly, Vincent said, "Really? You do that?"

"Of course," I said.

Vincent began to glow, and he immediately raised his glass and toasted, "To future business together."

Vincent understood this introduction would breathe new life into his struggling operation. As Vincent's gratitude washed over me, I couldn't help but feel a twinge of something darkly akin to pride. Then, as if the relationship or the mission itself couldn't have gotten better, Vincent recalled the deal we had agreed upon, part of why he was in Phuket.

He gently reached toward me and said, "I have the plastic you order. But not here. Tomorrow, we go to Bangkok. I get them for you."

Confused, I asked, "We need to go to Bangkok?"

"Yes," Vincent said. "Book your flight, tell me details, and we go together."

I knew this wouldn't be well received by leadership, but I had little choice. Refusing or balking at this offer could send a negative message to Vincent. I swallowed hard, trying to put these thoughts behind me, saying, "Okay. I will do it when we get back to the hotel. But now it is time to hit the mean streets of Phuket."

Immediately, Vincent put his hand up and said, "No, no, not me. I need recover. I go hotel."

"Really?" I sadly stated. Then I turned to Sone and said, "What about you?"

Sone, not one to go to clubs, said, "No, not for me."

"Okay," I replied. "Take care. I will send you my flight details soon."

Sone interjected, "Not me. I'm still sick. I'm flying home tomorrow. You two have fun in Bangkok."

"Hope you feel better," Vincent said. "See you tomorrow."

Once Vincent departed, his footsteps fading into the night's silence, I took a moment to gather myself. With a mix of trepidation and determination, I reached out to the team, "Op over. Vincent headed back to the hotel."

Typically, the response is quick, but this time it lagged. I didn't give it much thought as I pondered my next move. I could turn in for the night, or since I was already out, check out the scene on Bangla Road. As my options played out in my head, the reply appeared on my phone. As I read it, a wave of depression washed over me. It was a cold reminder of their indifference, leaving me feeling exposed and vulnerable in the neon-lit jungle that surrounded me.

Their surveillance duties had ceased a while ago, their once unwavering dedication giving way to the relentless grip of fatigue and complacency. Frustration gnawed at me; a bitter companion clawed at my insides as I replayed the day's events in my mind. The diligent eyes that should have been watching my back had succumbed to the allure of slumber, abandoning their post without a second thought. And yet, I remained in the dark, unaware of the true extent of their negligence until the late evening hours.

With the weight of disappointment settling upon my shoulders, I decided it was time to immerse myself in the pulsating energy of Phuket's nightlife. I got up and left the confines of the restaurant and ventured into the beckoning night, guided by the intoxicating allure of the local disco.

As I walked toward Bangla Road, I texted Dok Mai, my reliable confidante, saying, "You want to meet me at discotic?"

The reply from Dok Mai was almost instantaneous, "Yes! I come now."

With the clock ticking toward the early morning hours, Dok Mai and I once again found ourselves amidst the swirling sea of bodies on the dance floor. I was captivated by her beauty, but amidst the kaleidoscope of neon lights and pounding music, I caught a glimpse of ASAIC DuBois.

There he was, a figure I had once idolized, dancing away the evening with a captivating lady. The revelation struck me like a lightning bolt, shattering the illusion of loyalty and trust that I had held for so long. At that moment, the lines between duty and personal desire blurred, leaving me with a bitter taste lingering on my tongue.

Being intoxicated, I waited until I caught ASAIC DuBois's attention and then waved him over. The club was chaotic; individuals blended into a sea of anonymity, and no one paid attention to anyone. It was a perfect place to debrief him on the next steps.

I pulled ASAIC DuBois toward me and in a normal voice explained, "The meeting with Vincent went well. I learned a lot about his relationship with Andy, Sun, Leon, and P0l1c3D0g. The most important item, Vincent does not have one hundred credit cards with him. I need to go with him to Bangkok to get them."

ASAIC DuBois did his best to focus, but his newfound friend was tugging at him. "Anything else?"

"Yeah," I continued, explaining. "In the morning, I will book my hotel and flight. Brief the team. Please let them know about the change in plans and inform them that you will be traveling to Bangkok. Oh, also, Sone is heading back to San Diego. He is still feeling sick."

ASAIC DuBois, doing his best to fend off his lady, replied, "Copy that. I will brief Montaña and Headquarters."

With the Cliff Notes of Vincent and my meeting done, curiosity got the better of me. I asked, "How long have you been here?"

ASAIC DuBois, arms around his friend, said, "A couple of hours."

I shook my head, knowing he was well into enjoying his evening while I was at dinner with Vincent. Ignoring the obvious, I laughed, saying, "Awesome. Well, I can tell you have your hands full. Let's talk in the morning."

ASAIC DuBois winked, saying, "You as well."

As the night ended, Dok Mai and I retreated to my suite. Once inside, with her approval given, our lips locked, and the rhythmic movement of her hips drew me in. I took hold of her dress and pulled it over her head. She followed suit, pulling my shirt off. I paused to catch a glance of her body, then I drove my hands forward, undoing her bra.

Her near-perfect breast was exposed, nipples pointing in my direction. I leaned in for a mouthful, caressing and kissing her body, my tongue following her curves. The room got hotter, the rhythmic motions were more meaningful and purposeful, and the moment was right.

With passions at a climax, the last hurdle needed to be overcome. Panting with anticipation, with a quick twist, she was on her back. I dipped down, continuing to follow from her breast past her flat stomach. I knew there was something warm and delightful waiting for me.

My hands working together with my teeth, I pulled her silky underwear off her body. Her passion and desire reached her limits. Just from taking off her lingerie, Dok Mai was already wet from lust. Her want was more intense than ever. Her genitals were moist, wet from desire, my cock hard, ready for what would soon follow.

Starting from her lower legs, desiring to procrastinate just a little, I slowly worked my way back toward her pelvis. I kissed her defined leg, inch by inch, moving closer and not wanting to move too quickly, but enough to entice her more. As I approached mid-thigh, a slight quiver could be felt. Inch by inch and just close enough, I was sure not to dive right in but rather start lightly.

A tiny lick, followed by a kiss. Another longer, slower lick, and she quivered from excitement. I toyed with her, rolling and circling my tongue in the right spot. Every movement brought her closer to that anticipated ultimate feeling. Sensing the excitement, her body tensing up, touching her hardened nipples, the time was just right.

I slide between her legs and slide my cock in gently. She moans, her hands grabbing my ass, thrusting my cock deeper inside her. Wanting to tease her, I pulled back, delaying her orgasm and pushing her desires to the limit. Gentle, slow teasing wasn't in Dok Mai's plans tonight. Dok Mai wanted it all, brutal, not soft.

She was more than ready for everything. I pulled back she pulled me forward, deeper inside cock, rigid bodies sweating, desire urging for more. Our minds were on different paths, yet we shared the same goal.

No need to fight her. If Dok Mai wanted it hard, I would give it to her. Every thrust forward and further back, force forward, hitting her just in the right spot. Dok Mai moaned and wanted faster still.

Working up a sweat, driven to satisfy her wants and desires, she knew from her head tilting back that she was near climax. My body wanted more, and hearing her moans filled it with pleasure. Each thrust forward, her grip tightened around my arms, then moved her head forward ever so slightly.

Finally, her body releasing the inner pleasure it so desperately held onto, Dok Mai let out a passionate and delightful moan. Dok Mai's body tensed, and I felt her quiver, my cock just as sensitive. I felt everything inside her the moment Dok Mai came.

With every ounce of resistance left, I continued a little faster, a little harder, knowing with each thrust, the sensitivity from within would drive her wild. The last moments of Dok Mai's orgasm were finally complete, and my desires were no longer controllable. I pushed forward with one final thrust.

My passion reached its climax as well. I quickly pulled out and moved back slightly. As she watched me, I grabbed myself, sliding my hand back and forth. The final stage was completed in a burst, sending a stream of cum all over Dok Mai's breasts and stomach. Dok Mai had positioned herself just right, welcoming the experience, and licked what she could with her tongue.

We felt relaxed and comfortable. As I felt tired, knowing the morning alarm clock would soon ring, we moved from the couch to the bed. Naked, our bodies pressed against each other, the heat generated between us lulled me closer to sleep. Our bodies fit perfectly together.

I gently stroked Dok Mai's hair, rolling down her back and occasionally drifting to caress her firm buttocks. Comfortable in Dok Mai's grasp, safe sleep came quickly. The final thoughts focused my mission and tomorrow's plan.

As morning dawned, I woke with a determined purpose. With no time to dwell on pleasantries, I quickly bid farewell to Dok Mai, promising I would see her again soon. Once she departed, I swiftly navigated the web of flights from Phuket to Bangkok and found one that suited me. However, just as I was on the verge of finalizing the arrangements, the shrill ring of the telephone pierced the air, jolting me from my concentration. I answered the phone.

On the other end was ASAIC DuBois. His voice crackled with tension, words laced with panic. ASAIC DuBois stated, "Everyone in San Diego and DC is panicking. You can't be on the same flight with Vincent."

Mystified by the panic, I reasoned, "Wait. What? You mean to tell me, I am to tell Vincent he can't be on the same flight as me?"

Dramatically, ASAIC DuBois said, "Yes. You have to book separate flights."

"Just how am I going to do this?" I flippantly retorted. "Explain to me how a friend who is in the same city, going to the same destination, is supposed to plan separate flights purposely? Do I say, 'Hey, Vincent, what flight you on?' Yeah, I booked a different flight. See you in Bangkok."

Angrily, ASAIC DuBois stated, "I don't know, but figure it out."

Frustrated, I hung up the phone without saying another word. I then turned to ICQ and pinged Vincent. "What up, bro?"

Vincent wrote back, "What up? How was last night? ☺"

"Good, ☺" I wrote. "I have my flight. Thai Airlines departing at 2. You need the flight number?"

"Nope," Vincent replied. "My flight departs at 1."

A surge of relief washed over me once I knew Vincent had already booked a flight. This allowed me to proceed with planning my flight separately. As I started booking, my phone began to flash and buzz. I knew it must be from ASAIC DuBois. I looked and was astonished to read, "DO NOT take a taxi with Vincent. You must travel alone."

Instead of messaging ASAIC DuBois, I dialed his number. Once he answered, I pushed back, "Look, we aren't on the same flights, which is a win, but I can't naturally tell him NO I'm not sharing a ride to the airport with you. If he asks, I must ride with him to the airport."

The phone went silent. The pause felt like an eternity, and when it came back to life, ASAIC DuBois begrudgingly said, "Fine. Take the taxi together."

I took a deep breath and read Vincent's following message, "Meet at 11. We take taxi together."

"See you at 11," I replied.

Chapter 20

Vincent and I go to Bangkok

As Vincent and I embarked on the journey to the airport, a palpable tension enveloped me, wrapping around my being like a suffocating shroud. The distant voices of authority, my supervisors, resonated in my mind like a cacophony of panic and directives. Their desperate desire for distance and separation clashed vehemently with the magnetic force of human connection, defying their anxious orders at every turn.

Once at the airport, a wave of relief washed over me like a cool breeze on a scorching summer day. Bound by separate flights, I found solace in the fact that our gates were far from each other. As we went through the check-in process, our eyes mirrored the bittersweet emotions swirling within us. We exchanged temporary goodbyes, clinging to the promise of reuniting in the bustling city of Bangkok.

With Vincent's departure preceding mine, I promised to send him a message upon my arrival. His face lit up with an infectious delight, his eyes sparkling with anticipation. "See you soon," he said, his voice filled with a sense of longing and excitement. In that fleeting moment, I couldn't fathom when our paths would intersect again, but little did I know that Vincent had a surprise in store for me.

Just then, Vincent turned back and said, "I pick up when you land. Take you hotel."

I took a deep breath, momentarily closed my eyes, and said, "Of course. I will send you a message when I land."

Vincent's insistence on personal hospitality, picking me up in his vehicle, was a maneuver that had ASAIC DuBois wringing his hands yet again. Lacking time or opportunity to protest what was natural, he conceded, perhaps a silent acknowledgment of demanding the unnatural, shunning a friend.

Strangely, I appreciated Vincent's determination to be there for me. It was a gesture of our connection and his support that spoke volumes about the depth of our bond. It was a silent affirmation of his loyalty and an unspoken declaration of the rapport we had built over the last two days.

Once my flight touched down, I sent a message to Vincent, and as promised, he was waiting for me just outside the arrival doors. He guided me to his car, and in a flash, we were off.

As Vincent's car glided through the bustling streets, I sent a message to the team: "Landed, heading to hotel. Green Toyota."

Lost in my thoughts, I glanced at the passing sights, their significance fleeting as we made our way to my next hotel. The journey from the airport felt like a mere blur, as if we had just departed moments ago. Along the way, I kept the team up to date, but uncertainty clouded my mind.

Did anyone follow? Was the team behind us? The replies provided no confidence as they were curt and evasive, a chorus of "Copy." Yet, deep down, I understood that their presence or absence held little weight. In the dangerous world I operated in, there was rarely anyone

DOI: 10.1201/9781003680390-20

close enough to offer protection should I find myself in a bind. A harsh reality forced me to acknowledge that I was on my own.

Vincent skillfully maneuvered the car into the hotel's underground parking, ending my tumultuous taxi ride to the airport, flight to Bangkok, and journey in Vincent's car. As we both stepped out, I let out a sigh of relief. As we walked toward the elevator, our footsteps resounded in the stillness. The excitement of what was to come lingered in the atmosphere, fostering an unspoken connection between us.

Not only had I secured a room for myself, but I had also taken the liberty of booking one for Vincent. As we checked in, I knew ASAIC DuBois would be disappointed in me. Yet, as I looked at Vincent, I couldn't help but notice the astonishment that flickered in his eyes. Like a shimmering facade of luxury, the opulence of the hotel captivated him, along with his appreciation of my generosity. It starkly contrasted with the danger that lurked beneath the surface of our lives.

Vincent broke the silence, speaking with a sense of urgency. "I have errands to run. Let's meet at this restaurant. Seven, okay?"

I checked the time and noticed that I had several hours to kill. "Sounds good. See you soon," I answered, maintaining a calm and collected tone.

As Vincent left, I made it my first goal to find a moment of respite. I needed to relax and gather my thoughts. But first, I had to ensure the team was informed of my safe arrival at the hotel. Vincent remained oblivious to the underlying currents, his trust in me seemingly strengthened by our journey from Phuket.

While I waited, I enjoyed a drink at the hotel lobby bar. My thoughts turned to the surveillance team, and I felt assured that everything would proceed smoothly since they had plenty of time to prepare.

As I checked the time, I reflected on how traffic in Bangkok is notoriously unpredictable. Additionally, in 2006, smartphones that provided real-time traffic updates weren't yet available. Aware of this, I arranged to leave early. Once I was prepared, I sent a message to the team, saying, "Heading out to meet Vincent."

I walked through the hotel lobby toward the entrance. After stepping outside, I hailed a taxi. The ride was smooth, and the anticipated traffic was nonexistent, allowing me to arrive early. I thought this would be great; I could check out the restaurant before the target arrived. However, to my surprise, Vincent was already there waiting for me.

Once I got out of the taxi, Vincent hurried over and said, "Welcome."

His swift approach gave me no chance to message the team about my arrival. With no other choice, I replied, "Greetings."

"Ah," Vincent said excitedly. "My favorite restaurant. Come, follow me."

When we walked into a traditional Chinese restaurant, I immediately noticed it was bustling with customers. It was a locals' only place, and this vibrant atmosphere made me confident that the food would be delicious. As we enjoyed dinner, we engaged in the usual small talk about carding. I did my best not to get involved in any type of criminal scheme with Vincent, although I sensed that was his intention.

Once dinner ended, Vincent had a plan. He leaned toward me and asked, "You want massage? I know a place women are always beautiful, and most importantly, know how to attend to a man's every desire."

How could I resist? With a smile, I replied, "Let's go."

Vincent's car resembled a shard of the night itself, a nondescript green Toyota that seamlessly blended into the vibrant tapestry of traffic. As we left the restaurant behind, his focus shifted to navigating the ceaseless swarm of mopeds weaving through the sea of cars, disregarding any semblance of order.

The city, alive and pulsating with the energy of a million souls, enveloped us in its embrace. Neon signs flickered like captured fireflies, casting an ethereal glow amid the urban jungle. The air was thick with the mingling scents of sizzling street food and exhaust fumes. As we navigated the chaotic maze, the city's arteries tightened around us, constricting our path.

The road ahead stretched like a ribbon of endless possibilities, hinting at hidden corners and untold stories. In the haste of our departure, I had forgotten to notify my team, but I trusted that they had witnessed our abrupt exit. With Vincent expertly maneuvering the car, I felt at ease sending them an update, "Left restaurant. Destination unknown."

Although I knew the type of service we sought, there was no point in saying, "Headed to a massage parlor," as they were abundant in Bangkok. Nonetheless, Vincent gracefully maneuvered through the streets of Bangkok. As he searched for the elusive massage parlor, the turn we needed materialized like a fleeting apparition, vanishing before our eyes.

Once we passed the point of no return, our only option was to follow the relentless traffic flow, unable to turn left or right. A muttered curse slipped from Vincent's lips as his eyes darted around, sharp and calculating. He looked for a break in the unending stream of cars, a gap that would allow us to circle back and correct our mistake.

The U-turn we urgently needed transformed into a strategic withdrawal, allowing us to move forward with a graceful arc that retraced our steps down the long and winding street we had just traversed. Bangkok, a labyrinthine maze of possibilities, challenged even the most skilled navigator, but Vincent was like Theseus—not just armed with a sword but also atop a steel chariot.

One U-turn took us to a one-way street that led to another turn. I tried to help by watching for wayward mopeds or unsuspecting pedestrians. Finally, Vincent saw his chance. With a quick jerk of the wheel, the car spun gracefully and got back on track. I could see the destination ahead, but my phone suddenly came to life. At first, I thought my team was trying to catch up, but to my surprise, they were already following closely behind us.

The message that illuminated my screen read, "Are we burned?"

Training at the Secret Service Academy, characterized by strict discipline and a disconnect from reality, became a fertile ground for ignorance. Sometimes, it was assumed that when a suspect made a U-turn, it signified an awareness of being watched. During surveillance with fellow agents, they frequently abandoned the "eye" after just two turns, fearing that a third would expose them.

As I recall the many nights I spent stuck in heavy traffic, I remember the difficulties I encountered. I would pretend to be the "target," picking a specific car and convincing myself it was a cop. Maintaining visual contact while tracking its every move was no easy feat. Life constantly interrupted my focus—phone calls, sudden maneuvers from other cars, or unexpected lane changes would distract me repeatedly.

However, the situation flipped. I found myself in Vincent's car beside the unsuspecting "bad guy." The team thought they had been compromised, but we were just lost. We had to make unusual turns to maneuver through Bangkok's exceptionally complex road network.

Understanding how quickly stress can escalate, I promptly responded to ASAIC DuBois's text: "Not burned. Lost. Destination ahead."

The massage parlor we sought was discreetly nestled amidst the bustling facade of buildings. In one fluid motion, Vincent deftly maneuvered the car into the parking lot and seamlessly, without effort, parked. We stepped out into the balmy night, the humidity wrapping around us like a second skin. The massage parlor was a nondescript door among a wall of commerce, sandwiched between laundromats and clothing storefronts.

Stepping inside, we were greeted by a sanctuary of tranquility. The air was refreshingly cooler and delicately scented with hints of lemongrass and jasmine. Soft, subdued lighting bathed the space, seamlessly blending traditional Thai aesthetics with modern comfort.

Polished wood paired with soft cushions, while gentle yet sensual music floated effortlessly, serving as a soothing balm for the frenetic energy we had left behind.

As the attendant approached us, her hands pressed together in a gesture of respect, and her smile exuded a professional warmth. She presented us with a binder, its pages a tantalizing catalog of choices, a testament to the parlor's profound understanding of physical allure. Each photograph of the massage therapists, though devoid of vulgarity, possessed an undeniable frankness, extending an invitation to indulge in the realm of relaxation and pleasure.

Vincent and I meticulously perused the pages, our eyes locked on each woman's captured gaze. We scrutinized them with the discerning eye of an appraiser in search of a rare gem. The gallery before us was an enigma: an assortment of women whose bodies exuded an alluring promise of skilled hands ready to offer their services.

After careful consideration, we made our selection. The women were introduced, their professional demeanor emanating a sense of grace, as practiced smiles graced their faces. They led us further into the depths of the parlor, where our anticipation grew, knowing that the rooms awaiting us were sanctuaries of tranquility. Before we entered the massage room, we were issued lockers, where we were expected to shed our clothing, leaving behind the layers that shielded our vulnerability.

My first thought was a mixture of gratitude and apprehension. I was grateful that I wasn't required to wear a wire, but I was anxious about parting with my cell phone, my only connection to the surveillance team. Reluctantly, I undressed and donned the robe they provided, feeling a sense of vulnerability settle over me.

Once ready, our masseuses welcomed us, their presence commanding yet gentle, like a whisper of silk against the skin. Leading us to our rooms, I waved goodbye to Vincent, wishing him a pleasurable experience. As my masseuse and I entered the room, a sense of solitude enveloped us, and the air was thick with anticipation of what was to come.

A solitary table stood in the center, bathed in warm lighting that cast a soft glow on the fully tiled floor and wooden walls. The room exuded serenity, a sanctuary from the chaos of the outside world. The sound of running water from a basin in the corner mingled gracefully with the scent of incense, creating an intoxicating atmosphere that beckoned one to relax.

My masseuse, with gentle grace, helped me remove the robe. She motioned for me to lie on the table, the cool surface against my skin sending shivers of anticipation down my spine. As I followed her commands, I looked back at her, and to my surprise, she, too, shed her gown, bearing her own body before me.

The sight was tantalizing and empowering, a reminder of the sensuality that awaited me. Before the massage began, she washed me from head to toe, a ritualistic cleansing that invigorated and soothed me. With skilled hands, she started the process of washing my body, each touch a deliberate caress that awakened my senses. The salt tapping against my skin created a tingling sensation as the moisture was quickly absorbed, leaving a trail of rejuvenation in its wake.

As I surrendered to the experience, she began a vigorous yet sensual scrubbing, her hands moving with purpose and precision. With an almost erotic intention, she climbed atop me, her legs wrapped around my body, pressing her form against mine. The pain of each stroke faded into a refreshing sense of renewal, a shedding of the old to make way for the new.

After the ritual salt washing, she helped me put on the gown again, her touch gentle yet lingering. Side by side, we walked to the next room, a space adorned with traditional Japanese aesthetics reminiscent of a geisha's private quarters. The subsequent massage was a sacred ritual, a dance of healing that unfolded with each deliberate motion of the therapist's hands. Every touch and stroke was a step along the path to serenity, an exquisite symphony aimed at releasing the tension buried deep within my body.

As I sank into the table, my muscles surrendered to her expert ministrations, and tension dissolved like smoke. At that moment, time seemed to stretch and fold upon itself, the universe conspiring to grant me respite from the chaos outside. The weight of the city of Bangkok, with its relentless pulse, faded into a distant drumbeat, a forgotten melody swallowed by the serenade of the methodical pressure of her knowing fingers and the gentle brush of her smooth, warm body.

Within the confines of this haven, aliases and missions were merely whispers of a forgotten past. The only reality that mattered was her skillful touches, the gentle breath of peace that enveloped us, providing a respite from the trials and tribulations of my daily life. In this place, deliberately crafted for escape, I reveled in the solace of the present, immersing myself in the quiet sanctuary where worries melted away and the essence of my being found tranquility.

The soothing touch of the masseuse's hands lingered on my skin as she led me back to the locker room. The air was thick with the scent of essential oils, and the soft glow of the dimmed lights enhanced the ambiance of relaxation. With a graceful bow and a whispered goodbye, she faded into the shadows, leaving me in a state of peace.

As I hastily dressed, my mind was preoccupied with thoughts of Vincent. Would he be waiting for me, or lost in the pleasures of the hidden paradise secluded behind the lobby walls? I had been out of contact with my team for several hours, and as a result, I felt a surge of nervousness. I needed to connect with them and let them know that all was okay.

When I pulled out my cell phone, I was surprised by the number of messages I had. Without even opening them, I guessed they were inquiries about my location. However, they weren't about my whereabouts or activities at all. As I read through the messages, I realized they contained something equally significant: news of a developing storm back in the United States. Seeing that I had some time, I called ASAIC DuBois.

"I don't have much time. What's going on?" I said quickly to ASAIC DuBois.

ASAIC DuBois answered, "I'll be brief. I just got off the phone with Headquarters. Some believe you're on a 'boondoggle.' They also mentioned Vincent, claiming he's of no value."

"No value?" I exclaimed. "Without Vincent, I'd be in the dark about Slim. Without him, I wouldn't have an advocate. Are they even aware of this?"

"I did inform them," ASAIC DuBois replied sheepishly. "But as you know, I'm a protection guy. I'm not sure what else to say."

Shaking my head, I said, "Tell them Vincent is our way back into Slim's good graces. Vincent is connected to P0l1c3D0g and Leon. Let them know that late nights, drinking, and relaxation are part of the undercover lifestyle. I can't believe they are scrutinizing my actions five thousand miles away."

"I understand," ASAIC DuBois sympathized. "I wanted to give you a heads up so you can prepare, but they're deciding now and seem to be leaning toward ending the op early. I'm sorry."

"Whatever," I said dismissively. "I gotta go before Vincent shows up. Later."

"Later," ASAIC DuBois replied.

The news deeply upset me, but it was an ominous warning that the operation was about to abruptly cut short due to the target's perceived low value. Now, I was left grappling with how to conclude the mission without losing face. Though no official decision had been made, my experience told me to plan accordingly.

Now, I had to find a way to withdraw gracefully. This task proved challenging, as I needed to maintain a facade of a free spirit, unbound by rules, even as I departed prematurely to fulfill an unwise decision. It was an extraordinarily dangerous situation, but it wouldn't be the worst situation I would encounter due to Secret Service leadership.

Sitting back, I contemplated my next steps with Vincent. It seemed like only a few minutes had passed, but in reality, I had been absorbed in conversation with ASAIC DuBois for nearly thirty minutes. Distracted by the unfolding situation, I hardly noticed when Vincent entered the lobby.

"Hey," I said. "You were in there quite a while. How was it?"

Vincent chuckled and replied, "It was good. I like this place."

I nodded in agreement and said, "I'm happy to hear that. Let me take care of the check."

"Don't worry about it. I got this," Vincent said, waving me off.

After paying the bill, we headed toward Vincent's car. As we walked side by side, he suddenly asked, "Do you play pool?"

I glanced over at him and replied, "Huh? You must have been really wasted in Phuket. Remember? That was my favorite in college."

"Right, I remember now," Vincent nodded. "Let's go play some pool."

While sitting in Vincent's car, I quickly texted ASAIC DuBois, "We're on the move," and then put my phone away.

As Vincent drove to his favorite bar, I considered my next move. I knew the operation was likely ending, and I needed a solid plan. I hoped the bar was further away, but instead, it was nearby. It was nestled in an area called Nana, a popular spot in Bangkok known for its many bars and party scene.

As Vincent parked, I felt it was the right moment to speak up, so I said, "Hey, I have some unfortunate news. My team has a problem. I'll need to leave early."

Surprisingly, Vincent remained unfazed. He casually suggested, "Just let me know, and I'll take you to the airport."

"Thanks, man. I appreciate it," I replied.

Though Vincent remained oblivious, I knew ASAIC DuBois would not appreciate my accepting his offer. To handle this, I just pushed it out of my mind. It was something to deal with tomorrow, and right now, I needed to focus on Vincent.

But everything changed once we got out of his car. Vincent's phone buzzed. He glanced at it and then faced me, letting out a sigh. "I go home. Wife nagging me. Let's hang tomorrow."

"Oh, sure. That works for me," I replied. We exchanged a solid handshake before parting ways.

I seized the moment as Vincent drove off and sent ASAIC DuBois a final message: "Vincent headed home. Op over for tonight."

Chapter 21

Doctor's orders—it's time to go home

I stood there watching Vincent drive away, contemplating my next move. Should I return to the my hotel or explore Nana? A single phone call solidified my decision. Knowing I had parted ways with Vincent, ASAIC DuBois called. Skipping the usual pleasantries, he said, "Book a flight to San Diego for the following day. The operation is over."

"Understood," I said.

ASAIC DuBois added, "If possible, avoid accepting any offer from Vincent for a ride to the airport. Make up any excuse. I don't care what it is."

Shaking my head in disbelief, I said, "I will do what I can, but I can't make any promises."

Returning to the hotel, exhaustion weighed heavily upon me. The day's activities had taken their toll. Without a girlfriend to keep me awake, I found solace in the peacefulness of the moment. I thought more about my next day's flight back to San Diego. I knew Rachel would be pleased with my early return.

Since I ended the night early, I woke up early the next morning. It was a rare opportunity for me to enjoy a full night's rest. Our flight wasn't until later in the afternoon, and it was too early to pack, so I intended to enjoy a leisurely breakfast in the hotel lobby. However, fate had a different plan in store for me.

As the elevator doors opened, I stepped into the expansive lobby. To my surprise, Vincent and his wife were there waiting for me. They had seemingly made use of the room I had booked for them.

While one might consider this unanticipated meeting a positive development, it presented a challenge for me. I had no support. No one was aware of this meeting. I was convinced that everyone believed Vincent and my final meeting was last night, but luck wasn't on their side.

I walked over to Vincent and greeted him, saying, "Good morning. I see you chose to stay the night."

"Yes, very nice. Thank you once more," Vincent replied. He then introduced his wife, saying, "This is my wife."

"It's a pleasure to meet you. I'm Rich," I responded. "I was about to head to breakfast. Care to join me?"

Vincent responded enthusiastically, "Yes. We join."

As we had breakfast, I realized that discussing my early departure wouldn't be easy. This prompted me to speak up, saying, "I spoke with my team last night. They got into some trouble. I must go back today. If I don't, it'll be bad news for me."

Vincent lowered his gaze, deep in thought. Then, he looked at me and asked, "What time?"

"In a few hours, I've already booked a taxi based on the hotel's suggestion," I answered.

"Cancel it," Vincent replied firmly.

"No, you've done enough. I can take a taxi," I insisted.

DOI: 10.1201/9781003680390-21

"No, I take you to airport," Vincent stated decisively.

"I don't want to inconvenience you. It's a long drive. I'll take a taxi," I urged.

"I have plastic. We need get from my people. We go now, then I take to airport. It's settled," Vincent insisted.

I knew ASAIC DuBois would be upset, but there was no alternative. Vincent was right; we had unfinished business, and I didn't have much to say. I conceded, "Alright. I need to pack. Give me twenty minutes."

"No problem," Vincent replied cheerfully. "I be in lobby waiting you."

As soon as I was out of Vincent's sight, I hurriedly messaged ASAIC DuBois about the unexpected encounter. I wrote, "Vincent was in the lobby this morning. The meeting was unplanned. He reminded me we need to recover the counterfeit credit cards and insisted on taking me to the airport afterward. I'm in my room packing. The meeting is in one hour."

I braced myself for an angry response from ASAIC DuBois, but to my surprise, only the words "Roger, we'll be ready" flashed across my screen.

The indifferent reply suggested a grim possibility: Would I face consequences upon my return home. With limited time to reflect, moments sped past, prompting me to gather my belongings and head to the lobby.

As I walked toward reception, Vincent sat patiently in the grand lobby waiting for me. I caught his attention and gestured that I needed to check out. Silently, I hoped he wouldn't insist on going with me to the counter.

I knew the hotel records weren't under the name Richard Druc. Instead, the room was registered under my name, Richard K. LaTulip. Fortunately, luck seemed to be on my side as Vincent remained seated, not even flinching.

Standing at the reception, I seized the opportunity to send ASAIC DuBois a quick update. I wrote, "Vincent in lobby. Going to get plastic. Then to the airport."

Once check-out was complete, I walked to Vincent and said, "Ready."

"Yes, let me take luggage," Vincent graciously offered.

Not wanting to seem awkward, I offered no resistance, saying, "Thank you."

Vincent gestured toward the elevators and said, "Follow me."

Once inside Vincent's car, a palpable shift in his demeanor became evident. His eyes narrowed, his jaw set with determination, and it was clear that he had mentally shifted gears. The weight of our mission, with its time-sensitive nature, pressed upon him, igniting a fire within his core.

As we embarked on the treacherous journey through the labyrinthine streets of Bangkok, Vincent's skillful hands danced across the wheel, effortlessly navigating the maze with the precision of a seasoned conductor leading an orchestra.

The city unfolded before us, a tapestry of bustling streets and endless crowds, as Vincent skillfully navigated the vehicle through the chaos. Each turn and each acceleration were executed with precise finesse, reflecting his unwavering focus. We had no time for mistakes and no room for error. We needed to be methodical and meticulous in our approach if I were to acquire the elusive counterfeit credit cards and catch my flight before it vanished into the afternoon sun.

After what felt like an eternity, we arrived at an industrial area, an enclave where the city's hustle and bustle gave way to the harsh realities of labor and industry. The buildings stood tall, bearing the scars of countless trucks and workers who had traversed these roads before us. The air was thick with the smell of machinery and sweat, a reminder that this was a place where illicit deals could thrive in the shadows.

In the distance, I spotted a solitary car, its presence an anomaly in this otherwise desolate landscape. As we approached, the figures of two Thai men came into focus, their stances revealing a mix of anticipation and caution. A third man sat inside the car, his posture radiating quiet confidence, as if he held all the cards in this dangerous game.

With purpose, Vincent brought the car to a halt, the engine's growl fading into the stillness of the afternoon sun. He turned toward me, his eyes burning with determination, and declared with unwavering resolve, "Let's go."

At that moment, the weight of the mission—my mission—felt overwhelming. Countless thoughts raced through my mind, and adrenaline surged through my veins. Vincent was familiar with these people; I wasn't. They were a mystery, and if tradition held, the conversation would unfold in a language that was foreign to me. The main thought that flashed through my mind was, "I hope they don't say, 'Kill the white guy.'"

This knowledge gap meant I would have no early warning signs of impending danger. What lay ahead would test my limits, challenge my ability to remain calm, and push me to the edge of my capabilities. The question remained: "Was I ready?"

Taking a deep breath and letting out a shallow sigh, I exited the car, a rush of anticipation flowing through me. The air was thick with uncertainty, and as I walked toward Vincent's friends, I prepared myself for what lay ahead. Time felt frozen, the burden of the unknown pressing heavily on my shoulders.

As we approached, they made their move, their silhouettes gliding forward in a quiet dance of mystery. When we met at the midpoint, Vincent and his new friends' words flowed like music in Thai, a secret dialect that slipped past my comprehension. The transaction unfolded before me, their hands meeting as a package changed hands. It was a brief moment, as if time paused for an instant.

And just like that, it was over. Vincent and I turned on our heels and began our retreat, the echoes of disappointment reverberating in my mind. There was no grand spectacle, no dramatic confrontation between rival factions. The scene unfolding before me defied my expectations, shattering the illusions crafted by movies and novels.

The vivid images of tense standoffs, where adversaries exchanged wary glances filled with fear and resolve, faded. Instead, a heavy reality crashed down on me, dispelling the romanticized ideas I once held. This was no Hollywood spectacle; it was the harsh reality of the criminal underworld.

There were no thrilling chases, no gunfire slicing through the air, and no unexpected hero triumphing against the odds. Instead, I found myself enveloped in the mundane reality of the situation, leaving a lingering sense of disappointment. The dramatic scenes, so commonplace in films, were starkly disconnected from the reality unfolding around me, prompting me to reevaluate my expectations.

Once inside Vincent's car, he looked at me, handed me the package, and said, "Your plastic."

Feeling obligated, I opened the package and thumbed through the counterfeit cards, pretending to "check" the product. At that moment, I couldn't help myself; I was mindlessly performing a task I believed was normal. Movies told me, "I needed to check the package."

The reality was I didn't care. I had no intention of using what had now been given to me; I only cared that it was the same plastic that carried the names and data I provided. Acting satisfied, I said, "Looks awesome. Thank you." Then, I handed Vincent the remaining $5,000.

Without checking the money, Vincent pocketed it and said, "Thanks. Now to the airport."

The drive to the airport was smooth, with no unexpected incidents. The seamless traffic flow allowed us to glide effortlessly along the road. As soon as we merged onto the highway, the bustling presence of mopeds faded into the periphery, and their exclusion from these thoroughfares ensured a sense of tranquility.

However, our peaceful drive was occasionally interrupted by the hulking presence of ancient trucks, burdened with loads that surpassed their recommended capacity. Lumbering along the road, these behemoths posed occasional obstacles on our path. As I gazed out into the horizon, a vast expanse stretched before me, inviting me to lose myself in its breathtaking beauty.

We arrived at the bustling Bangkok International Airport. The air was thick with humidity, and the scent of exotic spices mingled with the diesel fumes from the nearby taxis. My newest friend, Vincent, stepped out of his car and quickly unloaded the luggage. As we exchanged our goodbyes, a surge of emotion washed over us. We embraced, our bodies coming together in a heartfelt hug. It was a promise, an unspoken agreement that we would see each other again, no matter the cost or distance.

As I entered the airport, a surge of triumph enveloped me. Our mission was accomplished, and each step and every strategic choice had brought us to this point. I felt compelled to send one last message to RAIC Tran, FSNI Boonme, and Lieutenant Colonel Chaiwat, my fingers moving swiftly over the keyboard with a sense of closure: "At the Airport. Vincent departed. Op over. Thank you for your assistance."

As I settled into my seat on the flight back to the United States, the rhythmic hum of the engines turned into a calming melody. It was a lullaby that relaxed the adrenaline that had fueled me during the operation. With the world's noise fading into the background, I found myself alone with my thoughts.

Thoughts of the operation flooded my mind. The bonds I developed with Dok Mai and Vincent brought me both a sense of achievement and sorrow—yet I realized that I would miss Dok Mai the most. I recognized the delicate balance of trust and deception that kept me alert. This was just the start; it marked the first of many missions I felt would leave a significant mark on the history of the Secret Service.

Chapter 22

How nice it is to be home

Traveling takes a toll on the mind, body, soul, and home front. It's a relentless, grinding journey that chips away at the essence of your being, stripping away the familiar, the comforting, and the predictable. Being away from friends and family, especially for extended periods, can create a chasm in your mind and heart, altering you and those you hold closest. My experience, as it unfolded, proved to be no exception.

In the demanding world of the Secret Service, where shadows moved and secrets lingered, each day was a trial of resilience. I functioned as part of a system designed to protect, serve, and remain unseen. However, my position had gained an added layer of complexity; I was now operating undercover in a world of emerging technology, an unexplored domain called the deep and dark web. Beyond these complexities, I was more than just a Secret Service Agent. The allure has always captivated me, and I never expected the profound influence it would have on my life.

In my civilian life, I had someone special waiting for me, helping to keep my sanity intact. Rachel, with a heart as wild as her spirit, became the anchor of my tumultuous existence. Together, we forged a path through the chaos, weaving our stories into the fabric of our shared lives. In my home, which soon became ours, we created numerous memories shared by only the closest couples.

Many nights, our laughter resonated through the hallways while we entertained friends. Our home became a lively gathering spot, filled with camaraderie and warmth. We cheered for our favorite sports teams, yelled at the TV together, and celebrated significant and minor victories. Amid all this joy, we welcomed two amazing Labrador retrievers, Bella and Natasha, who embodied loyalty and companionship.

But life has a peculiar way of challenging our cherished connections. As the pressure from my undercover work grew, it eroded the foundation of our relationship. Rachel and I were no strangers to the trials of love; every couple experiences ups and downs. Yet, the burden of our responsibilities, the secrets we harbored, and the darkness enveloping us began to obscure the once-idyllic existence we shared. Each argument pushed us further apart, forming emotional rifts that seemed insurmountable to bridge.

Despite everything, we soldiered on, managing the delicate balance between our personal lives and work. We clung to the precious moments still shining brightly amidst the encroaching darkness. However, as the days turned into nights and the pressures of my covert mission intensified, the question lingered in the air like a storm cloud: Could love endure the tempest brewing on the horizon? Especially on this day, which had begun so blissfully for us.

Rachel and I journeyed from San Diego, driving south on Interstate 5 to Tijuana, with her friend Taylor in the back seat. It had become our routine to take this trip every Saturday. Taylor, who worked with Rachel, had also become a good friend of mine over the years. We frequently enjoyed watching our favorite NFL teams together on Sundays.

DOI: 10.1201/9781003680390-22

We parked near the border and walked across into the bustling heart of Tijuana. The vibrant city beckoned us with its colors and sounds. Street vendors hawked their wares, and the scent of sizzling tacos hung in the air. Much like my relationship with Rachel, this city thrived on life and adventure. As was our tradition, our first stop before the "Mercado" was the legendary Caliente Sports Book.

It was where dreams took form on betting slips, and fortunes were made or lost with a game's turn or a horse's nose. Caliente was a dimly lit oasis of suspense and enthusiasm. It beckoned to gamblers from far and wide, promising the allure of fortune and the sting of defeat.

A thick veil of cigarette smoke lingered in the air as we entered. The dimness inside was intentional, casting long shadows over the figures hunched over their betting slips, newspapers, and cheat sheets. These were the regulars, worn and weary, their cigarettes dangling precariously between their lips, a pencil in one hand and papers in the other. Their eyes carried the burden of countless losses and a faint spark of hope that one team or horse would grant them their fortune.

The facility was a relic of the past, a time-worn structure where the black checkerboard tiles bore the scars of countless footfalls. The fluorescent tube lighting overhead emitted a flickering, eerie light that cast grotesque shadows on the walls. The once-vibrant red paint, now faded and peeling, clung to the walls like a melancholy memory of better days.

Behind the counter, where iron bars resembled the old jail cells of a bygone era, the ladies worked with a suspicion that came from years of experience. They took bets with practiced indifference, their eyes measuring every patron who approached. Trust was a scarce commodity in this world of high stakes and deception.

Despite its rundown state and gloomy atmosphere, the southern Mexican sports betting venue had an unusual charm. We moved with intent, aiming to minimize our time spent, as our primary objective was to grab the NFL odds sheets. We planned to return later in the day to place our bets, but for now, we were focused on a brief visit. With the odds sheets finally in our possession, we headed straight to the core of Tijuana's vibrancy—the "Mercado."

The "Mercado" was a sensory explosion, an oasis of flavors and colors. We found our favorite open-air cantina, where the rickety wooden tables bore witness to countless meals shared. Buckets of Corona and margaritas flowed as freely as the laughter and conversation. Quesadillas, tacos, chips, and salsa adorned our table, and the food was a symphony of tastes that filled the air.

The "Mercado" in Tijuana, Mexico, reflected the passage of time. It was nearly encircled by aging two-story Spanish-style structures whose once-bright hues had faded, echoing a glorious past. Where stucco used to be, rebar jutted out, a stark reminder of the buildings' ongoing struggle against the elements. In the center lay a dry fountain, a relic of bygone days when water danced joyfully in its basin.

Children scurried around, tentatively approaching tourists with timid smiles, hoping to sell candies for some extra money to support their families. In the background, attentive parents could be spotted lingering in a corner or at the top of the staircase. They stayed close enough to ensure their children's safety while still granting them the independence to pursue opportunities.

Our chosen spot was a charming little restaurant located at the corner of one of the buildings. Having visited so frequently, we had become regulars. We settled into our favorite seats, holding NFL odds sheets in hand, and ordered our preferred buckets of beer and a pitcher of margaritas. The menu offered a delightful selection of Mexican dishes—including tamales, quesadillas, fajitas, and tacos—each presenting a delightful exploration of authentic Mexican cuisine.

As we exchanged stories, laughter, and the occasional spirited debate over which football team would win on Sunday, the Mercado sprang to life. It reflected Tijuana's vibrant tapestry of culture. The clinking of glasses, the sizzling grills, and the lively conversations of fellow patrons blended into a joyful symphony, celebrating the simple pleasures that united us all.

Rachel, Taylor, and I had transformed from mere customers into members of the family at this restaurant. Rather than purchasing the candies offered by the children, we requested the waiter to set up a table for them. Their excited expressions brightened as they realized their favorite meals would soon be served.

During those moments in the heart of the "Mercado," we found relief from life's complexities. We experienced the warmth of its people, the depth of its culture, and the enduring ties of friendship. However, time flies, and with the sun setting, our study of the wager sheets had to come to an end. It was time to head back to the Caliente Sports Book.

As we approached the counter, the attendants behind the iron bars displayed a weary yet vigilant demeanor. Their experienced and watchful eyes surveyed the patrons as they conducted their business. Trust was rare in this high-stakes gambling world, and every interaction carried an air of secrecy and suspicion.

With a mix of excitement and nerves, we placed our bets for Sunday's games. As the transactions unfolded, we found ourselves engaging in brief conversations with a few locals. These were seasoned gamblers, their stories as vivid as the worn checkerboard tiles beneath us. They shared insights, tips, and superstitions, but we built a connection through our shared goal of winning.

After placing our bets, we left Caliente for our next destination, the United States. As we got ready to cross the border, just like on previous weekends, thoughts of potential gains and the dread of losing swirled in our minds. The unusually long line lightened the atmosphere.

While discussing our chances of winning, Taylor reached into his pocket, intending to warm his cold hands, only to freeze mid-motion, his face going pale.

When he saw the border crossing station and the words "Welcome to the United States," the realization hit him like a sledgehammer. Off in the distance, U.S. Immigration and Naturalization Officers examined documents, while U.S. Customs Officers meticulously checked border crossers.

In a state of panic, Taylor grabbed my arm and exclaimed, "Rich, I have a problem."

Taken by surprise, I asked, "What's the issue?"

Pointing off into the distance, Taylor confessed, "Those people are following me. Actually us. They are following us."

Initially caught off guard, I thought, "Why on earth would someone be following us?" I dismissed it momentarily, but then thought, could it be the cartel. There were reports of agents being kidnapped south of the border. I became focused and said, "Where?"

Rachel, witnessing the scene, exclaimed, "What the hell?"

I turned to Rachel and asked, "Taylor, do you want to explain? I don't see anyone."

Taylor then started panicking, "There, you see them?"

Not seeing anyone, I said "Okay, Let me think this through."

Looking at Rachel with his eyes closed, Taylor screamed, "They are coming towards us."

"What the hell, Taylor?" Rachel reacted. "I don't see anyone, just a couple kids selling candy."

"We need to run," Taylor claimed. "They are getting closer."

I shook my head and said, "I work for the Secret Service, come on let's start swiftly moving to the border. What the hell."

Rachel turned to me, whispering, "Okay, something is not right. You need to help him."

I peered off into the distance, still not seeing anyone. I grabbed Taylor's arm pulling him towards me and said, "Let's Walk."

I kept alert the entire time, scanning for anything out of the ordinary, still nothing.

Then Taylor pulled back, fear in his eyes, "There, there he is again. Just in front of us."

Rachel and I looked ahead, not seeing anything strange, I said, "Those are just Immigration Agents."

"Yeah, they are in disguise. They aren't who they seem," Taylor whimpered.

Rachel, with a concerned look, pleaded, "You gotta help him."

"Help him?" I replied. "What can I do? 'Hey, Inspector, my buddy is having a mental breakdown. He thinks you're the cartel, but I work for the Secret Service, So, nevermind him."

Understanding the seriousness, Rachel insisted, "Well, we have to do something."

Deep in thought, I ran my fingers through my hair and finally said, "Alright. Taylor, stick by side. Nobody knows who we are, so stay calm."

"Rich, I'm freaking out," Taylor admitted. "I don't know if I can handle this. They are going kill me."

Rachel looked at him firmly and said, "Man up. You got this." Then she peered at me urging me forward.

Taylor composed himself and said, "Okay, but you promise to protect me."

"Look Taylor," I said. "If anyone tries to hurt us, I'll fight. But piece of advice, don't say anything to the Inspector unless someone starts hurting us."

Taylor still nervous, sweating bullets, complied and said, "Okay, I promise, but I'm staying right behind you."

"No problem," I said but my eyes peered at Rachel almost saying out loud, "Taylor wasn't just losing it, he was unraveling right in front of us."

As a Secret Service Agent, I knew that this situation could spiral into a disaster, but who was out there? Is someone threatening not only Taylor but us. Is there something more I don't know about Taylor? Could it jeopardize my career, Rachel's and I's relationship, or our cherished tradition. Or is it nothing. My wager was on that bet, but still we weren't in America. Here I was nothing, not a Special Agent, not a law enforcement officer, just an ordinary person.

As we approached the Immigration Inspectors, the intensity in the air was thick, and our hearts raced with apprehension. I was waiting for that phatom person to stand out, pull a gun, and start shooting. But nothing. Instead, the Immigration Inspector, a stern figure with a piercing gaze, studied our documents closely. His questions came rapid-fire, each word laced with suspicion.

Though strained, Taylor's demeanor remained steady, and his responses were measured. The tension was unbearable as the Inspector scrutinized our group, but Taylor's performance was convincing, and the officers, seemingly satisfied with our responses, let us pass. As we crossed the border, the relief was overwhelming.

It was a heavy weight lifted from our shoulders, but the intensity of the ordeal lingered. We had crossed safely, but the silence afterward said more than words ever could. With the San Diego skyline on the horizon, the familiar felt distant. Our tradition had endured, but something had changed.

Rachel hovered near Taylor, her concern genuine, her words soft and measured. I understood it. He had just unraveled in front of us. Whatever that was—panic, paranoia, something worse—it had rattled all of us. Still, I couldn't shake the feeling that I was on the outside of something I didn't fully understand.

She hadn't said much to me since we crossed. A glance. A nod. No anger, no cold shoulder—just distance. I tried to tell myself it was exhaustion, that we were all just shaken. But there was something else. Something quieter and more complicated to name.

Maybe Rachel knew more than she let on. Perhaps this wasn't the first time Taylor had gone off the rails like that. I didn't want to believe she had kept that from me. But the possibility hung in the air between us, unspoken. As I saw it, Rachel cared more for Taylor than for me.

Nonetheless, some of my experiences with Rachel and Taylor had helped prepare me for my undercover life. However, these two worlds were slowly pulling us apart. The tension between us was suffocating.

Our love, once the foundation of our relationship, had evolved into something that resembled family. Arguments have become a daily occurrence, and our relationship seems to be unraveling before our eyes. Taylor was becoming increasingly the catalyst for our most explosive arguments. The idea that his unusual breakdown was something more, something only Rachel understood, but also could have jeopardized my career, faded into an afterthought.

Home no longer felt like a refuge. To avoid my pain, I turned away from my relationship. Choosing to throw myself deeper into my covert operation. I had been living a double life: one as an agent tasked with infiltrating an international cybercriminal ring, and the other as Rachel's boyfriend. With each personal blow, my focus sharpened. Losing control in one part of my life meant I couldn't afford to lose it in the other. It forced me to navigate treacherous waters filled with criminals whose actions fascinated and concerned me equally.

No one I was meeting was known to be violent. Still, I was working in exotic places, where languages were unknown to me, and I hoped the conversation wasn't directed toward me in an unsettling manner. I never really thought about it when working. It was only afterward.

The success of the operation depended on change, and I was willing to do whatever it took to make that happen. The targets found me uninteresting. I knew drastic steps were needed to salvage the failed Macau operation. There was only one way to address this: I had to return to Macau.

I continued my meetings with SAIC Montaña and ATSAICs Carrington and Sheehan, where I fervently pointed out the shortcomings of their approach. Criminals could sense when something was amiss. Traveling halfway across the globe for a three-hour meeting wasn't just nonsensical; it was dangerous.

However, I was at a pivotal moment, caught between the slow collapse of my relationship with Rachel and the alluring pull of my undercover life. The decisions I made in the days ahead would determine not only the outcome of Operation Carder Kaos but also the fate of whatever was left between Rachel and me.

I was caught between two collapsing worlds, one personal, one professional, and neither willing to let me go.

Chapter 23

Take 2—rinse, refresh, repeat

My relationship with Rachel felt like an emotional rollercoaster—an unpredictable journey filled with ups and downs that kept us in a state of tension. The added stress from work only intensified our struggles. I faced ongoing second-guessing from leadership, which complicated an already intricate investigative operation.

Despite Headquarters' request that I acquire a database, when it came time to fund it, everyone—from administrative staff to agents to leaders—seemed to move at a snail's pace. Once obtained, this crucial information would advance the case and reveal the secrets we urgently needed to know. The bureaucracy and red tape felt suffocating, like a noose tightening around my neck, stalling my progress and leaving me frustrated and helpless.

Adding to my frustration, Maksik, whom I intended to meet in Thailand, reappeared only to inform me that he had altered his plans. He expressed a lack of connection and trust, particularly since we hadn't exchanged money for the promised database.

This revelation shifted my anger toward Headquarters. After all, ATSAIC Sheehan approached me to purchase the database from Maksik. Now, facing uncertainty, SAIC Stokes and ATSAIC Sheehan retreated, leaving me to shoulder the burden of their indecision.

My conversations with Maksik focused on this one deal, and I had to justify my unpreparedness each time. Daily discussions only increased the strain on our relationship. However, on this day, despite the potential consequences of further damaging Maksik's trust, leadership made another choice that left me in an even more precarious position.

I noticed a flashing message as I sat in the forensic lab, gazing at my undercover computer and mulling over my dilemma. I wondered who it could be—Maksik, of course. Even before clicking on the notification, I anticipated the questions that would follow. Still, I felt compelled to look. Upon reading the message, it said, "What up, Brat?"

Uncertain if he was online, I typed back, "Hey. What up, Brat?"

In no time, Maksik replied, "Busy ☺. U?"

Sensing where the conversation was going, I responded, "Same ☺. My guys work every day. Almost ready with the 💰💰💰."

Maksik then said, "Good ☺. I have something I need to ask."

My curiosity piqued, I typed, "Yes ☺ ask."

Maksik replied, "My team decrypt dumps with PIN. R u interested?"

Now, I was focused. This was a breakthrough. Maybe Maksik wasn't put off; I hurriedly typed, "Maybe. Tell me more. ☺"

Maksik responded, "I can offer 10 dumps+PINS for 3k."

Once I saw the price, I cringed. I immediately feared ATSAIC Carrington would disapprove, but I pressed on, "3k? Only 10 dumps? That's a lot of money."

"Yes," Maksik replied. "But you get money straight from ATM. You don't have to buy and then sell online. ☺"

I understood his point and replied, "Let me think about it."

DOI: 10.1201/9781003680390-23

Maksik typed back, "Okay. But hurry; I don't know how long this will last. ☺"

Thoughts raced through my mind as I considered the seriousness of the offer. Maksik's choice highlighted the trust I had built within the criminal underworld. However, I couldn't overlook the notorious stinginess of the Secret Service.

Typically, a dump without a PIN costs around $15, meaning I could buy 200 dumps for the same amount. The math was straightforward, but the bureaucracy remained baffling. I took a deep breath and softly said, "If you want to play with the big dogs in the tall green grass, you have to get off the porch." Then, I headed to ATSAIC Carrington's office.

As I entered ATSAIC Carrington's office, I knocked and said, "Hey, boss, do you have a moment?"

ATSAIC Carrington was on a call but waved me in, gesturing to a chair.

Once I sat down, he finished his call and asked, "What's up?"

I held back my excitement and said, "I just spoke with Maksik. Standard question: any updates on the money?"

ATSAIC Carrington clicked his teeth, replying, "No news yet."

"Of course," I shot back. "Maksik offered me an insider deal. He's willing to sell me ten dumps along with their associated PINs."

ATSAIC Carrington's eyes widened at the news. "Really? He has the card PIN?"

"To be fair, I'm not sure," I answered. "This is new information."

"Okay," ATSAIC Carrington said. "What's the cost?"

I took a deep breath and responded, "Three thousand dollars for ten dumps and their PINs."

Stunned, ATSAIC Carrington repeated, "Three thousand dollars? For ten dumps and PINs? What do we currently pay per dump?"

I explained, "Right now, depending on the type, we average about fifteen dollars per dump."

Looking thoughtful, ATSAIC Carrington reached for his Tums, popped one in, chewed quickly, and remarked, "Hmmm, then for three thousand dollars, we could obtain around two hundred dumps."

I quickly interjected, "Yes, but keep in mind this is like cash. I can withdraw the money directly from the ATM."

Casually, ATSAIC Carrington replied, "I doubt the courts care, besides, two hundred is better than ten, right?"

I cautiously responded, "I mean yes and no. Besides don't we have an obligation to protect the public?"

Deep in thought, ATSAIC Carrington replied, "Yeah, but I know no one will endorse it. Let's stick with the fifteen-dollar dumps."

With great reluctance, I returned to Maksik to decline the offer, fully aware that it could jeopardize our growing relationship. This decision haunted me as I recognized the significant consequences of passing up such an alluring opportunity. As this horrible situation unfolded, one would think, "Can it get worse?" The answer is, "Yes, it can."

Sone arrived at the office to pick up his reimbursement check and chatted with SA Mason in the lobby. The thin walls make it easy to hear the latest gossip.

As I got closer, I greeted, "Hey, what's up, Sone?"

Laughing and rubbing his head, Sone responded, "I was just telling your boy I found it hilarious seeing ASAIC DuBois walking down Bangla Road with a girl. It was that night I left you and Vincent early."

I knew precisely what Sone meant, but I feigned ignorance. "Huh? Really? Are you certain it was ASAIC DuBois?"

Sone replied confidently, "Yeah, I know what DuBois looks like. And from the look, he wasn't on his way to a bar. He was so engrossed with that girl that he didn't notice me."

Not wanting to prolong the conversation, aware that it had already been damaging enough, I said, "Okay, did you get your money?"

Sone responded, "Yeah. But man, you know the Government is cheap these days."

"Alright," I replied. "I'll call you regarding the next steps. Take care."

As soon as Sone departed, the news related to ASAIC DuBois spread throughout the office. The murmurs intensified, and discussions grew more elaborate. With each retelling, the story grew, as each agent contributed their embellishments, turning it into an extraordinary tale, making ASAIC DuBois the focal point of that operation.

Eventually, the story reached SAIC Montaña. Upon learning about his actions, ASAIC DuBois became the focus of his anger. Just the mere suggestion that his ASAIC was spending time with local women rather than overseeing the surveillance could inflict lasting harm to SAIC Montaña's career, the office, and the operation.

Adding flames to the fire, those who knew ASAIC DuBois often watched in awe as he effortlessly charmed his way through the bars. Now the claims were he cut his surveillance duties short, leaving the rest of the team to bear the weight of the operation on their shoulders. I couldn't help but notice the irony in their claims, considering rumors were they too frequently concluded their surveillance duties prematurely.

As I walked past ASAIC DuBois's office, he called out to me, "Hey Rich, could you step in for a moment? I have a question."

"Yes, sir. How can I assist?" I replied, taking a seat across from ASAIC DuBois.

He looked down before saying, "Have you heard the rumors?"

"I'm not sure what you mean, Mr. DuBois," I responded.

"The SAIC called me into his office," ASAIC DuBois began. "Rumors are that I ended surveillance early to chase women. Do you know anything about this?"

ASAIC DuBois was aware that I had firsthand knowledge of his escapades. After thinking it over, I replied, "The SAIC already asked me what I knew, and I told him I had no idea. I was occupied the entire time. Besides, how could I possibly know what you were doing during surveillance?"

"Right," ASAIC DuBois replied with excitement. "Still, rumors are spreading. If you find out who's behind it, let me know right away."

I shook my head slightly, knowing I wouldn't be reporting another agent, but said, "Of course, sir. Anything else?"

"No," ASAIC DuBois replied.

Ultimately, ASAIC's actions would have repercussions. SAIC Montaña concluded that ASAIC DuBois's trip to Thailand marked his final operation in that role. The consequences of the office drama and the ensuing rumors would leave marks on the workplace but would likely recede just as swiftly as they emerged.

Amidst the unfolding office politics, I maintained my discussions with SunCredit, Slimbady, and Vincent, clearly expressing my intention to return to Macau. These conversations aim to confirm their availability, especially SunCredit and Slimbady, whose participation is essential for the success of our mission.

I reiterated my intention to purchase one hundred embossed credit cards in Macau to entice them further. I will supply them with the names and stolen credit card information. SunCredit and Slimbady would only need to create and emboss the counterfeit cards. The agreed-upon price was $10,000, which Slimbady and SunCredit happily accepted.

While their response was positive and eager to meet, the true challenge lies in obtaining Headquarters' approval. I believed that showcasing our achievements, previous successful missions, and the support from the local U.S. Embassy and law enforcement would be sufficient. However, to my dismay, despite every accomplishment, success, or endorsement, I was continuously caught in a struggle. For each operation, I had to start from scratch as if it were an entirely new endeavor.

While the discussions seemed hopeful, issues arose when Slimbady requested items like cameras or computers, which Headquarters deemed unnecessary for my achievements. Once approval was secured, ASAIC DuBois emphasized that we shouldn't give gifts without expecting something in return. He pointed to our government form that specifies in section seven that we must provide information about the type of contraband received. If we fail to obtain contraband in exchange for confidential funds, section seven would be blank, undoubtedly raising questions from Inspections.

Once all obstacles were navigated, the plan was thoroughly outlined and executed. I planned to meet Slimbady, SunCredit, and Vincent in Macau for three days each, with a day's break between each meeting. Including flights and country briefings, I estimated we would spend fourteen days in Macau. However, this plan would be fleeting, as unexpected events would soon unfold.

Somewhere between Maksik's dumps and PINs proposal and amid discussions about operations in Macau, an urgent meeting occurred at Headquarters. Representatives from the larger payment card networks, and their most influential member banks convened, seeking an audience. They revealed a troubling discovery: a significant surge in cash withdrawals from ATMs. The member banks were left stunned, unable to comprehend how such a phenomenon could happen, and they came to DC to explore options of what can be done.

During the meeting, they reported that cybercriminals had decrypted the PIN block and were targeting ATMs worldwide. What was concerning about the PIN block was that it was thought to be impossible to decrypt due to advanced encryption standards. The last piece of the puzzle shared was that all the affected credit cards had a common point of purchase.

The banks feared that the entire encryption system had been compromised, and they were now relying on the Secret Service to take action. ATSAIC Sheehan played it cool; they listened, took notes, and didn't disclose their plans, but quietly, they knew just the person to speak with.

As I immersed myself in the detailed planning of the operation in Macau, I remained unaware that the "planners" at Headquarters were having discreet discussions about my upcoming operation. Soon, I would learn my initial proposal was too lengthy. Instead, I would have just two days with Slimbady and only one day each with Vincent and SunCredit. The breaks between meetings were eliminated, resulting in a schedule packed with back-to-back encounters. Lastly, I was instructed to travel, conduct my meetings, and dive directly into my undercover work.

To make matters worse, even after Chief Superintendent Weng-Hou Chen's warnings, I was allowed a pitiful gambling budget of just $1,000. With such a limited amount, convincing others that I was a successful Carder was difficult. I needed to devise a credible situation in which spending extravagantly on gambling, dining, hotels, or women wasn't my style.

From the outset, I recognized that long-term, deep-cover operations entail substantial risks. Experts in this area will consistently highlight these dangers. Yet, the operation's complexity intensifies into a more significant threat when an agent operates in a foreign country, where dependable resources may be scarce.

They are isolated from their typical support networks and must navigate treacherous waters. Every choice they make could be the difference between success and failure or even life and death. The pressure was enormous, the consequences severe, and my leadership's decisions were not helping.

While I frequently received assurances of my safety, doubts emerged as I reflected on the brilliant strategies that were being pushed onto me. Were these instructions genuinely created for my benefit, or was there a hidden agenda? Despite these concerns, I faithfully adjusted my plans and moved forward, my determination steadfast.

In my final conversations with Slimbady, SunCredit, and Vincent, I clarified the details of our illicit agreement. I carefully shared my arrival dates and provided them with the necessary money transfer information, ensuring they had half of the promised funds. By doing so, I ensured that I complied with AUSA Peña's directive to initiate the criminal activities in San Diego and conclude them in Macau.

Before heading to Macau, Vincent shared intriguing snippets of his chats with Maksik, highlighting their shared connections. However, my primary interest was in the discussions I had with Slimbady and Maksik.

Slimbady reached out to me on ICQ, saying, "What's up, bro ☺"

I replied, "All good, bro. You get my details about Macau? 😎"

"Yes, I ready. Wait you ☺," Slimbady responded.

"Great," I replied.

"BTW, Maksik ask about you," Slimbady continued.

This immediately intrigued me. What could Maksik be curious about? I eagerly replied, "What did he ask? ☺"

In that instant, the most alarming message appeared on my screen: "He ask if you a cop."

Panic gripped me as I imagined the various responses Slimbady could have given. I typed back, "What did you say?" and anxiously awaited his reply.

"I tell him no way Surfrider cop ☺," Slimbady answered.

Relief washed over me as I responded, "😁."

As I sat there, I thought, "This is perfect. Slim vouched for me. It's where I need to be." Just then, Maksik came online and messaged me, asking, "What up, Brat?"

Seizing the moment, I quickly replied, "Not much. Planning my trip to Macau. U? ☺"

I knew Maksik had recently spoken with Slim, and I wanted him to understand that I was heading to Macau for a party with Slim. Jealousy can be a powerful weapon if used appropriately.

Maksik responded, "Work ☹. I could use a holiday."

Seeing an opportunity, I replied, "Join us ☺."

"I wish," Maksik said. "Later I will, but only once our business is finished. How is it going? 🤔"

"My team is working every day. I'll be ready soon. You know it's a lot of money," I messaged, hoping to highlight the significant sum that was about to be transferred.

To my astonishment, Maksik replied, "$75k not much money, bro. 😎"

His response took me by surprise, and I thought, "If $75,000 isn't significant to Maksik, then what does he consider a lot of money?" Still, I responded, "Well, to me, $75k is a lot of money. 🤪"

"Well, I'm waiting," Maksik wrote before going offline.

By the end of my conversation with Maksik, I could feel his frustration, yet I praised his patience. If I had the funds, I would have sent the money to him immediately. Sadly, even though I had verbal authorization, the $75,000 hadn't yet arrived. All I could provide were excuses.

My next move was to once again raise my concerns to SAIC Montaña regarding the funding delays, hoping he would reach out to Headquarters. However, I knew in my heart that nothing would change. My feelings were SAIC Montaña was far too focused on his career to address the issue.

As the days passed, the final decision about staffing was reached. ASAIC DuBois made a fledgling attempt to be San Diego's onsite supervisor in Macau, but SAIC Montaña rejected the idea. Instead, he nominated himself.

The team would consist of SAIC Montaña, SA Mason, Sone, and me. As we boarded our flights to Hong Kong, I thought about my delicate relationship with Rachel and the tasks I would need to handle upon our arrival. As the plane took off, I drifted into a delightful slumber. My next stop, China.

Chapter 24

Time to fix what was screwed up

On a crisp February morning in 2006, Sone's and my plane touched down in Hong Kong. Due to our early arrival, we had ample time to meet with RAIC Stone and the staff at the U.S. Embassy. Unlike my last visit, where I worked alongside SA John Butters, I was eager to collaborate this time with our Foreign Service National Investigator (FSNI), Luna Li.

FSNI Li earned recognition for her in-depth expertise and dedication to her role, providing valuable insights that enhanced our collaboration with the U.S. Embassy and our local counterparts. Her professionalism ensured a more effective and streamlined operation.

FSNI Li updated us on her preparations, which included organizing transportation to Macau and our meeting with Chief Superintendent Weng-Hou Chen. Afterward, we proceeded to the U.S. Embassy, where I briefed the Regional Security Officer and Deputy Chief of Mission. Cybercrime was still on the rise, and many leaders were eager to learn. Once I addressed their curiosity and responded to more general inquiries rather than those about specific operations, they expressed their support and wished me good luck.

Having completed my official responsibilities, it was time to unwind. Some team members gathered for dinner and drinks in the Wan Chai District. This would be my last opportunity to relax with the team before heading off to Macau. Once I get there, I will shift from Richard LaTulip, the Secret Service Agent, to Richard Druc, the online cybercriminal. However, a strange unease settled within me. Despite the odds being slim, I understood that there was always a possibility of unexpectedly encountering my target.

After dinner, everyone chose to head back to their hotel rooms for some rest. Meanwhile, I craved adventure and set out to discover Hong Kong's lively nightlife. The evening held great potential, and I had the perfect destination in mind.

As Sone and Grant said their goodbyes, Grant reminded me, "Don't forget, we've got an early boat to Macau."

I winked and smiled, assuring him, "Don't worry about me. I'll make it there."

With determination, I set off to continue my journey. I departed from Wan Chai District, primarily filled with restaurants and pubs, and made my way to Lai Kwai Fong. This area was famous for its discos and party lifestyle. The appeal of one of the more famous clubs drew me in, known for being a place filled with hidden secrets waiting to be discovered.

As I approached the bar's entrance, the club's neon lights flickered against the busy streets, casting an otherworldly glow. Crossing the threshold, I prepared for the customary scrutiny of the doorman, a ritual rooted in the fabric of Southeast Asian nightlife. While it seemed to be a security measure, it wasn't. Its true purpose was to ensure that only those deemed acceptable were allowed in, perpetuating a complex web of societal norms and biases that left behind tales of exclusion and prejudice.

After passing through security, I moved forward, eager to explore all it had to offer. The club's interior instantly caught my eye. The central bar thrummed with energy, while to my

DOI: 10.1201/9781003680390-24

far left, a DJ crafted beats that resonated through the crowd. It embodied the quintessential nightlife experience reminiscent of a movie scene.

Beneath its appealing exterior lay a more intricate environment. The bar featured distinct areas, each with its unique allure. As I glanced from left to right, I noticed Eastern European women gathering near the DJ; they appeared poised and confident, yet their eyes scanned the room in search of a companion.

Nearby, exotic Middle Eastern women captured the attention of onlookers with their charm. Completing the scene, Southeast Asian women beckoned, waving and blowing kisses to invite guests into their area.

I was told unspoken rules of the establishment governed these divisions, ensuring a delicate balance of power and territory. It was a world unto itself, where lines were drawn and boundaries enforced with unwavering precision. And yet, amidst the structured chaos, there was one place of unity—the dance floor. Here, everyone was welcome, regardless of their background or origin.

When it came to where I wanted to settle, it felt obvious. After traveling extensively, I found that my interests were strongly aligned with those of the women from Southeast Asia. I approached their section intently, excited to start conversations and make a new friend. I intended to rely on my charm since paying for sex wasn't something I wanted to do.

Yet, the challenge remained consistent. Recognizing genuine attraction proved difficult; every woman glanced your way, particularly as you moved among them. Their enthusiasm made sense—it represented a chance to earn money. Thankfully, those who desired only money were easy to spot; they didn't play games with you but approached you with clarity and purpose.

As I navigated the sea of faces, a hand touched mine. Looking toward the lady, she smiled and said, "Hi. You like me? You wanna have sex? One hundred dollars."

I smiled and replied with a excuse, "I just arrived. No, thank you."

Those offers were not for my liking. I wanted to enjoy drinks, engage in conversation, dance, and see where the night would lead. Then, across the bar, I noticed someone who stood out—a woman different from the rest. Her demeanor was both shy and captivating.

With shoulder-length jet-black hair and subtle peach lipstick, she radiated a sense of quiet elegance. Although petite, she carried herself with poise, drawing attention from the crowd. Her attire was classy and distinctly different from that of those around her, who wore short mini-skirts, tight blouses barely buttoned, and pigtails, attempting to embody the male schoolgirl fantasy.

She seemed out of her element, possibly inexperienced in the game or simply new to the bar scene in Hong Kong. Seizing the moment, I approached her and said, "Hi. I'm Rich."

She looked at me, smiled, and replied, "My name is Angela."

Having visited Southeast Asia enough, I knew that wasn't her name, so I asked, "American name? Why do you have an American name?"

Lai replied, "American can't say Chinese name well. This just easy. So, I say, Angela."

"Nope, I don't like it," I said. "I'm in Hong Kong, visiting your country. What's your real name?"

Lai smiled shyly, giggled, turned her head, looked directly at me, and asked, "You sure?"

I confidently replied, "Yes, I want to know your name. Not a name typical of America."

"Ok," Lai said, "My name is Lai."

"Lai? What a beautiful name," I said. "I prefer to call you Lai if that is ok with you."

Lai smiled, blushing as she spoke, "Yes, it fine with me."

"Lai, may I buy you a drink?" I asked.

She nodded and replied, "I like Cosmopolitan."

"Absolutely," I replied, taking her hand and leading her through the crowd to the bar.

I looked at the bartender and shouted over the music, "One Cosmo and one double Johnny Walker Black Label."

The music pulsated around us, the crowd pushing everyone closer, but I didn't mind. This opened the door for us to be closer, to be more intimate. To help protect her, I put my hand around her lower back and pulled her close, our bodies lightly touching. Lai stayed firm, moving closer toward me, letting me know she was interested.

The bartender caught my eye and handed me our drinks. I turned and said to Lai, "One Cosmo."

"Thank you," Lai said.

I then offered a toast, "To new friends."

Lai smiled, raised her glass, and repeated, "To new friend."

As the night progressed, our connection deepened with each shared moment. Every brush of skin, every knowing glance, spoke volumes without words. It was a dance of its own, a silent language of desire and curiosity that drew us closer together. When the invitation to dance was extended, Lai's eyes sparkled with anticipation, and we moved as one on the crowded dance floor, finding solace in each other's presence.

With the music as our backdrop and the rhythm guiding our steps, I felt an undeniable pull between us. In a moment of shared understanding, our gazes locked, and I closed the distance between us, seeking solace in the soft press of her lips against mine. In that fleeting moment, the world around us disappeared, leaving only the echo of our connection lingering in the air.

The night was growing late, and I knew our connection was shared equally as I asked, "Would you care to join me at my hotel?"

Without hesitation, Lai said, "Yes, but you mind me take you on my bike?"

My mind immediately conjured up images of my Honda VFR750CC motorcycle, but I quickly realized she was referring to a moped. Not wanting to miss out on the adventure, I responded, "Not at all. Let's go."

I watched in awe as Lai effortlessly donned her helmet, mounted the moped, gestured for me to join her on the back, and said, "Get on."

It was undeniably enticing, and despite my years of riding experience, I relinquished control and embraced the thrill of being a passenger. Lai skillfully navigated the bustling streets of Hong Kong, her familiarity with the city evident in her confident maneuvers.

The short ride from the club to the hotel was a tranquil journey in the early morning hours, allowing us a moment of peace amidst the city's chaos. As we neared the hotel, Lai expertly found a parking spot for her moped. We disembarked and walked hand in hand, entering the hotel's grand lobby together. A quick elevator ride took us to my floor, where I led her to my room.

Once inside my room, we passionately embraced each other. As we kissed, our hands went to work, exploring each other's bodies. Piece by piece, we removed each other's articles of clothing. I guided her to the bed, where we fell into its comfort. After a passionate embrace, our naked bodies soon tangled together as one. As the passion grew assertive, I rolled over on top of her. Staring down at her, our eyes locked, taking the opportunity to enjoy each other.

Passion erupted together, and then the lull, tired from the night's dancing and passionate embrace, I collapsed into her arms. She held me close to her, and then I rolled over; both exhausted, we fell asleep next to each other. The rest didn't last long; my alarm brought me back into reality. The purpose of my visit to Hong Kong is an undercover operation. The fast boat to Macau awaited me, and I couldn't be late.

I hurriedly showered and, while I was dressed, took one last glimpse of Lai. The knowledge that it would be our final meeting weighed on me as I left Lai undisturbed in her slumber and made my way to the hotel lobby. In the lobby, the team boarded the van bound for Hong Kong Port. Once we arrived at the port, Sone and I said our farewells, and solitude settled in as we parted ways to our separate destinations.

Sone and I took a taxi to our hotel in Macau. Memories of past mistakes reminded me to be discreet, but I booked the hotel under my real name because ASAIC Carrington wanted to bypass governmental red tape. This was a risky decision that any junior spy would typically avoid, as it raised the risk factor to unacceptable levels. Nevertheless, I pressed on, keeping my exact whereabouts hidden, praying those I would soon meet wouldn't check up on me.

Chapter 25

Time to rebuild damaged relationships

Sone's and my meeting with the police was less than an hour away, but time was a luxury we couldn't afford. Immediately afterward, we were scheduled to meet with SunCredit, and every second counted. I made a mental note to inform him during my meeting with the authorities, anticipating his timely arrival on the island later that afternoon.

Fortunately, the police station was just a brisk ten-minute walk from my hotel. When Sone and I arrived at the back door, I messaged SAIC Montaña. Moments later, Chief Superintendent Weng-Hou Chan appeared, his familiar face a reassuring sight. With a firm handshake and a nod, he said, "Follow me to the briefing room."

Weng-Hou wasted no time leading Sone and me to the briefing room, his brisk stride indicating the urgent matters awaiting us inside. The atmosphere inside the room was stark yet purposeful. It featured a large conference table, several chairs, a distant whiteboard, and the harsh glare of fluorescent lighting. After exchanging pleasantries, a secretary offered the customary coffee or tea. Perfectly arranged on the table were the pastries and candies.

Following the introductions, I began to outline the strategic shift: "Weng-Hou, as you may recall from our last meeting, I wasn't permitted to leave the meeting location. However, this felt unnatural and unsettling. After considerable discussion, leadership has approved a more natural engagement. I can move more fluidly and go wherever necessary."

Weng-Hou's eyes lit up with interest as he said, "That's great news! I agree that it's more natural. I'm sorry to bring this up, but your response last time bothered me. Can you tell me what you will do if any of them decides to gamble?"

I shrugged and replied, "It remains the same as before. I've been authorized to gamble up to $1,000."

Weng-Hou then addressed his colleagues, sharing the story in Mandarin. As he spoke, I observed their previously stoic faces change to expressions of intrigue and surprise, their eyes lighting up as they engaged eagerly. Mid-conversation, Weng-Hou raised his hand, signifying that he had heard enough.

Weng-Hou paused, glanced back at his colleagues, then refocused and said, "As I mentioned, we advise against gambling with them. You must be prepared to wager thousands of dollars. If you don't gamble like they do, they'll suspect you're a cop. Avoid gambling at all costs."

I recognized that Weng-Hou's concern was authentic and heartfelt, but the complexities of my undercover mission were beyond his comprehension. He couldn't see that much of my leadership was disconnected from reality, and didn't understand the nuances involved in undercover operations. Consequently, his good-natured advice only scratched the surface of the high-stakes gambling I faced every day.

Unfazed by Weng-Hou's warning, I replied, "I appreciate your concern, but I have a plan for how to handle it."

DOI: 10.1201/9781003680390-25

Just then, the familiar buzz of my undercover phone disrupted the conversation, capturing everyone's attention at the table. I reached for the device and scanned the words on the screen. Ready or not, they signaled the next phase of our operation.

I mentioned, "The message is from SunCredit. He's waiting for me at a nearby hotel. Sone and I have to leave."

Weng-Hou quickly responded, "We need thirty minutes. After that, you can meet him."

I shook my head and replied, "Alright. We'll meet him in thirty minutes."

As I exited the police station, I began to reflect on everything. A surge of anticipation flooded over me. This was my chance to make things right with SunCredit and redeem myself in his eyes.

While Sone and I headed toward the meet location, I asked, "Do you think that was SunCredit on the jet-boat?"

Sone responded with a puzzled expression, "No. I didn't see him."

I questioned, "Are you certain?"

Sone laughed, "Yeah. I'm good with faces, and Sun wasn't on board."

Smiling, I said, "Alright. I believe you. Besides, it doesn't matter since we didn't speak with the team."

I checked my phone for the time. It was still too early, and I realized the team wasn't ready yet. I pointed to a small ice cream shop and said to Sone, "Let's wait here for the team's signal."

After around five minutes, I received the go-ahead message from SA Mason, indicating it was time. I turned to Sone and asked, "Are you ready?"

Sone responded quickly, "Yup."

"Alright, let's go meet Sun," I said.

As Sone and I walked into the luxurious hotel, a wave of anticipation and excitement washed over me. The lavish lobby enveloped me, amplifying the significance of the moment. I quickly sent two messages—one to SA Mason and the other to SunCredit. The messages were almost identical: "We are here."

SA Mason responded, "Roger," instilling a sense of reassurance. Looking up from my phone, I noticed a familiar figure approaching. It was SunCredit, accompanied by a woman, walking toward us.

Excitement and determination flooded through me. I stepped forward, reached out my hand, and said, "Great to see you again, my friend."

SunCredit replied, "Likewise." He gestured to his companion, encouraging her to step forward, and said, "This is my wife."

I greeted her with a slight bow, "I'm Rich. Nice to meet you."

After the introductions, SunCredit pointed toward the hotel entrance and said, "Let's go to the nextdoor Hotel. They have the best restaurant."

I glanced at Sone before returning to SunCredit and said, "Lead the way."

The unexpected shift in plans caught me off guard, but it was refreshing. As SunCredit walked ahead, I quickly messaged SA Mason: "HEADED NEXT DOOR."

SunCredit exhibited a heightened caution, which distinguished him from Slim or Vincent. I wondered, "Did SunCredit arrange for his team to conduct countersurveillance again?"

As we climbed the grand staircase of the hotel, the enticing scent of savory Chinese cuisine drew us to the restaurant. The restaurant's refined atmosphere was perfect for our surreptitious meeting. SunCredit's wife's presence brought a sense of intrigue.

I wondered how much she was aware of her husband's affairs and whether she genuinely cared about them. What likely mattered most to her was that SunCredit provided her with a comfortable lifestyle. How he did it was less relevant.

Once we moved past the pleasantries, SunCredit cut straight to the chase and asked, "While you're here, are you also meeting with Slim?"

The directness of the question surprised me, but I was prepared. I understood that keeping it under wraps was unlikely. Rather than dodging around, I decided to be upfront and replied, "Yeah. I think we'll meet either tomorrow or the day after."

To steer the conversation elsewhere, I reached down, picked up the bag I had been carrying, and handed it to him, saying, "Here are the items you requested."

SunCredit opened the bag, glanced inside, nodded, and said, "Ah, okay. I almost forgot. Thank you."

Then, I reached into my pocket and pulled out a bundle of cash. I handed it to him and stated, "Here's the five grand I owe for the plastic."

Shaking his head in satisfaction, SunCredit reached inside his jacket pocket and pulled out a pack of cigarettes. He handed them to me and said, "Why didn't you just ask me to make two hundred? Why get one hundred from me and Vincent?"

I had expected questions about meeting Slim and Vincent, but this completely threw me off. It was apparent that SunCredit was aware of my parallel deal with Vincent. My internal clock shouted to me to answer as my mind raced, desperately searching for a believable response.

"It's just business," I finally responded, my tone steady despite the chaos. "Vincent has a source. You have a source. Which one is better? I need to know the answer. Although now it seems to me you have the same source."

SunCredit's expression changed, and a brief understanding flashed as he responded, "Yeah, this business is a small world. Everyone knows each other."

In that tense moment, a simple yet profound truth emerged. Headquarters' quest to achieve operational brevity forced me to expose myself to unacceptable levels of risk. The hasty consolidation of operations into a seamless succession had left me vulnerable to scrutiny and suspicion.

Had they allowed for more space, time, and distance between each operation or transaction, these unsettling questions would have never surfaced. Yet here I stood, the architect of intricate schemes, left to navigate the treacherous waters alone.

As I stood face to face with SunCredit, the air between us crackled with uncertainty. I felt the possibility of months of messaging and virtual interactions hanging in the balance. The online world, with its sterile black fonts and white backgrounds, lacked the depth of real-life interactions. Emoticons attempted to bridge the emotional gap, but here, in the presence of SunCredit, the unspoken language of gestures and expressions painted a clearer picture.

I could see the flicker of emotions in his eyes, the subtle shifts in his demeanor that spoke volumes. His calm demeanor reassured me; however, the conversation swirled around business and collaboration. This idea clashed with my need for separation. Despite his frustration at our diverging paths, SunCredit made one more point. He held the camera in his hand, and then looked at the laptop and said, "Why such shit?"

This marked the second time I was confronted about the standards of electronics I was allowed to purchase. And yet again, they fell short of my standards and I knew they were "shit" when I purchased them, but I had little choice. This was now the third tricky question from SunCredit, and all of it was within the first hour of our second meeting.

I was a storyteller by trade, but rather than weaving a confusing tale, I said, "That was all that remained after I sold the rest to my partner in LA. They didn't want them, so you get them."

With an unsatisfied look, he handed the lackluster devices to his wife and said, "Go home."

SunCredit then said, "I know a good bar. Shall we go?"

Sone, uninterested in drinking, replied, "Not me. I'm tired. I'm headed back to the hotel."

SunCredit said, "Okay. Good night." Then he looked at me and asked, "Shall we?"

Once again, I responded the same way, "Lead the way."

As we entered the elegant hotel lobby and made our way to the bustling bar, I couldn't help but feel a sense of anticipation mingled with a hint of unease. Seated at the bar, feeling the effects of a satisfying meal, I opted for two Johnny Walker Black Labels with a single ice cube for SunCredit and myself. The lively ambiance, complete with the melodic strains of a band in the background, set the stage for the evening.

As I scanned the room, my eyes alighted on potential conversation partners, igniting a spark of interest within me. There was energy in the air, a promise of possibility, as the night unfolded in the new vibrant setting.

As fate would have it, SunCredit, much to my dismay, expressed a keen interest in persisting with our discussion on work. Cognizant of my role, I willingly plunged into the conversation. With a clear objective in mind—to deftly steer the dialogue onto a different course. I navigated through topics relating to his operations, the intricate world of other Carders, and the swirling drama that enveloped them.

Even as I exchanged words with SunCredit, my eyes surreptitiously scanned the bustling crowd, a habit borne out of necessity. When the last remnants of my drink vanished, a sudden realization pierced my consciousness—I had neglected to check in with the surveillance team. If the mission ever became confrontational, this misstep could prove costly.

As my drink sat empty on the bar, I signaled to SunCredit for another round before excusing myself. Now was the perfect time to message SA Mason. After I sent the message, I checked my watch and noted that it aligned perfectly with San Diego. Without hesitation, I dialed Rachel, knowing she was likely at home.

The phone rang twice before Rachel answered with, "Howdy, stranger."

Laughing, I responded, "Right back at you. How are you?"

Rachel replied, "I'm good. Nothing special happening."

I asked, "What about Bella and Natasha?"

Rachel responded, "I just got back from the beach with them. I need to rush to wash them before heading to work."

"Ok," I said. "I won't keep you. Have fun at work. See you soon."

Consistent with her nature, my conversation with Rachael was short, and, most importantly, we avoided our usual argument. Now, I could focus on the task and return to the bar, ready to dive back into the undercover assignment awaiting me. As I settled back into my seat, a glass of Johnny Walker Black awaited me, its golden color shimmering in the dim bar light.

SunCredit, my companion for the evening, was keen to explore our mutual interest in carding. Yet, my thoughts wandered away from our chat, preoccupied with what was to come. Having already consumed several drinks, I knew I needed to steer the conversation in a different direction.

I had taken care of all essential business matters before I indulged in excessive drinking. My goal was to avoid the defense's argument, "How could you possibly remember what my client said or did after seven whiskeys?"

While SunCredit spoke, I scanned the crowd. Two Asian women caught my eye over his shoulder. One of them commanded attention with her authoritative presence, yet it was her companion who truly captivated me.

Her jet-black hair flowed down her back, gently resting on her bare shoulders. The royal blue dress she wore fitted her perfectly, with white edging that added an elegant touch to her figure. In contrast to the other bar patrons, her outfit fell below her knees, featuring a daring split on the right side that hinted at her leg. She completed this refined look with white gym shoes, creating a mesmerizing mix of sporty and sensual that left me spellbound, a combination that challenged conventions.

As she moved with effortless confidence, the interplay of light and shadow enhanced her features, casting a captivating charm. Her presence radiated a quiet strength, a magnetic draw that invited curiosity. A flicker of hope sparked within me as I considered the possibility that they were not part of the transactional world of solicitation.

My attention shifted to them, even as SunCredit kept talking. I interrupted him, gesturing toward the two women, and asked, "What do you think of those two?"

SunCredit turned his head, noticing the two ladies, and remarked, "They're very pretty."

I focused on them, searching for subtle hints that indicated their intentions. Then, it happened. The woman who had caught my interest met my gaze and gave a nod of acknowledgment. With an air of nonchalance, I gestured for her to come over. As she approached, I added casually, "May I buy you and your friend a drink?"

Her cheeks flushed a soft pink, and she replied graciously with a smile, "You may."

I waved to catch the bartender's attention, ordered their favorite drinks, and said, "Nice to meet you. My name is Rich." Then, I glanced at SunCredit, realizing I didn't know his name, and invited him to introduce himself, "And this is my friend."

Still blushing, she responded, "I'm Ha-eun, which means 'great kindness' in Korea."

Intrigued, I delved into a conversation, eager to discover the purpose of her visit, so I said, "I like your name. Since it's Korean, I'm curious, what brings you to Macau?"

Ha-eun shared, "My friend and me not stay here. We traveling to Singapore."

Sensing a spark between us, I handled some groundwork for SunCredit, as I didn't want her companion to feel left out. However, my primary focus remained on Ha-eun. I appreciated the opportunity to bond further over drinks. The lively atmosphere inspired me to ask, "Ha-eun, would you care to dance?"

Ha-eun nodded and said, "Yes. I want dance."

I quickly took her hand and said, "Let's go," leading her to the dance floor.

Dancing created an unvoiced bond between Ha-eun and me. Our bodies moved in sync with the music's rhythm. Our silent dialogue intensified with every twirl and dip, and our eyes met meaningfully as the tempo slowed. Although I desired to lean in for a kiss, I held back, reluctant to rush our moment. The night was still young, and there was no reason to hurry.

After a few songs, our energy began to fade, our clothes grew damp with sweat, and feeling thirsty, I leaned in to ask, "What do you think? Are you ready for a drink?"

Ha-eun wiped the sweat from her forehead and replied, "Yes."

I guided her back to the bar for a refreshing drink. While we cooled off, SunCredit tapped my shoulder, signaling me to lean closer. He then suggested, "We should switch venues. I know a great spot for karaoke—98 Bar."

I acknowledged his suggestion and turned to Ha-eun, asking, "Do you want to go sing karaoke?"

Her eyes lit up at the thought as she quickly responded, "Yes, I love to sing."

With her affirmation, I leaned back toward SunCredit and asked, "Should we walk or take a taxi?"

SunCredit answered, "We need a cab. Follow me."

With Ha-eun beside me, we walked to the taxi stand outside the hotel for a short ride to the karaoke bar. Once we arrived, the atmosphere changed significantly. The hotel radiated luxury and charm, while this place was dimly lit, enhancing its visitors' drunkenness. The hostess escorted us to a semi-round table with a view of the stage.

I kept my attention fixed on Ha-eun, but amid the chaotic karaoke sounds, a drama was starting to unfold. As we talked, her friend's sudden signal made her stand up, hinting at an unexpected development. I glanced at SunCredit and, grimacing, asked, "What did you say to her friend?"

SunCredit chuckled, remarking, "Nothing. She mentioned it would cost me eight hundred Hong Kong dollars for her."

I nodded and said, "So she is a working girl."

"It seems that way, my friend," SunCredit replied.

I thought for a moment and then said, "What do you think?"

"Too much," SunCredit replied candidly.

Contemplating the turn of events, I gazed toward Ha-eun. From a distance, I knew they were in a heated exchange, and Ha-eun didn't look happy. As quickly as they stood and left the table, the debate ended. Ha-eun's frustration was palpable. She swiftly returned to the table and sat beside me, her irritation evident.

Playing coy, I said, "What happened? Are you ok?"

Her face showed apparent frustration and anger as she inhaled deeply and spoke, "My friend. She angry with me."

Without hesitation, I replied, "Why."

"Your friend not want to pay," Ha-eun said. "She want me leave with her."

I put my hand up and said, "I'm not paying for anything."

"You not let me finish," Ha-eun explained. "I not want money. Only her want. I only want go with you."

Flattered and concerned, I said, "I don't want to cause trouble. Are you sure?"

Ha-eun said with a sad look, "She be mad with me. But I no care. I go with you. No want money. I no need it."

It was a surprising turn of events that had initially felt like a transaction but transformed into two people seeking each other's comfort and warmth. As the early morning hours approached, I asked SunCredit, "What are you thinking? Are you going to pay her friend?"

SunCredit said, "Look at me. She will not go with me unless I pay. She wants her money, but I'm not paying her. I will go to a club and sleep before catching the boat back to Hong Kong."

Realizing his intentions, I said goodbye to SunCredit and Ha-eun and I retreated to my hotel. The walk was filled with a range of emotions. During that night we spent together, I desperately wished for time to freeze, cherishing every second we shared. Yet, I knew that this joy wouldn't last forever.

The morning revealed a brutal truth. Ha-eun had to move on to Singapore, a direction different from mine. The thought of her traveling with a woman of dubious profession troubled me, making me wonder about the uncertain future ahead of her. While she got ready, I told her, "Ha-eun, you don't have to go. You can stay here with me."

Ha-eun paused for a moment, seemingly considering the proposition. Despite my offer of sanctuary, she remained resolute and said, "I must go. My friend waits."

Realizing I couldn't make her stay, I rose, and we shared one last embrace, our farewell words lingering in the air. It was an unspoken understanding that our lives would not intersect again. With a heavy heart, I watched her depart, carrying with her a piece of my soul. Ha-eun left an indelible mark that would forever linger in the recesses of my thoughts.

I climbed back into bed, saddened by Ha-eun's departure, when I received a message from the team. They had successfully acquired SunCredit's passport details. Once he left the karaoke bar Weng-Hou's surveillance team shadowed SunCredit's every move until he left Macau. From the moment we said "go," everything unfolded seamlessly, a stroke of luck that felt almost too good to be true.

Amid unfolding events, I had developed a distinct bond of camaraderie with SunCredit. However, with Slimbady's arrival just hours away, there was no room for complacency or celebration. The weight of the impending task felt significant. With a renewed sense of purpose, I began to strategize and prepare for the upcoming challenges, aware that the real test of my determination was just on the horizon.

Chapter 26

One down, two to go

Last night's operation went smoothly, with every detail aligning perfectly. SunCredit's satisfaction was evident, and my ability to establish a good rapport with him was crucial. Furthermore, the local surveillance team worked without issues, providing valuable insights into SunCredit's identity.

That night, in my opinion, a minor issue occurred. SAIC Montaña turned down a dinner invitation from the Police Chief and opted to stay in his hotel room, a significant contrast to ASAIC DuBois's more sociable style. I knew SAIC Montaña overlooked a chance that was as crucial as my role, which involved fostering relationships with the police. Regardless of this oversight, I kept my eye on my next target, Slimbady.

I wasted no time and messaged Slimbady, "What's up? ☺ I'm in Macau."

Slimbady responded immediately, "☺ I arrive by helo from Shenzhen soon. Meet at 6. There is a Chinese restaurant at Mandarin Oriental."

I quickly typed out, "Okay, see you soon."

I grabbed my phone and messaged SA Mason, "Slim will arrive by helo. The meeting is at 6 at a Chinese restaurant."

SA Mason replied, "Roger. Will pass to police."

When Slimbady's helicopter landed in Macau, a wave of urgency washed over me. Sone and I departed our hotel and took the familiar route to the Chinese restaurant. Upon arrival, I nudged Sone and remarked, "You missed a wild night."

Sone laughed and said, "I bet."

Fond memories and images of Ha-eun filled my thoughts as I sat in the lobby, her journey to Singapore playing like a silent film. I contemplated several scenarios for her, hoping for the best to unfold. Then, suddenly, I was pulled back to reality. Slimbady walked in, bringing a glimmer of hope for a new beginning. Though regrets from our last encounter loomed, it was time for redemption. After some small talk, we headed to the restaurant, the air heavy with anticipation and unspoken truths.

While we dined, our conversation blended business discussions with online drama, shifting toward the effectiveness of the dumps. I trod carefully, ensuring I shared limited information, as I had to manage the fine line between trust and confidentiality. Keeping the broader expectations of the carding community in mind, my story resonated with him, aligning perfectly with the many others he had encountered.

It was a silent reassurance, a nod of approval that whispered of shared experiences and unspoken understanding. I wasn't the typical "Carder."

As the conversation ebbed and flowed over dinner, valuable insights were exchanged, yet it all felt like a repetitive dance. The same topics looped in endless cycles, but a sense of consistency lay in that repetition. Once Slimbady had heard enough, he changed the subject and asked, "You go gamble now?"

DOI: 10.1201/9781003680390-26

Being fully aware of my strict budget, I said, "Sure, we can go. But you know the casino isn't the place to win money. I make my money on the NCAA tournaments."

Slimbady's eyes widened, and his curiosity piqued, "How much you make?"

"It depends. Some weekends, I crush it. Then others not so much. But you know, if they called it winning, everyone would play."

Laughing, Slimbady said, "We go now to Cotai Strip. Okay?"

I looked at Sone and then said, "Yeah. Let me get the check."

I caught the waiter's attention and signaled for the bill. Once the check arrived, Slimbady reached for it and said, "I pay."

I grasped Chinese customs, where splitting bills does not exist; offering to pay signifies goodwill, and refusing this gesture is considered an insult. I attempted to convey this cultural nuance to SAIC Montaña, but it proved challenging. His perspective was shaped by a world that frequently conflicted with the complexities of tradition and etiquette.

As we embarked on our journey to the glitzy casinos of the Cotai Strip, I realized the moment had arrived. What would Slimbady think of my "low-stakes" gambling? I had laid the groundwork for my cautious strategy, but was it sufficient? Slimbady played by a different set of rules. To him, gambling was tied to a cosmic force akin to karma or luck. The fortune one experienced in a casino spilled over into other parts of life.

As we raced through the neon-lit avenues of Macau, I felt the pressure of carrying just $1,000 in my pocket. This small amount, given to me by SAIC Montaña, loomed large as I caught sight of the dazzling Cotai Strip in the distance. I pondered how long this money would last, intertwined with fragments of my discussions with Chief Superintendent Weng-Hou. The only relief came from the haze of alcohol that calmed my nerves.

As I stepped out of the taxi and entered the Venetian Casino, I felt as if I had been whisked back to the luxury of Las Vegas, though everything appeared even more extravagant and surreal on the Cotai Strip. Surrounded by familiar statues and elaborate floor tiles, it created a sense of familiarity amidst this grand atmosphere. Slimbady, an experienced visitor of the Venetian, took the lead with a resolute focus, directing us directly to the Baccarat tables.

The casino's low hum surrounded us as we settled, creating a deceptive calm before the excitement began. With my limited understanding of Baccarat, I took on the role of an observer, soaking in the atmosphere as the cards were dealt. Slimbady quickly turned to Sone and me and urged, "Come on."

After sitting down, Slimbady immediately reached into his pocket and boldly placed 20,000 Macau dollars on the table. In contrast, Sone and I opted for a more modest entrance with 500 Macau dollars. I observed Slimbady enter the game, cautiously betting $200 per hand. He remained still, intensely focused on both the cards and the dealer. I noticed him pulling money off the table.

Seeing his success motivated me, so I decided to join the game, hoping that elusive beginner's luck would smile upon me. I bet fifty Macau dollars against Slimbady's 500 Macau dollars. Sone was a bit more aggressive, betting one hundred Macau dollars. As we played, the table became crowded, and soon I found myself at the center of an unexpected twist: other players began putting money on top of my bet.

This was new to me, but it was clear that Chinese tradition allowed players to bet on each other's hands. If only they knew I was clueless about the game of Baccarat. Deal after deal, losing hand after losing hand, it became evident that my hope for beginner's luck never materialized. I held my own, but in the end, as I had many times before, I was out. I reached my authorized limit. I looked at Slimbady and said, "This game is rigged. I'm done."

Slimbady remained focused but recognized the writing on the wall and replied, "Me too. Let's find women."

Laughing, I said, "That works for me."

Sone, scratching his head, responded, "Not me. I'm going back. This is too much."

"Sone, are you sure?" I replied. "You gotta stay out one night."

"No, no," Sone replied. "I'm too tired. You two have fun."

"Looks like it is just you and me, Slim," I replied. "Where shall we go?"

Slimbady looked up and then said, "I know. Karaoke."

As we walked to the taxi stand, I grabbed my phone to send an update, but instead, I saw a cryptic message from SAIC Montaña. The message read: "What are you doing?" This left me unsettled as I thought, "What do you think I'm doing?" I was put off by the message, and I didn't immediately respond, figuring this was information SA Mason could provide.

As I said goodbye to the neon-drenched streets of the Cotai Strip, I felt an exhilarating sense of anticipation. The lively energy of Macau welcomed me, offering endless avenues for exploration. Each hotel promised a unique experience, bustling with possibilities, yet the main attraction lay in the illicit activities.

Prohibited in Las Vegas, these activities thrived here. Men roamed the bars, casinos, and streets in search of companionship. Slimbady seized the moment to introduce me to the "walking" tunnel, a passage connecting two hotels with an unspoken secret.

Slimbady invited me, saying, "Come sit here."

Intrigued, I responded, "Sure, but I thought we were headed to a karaoke bar?"

"Yeah, yeah," Slimbady said, "First, I show you this. See lady. They walk from one hotel to next."

"Okay," I replied, sounding uninterested.

Slimbady realized I was struggling to understand and elaborated further, saying, "All lady for sale. You pick what you want. But they not stop. You must get them."

This caught my attention, prompting me to ask, "So every lady just walks back and forth until a guy chooses them? And then what happens? They negotiate a price and that's all?"

Slimbady enthusiastically confirmed my question, saying, "Yes! You want?"

"No," I replied. "This isn't my scene. I enjoy going to bars instead. Didn't you mention there's a karaoke bar we need to check out?"

The disappointment was evident, but Slimbady dismissed it, saying, "Yes. We go now. Come on."

Slimbady led the way to the karaoke bar, moving with a sense of purpose through the hotel to a secluded elevator. We stepped in and rode up to the third floor, my anticipation growing with each moment. As the doors slid open, a hostess greeted us warmly, setting the stage for what was to come. At first glance, the entrance to the karaoke bar resembled a high-end restaurant more than a place for belting out tunes. Yet, Slimbady's familiarity with the venue reassured me that we were in for an unforgettable experience.

As the hostess led us through the winding corridors, I couldn't help but admire the ingenuity of the design. Every twist and turn resonated with the unspoken stories of past adventures and covert activities. The private karaoke rooms were a true find, each thoughtfully crafted to accommodate groups of different sizes. With Slimbady in charge, I felt a rush of excitement, ready to discover the surprises that lay ahead at this surprising karaoke venue.

After a seemingly half-mile walk, we finally arrived at our designated spot. Looking around, I realized this experience would be different from any karaoke bar I had ever visited. I was excited to see how the night would play out within these walls. Once we settled in, a waitress came over with two bottles of Johnny Walker Blue Label, setting the stage for an unforgettable evening. The energy in the air was palpable, hinting that this was just the start of what promised to be a wild night.

The atmosphere changed when the Hostess arrived, engaging in a tense conversation with Slimbady. Although I couldn't make out their words, the intensity of their exchange hung palpably in the air. My mind drifted to whether the surveillance teams could surveil me, especially given the hotel's complex layout. A wry thought crossed my mind; something I half-joked about later was my only hope that Slimbady wasn't saying, "Kill the white guy." Regardless, at that moment, I knew I was on an island.

After the Hostess left, I turned to Slimbady and asked, "What did she say?"

Slimbady looked at me and said, "I say to her I want lady who speak English. She say only Mandarin. Such a big place, and they no have lady speak English. Sorry."

I replied without hesitation, "It's all right. I'm a social guy. Who knows, maybe they speak just enough English. I wouldn't worry about it." I then raised my glass and said, "To good friends and good times."

Slimbady followed suit saying, "To good friends."

After our toast, a knock echoed at the door, and in walked the Hostess. With a swift command, she ushered in a procession of eight captivating Asian women, their allure accentuated by their lingerie. The women formed a line, presenting an enticing display for Slimbady and me.

Slimbady, with a playful grin, said, "You pick one."

This ignited a flurry of thoughts and feelings in me. As excitement grew, I focused on selecting someone whose body type specifically appealed to my desires. I fumbled for words, thoughts racing through my mind. I said, "Just one?"

Slimbady laughed, "Yes, pick one."

I looked at the Hostess and said, "The lady in pink."

Slimbady made a choice that surprised me, given his slender physique. The differences between his lean frame and the tall, curvaceous woman he selected suggested a more profound complexity beyond simple physical attraction. Our selections showcased our likes and reflected the nuances of our desires.

As the ladies settled beside Slimbady and me, I tried to bridge the gap with a few questions in English. However, it was clear that my words fell on unfamiliar ears. Opting for a more universal gesture, I motioned for her to join me for a drink. Without hesitation, she understood, gracefully pouring herself a drink and refilling mine, a silent yet thoughtful act.

As she passed me my glass, I introduced myself, saying, "Rich. My name is Rich."

She nodded in recognition and responded, "Crystal."

The atmosphere was alive with energy, and the music pulsed through the room as we sang and danced the night away. We were all in our element, taking turns on the karaoke machine. When my turn came, I playfully glanced at Crystal while performing my favorite tune. Our chemistry was building, but it also felt flat; we sang, danced, and drank, but couldn't speak to each other.

The hours flew by like a whirlwind, and just as quickly, they came to an abrupt stop. The door opened, and the Hostess entered. The music stopped, and silence enveloped the room.

The mere act felt like a huge buzzkill. She signaled a change in the evening's events. Slimbady, in his intoxicated state, tried to keep his composure as he leaned shoulder-to-shoulder with me, a mischievous glint in his eye as he slurred out a command in his best attempt at English, "We go my hotel now."

Under the influence of the whiskey I had downed, I slurred, "What about the ladies?"

Slimbady reclined and replied, "They come too."

The journey to Slimbady's hotel was quick, the dimly lit streets devoid of any signs of life at that late hour. Upon our arrival, we headed to the elevator and went to his room. As we entered, Slimbady dashed to the minibar and started pouring drinks for everyone.

Rather than following Slimbady, I scanned his room. My gaze landed on Slimbady's computer, which was open on the small hotel desk. My curiosity piqued, I asked, "Hey, Slim, are you online?"

Slimbady, who was too interested in the ladies and whiskey, replied, "Maybe."

The computer wasn't interested in him, but undeterred, I pressed on, asking, "Mind if I use your computer to check my messages?"

With a nod, Slimbady slurred, "Sure."

Seizing the moment, I hit the space bar, bringing the computer to life. I looked for his ICQ instance, as Jabber wasn't widely used. I observed a mix of QQ, ICQ, and Yahoo Messenger in his programs folder.

A surge of adrenaline coursed through me. Despite Slimbady's approval, I realized my aim was to betray his trust in me. It compelled me to look at Slimbady, hoping he wasn't observing my actions. Fortunately, he was busy moving toward the radio. Excited to begin the festivities, he turned on the music and cranked up the volume. Slimbady then swiveled around, and, grasping a glass of whiskey with one hand, he reached for a lady with the other.

At this point, Crystal felt left out. However, she was determined to pull me onto the makeshift dance floor, but I quickly waved her off, saying, "One minute, almost finished."

Crystal, now with a sad look, replied, "Please. Come. Dance."

I barely heard her words because I was focused on searching Slimbady's ICQ friend list. Each user sets up their list according to personal preferences, but by this time, I had memorized Maksik's ICQ number: 466-166. I scrolled to the "M's" and found Maksik as the first friend. Slimbady organized his list alphabetically, just as I did.

I checked the indicator status to determine if it was red, yellow, or green. It was a straightforward tool that indicated who was present and who was absent. Fortune favored me that day; Maksik was online. The question lingered: was he genuinely online, or had he forgotten to change his status?

I considered this for a moment, but ultimately, it didn't matter. My chief concern was whether Maksik would see my message from Slimbady's account. Once that occurred, it would be clear that I was with Slimbady. Instead of dwelling longer, knowing my time was limited, I started messaging Maksik, "What's up?"

I expected a lengthy wait. Instead, I quickly noticed the typing bubble, followed by the message: "What up, Slim?"

I felt immediate joy as I responded to Maksik, clarifying that it wasn't Slimbady: "It's Surfrider. ☺ I'm with Slim."

Maksik then asked, "Where are you?"

I quickly replied, "Slim and I are having a party in Macau. I needed another holiday."

Maksik responded, "You go on many holidays."

"True, but you know you can't take your money with you, so might as well enjoy it," I replied.

Maksik answered, "You're right."

At that moment, Crystal had given up and joined Slimbady and her friend. Then, Slimbady noticed that I had been messaging back and forth. To prevent any paranoia, I shifted my focus. It was important for me to convey that I wasn't tampering with his computer but rather having a conversation with Maksik.

In a casual tone, I said, "Maksik is online. I told him we were hanging out in Macau with some ladies."

Slimbady in a drunken state slurred, "Okay."

With Slimbady's curiosity satisfied, he shifted his focus back to his drinks and the company of the women nearby. He was indifferent to Maksik at that moment. Aware that I needed to return to the party, I told Maksik, "Just wanted to say hi. Going back to party with the ladies. Take care. 😎"

Maksik gleaned two insights from those messages: first, that Slimbady and Surfrider were on holiday together, and second, that Slimbady trusted me enough to let me use his computer. I hoped the message helped him create a picture of Slimbady and me surrounded by women and drinks. All the while, Maksik remained tethered to his computer in Ukraine.

This wasn't merely about planting a seed in Maksik's mind; it was a calculated strategy to instill jealousy and a sense of missing out, which I believed was slowly taking root. Although the $75,000 deal hadn't materialized yet, discussions surrounding it continued to resonate.

Amid a vibrant party, I found myself plotting an escape. I wanted to avoid having Crystal join me. I wasn't interested in paying for her company, yet I knew she was eager to earn her keep. I considered pretending to be too drunk to sneak out unnoticed through the hotel room door.

Unfortunately, my plan was hampered by a communication breakdown. My words failed to connect with Crystal, and I suspected that Slimbady, who was intoxicated, hadn't understood my intentions either. Instead of reacting, he continued to dance—or rather, stumble—cheerfully, clearly having a great time.

Despite everything, I stepped into the hallway, eager to escape. I rushed to the elevator bank and pressed the button for the ground floor. When the doors opened, I stepped inside and hit the ground floor button again, followed by the close door button. As the doors slid shut, I thought I was halfway there; Crystal was nowhere in sight. My focus was on getting away from the hotel as fast as possible.

When the doors swung open, I dashed through the lobby, eager to vanish into the night. While crossing the street, I heard a familiar voice calling out to me. It was Crystal. Now, I faced a dilemma; running away now would only send her back to Slimbady. I decided I had to lead her away from the hotel instead. My goal wasn't to take her to my place, but to create enough distance from Slimbady's hotel, hoping she'd forget how to return.

After walking a few blocks and navigating intentional twists and turns, I felt far enough from Slimbady's hotel. I let go of her hand, feigned drunkenness, and said, "Go home!"

Initially taken aback, Crystal seemed uncertain. "No. I come," she uttered.

I blurted out, "No, go home! I'm not interested."

With determination, Crystal responded, "I with you. I come."

Frustrated, I dismissed her, saying, "Go away. I don't want. Leave."

After some hesitation, she followed me for a block before turning away. As I glanced back, I felt a sense of relief, certain she wouldn't be able to find her way back to Slimbady. Even if she did, the chances were high that he was either passed out or making love to her friend. However, I was sorely mistaken.

Chapter 27

Vincent joins the party

I woke up the following day feeling rejuvenated. Although Vincent was on his way, I first needed to attend the debrief at the police station. Eager anticipation filled the air as my colleagues eagerly awaited news of the progress made over the past two days. I entered quietly through the back entrance, staying alert because Slimbady was still in town, and Vincent could show up at any moment.

As I entered the meeting room, Chief Superintendent Weng-Hou greeted me with a broad smile. He walked over, bowed slightly, and said, "James Bond. I apologize for doubting you. Please, how did you manage it?"

At first, I was surprised by his admiration, but then I realized he praised my successful gambling strategy. I replied modestly, "I anticipated it. I kept telling Slim and the others that this kind of gambling isn't for me. They also know about my vices—women, sports betting, whiskey, and, of course, wine."

Still smiling, Weng-Hou said, "Please have a seat. First, let's go over last night, then we can plan for today's meeting."

I placed the fake credit cards on the table, saying, "Here's the plastic I mentioned earlier."

Intrigued by the counterfeit credit cards, Weng-Hou asked, "Could we take a look? Can you tell us what makes them so valuable?"

"Absolutely," I replied. I gestured toward the security features, saying, "Here you can see the stylized symbol. Next to it is the hologram, which is nearly perfect. Then, if you use a UV light, you can observe the UV feature on the plastic. You'll notice the micro-printing when you flip the card and examine it closely. It's all very professional."

Intrigued, Weng-Hou asked, "And these work in the United States?"

I answered, "Sure, a nineteen- or twenty-two-year-old won't recognize the difference. They'll only be declined if the credit card processor rejects the transaction."

Weng-Hou remarked, "This is quite intriguing. So, shall we discuss tonight's agenda?"

SAIC Montaña seized the opportunity to say, "Tonight marks the final night of this operation. Everyone from the United States will head back tomorrow."

I sat motionless, doing everything I could to show any emotion, as the news surprised me. After SAIC Montaña's declaration, Chief Superintendent Weng-Hou said, "You will not continue the operation as planned?"

SAIC Montaña replied without emotion, "No. It's over tonight. I need to be back in San Diego."

Weng-Hou glanced at his team before saying, "Alright, tonight will be the finale." He shifted his focus and asked, "When will Vincent arrive?"

With my voice trembling with anger, I stated, "I haven't heard from Vincent or Slimbady, but I suspect I will later this afternoon."

"Alright," Weng-Hou replied. "We'll be prepared. Please notify us when you have updates."

DOI: 10.1201/9781003680390-27

"Absolutely," I replied, rising to my feet. I swiftly pivoted and headed toward the exit without uttering another word.

Frustration and anger consumed me. I had questions, yet voicing them in that meeting would have been unwise. I also refrained from addressing SAIC Montaña publicly in front of the team. Nevertheless, I was seething inside, contemplating, "What prompted this sudden decision?"

My thoughts raced as I wondered if Headquarters had intervened or if there would be a visit. Either way, the notion that this required my attention seemed absurd. If a protective visit was scheduled in San Diego, SAIC Montaña could quickly return, allowing RAIC Stone to assume his responsibilities. After we left the police department, once SAIC Montaña and I were out of earshot, I could no longer contain my curiosity.

"What's the reason we're leaving tomorrow morning?" I asked.

SAIC Montaña stated, "I must return to the office."

"Is there a particular reason?" I inquired.

SAIC Montaña, taken aback by the question, responded, "Your meetings with Sun Credit and Slimbady were successful. Vincent isn't especially significant."

"Alright," I replied. "We talked about this earlier. Traveling halfway around the world and spending hours instead of days is wrong. It's not normal. As for Vincent, there's an intelligence gap. We don't know his value. Besides, he's a Carder who supports me. How's that not significant?"

Unfazed, SAIC Montaña, his tongue flicking between his lips, remarked, "As for tonight, it ends at midnight. We have early flights to catch."

Following a tense exchange with SAIC Montaña, I was in turmoil yet remained composed. I never considered ending the mission prematurely; however, while I was focused on my role as a Carder, political dynamics were unfolding behind the scenes. I now understand that SAIC Montaña's probing message served as a warning that ultimately cut the operation short. What was meant to be a multiweek mission turned into just a few short days.

Even though I felt frustrated, I recognized that resisting was pointless. Letting anger take control would only cloud my judgment. I needed a strategy to "soften the blow" of the unexpected turn of events. While at my hotel, I logged into my ICQ account, determined to contact Slimbady and Vincent. Among the many messages in my inbox, one stood out to me.

SunCredit messaged me, "Hey, are you still in Macau? Would you like to meet tonight?"

A flicker of positive news following the recent turmoil. Yet, I had to share the unfortunate update and wrote, "I'm sorry, my friend, but I can't. I must head back to San Diego tomorrow due to an emergency."

SunCredit replied, "I hope everyone is okay."

That was a good sign. It seemed SunCredit cared, so I typed back, "I will find out soon. ☹"

SunCredit concluded with, "Let me know when you return."

"Absolutely, my friend," I replied.

I was aware that Slimbady, Vincent, and SunCredit communicated, so it was crucial to maintain a consistent story. I created a narrative about one of my "guys" getting arrested while attempting to cash out some cards. Considering the nature of our work, it was a believable account.

As I crafted the story in my mind, Slimbady messaged me, "Meet for dinner?"

"Yes," I shot back. "Where?"

Slimbady replied, "Same place. 1800, okay? Vincent joins us."

"Works for me. See you soon, 😁" I messaged.

With tonight's meeting agreed upon, I quickly sent the update to SA Mason. Then, I pivoted. I knew I had time, so I messaged ATSAIC Carrington. I was curious to see if he was aware of the sudden changes. I didn't need to wait long.

My phone rang once, and I answered, "Do you know what's happening?"

Letting out a tired sigh, ATSAIC Carrington explained, "Yes."

I asked with sarcasm, "Can you explain why?"

ATSAIC Carrington asked, "Didn't he tell you?"

"What do you mean?" I asked.

"So, you don't know," ATSAIC Carrington stated.

"Why would I know?" I replied. "I only know I have to leave tomorrow morning."

After taking a deep breath, ATSAIC Carrington remarked, "The SAIC couldn't book a first-class ticket. The soonest option is tomorrow."

Frustration seeped into my voice as I replied, "So, you're saying our entire operation is being cut short because the SAIC couldn't get a first-class ticket to San Diego in two days?"

"I'm afraid so," ATSAIC Carrington replied.

Frustration permeated from within as I said, "We preach about prioritizing my safety above all else. Yet, ASAIC DuBois is god knows where, surveillance teams seemingly are in bed by midnight, and now operations are being cut short for first-class tickets."

ATSAIC Carrington attempted to console me, acknowledging, "I understand. It's far from ideal."

Interrupting him, I went on, "You know what's worse? I'm told I must be in bed by midnight. Midnight? Who in the hell, especially a Carder who isn't the most 'responsible' anyway, goes to bed by midnight?"

ATSAIC Carrington could only manage, "I understand. It sucks."

As I calmed down, I said, "It's just insane. Going to bed by midnight—why? Is it so I can 'stay awake' for the ten-hour flight back? Who wants to be awake for that long? This is absolute madness!"

ATSAIC Carrington felt frustrated and powerless. He knew there wasn't much he could do, so he ended with a simple, "I'm sorry."

After the call, I immersed myself in my planning and waited patiently. As six o'clock neared, Sone and I headed to Slimbady's hotel to meet them again for Chinese food. This aspect is one part I found amusing. The often-heard phrase was that Americans only like American cuisine, meanwhile it appears that the Chinese exclusively only enjoy Chinese dishes.

When Sone and I arrived at the hotel, Slimbady and Vincent were waiting in the lobby. As we approached, Slimbady remarked, "I very hungry. No eat all day."

I laughed and asked, "Hungover?"

Slimbady rubbed his forehead and replied, "Yes."

As we sat down, Slimbady asked, "What happen? She come back."

Puzzled, I inquired, "Crystal? She came back?"

Slimbady said, "Yes. She come to my door. Tell us you don't want her."

This news surprised me. Crystal wasn't supposed to return to Slimbady's hotel, yet she did. I had to think fast about how to explain the situation, so I responded, "Yeah, I wasn't fond of her, so I told her to leave. But are you saying she showed up at your door?"

Slimbady nodded and grinned as he replied, "Yes, I had threesome. Thank you."

I fully recognized that wasn't my intention, yet I couldn't resist chuckling as I replied, "You're welcome."

During dinner, we discussed carding, gambling, sex, and more carding. When the opportune moment presented itself, I let everyone know our change in plans and said, "Oh, before I forget. Sone and I have to leave tomorrow morning. The guys ran into some trouble."

Vincent said, "Is it serious?"

"I'm not sure," I replied. "All I know is one of the guys got caught cashing out."

Vincent said, "That's serious. What time is flight?"

"In the morning, first one," I said.

Vincent shook his head and said, "Then tonight we have good time."

Slimbady, feeling the effect of his hangover, said, "No me. I sleep."

Sone latched onto Slimbady's statement, declaring, "Me too. I'm exhausted."

Vincent then pointed at me and said, "Rich? Come on, we go out."

"Sure," I replied. "I'm not going to bed, but I can't stay out all night."

Vincent pounded the table and declared, "I know just the place."

After settling the bill, Sone and Slimbady said goodbye, and Vincent remarked, "We need taxi."

"Lead the way," I said.

The taxi driver expertly maneuvered through the streets of Macau, first steering away from the city. Then, he suddenly turned and climbed a hill that provided stunning city views. The journey piqued my curiosity as I pondered what secret surprise Vincent had in store for me. Concurrently, I quietly wished our journey wouldn't lead us to Mainland China, a scenario I wanted to avoid.

Pulling away from the stunning scenery, I casually remarked to Vincent, "Just remember, my flight is early, so I plan to head back around midnight."

Vincent's reaction was immediate and adamant, "No. This your last night. We stay out all night. Besides, you can sleep on flight."

I knew that would not go well with SAIC Montaña, so I tried again, firmly stating, "No, I need to head back early. I can't afford to miss it."

Vincent remained resolute, defiantly shaking his head and saying, "You not leave at midnight."

It was evident that this was shaping up to be a challenge. Balancing Vincent's expectations with the obligations set by SAIC Montaña felt like an impossible task. Nonetheless, I consciously chose to set aside the issue for the moment, opting to change the subject of our conversation. As we engaged in discussion, the car suddenly veered to the right and came to a stop. Vincent announced that we had arrived at our destination.

I stepped out of the car eagerly, my excitement rising as I absorbed the scene. Vincent, being familiar with the location, made me feel relaxed as he guided me. When we reached the karaoke bar on the third floor, I was enchanted by its Asian-themed decor: bamboo details, dangling gold coins, a tranquil koi pond, and elaborate Asian calligraphy.

A young lady escorted us down the hallway to an elevator. After we ascended three floors, we navigated a winding corridor, went up another flight of stairs, and took a few more turns until we reached our destination. The room was simple yet enchanting. It featured a TV mounted on the wall, an L-shaped couch facing the TV, and a coffee table in the center.

Vincent and I made ourselves comfortable in the room; he understood what would happen, while I was filled with curiosity and anticipation. When the Hostess arrived, she and Vincent conversed in Mandarin. I sat quietly, watching their exchange, even though I couldn't grasp the details. After their conversation ended and the Hostess left, I wondered what it was all about.

"What did you tell her?" I asked Vincent curiously.

Vincent, with a wry smile, said, "Relax. I arrange everything."

"Alright," I replied with a grin. "So, enlighten me. I know your history with SunCredit, but I believed you and Slim weren't on friendly terms."

Vincent looked at the wall and said, "SunCredit I not like. We not friends. Slim, he different. We no work together but we no problem hang out together."

"I see," I said. "You talk with Maksik?"

Vincent's eyes lit up as he said, "Yes. Thank you for meeting him to me. His dumps very good."

"That's great," I said.

As Vincent and I discussed the digital world, the Hostess returned with a generous offering: two one-liter bottles of Johnny Walker Blue Label, complete with mixers, glasses, and ice. I was taken aback by the sheer quantity of liquor Vincent had ordered, wondering if there had been a mistake.

"Vincent," I said, astonished, "Don't forget I have a flight tomorrow morning. There's no way we can finish all this and still walk out of this place."

Vincent chuckled, "No worries, we no need drink it all."

I gave him a look and joked, "Of course not, but leaving it behind would be alcohol abuse."

I glanced at my watch and realized I had plenty of time. Perhaps two liters of whiskey weren't such a terrible thing after all. I was directed to conclude by midnight, but there was no defined path to get there. With our glasses raised, we toasted, "To new friends."

Taking advantage of the moment, Vincent turned to me and disclosed, "Earlier, I say girls must speak English. If not, no bring."

Puzzled, I responded, "You didn't have to do that. I can manage, and as a guest in Macau, I shouldn't expect everyone to speak English."

Vincent politely waved off my concerns, stating, "They must speak English."

A sudden knock at the door disrupted our conversation, and as I turned to look, the Hostess walked in, delivering sharp orders in Mandarin. I sank back into the soft couches, astonished as eight women dressed in lingerie entered the room.

Once everyone was aligned perfectly, and the Hostess was pleased, she addressed Vincent. Vincent then faced me and said, "Choose one. They all speak English."

As I stood in awe of the beautiful women before me, I wondered who would capture my interest the most. The only variations among them were the color and style of their lingerie. Height, breast size, and hair color were noticeably visible. However, the most important factor I couldn't identify at that moment was their personality. Were they playful? Did they enjoy dancing? What type of music did they like? All of this was still a mystery to me.

"No, Vincent, you go first," I said, trying to defer the choice.

Vincent waved me off, insisting, "You my guest. You must pick first."

"Okay." I pointed at the young, petite lady in light blue lingerie and said, "Would you care to join me?"

She replied, "Yes," and sat down beside me.

Vincent quickly decided, saying to the lady in pink lingerie, "You," and she sat next to him.

With a clap of her hands, the Hostess dismissed the lineup of ladies in lingerie. As the door closed behind them, our two new friends began their preparations, filling our glasses with scotch and ensuring we lacked for nothing. After they served us our drinks, we all raised our glasses and toasted to the evening.

After our toast, I asked, "You speak English?"

My new friend smiled and nodded, saying, "Yes, I speak English."

"That's great! What's your name? I'm Rich," I replied excitedly.

"Nice to meet you, Rich. My name is Katie," she replied.

My encounter with Katie in Macau was a stark departure from my previous escapades with Slimbady. As we exchanged introductions, it quickly became apparent that Katie's vibrant spirit and captivating presence made her stand out. She exuded a charm that was impossible to ignore.

Yet, a nagging thought lingered amid the celebration: SAIC Montaña's midnight deadline. This obligation felt unreasonable, threatening to overshadow the night's enjoyment and distract me from my primary goal. Meanwhile, the karaoke session was in full swing, with Vincent taking the lead and passing the mic around.

Though I hesitated, still sober enough to shy away, Katie eagerly seized the microphone. She sang her version of Britney Spears' "Oops!... I Did It Again," energizing the room with her voice, which struck a captivating mix of strength and grace. Witnessing her performance was inspiring, with each note evoking a magnetic allure that captured my full attention.

As Katie's friend joined her for a duet, the atmosphere grew even more enchanting. Vincent and I found ourselves fully immersed in the moment, relishing the contagious energy of the evening. Thinking about our absent friend Slimbady, I couldn't help but picture how much he would have enjoyed the karaoke experience. With Vincent now wholly absorbed in the festivities, it was clear that my turn to take the stage had arrived.

With a mischievous glint in his eye and a playful grin, Vincent turned to me and declared, "Rich, your turn. You sing next."

I resisted as best as I could, but Vincent and Katie were relentless. "Rich, sing for us," they insisted in unison.

Sighing, I reluctantly agreed, "Okay. Okay, I'll sing."

Vincent's eyes sparkled with excitement as he proclaimed, "Now, every time we sing, we must drink our glasses."

I paused before saying, "Wait, you want me to down the entire glass of top-shelf whiskey? This isn't meant for shots."

Vincent repeated firmly, "You sing, you drink."

With a sense of resignation, I jokingly replied, "Fine, but just know I'm doing this under protest."

As I hesitantly agreed, memories surged of dinners with the police, where wine flowed like shots. It felt ridiculous to me. I often attempted to take a sip discreetly, but Chief Superintendent Weng-Hou's vigilant gaze prevented my efforts. Though my colleagues were not pleased, I remained unfazed, as I was already used to drinking heavily. The only drawback was hastening the delightful taste of quality wine.

I selected "Secret Agent Man" by Johnny Rivers for my performance. After a few drinks, it was the perfect choice to honor the trip. I had already thought of the name "Operation Carder Kaos"—a lighthearted reference to stirring up trouble in the carding scene, inspired by the villainous organization from "Get Smart." Now, I found myself convinced to take the stage for karaoke. What better way to keep the momentum than to sing "Secret Agent Man?"

As the music began and I started to sing, Vincent and Katie cheered with recognition. Vincent took his lady's hand and began dancing and singing along with her. I took Katie's hand, pulled her close, and we danced together in response. At that moment, I felt like an international man of mystery, with everyone in the room knowing my name but being unaware of my true intentions.

When I wrapped up my song, Vincent immediately clinked glasses and insisted I drink my whiskey. Katie stood nearby, ever prepared to refill any empty glasses. Vincent was singing once more, his glass slightly overflowing. It was clear he was drunk. The clock chimed eleven at night, leaving an hour until midnight. Would Vincent's impulsive plan for whiskey shots benefit me?

I felt the effects of the whiskey, but Vincent, who was smaller than I, was struggling. His balance was wavering, and his speech was slurred. I thought, "Maybe it's time to call it a night before things get out of hand."

With each song sang, another shot demanded, but now it wasn't just the singer; it was for everyone. Vincent was insistent and having the time of his life. I glanced at the two bottles and noticed one was already empty, and the other wasn't far behind. Vincent's balance was nonexistent; it was clear he would not last much longer.

I seized the opportunity, took the mic, and launched into "Sweet Caroline." While I sang, Vincent sank into the couch, unable to stay upright without help. Although he attempted to take the mic, he was finished for the evening. The final bottle of whiskey had been drained, and the hour was approaching midnight.

When I thought things couldn't get any more chaotic, the Hostess entered, curious about the party's fate. Noticing Vincent's sorry state, I turned to Katie and firmly said, "We'll take the check."

Katie quickly relayed our decision to the Hostess, confirming that we were calling it a night. She then turned back to me and inquired, "We come too?"

I knew Vincent wasn't in any shape to return on his own. With only twenty minutes left to finish the operation, there was no time for delays. "Yes, Katie, you and your friend are welcome to come, but she has to ensure he gets back safely," I instructed.

Katie's eyes gleamed with excitement as she hurriedly shared the message with Hostess, then turned to me and said, "Wait for us here."

Naturally, I reflected. It was clear that Vincent needed substantial help. While I monitored Vincent, my thoughts drifted to Katie. We built a genuine connection in a few hours, and I truly enjoyed her company. As Katie changed, the Hostess returned with the bill.

I paused briefly when I looked at the total—$1,754.74. I recognized that Vincent couldn't pay, so I pulled out my undercover credit card to pay the bill. I knew I'd have to explain this expense later, but my instructions were straightforward: conclude by midnight.

As the Hostess departed, I glanced at the clock and noted it was fifteen minutes until midnight. Katie and her friend appeared, now clad in street clothes instead of lingerie. I was surprised by how much Katie had changed, yet I admired the transformation. I said, "Remember, you need to take care of Vincent and get him home safely."

Katie quickly replied, "Yes, she will. She knows. Where do we go?"

I knew I was on the clock, so I said, "There is a bar at my hotel. We'll go there."

Katie excitedly replied, "Okay."

As we left, I watched Katie's friend struggle to help Vincent walk. Despite my guilt, I knew time was short. I bid farewell, hoping for Vincent's well-being. As Katie and I walked to my hotel, I sent the final signing-off message to the team. I looked at the time and noted it was three minutes past midnight.

Katie and I walked hand in hand to the hotel, sharing laughter and conversation during our brief five-minute stroll. Upon entering the hotel lobby, a wave of accomplishment washed over me. I had fulfilled all the requirements of SAIC Montaña, and the operation had smoothly concluded eight minutes past midnight. Although I arrived a little after the scheduled time, it was close enough.

The band's music in the hotel bar caught my attention, so I asked Katie, "Shall we dance?" With a nod of enthusiasm, we walked toward the dance floor.

The hallway to the bar was narrow, and Katie and I were captivated by our conversation. However, as I glanced ahead, I saw Chief Superintendent Weng-Hou accompanied by another officer, who both were supporting Chief Ng Ka Ho. I laughed, noting that Chief Ng was experiencing the same challenges as Vincent, but he didn't have a woman assisting him to his hotel room.

I knew that evening a special event was planned between our teams. It was a celebration to acknowledge our work together. However, as I would hear later, like ATSAIC Carrington,

SAIC Montaña had little patience for Chief Ng's drinking. Once the main course was finished, SAIC Montaña departed. International liaison wasn't for SAIC Montaña or ATSAIC Carrington. Once again, SAIC Montaña chose to sit in his room rather than build relationships.

Even though Vincent was far away, I was still with Katie, making interactions with Chief Ng or Chief Superintendent Weng-Hou less than ideal. Katie and I were getting to know one another, and I didn't fully trust her. Slimbady and Vincent frequently visit Macau, and I worried that one of them might randomly run into Katie. A simple question could quickly reveal a significant secret.

As a result, I lowered my head and glanced at the wall. Katie and I moved quickly past the crowd. Chief Superintendent Weng-Hou was so preoccupied with carrying Chief Ng that he didn't see us. As I slipped by undetected, I couldn't help but chuckle at the similarity between Chief Ng and Vincent.

Inside the pulsating club, vibrant lights and energetic music filled the air, creating a lively ambiance. Still buoyed by the effects of whiskey, Katie and I swiftly made our way to the dance floor, eager to continue the festivities.

With spirited joy, we danced until a slow song played, allowing us to catch our breath and embrace. Amidst the celebration, fleeting thoughts of the recent stressful nights plagued by unreasonable superiors crossed my mind. However, my well-executed operation overshadowed any lingering worries.

The crowd thinned as the evening wore on, leaving Katie and me on the dance floor. When the last dance was announced, we held each other close, cherishing the night's final moments. Acknowledging that time was slipping away, I realized I had to leave soon for the port to board a jet boat to Hong Kong International Airport.

When the song concluded, Katie and I quickly headed to the exit, entering an empty lobby featuring only a sleepy clerk at the check-in desk. We rushed by him, hardly acknowledging his presence, and went directly to the elevator, aiming for my hotel room.

Once inside the room, the passion that had ignited on the dance floor continued to blaze between Katie and me. Shedding our clothes, we sank onto the bed, with Katie beneath me as I took charge for the last time. No words were necessary; our desires spoke volumes as we moved as one, synchronized in our passion. As much as I wished for time to freeze in these euphoric moments, the reality of impending departure loomed.

My phone's alarm shattered the tranquil air, reminding me that my departure for San Diego was near. Refraining from sleep, Katie and I clung to each other until the final moments, when I reluctantly tore myself away from her embrace. After a quick shower, I packed, and we retraced our earlier steps back to an empty lobby.

There, amid the silence, we exchanged our last kiss, our lips embracing one final time. I held her close a final time and then bid farewell as I turned and headed toward the Macau port. The hotel's proximity to the port provided a fitting backdrop for our farewell, and the crisp morning air signaled the start of a new day.

As I approached the port, I knew I would soon reunite with the team, but a sense of caution lingered within me. The buzz from the whiskey, the pulsing rhythm of the dance floor, and the thrill of being with Katie were slowly fading away, leaving me struggling to stay awake long enough to board the jet boat with my luggage. Desperate for a boost, I grabbed a cup of coffee, hoping it would deliver the jolt. Thankfully, it did the trick.

As we set off, I maintained my distance, merely exchanging a nod with SAIC Montaña and SA Mason, a silent yet respectful acknowledgment. I took my seat, looking forward to the rest I desperately needed. Before long, I drifted off, impervious even to the rough ride of the jet boat. I remained unaware of the journey, only stirring when the boat reached the

Hong Kong International Airport. Sleepiness clung to me as I trudged through the terminal like a zombie, trailing the crowd toward the gate, my mind clouded, yearning for more sleep.

After I boarded, I found my seat and quickly fell asleep. For the next few hours, I slept soundly, dreaming of mended relationships, renewed friendships, and the hope of meeting Maksik soon. However, despite my happiness, not everyone was pleased, and I wouldn't hear the news until Monday.

Chapter 28

An advocate, antagonist, and a deal!

The plane landed, and I was finally back in San Diego. After stepping off, I hurried to the taxi stand. Outside, I basked in the familiar comforts of home: the sun warming my skin, the salty air, and the iconic skyline. I eagerly anticipated this weekend with Rachel and my two beloved chocolate Labradors, Bella and Natasha. However, like many weekends, it began well but ended in arguments. Before I knew it, I was back at work, sitting in ATSAIC Carrington's office.

"Hey, Rich," ATSAIC Carrington said. "Come, take a seat."

"Good morning, Mr. Carrington," I said.

ATSAIC Carrington looked confused before saying, "Where should I start? I don't know. I suppose the jet boat."

I was now confused, thinking, "The jet boat?"

"I received a call from the SAIC," ATSAIC Carrington began to clarify. "He was quite upset. Did you sleep during the ride to the airport?"

"Excuse me?" I said. "Yeah, I slept. What's the big deal?"

ATSAIC Carrington stated, "While you were in Hong Kong, the SAIC reached out and reprimanded me for you sleeping on the boat. Later, he called me from LA and mentioned that you slept again during the flight from Hong Kong to LA."

"Are you kidding me?" I said in disbelief.

ATSAIC Carrington said, "He felt you showed a carefree attitude, were unprofessional, and, worst of all, disrespectful."

I shook my head in disbelief and said, "Let me get this straight. The SAIC was mainly worried about my sleeping on a boat and a plane. Meanwhile, I was left alone with the bad guys, explaining that I had to cut my holiday short. I tried hard not to mention the real reason—my SAIC couldn't upgrade to first class. Aside from the required meetings, he seldom left his hotel. He only contacted me once to ask what I was doing. And that was a text message."

ATSAIC Carrington empathized with my concerns, saying, "I understand your frustration. I feel the same way. I can't comprehend why he calls to yell at me because you napped during the flight."

I was caught between a rock and a hard place. San Diego needed an on-the-ground supervisor, but ASAIC DuBois was grounded, and ATSAIC Carrington disliked traveling. That left SAIC Montaña, who didn't know how to call me from Macau, and a surveillance team that was rumored to be "tucked in" by midnight. It was a classic case of bureaucratic incompetence.

If there had been genuine concern, the operation would have had the necessary support. I wanted the best, but I was left with SAIC Montaña. Although he held the SAIC title in the San Diego Field Office, he was a liability in every other respect.

DOI: 10.1201/9781003680390-28

My only chance to change the odds was to complain to Headquarters, so I ensured they were aware of my challenges whenever the opportunity arose. While this happened, online criminals thrived, making headlines with each network compromise. As a result, industry leaders scrambled, seeking help from the Secret Service and the FBI. It was turning into a global crisis, and the competition was intensifying.

In my opinion, the Secret Service had the upper hand. I was conducting the only in-person undercover operation, and if it went smoothly, we would soon have access to invaluable intelligence. Maksik supplied me with the freshest data, and I had my sights set on completing our deal and acquiring an entire database.

The only major hurdle was the promised funding, which had yet to come through. Government bureaucracy or a lack of care was the bane of my goal, but my luck was about to turn. ATSAIC Carrington and I were summoned to Headquarters for an operational briefing. They sought firsthand updates from the field on carding cases.

Before I left, I found myself in ASAIC DuBois's office. ASAIC DuBois handed me my recently submitted expense report. I looked it over as ASAIC DuBois asked, "Can you explain that $1,754.74 expense?"

"Easy," I explained. "This is the bill from Vincent and my karaoke night. He was in no shape to pay, and I was told to wrap up the operation by midnight, so I paid."

Although sympathetic, ASAIC DuBois asked, "Why didn't you split the bill?"

The question caught me off guard, and I replied, "That's not how things operate in Asia; you either pay the bill or you don't. Furthermore, I'm playing the role of a 'big-time' cybercriminal. Why would I share the check?"

With a look of concern etched on his face, ASAIC DuBois said, "The SAIC is unhappy. He is thinking of having you cover the expense."

Struggling to maintain my composure, I said, "If that's the decision, please let me know who I should pay. But you need to know that this is bullshit. I'm out there alone, with no backup. Making split-second decisions, including covering costs, is part of the job. My life is on the line, and if I faced the same situation again, I would do it all over."

ASAIC DuBois nodded and said, "I understand. Let me speak with Montaña."

I couldn't wait to leave the office, even if it were just for a couple of days and back at Headquarters. At the time, word about my undercover operations in Thailand and Macau had not yet circulated. The information was closely guarded and known only to a select few, but soon, I would share these stories with a broader audience.

As the conference progressed, essential information was shared, and optimism regarding future operations increased. However, during a break with ATSAIC Carrington, everything shifted when Assistant Director (AD) Rookwood, a familiar face, approached me and said, "Hey Rich, how's it going? I'm curious to hear about Macau."

"Macau was a success," I responded, excitement clear. "I met with Slimbady, Vincent, and SunCredit. They're all on my side now. I even got to use Slim's computer to message Maksik."

AD Rookwood nodded with approval. "That's great news. Operation Firewall has been our cornerstone; I've been discussing this case with anyone in Congress willing to listen. There is plenty of funding available, and network breaches are a key topic of concern right now. The Service needs another big win to maintain momentum. Do you need anything?"

I caught ATSAIC Carrington's eye and sensed his reluctance for me to speak. Nevertheless, I said, "It's been two months since Headquarters instructed me to acquire a database. I've made all the necessary preparations, yet I'm still awaiting the funds despite previous assurances. Maksik messages me daily, and I continually delay putting the operation at risk. I need the money."

Surprised by the delay, AD Rookwood shifted his expression and said, "I approved those funds over a month ago. Let me handle it. You'll get your money."

AD Rookwood then spun around and made a beeline for the elevator bank. ATSAIC Carrington's look was intriguing. Although his preferred approach differed from mine, the hope that someone would finally deliver on their promises was worth it.

Once we were back in San Diego, ATSAIC Carrington and I found ourselves in the familiar confines of our office. My focus shifted to the challenging tasks of report writing, case management, and organizing the extensive case details. As I considered how to continue delaying Maksik, ASAIC DuBois summoned ATSAIC Carrington and me to his office.

Once inside ASAIC DuBois's office, he whispered, "It's Gale from Headquarters. She works in our finance department. She needs some case-related details for their records."

I listened intently as Gale, a stranger to me, said, "I'm working on transferring the $75,000. Can you provide me a quick blurb of the case?"

"Absolutely!" I replied with enthusiasm. "The case targets a multinational hacking group that has compromised the various networks, including Office Depot, Wal-Mart, Forever 21, and TJ Maxx."

Gale replied with a hint of contempt, saying, "That should suffice. I'm unsure why they approved this, but you should receive the funds within two days. It's unfortunate because this money would have been better spent on overtime. Just know, you're depriving them of food for their family's table."

I brushed off Gale's remarks and said, "Thank you. I will put the money to good use."

Finally, I was just a few days away from finalizing the agreement with Maksik and potentially arranging a face-to-face meeting with him. The viability of my operation heavily relied on AD Rookwood's steadfast support. I understood all too well that this case would never have gained momentum without his backing. However, to my disappointment, Headquarters decided to throw a wrench in the works just before the funds were transferred to my account.

After waiting two days, I was summoned again into ATSAIC Carrington's office. Inside were SAIC Montaña and ASAIC DuBois, with Headquarters on the other line. They wanted to discuss the pending deal with Maksik. San Diego leadership lacked sufficient case details; naturally, it fell on me to provide the answers.

ATSAIC Sheehan initiated the call by stating, "We recently spoke with some large banks, and they disclosed a significant issue costing them millions. Carders are accessing ATMs throughout the United States and withdrawing cash. Getting to the bottom of this is a top priority. None of our operations have access to this data, but I recall you were once offered dumps and PINs from Maksik. Is that accurate?"

I smugly replied, "Yeah, I told you about that months ago. I also told you that passing on this deal was a bad idea. However, no one was willing to spend the money. Anyhow, what do you need?"

The phone fell silent, and I almost thought we had lost the connection. Then it came alive with ATSAIC Sheehan's voice saying, "We want you to buy a database of dumps and PINs with the $75,000."

As it turned out, they believed my deal with Maksik wasn't finalized, and I could alter the arrangement. If I were to purchase a database of dumps and PINs, ATSAIC Sheehan thought it would enhance our reputation within the credit card industry. I wasn't about to back down and said, "Are you kidding? Maksik and I have a deal. I can't just change it. How about this: I can probably get ten dumps and PINS for $3,000."

ATSAIC Sheehan clicked his teeth together and said, "No, we don't want to spend confidential funds. We want you to use the $75,000."

My instincts screamed with resistance. I thought, “No way you’re fucking up my deal for your priorities.” Besides, I knew that abandoning the original deal wasn’t wise. I reiterated, “Look, I can’t change the deal. It would not be honorable.”

ATSAIC Sheehan shot back, “Honorable? What do you mean? They’re criminals. They often take advantage of people. Simply tell him you no longer want that deal. You want this one that includes dumps and PINs.”

I found myself torn between a moral dilemma and the survival of my operation. While I comprehended it, their argument relied on labeling me a “bad guy” with no honor among thieves. However, I took pride in my reputation for never complaining or stirring up chaos online.

From the intelligence I’d gathered, Maksik was viewed as one of the more trustworthy cybercriminals in the digital world. Yet, I didn’t want to escalate tensions or create unnecessary drama. With a sigh, I said, “Let me reach out to him. I’ll see what I can do.”

I left the room feeling once again betrayed by leadership, but I was determined to prove that my instincts were right. True to my word, I went online and messaged Maksik, saying, “What’s up, Brat?”

Maksik replied quickly, saying, “Hey. What’s up?”

I replied, “I need to ask you a question. Can I buy d+p? 😁”

Maksik messaged back, “Yes. 😎10 for 3k.”

I replied, “Hmmm, well, I have the money for the DB. However, I would like to modify the deal. Can I buy all d+p?”

Maksik took some time to respond but finally said, “This is not possible.”

Curious, I asked, “Any reason why?”

Maksik replied, “Because that is a different person.”

I thought about it and said, “How about we do 50% dumps and 50% d+p?”

Maksik replied, “No. As I said, that is a different person.”

I was running out of options and replied, “Seems I have little options. 😏”

Maksik said, “Yup.”

I had given up trying and wrote back, “Okay, let’s keep it the same.”

After my conversation with Maksik, I emailed ATSAIC Sheehan to clarify that Maksik obtains data from various sources. He was unwilling to adjust the terms of the deal.

I was asked into ATSAIC Carrington’s office for another call with Headquarters the following day. During the call, ATSAIC Sheehan stated, “Here’s the situation: You have three options. First, revise the deal to exclusively include ‘dumps and PINs,’ which we prefer. Second, adjust the deal to feature a mix of “dumps and PINs’ along with regular dumps, which we can accept. Finally, retain the original deal, which isn’t our preferred choice. Also, be aware that choosing option three means that if Maksik doesn’t meet with you, your operation ends.”

Quickly, I found myself tiptoeing through a treacherous minefield, acutely aware of the scrutiny from above. If I chose the first option, Headquarters would continue supporting the operation, even if Maksik failed to attend a face-to-face meeting. However, if I choose the final option and he does not meet me, support from Headquarters will be withdrawn, leaving the operation dead.

The tension was palpable as we discussed the three options in ATSAIC Carrington’s office. I started by asking, “What does everyone think?”

ASAIC DuBois emphasized, “I’m not an investigator. You are closest to this case, and I trust your judgment. I will defer to you.” With that, ASAIC DuBois stepped out of the decision-making process.

ATSAIC Carrington remarked, “I prefer option two. If you can manage this and Maksik doesn’t meet, we can still have a chance.”

I shook my head and replied, "I'm not convinced. I believe ATSAIC Sheehan and others are searching for any excuse to dismiss the case." I then asked SAIC Montaña, "What are your thoughts?"

SAIC Montaña held the authority, and ultimately, nothing else mattered. Whatever he thought or decided would become our path. What happened next caught me off guard.

SAIC Montaña declared, "It's up to you. I don't care." Montaña stood and walked out of the room, leaving ATSAIC Carrington and me exchanging worried glances.

Sensing the tension, ASAIC DuBois looked at us and said, "I'm on your side, boys. I'm good with whatever choice you make." He then stood up and followed SAIC Montaña out of ATSAIC Carrington's office.

ATSAIC Carrington said, "What's your choice?"

I replied, "Option three: I'm not changing the deal."

"Ok," replied ATSAIC Carrington.

ATSAIC Carrington called ATSAIC Sheehan, who answered, "Hey, how can I assist you?"

ATSAIC Carrington said, "We made our decision. We aren't changing the deal. We take option three."

"I understand," ATSAIC Sheehan said. "I will inform SAIC Stokes. Good luck."

The success of Operation Carder Kaos hinged on my ability to finalize a deal and arrange a meeting with Maksik. Without this, the operation would come to a screeching halt. The risks were considerable; without backing from Headquarters, there was no funding or the required authorization for my international undercover meetings. My next challenge was to figure out how to arrange the purchase.

SAIC Montaña invited me into his office. As I entered, he said, "Please take a seat. I understand you picked option three."

I replied, "Yes, it was the only logical choice."

SAIC Montaña glanced at the desk before looking up and remarked, "I can't say I'm pleased, but it's your case. What's your plan for sending him the money?"

"I'm not sure yet," I said. "I need to talk to him, but once I have the money, I'll send it to him."

SAIC Montaña gasped and choked on his saliva before saying, "You're going to send him all that money? Are you crazy? No, that won't work. You need to send it to him in small amounts. You can send him more if he proves he's trustworthy."

"Sir," I said. "With no disrespect, Maksik has never ripped me off in any of our many deals."

SAIC Montaña interjected, saying, "Yes, but we have never before sent him $75,000."

"I'm not quite following you, sir," I responded. "Are you suggesting that Maksik is waiting to rip me on this deal?"

"You never know," SAIC Montaña replied.

"I guess," I said. "But it doesn't make sense. Anyhow, I'll figure out a payment plan."

"Okay," SAIC Montaña said. "Keep me posted. It is a lot of money."

SAIC Montaña's worries were valid, given the nature of criminals and the budget constraints of the Secret Service. While I disagreed, there was still a slight risk that Maksik might take advantage of me. Hence, I concentrated on negotiating the details of the exchange.

I wrote Maksik, "Hey, I'm ready."

Maksik wrote back, "Hey 😉."

I messaged, "How do you propose we complete the deal?"

Maksik replied, "Send me the money ☺ I send you dumps."

Knowing I couldn't send all the money, I replied, "$75,000 is a lot of money. Can we split it up?"

Maksik paused before writing, “It’s not a lot of money. Honestly, I don’t care about the money. People send me twice that amount all the time.”

This revelation provided insight into Maksik’s world and the scale of his financial transactions. For him, $75,000 was inconsequential, dwarfed by his regular payments, which amounted to hundreds of thousands of dollars.

I had to think fast and then responded, “To me it is a lot of money. ☺”

Maksik then wrote, “Can we use Slim as an escrow? You send him money. I send him dumps. Then he transfers the dumps and the money.”

This didn’t sit well with me. Additionally, I knew ATSAIC Carrington would not want Slimbady as an escrow agent. However, Slimbady was Maksik’s and my common denominator, so his suggestion made a lot of sense. Yet, my gut told me to send the funds directly to Maksik.

I replied, “No. I send you the $$$$.”

Maksik replied, “Ok, do you have a business bank account?”

“I do not,” I wrote back.

Maksik persisted, “Can you open one? To send over WU takes too long.”

To his point, Western Union had become increasingly aware of criminals exploiting its services for money laundering. As a result, Western Union and MoneyGram implemented new policies. These changes made sending international money transfers significantly more challenging, and I wanted to avoid this at all costs.

I replied, “You are right. I will look into opening a bank account.”

Maksik said, “It MUST be a business bank account to send the money.”

I replied, “Okay. Let me get this set up. I need only one or two days.”

Maksik replied, “😁. While you do that, here is the BIN list. See ya.”

Over the next few days, I meticulously sifted through Maksik’s BIN list, carefully selecting the BINS I knew would garner a swift response from my banking contacts. Then, I set up my business bank account. Given the volume of business Maksik and I were about to undertake, it provided suitable cover and ensured less scrutiny. It certainly beat the alternative of using Western Union.

The next step was to negotiate with Maksik. Eventually, we agreed to divide the database into three parts, and I would do the same with the money. Amidst all of this, we discussed meeting in Phuket. There was no outright commitment, but he would consider it if all went well. This instilled confidence in me and reminded me there’s still a chance things will go my way.

But the question remained: Would hope be enough? The ultimatum from Headquarters loomed heavily in my mind, reminding me that the continuation of my operation rested on this high-stakes face-to-face meeting. I was determined to prove those senior leaders wrong who believed that Russians would never meet Americans. The success of my tactics and the operation itself hung in the balance, and I longed to demonstrate that my judgment was correct.

Once the BINS were finally chosen, Maksik swiftly assembled the order. I informed ATSAIC Carrington of the plan and said, “I would send a substantial wire transfer of $25,000 to Maksik.” The atmosphere around us crackled with tension, whispers of doubt swirling in the background.

When I returned from the bank, I logged on to my ICQ account and sent Maksik the essential information. I ensured he had everything needed to receive the funds discreetly. However, this was largely irrelevant, as the receiving bank was in a former Soviet state, where there were no laws against money laundering.

With the money sent, I found myself at a point of no return. Now, all that remained was to wait for Maksik to come online. These moments were filled with tension, swirling doubts, and uncertainties. Were my instincts correct? Was Montaña's cautiousness justified? Would Headquarters' skepticism prove right? It was a torrent of thoughts I tried my best to push aside.

As the days passed, the tension among my supervisors grew palpable. I couldn't deny my restlessness, either. Despite my confidence, there was always that lingering possibility, that sliver of doubt. What if Maksik betrayed me, solely motivated by greed? What if he handed over a pile of counterfeit data? Waiting for his response was unbearable, a tightrope walk between hope and apprehension.

After three days, Maksik finally sent me a new message. My heart raced as I read it: "I've received the money. The dumps are ready. Here's the Dropbox link."

I was delighted to write an offline message back: "Thank you. ☺ I will let you know if I have any problems."

Downloading the file through the link proved to be quite a challenge. However, after considerable effort, I successfully obtained the file. True to his promise, Maksik supplied me with one-third of the database. A quick calculation revealed that I was missing 453 credit card account numbers. Nonetheless, I had secured the foundation of a database: an astounding 54,547 stolen credit card accounts.

Eventually, word trickled in from my banking contacts, confirming the authenticity of the data. However, they did mention that these credit cards were associated with an older database breach. The fact that these accounts were linked to a previous breach didn't concern me. After all, it was anticipated. Now, the question looming before us was how to move forward.

I entered ATSAIC Carrington's office and declared, "Maksik delivered everything as promised, although it was missing a few hundred dumps. Regardless, my contacts verified the data. It's authentic but old, which was expected."

"That's awesome," ATSAIC Carrington replied. "What's next?"

"Well," I began. "That's why I'm here. Look, Maksik honored his end. Screw this one-third nonsense. HQ sent us the money to give to Maksik. If he cheats us, the case is over. If he doesn't cheat us but doesn't meet, the case is over anyway. Either way, the case is over. Plus, Maksik already mentioned Phuket once. Let's send him the remaining $50,000 and move on. It's the only way."

ATSAIC Carrington briefly chewed on a few Tums before responding, "Alright, go ahead."

I sprinted to my computer and logged onto ICQ. I saw the indicator light next to Maksik and thought, "Great, he is online." I messaged, "Привет, как дела ☺. Dumps received.

Maksik replied, "Привет ☺"

I replied, "I'm ready to send the rest. No need to break it into parts."

Maksik commented, "😁 That's great news. Please share details here."

I replied, "Okay. I will take care of this today."

Maksik messaged, "Tell me about Phuket. I understand that the tsunami destroyed everything. Is it safe?"

The message was a pleasant surprise. Maksik asked me about Phuket, rather than me asking him. I quickly replied, "No, Phuket has been rebuilt. I was just there. ☺"

"Oh yeah," Maksik wrote back. "Tell me how it was."

"What can I say ☺," I messaged. "The beaches are nice, the water is warm, the temperature is hot and humid, the beer is cold, and the women are beautiful."

Maksik replied, "😊 That is good, my friend. What do you think about March?"

"March works," I replied. "I stay in Patong Beach. Here are some hotel links. I recommend Baan Thai Resort."

Maksik replied, "Okay ☺, I will look and let you know."

"Perfect. Пока," I messaged.

After signing off from ICQ, I updated leadership on my Phuket strategy, which excluded Sone. I concluded that Sone wasn't instrumental in establishing the relationship; thus, there was no operational benefit. Additionally, the Service was frugal, and I knew reducing costs would be appreciated.

During my conversation with Headquarters, I discovered that Ben Rogers, a classmate from the academy, was part of the team. This news energized me, as I anticipated that Ben would advocate for my cause.

When the briefings concluded, I went to the bank to transfer $50,000 to Maksik's company. It was all done under the guise of a computer parts transaction. After all, we had to maintain the appearance of a legitimate business, even if it was anything but.

After sending the money, I logged onto ICQ and left an offline message for Maksik. However, as before, I had to wait several days for the transaction to be posted and cleared through the necessary protocols. I found it odd that, despite the relaxed approach to anti-money laundering regulations, it was still required to process transactions in accordance with industry standards.

As the conversation shifted to our upcoming trip to Phuket, Maksik grew eager to make the necessary arrangements and messaged, "Привет. ☺"

His message surprised me, but I happily replied, "Привет, как дела?"

Maksik replied, "I'm well. Received money. I will put together final dumps."

"That is good news. Thank you," I replied.

"Also," Maksik continued, "I booked my hotel in Phuket."

Elated, I responded, "Awesome. The one on Patong Beach?"

"No," Maksik answered. "But it is nearby. ☺"

I had done my research on Phuket before his answer. I knew that meant either Laguna Beach or Karon Beach. But Laguna Beach was too far, at least for me, so I quickly ruled it out. This led me to reply, "You staying at Karon Beach?"

There was a noticeable pause before Maksik replied, "😲 How do you know?"

Knowing that Maksik and others who worked online were paranoid, I thought, "Damn, he might think I hacked his computer." I needed to think quickly and replied, "I don't. 😀 But you mentioned nearby. The only place is Karon Beach."

That wild guess and his reaction provided me with invaluable intelligence. Now, I only needed to find his hotel. Time flew by; before I knew it, it was March 2006. To my delight, ATSAIC Carrington was the supervisor for this trip. Carrington's dedication was unwavering, and he wouldn't let a first-class ticket alter the plan.

Chapter 29

Finally—a Russian Carder!

As I departed San Diego, Rachel and I found ourselves locked in an increasingly bitter cycle of arguments. Each fight drove us further apart, eroding the love I once had for her. The foundation of our relationship was shaky from the outset, as two individuals from entirely different worlds attempted to build something together.

If only I had possessed the courage to end it. Instead, I clung on, hoping against hope that she would be the one to break things off, freeing me from the responsibility of making that decision myself. Instead of doing the right thing, I opted for an easier path and ignored it.

Upon arriving at the beach resort, I decided to unwind. I put the problems with Rachel behind me, and Maksik wasn't arriving until the following day—assuming he was true to his word, and he didn't change his mind. There was one thing that bothered me: Maksik hadn't sent me the final data dump.

He still owed me at least 110,000 credit cards. ATSAIC Carrington, ever the nervous soul, was growing impatient, and I had no news to offer him. If the pressure couldn't be more intense, ATSAIC Sheehan issued another veiled warning: "If Maksik doesn't show, the entire case would be considered a failure."

Seeking solace from the mounting stress, I headed to the beach, carving a cold Singha beer. Over my previous trips to Phuket, I had developed a friendly rapport with several of the ladies, specifically Napat, who took care of the beachgoers. Stepping onto the sandy shores, before I even noticed Napat, she called out to me. Napat enthusiastically directed me toward a lounge chair and asked, "What can I get you?"

I replied, "A cold Singha, please."

"Okay," she cheerfully replied.

As I settled into my chair, a sense of relaxation washed over me. The soothing sound of the waves, the warm embrace of the sun, and the infectious friendliness of the people detached me from the burdens of life. The sun hadn't set, but the lure of tonight and the promise to meet Dok Mai consumed my thoughts.

She was a complex woman, but I pushed these thoughts aside, knowing that when we were together, nothing else mattered. I anticipated what the evening had in store, lost in thought. I finished my third Singha as the sun kissed the horizon, punctuating the end of the day and beginning of the night. I thanked Napat and said, "I'll be back tomorrow. Save me a spot."

Napat replied, "I always do."

As I stepped inside my room, I couldn't resist checking ICQ. I hoped to find a message from Maksik, but none were waiting for me. I determined the absence of communication meant one thing—Maksik was en route. It made sense, but wasn't scientific, and ignored any other reason. I remained optimistic and headed out for the evening.

My first destination after dinner was my favorite club where I knew Dok Mai would be waiting for me. Thoughts of her lingered in mine from our last encounter just over a

 DOI: 10.1201/9781003680390-29

month ago. I was eager to reconnect. As I stepped over the threshold, my gaze immediately fell upon Dok Mai. The sight of her vibrant face, illuminated by the glow of the bar, filled me with delight. Without hesitation, she hurried to me. Our embrace lasted longer than expected; two acquaintances were finally reunited after a prolonged absence.

Our conversation was brief, stripped of unnecessary formalities, and ended with me saying, "There are better places where we can drink and chat."

Dok Mai eagerly accepted and said, "Wait me here."

Dok Mai then disappeared into the back room. When she emerged from the back room, I couldn't help but stare at her beauty. Dok Mai was ready for a night out on the town and looked the part. Together we ventured onto Bangla Road, found a place to play pool, drank, chatted, and when we were ready, headed to the discotic.

It wasn't until five in the morning that we returned to my resort. Exhausted from drinking and dancing, we collapsed onto the bed and fell asleep in each other's embrace. The morning was interrupted by the ringing of my phone; it was ATSAIC Carrington. I answered, "Good morning, sir."

"You sound tired," ATSAIC Carrington replied.

I laughed and said, "It was a long night."

ATSAIC Carrington understood and said, "Any news?"

"No," I replied. "Not yet. I bet that later this afternoon, I will have something."

Sleep still clouded my mind, and Dok Mai was still sleeping. I figured before I start the day, I needed some coffee. I snuck out and took the two-minute walk to Starbucks. With a cup of coffee in hand, I could already feel a renewed sense of energy.

I wasted no time in firing up my computer, determined to see if my intuition was correct. I searched flights departing from Kyiv to Phuket and found there were only limited options. Most of these options left only one conclusion—Maksik would arrive late in the afternoon.

To kill time, Dok Mai embarked on a local gastronomic adventure, visiting a place I would never have dared to venture on my own. With her guidance, I likely enjoyed one of the more authentic and local meals while in Phuket. Once we finished, we bid our goodbyes, promising to stay in touch.

Feeling somewhat adrift, unsure of where to go or what to do next, I returned to my room. I felt the pull to sit beside my computer and pray for some sign of life from Maksik. Everyone was on edge, nerves frayed. Minutes turned to hours, stretching out like an eternity.

I was fixated on the indicator next to his name. Sadly, it still glowed red. I couldn't help but feel that at any given moment, that indicator would turn green, signaling the long-awaited arrival. Around seven in the evening, after what felt like an eternity, I noticed the indicator flashed from red to green. I resisted writing anything; I didn't want to seem desperate. Instead, I played it cool and waited for him.

While I waited, I messaged SA Mason, "Maksik online. Standby."

SA Mason messaged, "Copy."

Once I set my phone down, the computer came to life. "Kuku." It was a message from Maksik. I opened the message, and it read: "I'm in Thailand."

The relief washed over me like a wave; he had shown up. I wrote back, "☺ Welcome to Thailand."

Maksik replied, "Thanks. What are you doing?"

I responded, "Having a Singha near the beach."

Maksik, with a hint of apology, messaged, "Sorry for the delay. Long story. Meet in two hours?"

Without hesitation, I fired back, determined to solidify our plans, "Yes, ☺ Tell me where."

Maksik replied promptly, "La Luna Bistro. Near my hotel on Karon Beach."

I swiftly replied, "See you at eight."

I closed the laptop lid and wrote SA Mason, "Meeting at 8. La Luna Bistro in Karon Beach."

SA Mason responded, "We'll be ready."

I figured a Tuk-Tuk ride would take around twenty minutes. With that in mind, I headed to the main road. I thought I should arrive early, sit at the bar, and sip on a cold Singha. All the while, surveying the bar's layout.

Once I arrived, I looked around. It was an open-air bar catering primarily to tourists. There were plenty of empty spaces, definitely not overflowing like the bars on Patong Beach. What was pleasant: the absence of blaring music. I still had no clue how well Maksik spoke English, if at all.

I had shared the details of my clothing via ICQ, but Maksik said nothing. Not knowing what he looked like, I made my way to the bar. As I entered, I suddenly heard a voice calling out, "Surfrider?" I turned my head, and there was Maksik, trying fervently to catch my attention.

The first thought that flashed across my mind was, "I had proven that SAIC Stokes, the Segvec loyalists, and many others were wrong. Russians do meet Americans." This meeting would prove to be the proverbial slap across their collective faces. I had navigated the minefield, dodged their bullets, and now would be sitting across from the most prolific vendor of stolen data.

I acknowledged him with a quick wave, closed the distance between us, and once near enough, I extended my hand, saying, "Maksik, nice to meet you. My name is Rich."

Maksik firmly clasped my hand and replied, "Pleasure to meet you, I'm Maksik, and this is my girlfriend, Svetlana."

Wanting to build rapport and establish trust, instead of engaging in business, I said, "How was the flight?"

Maksik put in head in head and looked at me, saying, "My friend, it was long. You can't believe my problems. Almost Svetlana and I did not come to Phuket."

"Oh no," I responded. "Why?"

"You know Kaiser," Maksik said.

I replied, "Yes, of course."

"Well," Maksik began to explain. "Svetlana and I travel from my home to Kyiv the day before. When we arrive, we go shopping. Local store. Who do I run into?"

Taking a guess, I said, "Kaiser."

"Yes," Maksik exclaimed. "There he stood with the girl I was interested in. The one I want. I couldn't believe him. What a betrayal."

"That's messed up," I replied.

"Kaiser seeing me with big grin starts talking this and that," Maksik continued. "And all, in front of Svetlana. Now we in big fight. She yelling at me and I say, 'Not me.' You can't believe it."

"That sounds like a crazy story," I replied.

Maksik, reaching toward me, says, "You know, I almost invited Kaiser to come with me. Now I'm glad I'm not. He is no longer a friend of mine."

"I'm sorry to hear that," I responded. "I don't like friends who backstab."

Maksik nodded his head, saying, "You are right, my friend. But that only one problem. At immigration we need to wait hours for visa. Missed our flight to Phuket. We must take next one."

"Wow," I exclaimed. "Such bad luck. Look, let me buy you a beer."

"That would be nice," Maksik said. "What do you recommend?"

"The local beer Singha," I replied.

Maksik, lifting his thumb and forefinger, responded, "We take two. But it get worse."

Laughing, I said, "How can it get worse. You miss your flight, and your friend is stealing your girl."

Maksik and Svetlana grabbed their beers, raised their glasses, and proclaimed, "Nice to meet you."

I replied, "Nice to meet you."

"Okay, you ready?" Maksik confides. "I pack $3,000 in luggage. When I arrive in room I open luggage. $3,000 nowhere to be found. It gone. Someone steals it."

"Wait," I said, shaking my head. "You packed in your checked luggage $3,000."

Maksik shrugged his shoulders, saying, "Yes. I thought, who gonna steal it?"

I laughed, saying, "Any number of baggage handlers."

Maksik nodded and replied, "Yes, it seems so."

All in all, Maksik's tales left me both captivated and disappointed. I was disappointed because I missed a chance to meet Maksik and Kaiser. The chances now that Maksik will ever extend another invitation to Kaiser are near zero. In those first moments, a different picture of Maksik began to form in my mind.

I had always assumed he was well-versed in the ways of crime, an individual who knew the rules and operated fearlessly. But, to my surprise, Maksik turned out to be the exact opposite. He appeared to be new to the world of criminality, lacking experience or worldly knowledge. He seemed sheltered and naive, a far cry from the hardened criminal I had envisioned.

It became clear to me that perhaps Maksik's motivation for inviting Svetlana and Kaiser to Thailand wasn't to further any nefarious ends, but to have someone to travel with. He required the company of others and feared traveling alone. I knew now if no one were available, Maksik would stay home rather than venture out by himself.

Over Maksik's shoulder, an opportunity presented itself. A local vendor offered a chance to pose with a large iguana. It felt like the perfect moment to capture a memorable snapshot of Maksik, me, and this fascinating creature. I motioned for the vendor to approach and said, "Hand him the Iguana and take our photo."

The vendor readily agreed and gently placed the iguana on Maksik's shoulder. He then took his camera and snapped a few Polaroids, saying, "Say cheese."

He then handed us two Polaroids, but before I could react, Maksik swiftly grabbed them and handed the vendor ten dollars. Taken aback by his abruptness, I decided not to press the issue. Maksik turned toward me and said, "I don't like photographs of me."

Next, he looked toward the street and pointed at the Thai police officers, stating, "Cops make me nervous."

I couldn't resist and asked, "What's the issue?"

Maksik shook his head and said, "I don't like them."

"I understand," I replied. "But those cops are tourist police. They're here to protect you from the people who want to harm us. I would not worry about those cops."

I could see Maksik start to think about it, and he began to shake his head, confirming that I was correct. Nonetheless, he confirmed, "Still, I don't like cops."

Laughing, "I get you, man. Fuck 'em."

Maksik laughed and downed the last sip of his beer before saying, "We are tired from the journey. I must work in the morning, but what do you think about meeting in the afternoon?"

"Of course," I exclaimed. "When you're ready, hit me up on ICQ. I am nearby, only a fifteen-minute Tuk-Tuk ride."

As soon as Maksik and Svetlana left, I wasted no time in reaching for my cell phone. With a sense of urgency, I quickly messaged ATSAIC Carrington, "Maksik exhausted. Headed back to hotel. Follow them. Op over tonight."

Once work was finished, I reviewed my messages and noted that there was a message from Dok Mai. She wanted to meet. The exhilaration from my encounter with Maksik, combined with Dok Mai's note, only fueled my determination. Without hesitation, I replied, "Let's meet at the disco."

Chapter 30

Maksik wants to explore Phuket

The following day, I woke up lethargic from another long evening with Dok Mai. I messaged ATSAIC Carrington telling him to meet me at Starbucks. As we sat down to discuss the previous night, I learned that, yes, the team had tailed Maksik and Svetlana. They led the team to their hotel, and once inside, the team contacted the hotel's management. Management provided us with all of Maksik's vital information.

With this data in hand, the local police cross-checked it against the immigration records. The result: they discovered Maksik's real world identity. The team rejoiced as this proved to be a colossal achievement. With this triumph, I focused on setting up today's meetings, and since he was working, I messaged, "Good morning. You asked me to remind you about the last batch of credit cards. I still have not received. About today, let me know when you are ready."

Maksik replied, "Hey. Okay, I will get it and send it. Give me two hours."

About an hour later, my ICQ alerted me to a message from Maksik, "Here is link. We come to Patong Beach."

"Okay," I replied. "There is a bar next to my hotel. Meet me here."

Immediately, I clicked on the link, eager to start downloading the data. While the data was being downloaded, I messaged ATSAIC Carrington, "Meeting in 30 minutes at the bar near my hotel."

Once the data was successfully downloaded, I made my way to the bar. Settling in, I patiently awaited Maksik's arrival, ordering a Singha beer. As I sat at the bar, opposite me was SA Mason. I did everything in my power to ignore him and instead kept my gaze on the main road. As I sipped my Singha, I noticed a Tuk-Tuk pulled up. Then, two unmistakable figures emerged, Maksik and Svetlana.

I waved, and once Maksik saw me, he headed over and took a seat next to me. Once he sat down, I asked, "Can I get you a beer?"

"Yes," Maksik said. "We will have Singha. It is very tasty."

I caught the bartender's attention and ordered another round. Once Maksik and Svetlana had their Singha beers, I said, "The link worked. Thank you."

Maksik's face lit up with satisfaction, and he replied, "I was told there were 110,000 pieces, but please double-check it. If you have issues, let me know."

"Okay," I replied, raising my glass in a toast to Maksik. "Appreciate it, and I assure you, if there is a problem, I'll let you know."

While we continued our conversation, a burning question had been gnawing at me, and it involved Script. During his prime, he led a popular criminal forum named CarderPlanet. Moreover, the extent of his criminal operation became apparent during Operation Firewall. Post this operation, the U.S. Postal Inspection Service collaborated with the local police and they executed a search warrant at Script's residence.

DOI: 10.1201/9781003680390-30

According to "word on the street" Script anticipated that one day, the police might raid his apartment. As a result, Script fortified his apartment. When the day came, they beat on his door, demanding that Script open it, but undeterred, Script "cooked" the evidence all the while yelling, "You're on my payroll."

Eventually, the police gained entry, apprehending Script and seizing any potential evidence. However, at this pivotal point, a dark cloud appears, and the actions of those involved are shrouded in a cloud of uncertainty.

The U.S. government had delivered a legal document known as a Mutual Legal Assistance Treaty (MLAT) to the Ukrainian government, requesting that they collaborate and share the evidence seized from Script. However, months passed without an official response, prompting the Secret Service to send me to Ukraine to liaise with them.

During this time I met with the two prosecutors, one of whom was clutching the MLAT. He looked at me and said, "We have documents. Your MLAT is here. But we have nothing more to provide right now."

I replied, "Do you have a timeline? Or projections when you can share?"

"No," the prosecutor said. "The case is still in court along with the evidence."

I left Ukraine with no more or no less information than I had before I started the conversation. More importantly, everything grew chillingly quiet. Then, without warning, news arrived that shattered the silence. The case against Script was dismissed. He was a free man, vindicated by the system that had once accused him.

Now I sat next to Maksik, an individual who knew Script and may shed some light on the topic. And so, I leaned in and asked Maksik with a tone of curiosity, "Do you know what happened to Script?"

Maksik turned toward me and said, "Yes, I know what happened."

I exclaimed, "Really? You know."

"Yes," Maksik said. "Script paid the judge, two members of parliament, and the prosecutor."

"Hmmm," I said. "How much did that cost him?"

"I'm not sure of total," Maksik explained. "But if I understand, over one million dollars."

I laughed and said, "And what does that get you?"

"Well," Maksik responded. "Those members of parliament testified Script was an honest man. As for prosecutors, they lose the evidence. With deck stacked in his favor, judge rule in favor of Script, granting him his freedom."

I couldn't help but interrupt, my disbelief getting the better of me. "Wait a minute," I said, my voice filled with skepticism. "Are you telling me that one million dollars was enough to make the prosecutors just 'misplace' the evidence?"

Maksik shrugged nonchalantly, a wry smile playing at the corners of his mouth. "Yes, this is how it work in Ukraine."

"I see," I said. "And what happened to it?"

"If I hear correct," Maksik confided. "It just go away. Nobody knows where except for Script himself, of course. With no evidence what else can judge do, he walk away a free man."

As I absorbed the implications of Maksik's tale, I played my part, nodding my head in feigned agreement and said, "Fuck the police!"

Maksik's face lit up and reiterated, "Yes fuck the police!" He shifted his focus and pointed to a nearby vendor, "What do you think of hat?"

I looked at the vendor's hat and replied, "I don't know. What do you like?"

Maksik, contemplating his choices, said, "I like hat with white band and then the one with blue band."

I had no real knowledge of Maksik's hat preferences, but I pointed him in the direction of a hat with a dark blue band and the word "Thailand" written on it and said, "I like that one."

"Okay," Maksik said. "I buy. But what you think? Is it time? Can we go to Bangla Road? I think it is time for party."

I glanced at my watch and said, "It is still early, but do you play pool?"

Maksik's eyes widened as he responded, saying, "Yes, I like. Shall we go?"

That night, filled with newfound camaraderie, Maksik, Svetlana, and I ventured to the vibrant bar located on Bangla Road. Promising to show Maksik the best spots, we immersed ourselves in the atmosphere and engaged in friendly competition, playing pool and continuing to build our connection.

Between shots, Svetlana captured moments in photographs, much to Maksik's annoyance. Each time the camera clicked, he would turn to me with a resigned expression and mutter, "I don't like when she take picture, but what can I do?"

I understood his concern but reassured him, "Let her be. They are memories and only she has them."

"You are right," Maksik replied, laughing. "Hey, can you help? I'm want a blonde Thai girl for Svetlana and myself. Do you know, can we find such a girl?"

The question caught me off guard, I humorously said, "Blondes are a bit of a rarity around here. But I know a place. Follow me."

As a matter of convenience I chose the dance bar at the back of the pool hall. As we entered, I carefully selected a table one row back from the stage. Before long, a Thai girl appeared on stage, and as luck had it, she was precisely what Maksik wanted. Her blonde hair sparkled in the lights, as her uniqueness set her apart, attracting the attention of others.

I took the opportunity and explained, "Okay, you have two options. One is you can pay the bar fine, typically four hundred Thai Baht."

Maksik interrupted, saying, "Bar fine? What is that?"

I continued saying, "The bar fine is paid to the bar. Each girl is here to attract men. To have them leave early, you must compensate the bar. Once you pay, you leave with the girl and enjoy their company. If you want sex, you can it. If she likes you no problem, but you may also have to negotiate it. You never know with them."

Maksik, now curious, asked, "And she stay all night?"

"Yes," I responded. "Unless you don't want to, then say leave."

Maksik, shaking his head, said, "What is option two?"

"Ah," I said. "Option two: you negotiate what you want, pay up front, and leave."

"I like this option better," Maksik said. "I don't want to party. Besides, Svetlana still thinking. How much you think it cost?"

Shrugging my shoulders, I said, "Maybe four thousand Baht. But she is a rarity, maybe more."

Maksik turned toward Svetlana and started speaking with her about the proposition. They spoke in Ukrainian, so I was unsure if she was getting cold feet or had begun to think about it. I knew once the chance was in front of you, the idea could lose its luster. Maksik turned to me and said, "Can you talk to her? Ask her how much. Please be quick before Svetlana changes her mind."

"No problem," I replied.

I spoke with her for about five minutes before returning to Maksik, saying, "Five thousand."

Maksik nodded and said, "Do think she is worth it?"

"I have no clue, but she is blonde," I laughed.

Maksik teetered on the edge of a decision, his mind caught in a whirlwind of uncertainty. Svetlana encouraged him to take the leap, but there was an unmistakable quality about Maksik's character—an inclination toward excessive caution.

As Maksik contemplated, the blonde Thai girl grew impatient. When no offer materialized, she went to another table. I understood it was now or never, so I leaned in toward Maksik and said, "Hey, if you don't make a decision quickly, your opportunity will slip through your fingers."

Maksik sat there, lost in thought, deliberating his next move. He reached for his phone, perhaps intending to capture the moment for posterity, but then hesitated and put it down. At that moment, I could see the battle within Maksik's eyes. The tension in the air was palpable, leaving me on the edge of my seat, eagerly awaiting his next move.

But I was intrigued by how he handled his phone, which prompted me to ask, "Did you want to take a photo?"

Maksik sheepishly replied, "Yes, but they have a sign. No photographs."

"Wait," as I looked at the sign and continued, "That sign right there?"

Maksik nodded and verbally confirmed, "Yes."

"Let me get this straight," shaking my head, "You hack companies, steal shit tons of credit card account numbers, sell them to people all over the world, but it is that sign, saying no photos, that is stopping you from taking a photograph. Now, I might be wrong, but I'm pretty sure there is a sign somewhere that says DON'T STEAL."

Maksik decided to take a photo and laughed while saying, "You're right."

Regrettably, Maksik's opportunity slipped away as the blonde Thai girl found a match. I couldn't help but wonder what was holding Maksik back. Was it his moral dilemma? Perhaps it was the money, though I knew he had more than enough of it. It had to be the moral struggle that troubled him.

The sign that read "no photographs" seemed to momentarily weigh heavily on Maksik's conscience. I could only imagine the inner turmoil he experienced, questioning whether he could justify paying for sex. Coincidentally, as Maksik finally declared that he would take the blonde Thai girl home, Svetlana pulled away, clearly upset and surprised by his decision. This prompted me to jokingly quip to Maksik, "This is why you don't bring sand to the beach."

Maksik laughed, but Svetlana had had enough. Understanding that Svetlana was unhappy, Maksik said, "I'm sorry. We need to leave. I contact you tomorrow."

Once Maksik and Svetlana left, I messaged the team, "Maksik headed back to hotel."

Next, I messaged Dok Mai, but she didn't respond. I could only assume she must be occupied with work. Being undeterred, rather than heading in for the evening, I sought entertainment elsewhere. After all, this was Phuket.

As I wandered the streets, I stumbled upon a quaint little bar where a waitress took a particular interest in me. We engaged in conversation for a while, but I reasoned that it was pointless to chat while she served drinks to other patrons. This prompted me to ask, "Do you have to work all night? If not, we can have some drinks and chat."

"No," she explained. "My shift ends in fifteen minutes. Once I finish, I meet you outside."

I was surprised by her willingness to hang out and replied, "I will be waiting."

True to her word, the waitress emerged like clockwork, dressed in attire that was not meant for work but rather for a night out on the town. Taking my hand, she asked confidently, "Where shall we go?"

I looked at her and said, "I have a few places in mind."

The next morning, I woke up to a disheartening message from Maksik, which read, "Sorry, my friend. I don't feel well. Tomorrow, can you book a tour? Leave details here."

I wondered how badly his fight with Svetlana had turned out; nonetheless, I agreed to meet ATSAIC Carrington at our usual spot, Starbucks. There, at a table, sat ATSAIC Carrington. Giving him a nod to acknowledge his presence, I made a priority of getting a cup of coffee. Once I had my coffee in hand, I strategically chose a seat near him.

During our conversation, I provided ATSAIC Carrington with a thorough briefing. I shared details about the recent discussions regarding Script, the peculiar request to assist in selecting a hat, and my assessment of his personality. It was genuinely fascinating, delving into a side of the world that most never get to witness. I wasn't an outsider. I was gaining valuable insights from their perspective. The relentless stream of misinformation was no longer an obstacle.

As our conversation neared its end, I informed ATSAIC Carrington that Maksik intended to stay in for the day. He wasn't feeling well, but he wanted to take a tour the following day. I would work on this and then pass the details to everyone.

With no plans left for Maksik, I asked Dok Mai if she would be willing to meet me at the beach and spend the day together. My wait wasn't long for her reply. I was delighted to hear Dok Mai was happy to meet with me. Together, we indulged in a day of blissful relaxation on the sandy shores.

The next morning, determined to make the most of my time, I headed to the lobby and swiftly arranged for an island tour. The itinerary included a visit to the famous James Bond Island, among other attractions. As luck would have it, Maksik was feeling better, and I provided him with the necessary details.

Before embarking on the tour, I bid a fond farewell to Dok Mai, briefed the team on my plan, and without a second to spare, ran to the main road, hailed a Tuk-Tuk, and set off for Phuket Port, determined to make it in time for Phuket City Port. Upon arriving at the port, I swiftly located Maksik and Svetlana, eager to embark on our adventure.

Together, we made our way to the tour company, excitement building with each step. As we strolled across the sandy beach, the tour company snapped a few photos, capturing brief moments of the beginning of our journey. Neither Maksik nor I paid much attention to it; our focus was solely on the thrilling day ahead.

Soon, we boarded the boat, and that's when everything changed. The immense crowd of tourists squeezed onto the vessel overwhelmed me. Sensing my discomfort, I suggested to Maksik that we rent a private boat instead, ensuring a more intimate experience. However, he brushed it off, his frugality shining through once again. I decided to go along with it, determined to make the most of the day.

As our boat tore off toward our first destination, we joined the throng of other tour boats. It was an unspoken race to be the first boat to reach the same destination. The sight of them racing against each other, speedboats carving through the waves, was both captivating and chaotic.

Typically, I paid little attention to the surrounding world, focused on the mission, but as our boat slowed down, another boat paced us. It was the Secret Service surveillance team. They had secured a private boat. Maksik, absorbed in Svetlana's care, remained oblivious. My assumption was they paced us to get a quick photo. But instead of snapping a surveillance photo, one of the agents pumped his fist in the air and yelled at our boat, "Hell yeah, let's go!"

Internally, I cringed at the agent's display of enthusiasm, and a disapproving shake of my head betrayed my inward disapproval. Yet, I resisted the urge to react. Internally, I fumed, the surveillance team's primary objective was to blend in. Luckily, Maksik remained blissfully unaware of the situation, or at least he didn't show any signs of reaction.

At our next destination, an island resort, we were instructed that this was the place where everyone would have lunch. Because I was aware of our surveillance team, I looked out for them, and as such, I quickly found them when we arrived. It was a tactical error; upon spotting them, I noted that one agent chose to wear some questionable fashion—a shirt boldly emblazoned with the letters "F.B.I."

I had told everyone Maksik isn't comfortable with the police. However, the true meaning of these letters had no connection to the Federal Bureau of Investigation. Instead, it stood for "Female Body Inspector." Regardless, the choice was a clear display of a lack of discretion. I could only take a deep breath and shake my head.

The saga of our journey continued, spiraling into further complications. Our next destination was a small sand bar consisting only of a scattering of chairs and a bar. We were to spend the next two hours there. As I sat in a chair, I watched as the team's boat pulled onshore. I watched as each agent disembarked to join the crowd. But what caught my eye was the agent who sported the F.B.I. shirt.

Clearly, there was a conversation between ATSAIC Carrington and the agent about his choice in clothing. Now, instead of proudly wearing the shirt, he hastily turned it inside out, displaying the letters I.B.F. I could only dip my head into my hand and scream internally. Thankfully and to my benefit, Maksik and Svetlana remained oblivious to it all.

They never uttered a word, and I reassured myself that they probably had no clue about the subtle complexities unfolding around us. After we docked at the port, Maksik, Svetlana, and I shared a Tuk-Tuk back to our respective hotels. We agreed to connect later via ICQ. As I departed for Patong Beach, I planned to send a message with an update. Instead, there was one waiting for me, which read: "Meeting at Carrington's hotel."

I replied, "Be there in 30."

Once I arrived in Patong Beach, I wasted no time and made a beeline for ATSAIC Carrington's room. As I stepped inside, I was greeted by the entire surveillance team. My eyes were immediately drawn to the bed, where I noticed an assortment of cheap souvenirs.

I remarked, "You all wanted some souvenirs, I see."

SA Mason picked one up and handed it to me, "Nope. It is the best photo of Maksik and you. And it was taken by the tour company. Once we landed, we saw the table and bought them all. That one is for you."

The plain white ashtray was a photograph of Maksik and me strolling along the shoreline. It was the photo taken by the tour company's photographer that we paid no attention to at the start of the day. This photo turned out to be the most valuable photo of the entire operation. I was elated, but unfortunately, my elation was short-lived.

ATSAIC Carrington jumped in and said, "I spoke with ATSAIC Sheehan, and they consider the mission a resounding success. You met Maksik, developed rapport, but as they put it, there is little more to gain, so it's time to depart."

I scratched my head and bit down hard before saying, "We agreed to spend the entire time with Maksik in Phuket. That was the plan. Everyone agreed on that. I told Maksik I would be here for the entire time. Now you expect me to go to him and say, 'Hey buddy, it was great meeting you, but I'm leaving early?' I should be asking him, 'How many more days are you staying?'"

ATSAIC Carrington listened but replied, "I understand your concerns, but you'll have to rebook your flight. We're leaving tomorrow."

"I can't," I replied in disgust. "Headquarters may have cut this trip short, but as we discussed, I start my annual leave in two days, and it starts here."

ATSAIC Carrington, now rubbing his forehead, thought about it and said, "That's right. I forgot about it. Okay, but you must stay away from Karon Beach and book a different hotel."

"Of course," I flippantly replied. "I'll find another hotel."

Once again, Headquarters, sitting in their offices thousands of miles away, did everything to jeopardize my undercover operation. On one hand, they feign concern for my safety, but on the other, they are willing to throw it away in an instant. It was an absurd and perilous position to be in—pretending to be a criminal, all the while being expected to act like the most responsible and reasonable criminal in existence.

When I logged on to my computer, I was thrilled to find an offline message from Maksik inviting me to a charming Russian restaurant nestled near his hotel in Karon Beach. Considering it was my last night, I eagerly accepted the invitation and relayed the details to the team.

As I prepared to meet Maksik, my mind couldn't help but wander to a recurring theme of cutting my operations short. Instead of succumbing to despair, I resolved to find a way to make it work. It was my last night in Phuket, and I needed to be at the top of my game. As I entered the restaurant, I caught sight of Maksik and a radiant Svetlana already seated at a table. With a composed demeanor, I patiently waited for the customary exchange of pleasantries to conclude before delivering the news to Maksik.

It hurt me to say it, but I found the moment and said, "I need to leave tomorrow. I booked a flight for the morning."

Maksik cringed and replied, "No, please stay. Do not go."

A promising new friendship was on the horizon, yet unfortunate circumstances forced me to respond, "Sorry, my friend, I wish I could stay longer, but there are things I need to attend to back in San Diego."

Maksik reluctantly accepted the situation, his disappointment evident, and replied, "I wish you to stay. Once you depart, I know Svetlana and I not leave this hotel. I'll be bored beyond belief. We were having such a great time. Now, it'll be boring."

I did my best to uplift Maksik's spirits, but I knew deep down that true adventure requires a bold and audacious leader. Neither Maksik nor Svetlana possessed that fearless spirit. As dinner came to an end, we bid our farewells, and I couldn't help but say, "I look forward to our next adventure."

Maksik reciprocated the sentiment, but inwardly, I was consumed by a profound sense of melancholy. Once again, leadership failed to comprehend that those who lack excitement and charisma are often never invited back to hang with the cool kids. I feared that this could be my last invitation to the party.

The following morning, I checked out of my resort, walked down the street, and checked into the hotel next door. It was the only hotel that ATSAIC Carrington would allow me to stay at, as the brand name was recognizable to Americans.

I planned to spend the entire week with Dok Mai, taking my mind as far away as I could from the ineptitude of my managers. My disheartened soul had no desire to contemplate the unfortunate state of the operation further. I would kick the can for one week, but once I returned to San Diego, I had my next move figured out.

Chapter 31

Dumps and PINs anyone?

Upon arriving in San Diego, the relief from my holiday quickly faded. The burden of pending paperwork hung over me, threatening to engulf me in a tide of administrative duties. The pressure from the top to glean every ounce of intelligence from the database was overwhelming. While some mid-level supervisors extended their support, it was minimal in nature. AD Rookwood was the real ally, the one who held the most sway.

So far, all my previous operations have been micromanaged from a distance. The most frustrating aspects of the decisions included hasty judgments, a lack of foresight, and a cutback on operational days. Every part of me urged me to accept AD Rookwood's offer and "to reach out if I needed anything." However, the protocol required me to adhere to the chain of command.

I considered the repercussions of directly contacting AD Rookwood to voice my complaint. While it might resolve an immediate problem, it could create significant long-term disruptions to my operation. Still, the temptation continued to tug at me incessantly.

Adding to my frustrations, I spoke with SA Rogers shortly after returning home, who said, "Rich, do you know what happened last night?"

I replied, "No clue."

"SAIC Stokes walked the halls congratulating everyone on a job well done," SA Rogers explained. "Even the operation was his brainchild."

I replied, "Crazy as it sounds, but it doesn't surprise me."

"Yeah," SA Rogers continued. "And his boy, ATSAIC Sheehan, took the team out for celebratory drinks. Your name was never mentioned. It was CID this and CID that, talking about how great we are at CID."

I laughed, saying, "Well, I hope you got a few beers from it."

The Secret Service was filled with surrogate mothers eager to claim credit for my successes. Unsurprisingly, few reached out to express thanks, congratulations, and no one ever sent a simple apology. I tuned out the distractions, remained determined, and focused solely on advancing the case.

One of the online Carders I noted was Akihikatobe, or Tobe. Sone mentioned that during his heydays, he had shipped numerous stolen PlayStation 3 consoles to Tobe in the Philippines via DHL. I spoke with Tobe several times, but his sporadic online activity made me worry.

Since Tobe was mostly inactive online, I thought, "Maybe he was arrested." Therefore, I chose to promote international relations and share my investigative leads with the local police in the Philippines. After sharing, I patiently waited for an update.

Meanwhile, I continued working with Slimbady, Vincent, Maksik, Leon, and SunCredit, and as I worked, my network expanded. I met Delpiero, Kaisersose, Fidel, Zoomer, and Danny. The most exciting development was my work with Leon.

Leon messaged me, saying, "What up, Brat?"

DOI: 10.1201/9781003680390-31

I replied, "Leon, long time no talk. 😜 How are you?"

Leon responded, "Good. I talked to P0l1c3D0g. He may be out soon."

This surprised me because Leon was in Ukraine, and Diplomaticos was in a Belarusian prison. Leon couldn't go to Belarus, so I asked, "How did you talk to him?"

"A friend," Leon said. "They sneaked him a cell phone. ☺ He can talk on ICQ. His name is Diplomaticos."

I replied, "That is good news. ☺"

"My friend," Leon said. "He waits for you. ☺ His new ICQ number is 123-456-789"

After Leon provided me with the ICQ details, I sent him a friend request. Soon after, my request was accepted, and he responded, "Privet, Brat. It has been a long time. ☺"

I replied, "Privet. Kak dela?"

Since Sone was always generous, Diplomaticos quickly got to the point. "Sone, I have a favor to ask."

I responded, "What do you need?"

Diplomaticos replied, "Can you get Pirelli calendars?"

I wondered, "What does he want with Pirelli calendars?" Still, I replied, "I don't know what to get. Send me the links."

"Thank you, bro," Diplomaticos explained. "These are collector items from the '60s. Some are rare and expensive, but I will get you links."

Right away, I thought, "Great! I can already envision how this conversation will go with ATSAIC Carrington." I had no trouble sending the calendars, but I knew the real challenge would be getting them approved by leadership. Although I could play the bad guy, the government forms required a "tit for tat" explanation. Nothing was for free.

This meant every gift I sent needed to be exchanged for some type of contraband. Usually, I requested stolen credit card data. The data quality didn't matter to me. All that mattered was answering the question, "What did I buy for an August 1961 Pirelli calendar?"

What couldn't be recorded but was more valuable than contraband was the intelligence. Each time I sent a calendar to Diplomaticos, Leon instructed me to send it to someone in Kyiv. Over time it was clear that someone was Leon's real-world identity, the man behind the alias.

With Diplomaticos in prison, Leon struggled to make ends meet. His data was stale. If I had been a "real" Carder, I wouldn't have given him the time of day. However, he was connected to Diplomaticos, the organizer of DumpsMarket, and that connection kept Leon relevant.

Building on the intranational collaboration theme, I contacted an investigator in Belarus. This investigator provided me with an opportunity to uncover the truth. Many believed that cell phones were inaccessible to inmates in Belarusian prisons. Thus, I emailed a straightforward question: "Is it possible for Diplomaticos or others like him to possess a cell phone in prison?"

A few days later, I received my response, which was filled with unwavering certainty: "NO! This is impossible. No inmate possesses cell phones in Belarusian prisons."

It was a definitive statement, seemingly at odds with what I knew. Moreover, since I was working undercover and didn't know the Belarusian investigator, I refrained from providing them with evidence or challenging their claims. If they asserted that Diplomaticos didn't have a cell phone, then so be it—Diplomaticos didn't have a cell phone.

With rumors about Diplomaticos' release circulating, I focused on meeting another Russian-speaking Carder. If I met one, why not meet two? It was another opportunity to demonstrate that leadership's assertion that "Russians don't meet" was erroneous.

My concern was timing: how long would it take? His release could be days or months away, and then there was the question of his ability to meet. In the meantime, I would continue sending him almost anything he asked for, eagerly anticipating the day Diplomaticos would be free.

Until then, I concentrated on strengthening my relationship with Slimbady, Delpiero, Maksik, and Vincent while managing the internal drama. Unfortunately, while waiting for Diplomaticos' release, the latest promotion list was published. AD Rookwood was no longer in the Investigative Division; he had been elevated to Deputy Director (DD).

This news caused a sense of unease. On the one hand, DD Rookwood reported directly to the Director, marking a promising advancement for him; on the other hand, I realized that investigations could be lost among all the new priorities. He would no longer receive exclusive briefings on Operation Carder Kaos. This change put my operation in a state of uncertainty.

Amidst the darkness, a glimmer of light emerged. Cybercrime was rampant, sparking lively debates in the media and on Capitol Hill. A new unit was established at Headquarters to oversee the Service's cybercrime investigations. Field Offices worked diligently to create electronic crime task forces and specialized cybercrime operations.

Unfortunately for Maksik, the banks implemented new defensive countermeasures that diminished the value of his dumps and PINs operation. As a result, Maksik contacted me with an intriguing proposal: he would provide me with dumps and PINs, and in return, we would split the profits equally.

The essential takeaway from Maksik's proposal was his trust in me. He relied on me not only to share half of the profits but also to serve as a system of checks and balances. Despite being an honest criminal, Maksik had little faith in others. He turned to me to act as an arbiter.

I reveled in his trust and felt a sense of accomplishment from it. However, I had an issue: I no longer had control over the data I received. Instead, I was forced to work with whatever Maksik provided. Adding to the equation, SAIC Montaña and others were frugal, raising the stakes. Fortunately, Maksik's team decrypted credit card PINs slowly, so I received at most thirty dumps along with the corresponding PINs.

After receiving the data, I aimed to verify its authenticity with my industry contacts. Their input was essential for Maksik to view me as a credible source. If I presented a validity rate that was excessively high or low, I risked putting myself in a precarious position.

Dumps and PINs were a hot topic, so it was no surprise that SAIC Montaña became involved. However, another challenge arose—how much money could I send back? Obtaining the dumps and PINs was one thing, but sending back fifty percent was another matter. Ultimately, everyone wanted a Lamborghini, but they were only willing to pay for a Ford Escort. This placed me in a precarious situation, yet it was the typical situation I faced.

As a result, I encountered several challenges. First, I needed to navigate the dark web within a budget. Second, unreasonable demands evolved. Given Maksik's status, SAIC Stokes appeared to worry that someone else might apprehend him. Hence, I had to arrest Maksik. Although it seemed absurd, I was compelled to develop a counterargument or a compelling reason to prevent it.

My argument needed to acknowledge the risk of arrest while reminding everyone that I had only scratched the surface of this case. Arresting Maksik too early would hinder the objective of apprehending the hackers and disrupting cybercrime. I argued that even if another agency, like the FBI, arrested Maksik, he would return to me if my real-world identity remained undisclosed. This argument temporarily fended off the wolves, but deep down, I knew this discussion was far from over.

Then, fortune smiled upon me, and the timing was perfect. Maksik posed the question, "Have you ever been to Dubai?"

I replied, "Dubai? No. I haven't been. Why?"

"I have been researching the financial industry," Maksik explained. "I was thinking to visit. Would you want to join?"

The joy of being invited by Maksik pushed aside my depression from previous conversations. I happily replied, "Yes! ☺ When did you plan to go?"

My only fear was that Maksik would write back and propose something unmanageable. Contrary to my fear, Maksik replied, "I was thinking June, during the FIFA World Cup is near."

I let out a sigh of relief. The trip was over one month away. I messaged back, "That may work for me? I will look at hotels."

I ended the conversation and sprinted to ATSAIC Carrington's office. Without glancing, I rushed in, shouting, "Maksik invited me to meet in Dubai."

ATSAIC Carrington, caught off guard, replied, "That is good news, but as you can see, I'm in a meeting. Can we talk about this later?"

"Sure," I responded. "Call me when you are ready."

It was May 2006, and time wasn't on my side. I put my head down and began meticulously planning the June operation. Like the operation in Phuket, Sone was excluded from Dubai. Additionally, to help "kick the can" of arresting Maksik down the road, I devised a strategic plan that included imaging his computer.

I knew Svetlana was always prying into Maksik's affairs, driven by her concerns about his infidelity. This obsession would provide the cover I needed to image his hard disk drive.

The following challenges involved figuring out whether Dubai was a viable location for my operations. I began discussions with the Office of International Affairs, the Secret Service's Resident Office in Bulgaria, the Department of State, and Headquarters to assess the feasibility of the operation. Conducting due diligence was essential for obtaining approval.

With each meticulous detail of my plan falling into place, I couldn't help but feel a surge of accomplishment. While the risks were undeniably high, the potential reward awaited me among the endless towers that dominated Dubai.

Soon, I would be navigating a labyrinth of crime, deception, and power. The game had begun, and I was determined to come out on top, no matter the cost.

While planning the trip to Dubai, Vincent pinged me, asking, "Hey, you know Mona? She sell dumps."

I replied, "No."

Vincent got to the main point and asked, "I want know if she sell good dump. Can you test for me?"

The request was intriguing, showing that Vincent valued my perspective. Additionally, if Mona did sell good dumps, we needed to be connected. Consequently, I replied, "Please share her contact details."

After I had Mona's ICQ number, the next step was easy; I sent her a friend request with the message, "I hear you sell good dumps. Please send me the BIN list."

I was determined to purchase dumps from Mona, and once I received her BIN list, I knew she was likely a reseller.

"I received your BIN list," I messaged. "Do you resell?"

Mona took a few minutes before answering, "No, why do you ask?"

"I don't know," I started. "The list looks familiar. Do you know Maksik?"

"No ☺," Mona replied.

Not convinced by the answer, I felt compelled to test it. A relentless curiosity and a desire for clarity fueled me. I messaged Maksik, saying, "I came across a new dumps vendor, Mona. Are you familiar with her?"

As I spoke with Maksik about Mona, I forwarded the data to my banking contacts. In time, they provided me with critical information, such as the common point of compromise, which aligned with the data Maksik was selling. Soon enough, Maksik replied, "Why did you buy dumps from Mona?" This question all but confirmed my suspicions.

I answered, "I was curious if Mona's dumps were good."

Maksik responded, "☺ You can buy from Mona, but better if you buy from me." Translation: "Mona's dumps are my dumps."

Wanting to change the topic, I pivoted and asked, "Have you decided on Dubai?"

"Yes," Maksik stated. "June 8–15. Why don't you come to Ukraine? We can go together."

Leon invited me, and Kaiser had hinted at it, while Maksik was now urging me to visit Ukraine. This prompted me to dream about "fulfilling this task." Traveling to Ukraine would place me at the center of a significant carding hub. However, I knew that SAIC Montaña and others would likely have a panic attack if I brought it up.

I didn't completely rule out the idea of "picking Maksik up" in Ukraine; instead, I set it aside for now. I responded vaguely, "Visiting Ukraine sounds great. Perhaps after Dubai."

The operational goals were established based on the agreement from Headquarters. Although they didn't advocate for Maksik's arrest, I suspect it was a topic of discussion among them. The next challenge was negotiating the duration of the operation. Once more, I suggested extending the operation to cover the entire duration of Maksik's stay in Dubai.

Regrettably, Headquarters insisted on a maximum of four days or until Maksik's computer was forensically imaged, whichever came first. No one in San Diego objected; SAIC Montaña accepted it without protest. I could only watch in frustration.

During this time, I considered taking an unauthorized trip to Ukraine at my own expense, where I could act freely without interference from Headquarters. The only issue was that I generally followed the rules and showed no signs of insubordination.

After securing the necessary local approvals, the San Diego team and I were called to Dubai to brief the U.S. Embassy and the police officials. We intended to arrive one week before Maksik, but I couldn't shake my anxiety about the unforeseen hurdles Headquarters might present during this operation.

Yet, there was one advantage on my side. The shared desire to successfully image Maksik's hard disk drive. Completing this task benefited me because without it, we'd have continued working in Dubai. My only concern was how far I could push it.

Chapter 32

The magic of Dubai

Traveling from San Diego proved challenging, yet I felt a wave of satisfaction upon arriving in Dubai. Driving this satisfaction was knowing Maksik and I were staying at the same resort. However, due to preparatory briefings, we opted for the hotel recommended by the U.S. Embassy before heading to our more luxurious accommodations.

Our meetings with the U.S. Embassy reflected a repetition of earlier discussions. We informed the senior staff about our target and detailed our operational objectives. Furthermore, we addressed the day's critical topic: hacking. The U.S. Embassy's response was encouraging. They expressed their full support and gave us the go-ahead for the operation. The Regional Security Officer assisted in arranging our meeting with the police, ensuring all essential connections were in place.

I had never explored the Middle East in my career before. I yearned for firsthand experience and the opportunity to immerse myself deeply in its culture. Finally, an opportunity arose when I was connected with our police counterparts. I felt a surge of anticipation as I looked forward to our meeting.

Officer Ahmed picked up ATSAIC Carrington and me from our hotel in a stylish 2006 Mercedes S-Class. I couldn't help but think, "It must be wonderful to be a police officer in the UAE." Our initial meeting occurred at the police station, which felt rather formal and left us with a sense of unresolved matters. After our meeting, Ahmed took us on a cultural tour of Dubai. Once the tour was over, he assured us he would get in touch the next day.

As promised, our gracious host met ATSAIC Carrington and me at our hotel and took us to a shisha café. Upon arrival, he guided us into a private room where several colleagues were waiting.

Ahmed asked, "Do you smoke shisha?"

I had smoked cigars, but shisha was uncharted territory for me. I replied, "No, I've never smoked shisha. I'll take whatever it is you're smoking."

ATSAIC Carrington replied, "None for me. Thank you."

Ahmed responded, "You probably don't want what I smoke. It's better to take watermelon or a green apple with mint. Do you agree?"

I said, "Sounds wonderful."

Chuckling, Ahmed ordered the shisha and asked, "What do you hope to achieve?"

He got straight to the point, which I admired. I replied, "Maksik is a prolific vendor of stolen intellectual property. As I mentioned the other day, he's coming to explore the financial opportunities here in Dubai. While he's here, we propose forensically imaging his computer, if you can."

To my delight, Ahmed and his team exuded confidence, saying, "This is possible. I'm confident we can do it. But how are you going to get him out of his room?"

DOI: 10.1201/9781003680390-32

I replied, "Last time we met in Phuket, Maksik wanted me to book a tour. I imagine I can do this again. Once I check into the hotel, I will propose something that will take us on an all-day adventure."

Ahmed shook his head and said, "Good. This will work. My team will start gathering the necessary legal paperwork. We'll be ready."

The fragrant smoke enveloped us, enhancing our discussions. Ahmed and I spent an hour conversing, strengthening our bond. During our talk, it became evident that ATSAIC Carrington, initially tolerant of Ahmed's chosen meeting spot, was starting to show signs of impatience. Others noticed this as well, prompting Ahmed to kindly offer us a ride back to our hotel.

Upon our arrival, I sincerely thanked Ahmed and assured him I was available for anything he required. However, after Ahmed departed, ATSAIC Carrington, unable to hide his disdain, expressed his frustration, saying, "How long can one sit around smoking shisha? I have important work waiting. The meeting could have ended in fifteen minutes, yet we were there for hours. What a total waste of time."

I cautiously responded, "I don't know. I felt it was a productive use of time. We should respect that we are guests in their country. They approach things differently."

I believed this meeting was incredibly important, regardless of when or where it occurred. Like my meetings with Maksik, it focused on building rapport. In contrast, ATSAIC Carrington was a man of few words, lacking patience for further rapport-building.

In the days that followed, Ahmed and his team worked diligently on the warrant. Each day brought more meetings with our group, but to ATSAIC Carrington's annoyance, these meetings occurred at various shisha cafés. This experience deepened my immersion in Dubai's rich cultural tapestry. While Ahmed and I cherished these times, ATSAIC Carrington's patience began to wear thin.

With time slipping away, the warrant remained elusive, heightening the sense of urgency. Meanwhile, I felt compelled to change hotels since Maksik's arrival was imminent. Despite my satisfaction with our shisha café meetings, I realized that only ATSAIC Carrington was left to handle this task, and in my opinion, he lacked the necessary enthusiasm. This troubled me, but with little choice, I hoped for the best.

Stepping out of the hotel lobby, I hailed a taxi and departed for my new resort. Once I arrived I stepped into the grandeur of its distinctive wave-like architecture. I made my way to the front desk and checked in. The clerk assigned me one of the hotel's upper-floor rooms in Tower One. Settling in, I wasted no time to message Maksik, saying, "I arrived ☺ I'm in Tower One, room number 1721."

I expected Maksik to reply to my message once he arrived. As time ticked by, I diligently stared at the computer, waiting for the intoxicating ICQ messaging alert sound to play. Nothing. Then, as I was about to fall asleep, there was a knock at the door.

I shook the sleep from my eyes and I opened the door. On the other side, it was Maksik and Svetlana holding a bottle of vodka. Maksik grinned, "Are you hungry?"

"Sure," I replied.

"Then let's eat," Maksik replied.

While we walked, I sent a message to ATSAIC Carrington: He's here. We're heading to dinner.

Maksik chose the simpler restaurant, and over dinner and drinks, the conversation flowed easily. After dinner, Maksik looked at me and said, "Join us for drink upstairs?"

I had assumed, Maksik and Svetlana, were tired, and would call it a night, but not this time. Eager for the opportunity I said, "Of course."

Inside his suite, Maksik gestured towards the balcony. "Come. Let's sit. What do you want to drink?"

"What do you have?" I replied.

"Beer," Maksik laughed. "For now."

We settled in admiring the glow of the Burj Al-Arab flicker in the distance. Soon the vodka came out, and with each round the laughter grew. Feeling at ease I decided to tell Maksik a personal story, meant to deepen our bond.

I explained how my real life to my brother flipped over the car and broke both hands and legs. But instead of empathy, Maksik fixed his gaze upon me and said, "You told me you didn't have any brothers or sisters."

Immediately I thought, "Son of a bitch. Now what?" I was caught in a situation where my story conflicted, and unlike the academy, there was no "real stop." This was the real world. It was just Maksik, Svetlana, and me drinking on his balcony. I had no true undercover specific training to fall back on, not a practiced scenario of "What do you do if you are caught in a lie and challenged?"

Adding to my stress, I was alone in Maksik's room. The surveillance team was likely asleep in bed, not that it mattered. No one was getting to me on this balcony in time. Speaking of time, it was ticking, and Maksik was waiting for an answer.

Lucky for me, I was drinking, and I kept my calm composure. I looked at Maksik and said, "I lied. But that was online. I didn't know you. You didn't know me. There was no way I would tell you about my real life online. But now, we are sitting, drinking, and getting to know each other. Now, I'll tell you about the real me."

Maksik leaned back, tilted his head, and contemplated the remark. His changing expression felt like a glimpse into his thoughts, transitioning from doubt to acceptance. In our digital age, a person can identify as anything they choose, including a woman, a reptile, a fish, or even something else entirely. Maksik recognized this reality; dishonesty is routine in the shadowy corners of the Internet.

Maksik said, "Yeah, it's true. I understand."

With my stress relieved, Maksik and I relaxed on the balcony, chatting and sipping drinks until darkness gave way to light. We watched the sun rise over the horizon, rays of light shimmering on the Burj Al-Arab. Maksik poured the last of the vodka. After the last shot, we decided that now was a good time for a nap. After saying my good nights or good mornings, I left, promising to meet again for lunch.

On my way from Tower Two to Tower One, I texted the team to let them know I was clear of Maksik. Since it was around ten in the morning, close to the end of breakfast, I proposed a quick debriefing meeting with them. Since everyone went to bed around midnight, I felt they would be awake and ready to meet.

As I stepped into ATSAIC Carrington's room, I scanned to ensure SA Mason and Ahmed were there. I started by saying, "Sorry, Maksik and I were out drinking all night. I just left fifteen minutes ago. Maksik is in Tower Two, room twenty-two twenty-three. Upon entering, to the left in the closet is a safe. Inside the safe, Maksik has a fake law enforcement badge and a sum of cash. Beyond the closet, there's a desk where his computer is located. The beds are on the right side."

Ahmed replied, "Thank you. We'll use this for the warrant. It should be ready in two days."

Knowing the search warrant was only days away, I began formulating the next part of the plan: getting Maksik and Svetlana out of the hotel for at least six hours. I knew Maksik wanted to watch the FIFA World Cup games, but watching them would take about two hours. Furthermore, many guests at the hotel were from Europe, so they erected huge tents for everyone to enjoy the games.

While they weren't the coziest, you were surrounded by fans. This significantly lowered the likelihood of Maksik leaving the hotel to attend the matches. Additionally, since we couldn't execute a search warrant with Maksik onsite, I knew our adventure needed to be off-site and extend beyond six hours.

That's when it hit me. I remembered seeing a Jeep Tours advertisement in the hotel lobby. These tours took adventurers into the dunes of Dubai and the mountains of Oman. This seemed perfect, and I recognized it as a great opportunity. It made sense because Maksik loved the Thai island tours. With a plan set, I decided it was time for a quick nap.

My phone buzzed when my head touched the pillow, but I figured it was Rachel, so I ignored it. As I slept, my mind raced, making it difficult to stay asleep. After several hours, I still felt restless, so I got up. The excitement from the night's earlier activities kept me in a twilight state.

After shaking off the sleep, I remembered my phone buzzing and checked it immediately. I expected a message from Rachael but found one from ATSAIC Carrington instead. The message stated: "Target left the hotel. Police surveilling."

I thought, "Wow, Maksik left me behind." Maksik invited me to explore Dubai, stating he was looking for business opportunities but hadn't mentioned this appointment. We stayed up all night, yet there was no word of a meeting. All I could do was reflect on my mistakes. Where did I fall short? Would I have to start over? I wondered how I could foster the right relationship with Maksik.

Like my meetings in Thailand, I was acutely aware that my time was limited, and this operation was bound to be cut short. Supervision seemed to seize every opportunity to terminate it early. Now, with Maksik out in Dubai meeting nefarious individuals without me, I could only wonder who he was meeting and how this would be perceived as a failure on my part back at Headquarters.

I didn't have time to dwell on it and relied on receiving updates about Maksik's secret business dealings later. Moreover, I couldn't hold it against him, even though Maksik invited me to Dubai. Friendship has its place, but business is a different matter.

I intended to wait for Maksik to reach out or, if nothing, to contact him by mid-afternoon. When I met with Maksik and Svetlana again, I planned to bring up the desert safari and hoped he would share his experiences from the adventure in Dubai's city center. Patience was key, and by late morning, Maksik messaged me: "Meet me in the tents to watch Ukraine."

I responded, "See you soon."

My mind began to race. I hadn't heard from Ahmed or ATSAIC Carrington. My last update was that Maksik was "out" meeting with individuals in the city center. I couldn't help but wonder if he'd evaded the tail. Eager for more details about the meeting, I contacted ATSAIC Carrington.

"Hey," I said, "Maksik just pinged me. We're meeting at the FIFA tents at 1 pm. What happened in town?"

I waited for fifteen minutes before ATSAIC Carrington replied, "Disregard. They followed the wrong person."

I sat mystified, wondering, "How could this have happened?" I provided everyone with Maksik's photo and informed them of his tower and room number, but they still followed the wrong person. Then it struck me that surveillance isn't a simple task. I reflected on my experiences in Thailand and recalled moments when I was alone and no one followed me. I thought, "Let's just call it practice."

Meanwhile, I headed to the tents to watch the matches with Maksik and Svetlana. Stepping out of the hotel, the heat hit me like a brick wall. It was an excruciating forty-eight degrees Celsius, reminding me why I preferred to stay indoors. Inside the tent, I joined Maksik to catch the Ukraine match. We enjoyed a few beers while discussing my work in the United States.

Maksik changed the subject and said, "I don't think it will work out here."

I replied, "What do you mean?"

"My financial business," Maksik responded. "It's too regulated. There are too many laws."

"Ah, I see," I said.

Maksik shook his head in disgust as another goal was scored against Ukraine. He said, "Ukraine is done. I need to work. Let's plan to meet for dinner."

I shook my head and jokingly replied, "Don't worry, the United States didn't do better. It's not our game."

After Maksik departed, I reviewed the messages on my cell phone. They were from ATSAIC Carrington, primarily expressing his frustrations regarding Ahmed and the police. He vented that at each meeting, they smoked shisha. Adding to ATSAIC Carrington's anger was that he believed minimal progress was made on work-related matters. He felt it was time to "tell" the U.S. Embassy and inform Ahmed's supervisors.

Sensing this would not improve matters, I did what I could to "talk him off the ledge," but thankfully, good news arrived. Ahmed messaged the team, "We have the search warrant in hand."

Having this information in hand now meant I could start getting Maksik comfortable with the idea of a desert safari. I planned to offer the notion during dinner, a few hours away. In the meantime, not wanting to fall asleep, I needed to find something to entertain myself.

I thought I would go to the pool. I had seen some chairs half-submerged in water from the window. Thinking this was a good idea and a way to kill time, I ventured to the pool.

Unfortunately, shortly after my arrival, I realized what a mistake it was to go to the pool. The temperature was an uncomfortable forty-nine degrees Celsius. Even getting into the water, which I thought would provide some relief, proved unsatisfying.

My last option was to get a frozen Pina Colada, yet, upon receipt, the drink was more liquid than ice. Frustrated by the heat, lack of comfort, and a warm drink, I quickly returned to the hotel.

Once it was time for dinner, I strolled over to the restaurant of choice and connected with Maksik and Svetlana. Upon being seated, I suggested to Maksik we take a desert safari. Maksik and Svetlana agreed it would be cool to check out the desert landscape. I told them I would make the arrangements, likely tomorrow, but if not, the next day.

After dinner, Maksik, Svetlana, and I went to the hotel club. We sat at a table and ordered several drinks. The club was interesting, filled with primarily Western and Eastern European women who were being aggressively pursued by Middle Eastern men. I couldn't help but think about Ahmed's comments about fucking Western women. I knew this scene wasn't exactly where his story was focused, but the imagery was tangible.

While observing the club scene, I attempted to speak with Maksik, but his mind was elsewhere. He sat next to Svetlana, but his nonverbal cues made it clear something was amiss. I knew Svetlana had a trust issue with Maksik. I could only think that she must have wanted to view his cell phone, but was denied, which led to a dispute. Regardless, the overall UAE Club experience with Maksik was very blah and ended abruptly.

After two drinks, Maksik arose, fanning jet lag, bid farewell, and took Svetlana to his room. But before Maksik could depart, I told him I would be up early to arrange the desert safari tour. Maksik acknowledged and said, "Message me."

When Maksik was out of view, I messaged the team, saying, "Target is in for the night." I waited for a response, but none came. The following day, I woke up early to communicate with the team. I wanted to ensure everything was in order and the search warrants were not delayed. I obtained the necessary approvals and breathed a sigh of relief, knowing I didn't need to create an excuse. With that critical detail closed, I got ready and headed to the lobby for breakfast.

Upon arriving in the lobby, I spotted Maksik and Svetlana waiting for me. We had a quick bite before it was time to meet our driver for the day's adventure. Maksik, Svetlana, and I walked to the jeep, our chariot for the day, and departed the hotel. As we left the hotel, I sent a message to ATSAIC Carrington: "Departed." From this point, everything slowed down.

I imagined a well-oiled operation, primarily because of the movies or spy-based TV programs. Mission Impossible came to mind, and I wished I could witness the operation, but I had my role and would need to live vicariously through SA Mason.

As we drove away, I was hopeful for updates, but I had yet to receive any. I pinged the team, "Did you enter the room?"

The reply was, "No, still waiting for you to get far enough away."

I was shocked. What's the point of having a man on the inside if you don't trust them? They must have known, or at least assumed, that if we turned around, the first message I would send would be to the team indicating that we had turned around. They also knew that our tour would last several hours from the time we departed. What more do you want?

I shot back, "We departed. You are good to go," which was met with silence.

Another thirty minutes passed, and I sent another message: "Did you enter the room?"

SA Mason replied, "There is no computer in the room. Did Maksik bring anything?"

I replied, "Are you in the right tower? Maksik's room is in Tower Two."

My phone buzzed in my hand. I spun it around to read their reply. "Can you confirm the room number?" After reading their question, I was puzzled, thinking, "Shouldn't they already know that?"

Quickly, I typed, "Tower 2, room 2223."

SA Mason responded, "We are in Tower 1. Moving to Tower Two now."

So much for Mission Impossible. Despite my detailed instructions, the team entered a room in the wrong tower. Adding to my frustrations, it seems as if the local police didn't trust my guidance. Prefering to wait until Maksik and I were well over one hour away before entering the wrong room. I couldn't help but laugh, thinking, "While Maksik, Svetlana, and I took pictures in the dunes, the team was searching the wrong room." Laughing was my only outlet for relieving stress.

This was a small bump in the road. Regardless, the team regrouped quickly. They headed back to the lobby, retrieved the correct key from the front desk, and used the correct elevator for Tower Two this time.

As we continued our tour, the phone buzzed to life again: "Inside now, starting the forensic image of the computer."

Upon reading this message, I felt a mix of elation and nervousness, knowing we were approaching our second hour on the tour. I didn't even know the exact length of time for the tour or when we would return. Regardless, I provided the team updates as we traveled through the desert, taking in the sights.

Maksik, Svetlana, and I saw Dubai's dunes, Oman's alien mountain landscape, and a Sheikh's abandoned mansion. According to the story, the Sheikh abandoned it because it turned out to be haunted. The Sheikh was so hurried to get away that he even left the two limousines parked inside the gate.

As we headed back, I realized I needed updates from the team. I let ATSAIC Carrington know we were en route back to the hotel. No response. I waited fifteen minutes and pinged him again, saying our ETA was about forty-five minutes to the hotel—still nothing. I sent one more message, this time in a very concerned tone, asking the same question. Finally, a response: "They cleared the hotel room an hour ago. Image in hand."

I sat back, relieved yet a little offended. If it were me, I would have messaged the undercover once the forensic imaging was complete and the team cleared the room. Regardless, I had to be positive. After all, we had a false start, a recovery, and a successful launch.

Once the news of the successful imaging of Maksik's computer reached Headquarters, they instructed me to end the operation immediately. It was enough fun for one trip. That morning, we met for breakfast and said, "I decided to leave tomorrow morning."

Maksik said, "Hmmm, it's okay. I don't like this place. Too hot. We also want to leave."

I looked at Maksik and said, "I agree. There is no relief from the heat except inside. Do you ski? I was thinking we could go to Ski Dubai today. Any interest?"

Maksik looked at Svetlana, talked to her in Ukrainian, and confirmed, "Yes, we know how to ski. Let's do it."

"Great," I said. "Let's change and meet in the lobby in one hour."

Maksik replied, "Okay."

We shared a taxi to the Mall of the Emirates and checked in at Ski Dubai. The mountain wasn't huge, but it was divided into two distinct slopes: green and blue.

I got Maksik's attention and asked, "Which one do you prefer, blue or green?"

Maksik said, "We can do the blue."

I couldn't help but be super excited to ski in the desert. The mechanics of it all amazed me. Once we reached the top, I looked for an opening and skied to the edge. Looking back, I saw Maksik and Svetlana didn't look comfortable on skis, prompting me to ask, "Are you both okay?"

Maksik nervously responded, "We're okay."

"Okay," I shot back. "I'll see you at the bottom."

Feeling they were capable, I took off. The slope was relatively easy, but many people were on it. Each skier was at a different skill level, but I skillfully navigated between them and quickly arrived at the bottom of the slope. Once I was there, I waited. And I waited. I looked around, thinking there was no way I could have missed them going down the hill. Granted, everyone wears the same clothing, which means I could have missed them.

I waited another fifteen minutes, enough time for them to ski down the slope. I thought, "Even if I missed them, there was enough time to ride the lift and ski back down." So, I decided to head back to the top of the slope. I scanned the area. No signs of Maksik or Svetlana. I was utterly baffled. Where did they go?

This time, I didn't rush down. Instead, I moved slowly, just like I was taught eight years ago. I went back and forth, skiing the entire face of the slope. I hoped this would be sufficient to find them. Besides, they might have crashed and gotten hurt. Despite my efforts, I still didn't spot either Maksik or Svetlana, which made me anxious.

Determined to find them, I jumped back in line and got on the lift, planning to repeat my efforts. As the lift slowly rose to the top of the hill, I spotted two people and a guide walking down the slope, way off to the side near the Ski Dubai wall. I laughed; it was Maksik and Svetlana. Now, I wondered what could have happened.

I skied to the bottom and near where they would be arriving. Once they got close, skis in hand, I asked, "What happened? I thought you both knew how to ski?"

Dejected, Maksik looked at me and replied, "The last time I skied, I was seven. I thought I would pick it back up. But the ski patrol told me I must ski the little slope. We'll ski here for now."

I laughed and said, "You know, telling me that information would have been massively important. I would have never suggested Ski Dubai."

Maksik, Svetlana, and I skied for a few more hours, but after dinner, we packed our bags and all left for home the next day. As we were leaving, I wondered what lay ahead of us.

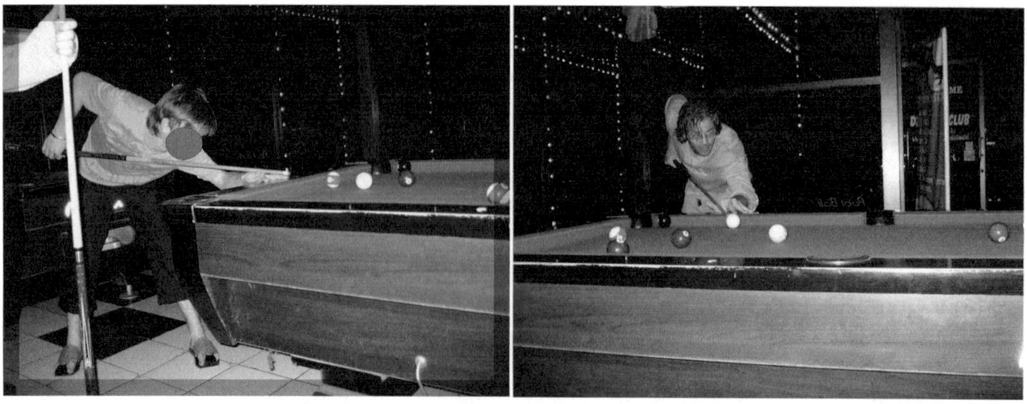

Photos 1.1 and 1.2 Maksik and I playing pool at a bar on Bangla Road, Phuket—captured by his girlfriend on the second night of our meeting. It was a rare moment of connection and trust, the kind that can only be built through time and shared experience. Despite Maksik's pleas for me to stay, I was forced to cut the trip short—another casualty of leadership's failure to understand the critical value of rapport in long-term undercover operations.

Photo 2 Captured by the U.S. Secret Service surveillance team, this photo shows Maksik and me during a stop on our boat tour in Phuket, Thailand. More than just a snapshot, it marked the beginning of a carefully cultivated relationship—one built on trust, deception, and the delicate dance of undercover work.

Photo 3 Maksik and I walking toward our tour boat in Phuket, Thailand—unknowingly captured by a local tour photographer during our first meeting. Later discovered by the surveillance team being sold as a souvenir, the image offered an unfiltered glimpse into our early rapport. Recognizing its value, the team discreetly purchased every available copy.

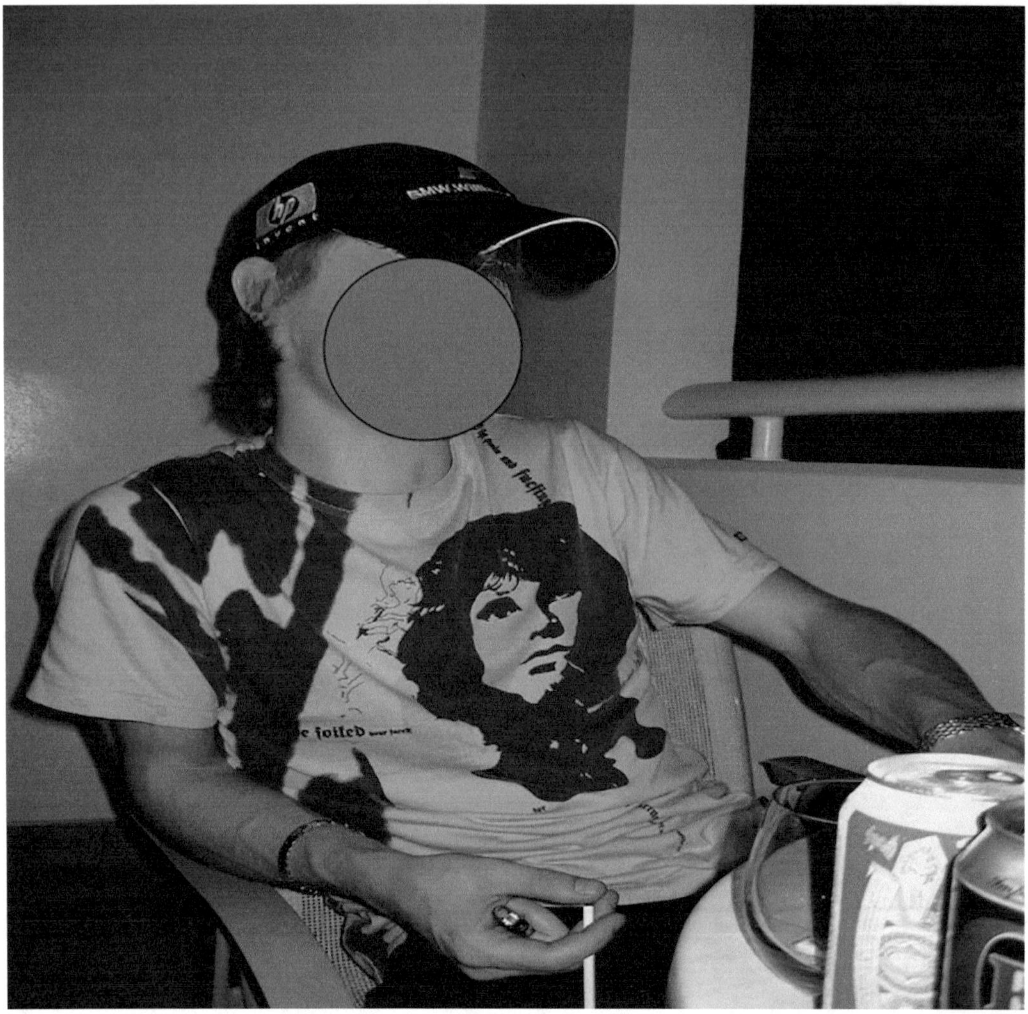

Photo 4 Maksik on his balcony of our hotel during our first night in Dubai. That evening, I recounted a story about my brother's motorcycle accident—a made-up tale intended to create rapport. Maksik, ever the skeptic, later questioned its authenticity. My response was straightforward and intentional: "I lied." In that instant, trust, control, and manipulation subtly converged beneath the shimmering moonlit sky.

Photo 5 Maksik and I are heading toward our desert jeep tour in Dubai, getting ready to explore the expansive dunes of the United Arab Emirates (UAE). While he viewed it as a carefree adventure, I understood it was a carefully orchestrated diversion, intended to keep him occupied while our team worked on a covert operation regarding his digital footprint in the city.

Photo 6 Maksik and I found ourselves deep in the United Arab Emirates (UAE) desert. A trip I orchestrated to keep Maksik occupied and away from our hotel, creating the ideal opportunity for U.S. Secret Service and Emirati officials to carry out a covert warrant on his computer in Dubai. Completely oblivious, Maksik continued on while the forensic team quickly imaged his hard drive. One important lesson learned that day: never wear open-toed sandals in the desert heat.

Photo 7 An Emirati official observes as a Secret Service Agent starts the forensic imaging of Maksik's hard drive. During a joint operation between the U.S. Secret Service and the UAE, the team encountered an early setback when they inadvertently executed the warrant at the wrong hotel tower. Nevertheless, this covert action marked a significant turning point in the effort to obtain digital evidence against Maksik, highlighting the scope of his criminal activity.

Photo 8 Maksik and I at Ski Dubai—our final meeting before the operation came to a premature end. After being helped down the slope by ski patrol, we shared a brief moment of levity as he revealed he hadn't skied since he was four years old. This setting, meant to deepen rapport and solidify trust, marked the last day of Operation Carder Kaos in Dubai—another critical opportunity cut short by leadership's decision to shut it down prematurely.

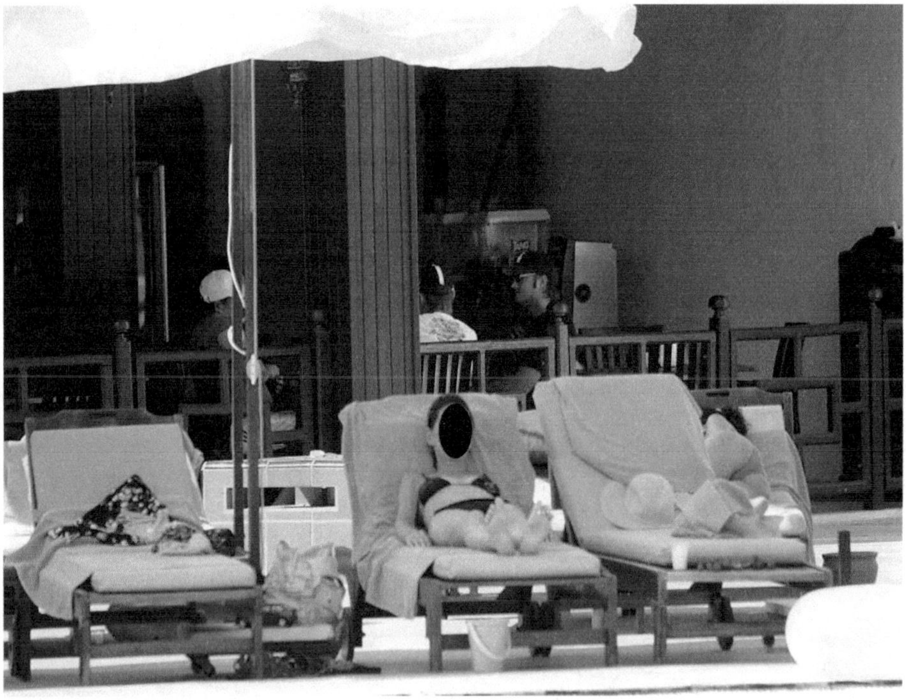

Photo 9 This photo, taken in Kemer, Türkiye, in July 2007, shows Maksik and me having lunch with his associates, just hours before his arrest. Our meeting was unexpectedly interrupted that evening when authorities learned Maksik had encrypted his laptop using PGP, alarming Turkish police and further straining an already tense collaboration with the U.S. Secret Service. His subsequent arrest marked the end of a precarious chapter and a turbulent international relationship.

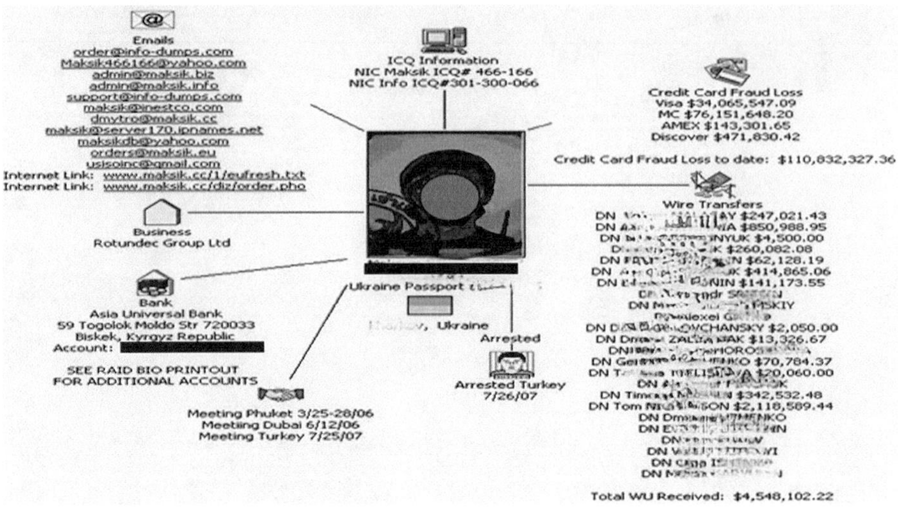

Photo 10 The post-arrest link analysis of the Maksik operation illustrates the knowledge held by the U.S. Secret Service at that moment. The chart highlights an extensive criminal network associated with Western Union transfers, banking activities, and fraud losses that surpass $110 million. Arrested on July 26, 2007, Maksik's operation stands out as one of the most thorough and significant cyber-crime cases of its era.

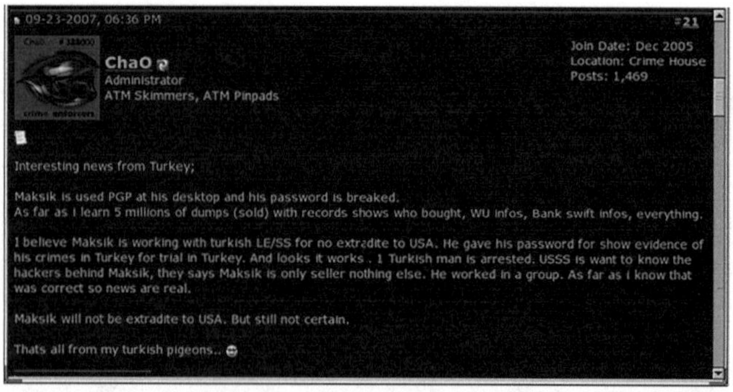

Photo 11 A forum post by "ChaO" breaks the news to the underground carding community by confirming Maksik's arrest and revealing that his passwords were compromised, thus exposing his closely held secrets, which could implicate many in the carding community.

Photo 12 Group award presented by the U.S. Department of Justice on October 27, 2010, in Washington, D.C., in recognition of contributions to Operation Sunburn. The group was nominated by the DOJ, not DHS, with my inclusion based on the critical evidence I provided from Operation Carder Kaos, which directly supported the successful prosecution. While the U.S. Secret Service did not independently recognize the long-term undercover work, this award served as a meaningful acknowledgment from the broader justice community.

Photo 13 Retirement plaque and U.S. Department of Homeland Security badges preserved in Lucite, commemorating the completion of my career with the U.S. Secret Service. Officially retired on December 31, 2020, this display honors over two decades of service, dedication, and duty in the protection and investigation of cybercrime.

Chapter 33

How many times can my family get sick?

In the days following the Dubai trip, ATSAIC Carrington expressed frustration over the long meetings held in shisha lounges. Although the official agenda rarely exceeded fifteen minutes, he felt they were ineffective and unproductive. ATSAIC Carrington even told me, "I eventually stopped going to the meetings."

I disagreed. The meeting's purpose was to discuss business and establish relationships. I valued the chance to experience a different culture, recognizing that no single system is flawless. Moreover, thanks to the collaborative efforts of our teams, the Secret Service would soon obtain the forensic image of Maksik's hard drive. However, San Diego would only receive its copy after Headquarters received theirs.

Once you accessed Maksik's hard drive, it was clear it held a treasure trove of carding information. That's when it occurred. I wasn't entirely focused, but you might have caught the call if you had listened carefully. Ready! Set! Go!

I missed the announcement because, at this point in my career, I was focused on sharing everything related to carding with the newly formed carding unit at Headquarters. The idea was simple: It was a force multiplier, and feeding to the mothership, as I referred to it, was necessary to maximize impact. Furthermore, the most significant Carders spoke and wrote in Russian.

Compounding matters, in 2006, Google Translate was of little assistance, and most everyone who could read, write, or speak Russian was assigned to Headquarters. This included support staff, such as Jack Jones. Since I consistently encountered language roadblocks, I would frequently call Jack Jones to ask questions.

"Hey," I said to Jack Jones. "Did you see the chat between Maksik and Lifestyle?"

Jack Jones, with a hint of frustration in his voice, said, "Which part?"

"Sorry," I said. "I know there are a lot of chats, but unfortunately, I can't read Russian. Anyhow, search for D&B."

"One minute," Jack Jones responded. "Okay, I see it."

"Excellent," I replied. "What are your thoughts? To me, it seems they are talking about hacking Dave and Busters."

Jack Jones paused before replying, "Yes, it seems to me that is what they are discussing. Please allow me some time to provide more details."

"Perfect," I said excitedly. "Talk to you later."

It didn't take long, but eventually, I was called into ATSAIC Carrington's office. "Rich, please take a seat."

"What's up?" I responded.

"SAIC Stokes called," ATSAIC Carrington started. "You need to stop calling Jack Jones."

I was confused and said, "What? I thought he was there to help with investigations."

"He is," ATSAIC Carrington replied. "However, you need to submit your requests via Headquarters."

 DOI: 10.1201/9781003680390-33

I was disgusted and said, "This is bullshit. How am I supposed to work my case? It is all in Russian. I don't speak Russian. If Headquarters will not help, I need an asset assigned to me to help with translation."

ATSAIC Carrington sighed and said, "Talk to SA Mason. Let's see if we can put together a translation quote and get it approved."

This concluded my direct collaboration with invaluable assets and, to put it bluntly, a divergence of goals. My objective was to climb Mount Everest, connect all the dots, find the crown jewels, and expose Maksik's hackers. I needed assistance to accomplish this task.

Headquarters understood this and made it their objective to dissect Maksik's hard disk before me. Once the hackers were identified, they would claim the most prolific ones. Meanwhile, they only helped me with matters involving Maksik and below. Despite my efforts, I was placed behind the proverbial eight ball.

Adding to my disdain, I felt as if Headquarters knew that SAIC Montaña's leadership was lacking. To me, it seemed everyone knew he was clueless about casework and only cared about climbing the corporate ladder.

While Headquarters pursued its agenda, I began exploring Maksik's drive. I anticipated seeing the "C" drive, typical for most computers. However, what drew everyone's attention was the volume labeled "Z." This was unusual. Still, since I was familiar with Pretty Good Privacy (PGP), I immediately knew it was an encrypted volume.

Maksik's use of encryption prompted me to contact SA Doug Bander, our primary forensics investigator. "Hey, I have another task for you."

"What do you need?" SA Bander replied.

"Maksik's computer," I responded. "He is using encryption. While I search for leads and evidence, I need you to compile a list of all passwords."

SA Bander nodded in agreement and said, "I'll get on it."

My desired outcome was to create a list of potential passwords that we could use to access the encrypted volume. Having these passwords could also prove helpful when unlocking other files or programs. It was a worthwhile endeavor.

With SA Bander laser-focused on uncovering passwords, I searched for investigative leads and found plenty. Buried in unallocated space were "golden nuggets of evidence" that linked Maksik to an extensive network of Carders, including Slimbady, Delpiero, Mona, Vincent, Kaiser, and hundreds of others.

While one hand was engaged in forensics, the other was on my undercover computer, responding to pings and advancing the case. My priority was getting more meetings with Maksik. I was willing to meet at any destination he was open to visiting.

Instead, this resulted in numerous invitations to Ukraine, but they centered on a single issue: Maksik disliked traveling alone. I couldn't help but keep thinking, "Despite his larger-than-life reputation in the carding world, he was timid. He was just a small-town kid." He needed a travel companion, someone to guide him on the journey. If he had one, he would have traveled more frequently, and I was elated that he trusted me.

I knew a trip to Ukraine would elevate me to the next level. My problem was that no one would ever give me the green light to take advantage of it. Whenever I brought it up, the go-to argument was that it was too dangerous, and they were concerned about my safety. This argument made me sick, and often, I thought, "Have you ever been on any of the undercover assignments? Because if you had, you'd know most were asleep by midnight."

My frustration was building, but I dared not voice my thoughts. I knew nothing good would come of it. Instead, I sulked and considered defying leadership by hopping on a plane to Ukraine. My counterargument is that, contrary to their beliefs, traveling alone to Ukraine would be safer for me.

I reasoned that bringing in a host country's law enforcement team, even if they were trusted points of contact, raised the risk of exposing my identity. The reason is simple: The more people who knew who I was and what my mission was, the higher the risk.

Unfortunately, many Secret Service leaders weren't ready to consider such a daring mission, and before I knew it, other matters captured my attention. I noticed Slimbady and SunCredit speaking to me less and less. I decided it was time to talk with ATSAIC Carrington. I walked into his office and asked, "Mr. Carrington, do you have a moment?"

ATSAIC Carrington responded, "Yes, of course. What do you need?"

"It is about Slim and others," I started. "They aren't speaking to me, and I think I know the issue."

ATSAIC Carrington ever committed to his Tums, grabbed the bottle, and replied, "What's the issue?"

"The purse strings are too tight," I replied. "Because I'm not doing business, they more or less only say 'hi' and 'bye.' It's not like when I first started."

"Well," ATSAIC Carrington responded. "We have spent a lot of money making many purchases. We have all the necessary evidence. SAIC Montaña and I don't see the point of spending more money."

I looked up at the ceiling, then cracked my neck, and said, "I'm not sure I agree with the philosophy. On the one hand, you're right; we have enough evidence against everyone. But this wasn't a buy-bust operation. It's a long-term undercover operation. My interesting personality only goes so far. It's the business side that keeps them talking to me. Without business, they won't take the time to speak with me. Remember, it was Slimbady who introduced me to Maksik. If we want intelligence, I need to spend money. If I want a cheerleading section, I must spend money."

ATSAIC Carrington took a deep breath and replied, "Your argument is that the relationship is built on business; without business, they aren't communicating regularly. I get your point. Let me speak with SAIC Montaña. I think I can get a modest weekly amount approved."

Fortunately, I was just enough of a pain in the ass that SAIC Montaña relented and loosened the purse strings. I restarted spending a modest amount of money, and while doing so, I always mixed in my planned holidays. My goal was to create jealousy, encourage my online friends to "spread the word" about the fun parties with Surfrider, and, in doing so, attract more people. Needless to say, as I predicted, spending money opened doors, and I got some bites.

While planning one of the trips to Bangkok, Thailand, I got a curious call from SA Rogers. "Hey, Rich. How is it going?"

I replied, "I'm doing well. What's up?"

SA Rogers responded, "I got a call from the RAIC of Bangkok."

"Who is the RAIC?" I replied.

SA Rogers laughed, saying, "Charlie Stonehouse, our old PT instructor."

I joined SA Rogers and laughed, saying, "I guess he got bored with the B team protection details. Anyhow, what did he say? I mean, why did he call?"

Ignoring my question SA Rogers responded, "What did you do in the academy to piss off Stonehouse?"

I was caught off guard and casually replied, "Nothing to my knowledge, why?"

Rogers explained, "Well, he was ranting and raving about many things, but ultimately, he said, 'There was no way SA LaTulip was coming to my district to have a party on the government dime.' He is demanding that the operation be canceled."

I quipped back, "Party on the government dime? What the hell does he care, and what business is it of his anyhow?" I had to ponder the dilemma, and then it dawned on me, and

I continued, "You know what? I think I know. Do you recall my blacked-out Chuck Taylor shoes?"

"Yeah, of course, those shoes were awesome," Rogers replied.

I continued, "Well, when I was back in San Diego, on a break from the academy, SAIC O'Reilly asked me some bizarre questions, including my footwear choice. Now it's clear who called him. Anyway, it isn't as if I can just be replaced. There is no other option but to send me despite Stonehouse's objections."

SA Rogers took a moment before replying, "Thanks for the information. And don't worry—I will handle it. The operation will get the approvals, and whether Stonehouse likes it or not, he'll support it."

I was thrilled to hear his response and tucked that conversation away in my mind. I focused on planning the trip to Thailand. Unlike my previous trips, I didn't plan to go to Phuket. It would only be Bangkok. Besides, Slimbady and others preferred casinos, restaurants, and girls over the beach.

Even with all the planning proceeding as I expected, there were several last-minute conversations to attend to, but none was stranger than my conversation with ATSAIC Carrington.

"Hey, Rich," ATSAIC Carrington said. "You got a minute?"

"Of course," I replied. "What's up?"

ATSAIC Carrington had an intense look on his face. Then he opened up and said, "What are your thoughts about bringing a female agent with you? She can pose as your girlfriend."

"I'm not a big fan of the idea," I shot back. "As I mentioned before, we'd have no chemistry. It wouldn't pass the smell test."

"Yeah, that's right," ATSAIC Carrington said, "But what about if Rachel posed as your girlfriend? You two have plenty of chemistry."

The first thing that ran through my mind was, "Are you fucking kidding?" Instead of blurting this out loud, I knew I needed a logical reason to say why the idea was terrible. It took me a second before responding, "Rachel is a U.S. citizen, not an agent. She wasn't trained to defend me if I got into a bad situation. Even worse, I won't allow Rachel to be placed in a dangerous situation. No, if there is "someone" then the only logical person is Dok Mai. She has been around them before. She's a known entity. It should be her."

ATSAIC Carrington tilted his head and acknowledged, "Of course, I understand. You're right. Forget it. We'll stick to what's been working."

With that disaster diverted, it was time to leave for Thailand. SAIC Montaña was the supervisor, and again, Sone wasn't invited. His role was reduced to local support or break glass emergency travel.

Everyone except SAIC Montaña met at the Bangkok Resident Office the day after we arrived. The first meeting was with RAIC Stonehouse, whom I hadn't seen since the academy.

Seeing him again was strange, but he looked pretty much the same after all this time. I did all I could to ask, "How was working on the B team?" Nonetheless, RAIC Stonehouse's demeanor was inviting and warm. It was like old friends meeting after many years had passed. But I was put off; I knew everything about this meeting was disingenuous. Regardless, I had to play along.

RAIC Stonehouse immediately invited SA Mason and me into his office. At first, I thought, here it comes, the lecture. You are in my district and had better behave in the best way. Just one slip-up and you are on a plane, persona non grata or PNG, forever. This would have been his dream, despite what Headquarters or I might have wanted.

Instead, the "lecture" RAIC Stonehouse asked, "Are you married?"

SA Mason and I looked at each other, but before we could speak, he continued, "Well, it does not matter. To each their own. There is a place called the Garden of Eden. They call it the seven levels of heaven, each level better than the last. Now I suggest when you go there you take two ladies. But here's the secret, you pick one lady and then tell her to pick a friend. This way, you know the one she picks is the girl she likes working with, and then what's your fantasy? Doctor? The slutty housemaid? Whatever it is, you tell them, and they will act it out in front of you. As they act it out, they go at it. Once they know you are ready, they come for you, and believe me, gentleman, you aren't cumming once if you know what I mean. Tell any cab driver, Garden of Eden; they'll know what you want."

I couldn't believe it one week ago; everything was being done to keep SA LaTulip out of Thailand. Now, it's where to go to have sex in Thailand. Needless to say, SA Mason and I replied, "No, thanks; we're good."

RAIC Stonehouse said, "Well, if you change your mind. That is the place to go. Now, regarding this operation, you should be aware that Bangkok is a dangerous place. Mopeds are all around. Anyone can drive up on you. POW. You're dead. Nothing you can do about it. So, you need to be alert all the time."

I was left speechless. His advice ranged from where to get laid to if you're not paying attention, you're dead. What a welcome to Thailand speech!

Later that evening, just before the operation commenced, I positioned myself in the center of the hotel lobby. I aimed for everyone to notice me and, more crucially, recognize Vincent as he arrived. Five minutes before his entrance, Vincent messaged me. I promptly relayed this information to the surveillance team.

Once I put my phone in my pocket, Vincent entered the lobby. Seeing him, I walked in his direction and greeted him. After exchanging greetings, Vincent pointed to the elevators and said, "Let's go eat."

I replied, "Sure. I can eat."

He led the way, and I followed. As we walked, I became curious and asked, "Where are we headed?"

Vincent excitedly replied, "I know seafood restaurant outside city. Local only. We go."

Vincent and I then entered the elevator and headed to his car. I immediately thought, "This isn't good." Once in Vincent's car, I texted SA Mason, "Green sedan heading out of east entrance."

My challenge in sending updates was primarily related to the street names. Nonetheless, as we exited, I texted SA Mason, "Heading east."

Vincent was flowing with traffic and moving swiftly. I didn't want to attract attention, but I became worried. SA Mason wasn't replying to my messages. I thought, "Come on, no way they didn't see me leave." Well, at least until I got a text message from SA Mason, "Are you still in the hotel?"

I thought, "What the hell? I guess for now, I'm on my own." I messaged, "No, departed, entering highway now."

SA Mason wrote back, "You left the hotel?"

I had to be careful. I was sitting next to Vincent and needed to control my emotions. Inside, I was furious, but outwardly, I had to remain calm. I typed another message, "On the highway, let you know when we exit."

SA Mason replied, "OK, going mobile now. Team on mopeds. Can't drive on highway." As I read this, I couldn't help but laugh.

Vincent, hearing me laugh, said, "What so funny?"

Realizing I laughed out loud, I replied, "Nothing. It was a message from my team. They hit it big."

I know we didn't plan for a longer journey, but because no one knew for sure, I would have thought there would have been at least one car. But that wasn't the case, and in Bangkok, it is easier to travel on mopeds.

Vincent finally exited, which prompted me to send the exit number to the team. Curiosity prompted me to ask, "Are you close?"

I wasn't surprised when I saw the reply: "No!"

Once Vincent and I arrived, I sent one last update: "Arrived. Advise when in position."

SA Mason's reply: "Roger."

Halfway through dinner with Vincent, SA Mason messaged me: "Team in place."

I was relieved to learn they had caught up; however, I wasn't sure what would happen next. Could they follow me? Or could they keep up? It remained a mystery. Nonetheless, as our dinner came to an end, Vincent remarked, "Hey, I want to show you something."

Curious, I replied, "What do you want to show me?" Initially, I thought he had something with him to show me, but his response didn't align with my thoughts.

"My home," Vincent said. "My stuff there, and I want your opinion."

Because my operation was "successful," Vincent wanted to show me his, to which I replied, "Of course. Where is it?"

"Not far," Vincent jubilantly replied. "Come, I will show you."

The drive was short, about four minutes away from the restaurant. As we arrived, Vincent said, "Come, follow me." Vincent dutifully escorted me upstairs and into his bedroom. Once inside, he opened a computer cabinet and turned on his computer. First, he navigated to his ICQ account and then looked at me, saying, "There are my friends. See, there is you."

I was in awe, amazed that I was spoon-fed his most private details. I could only reply, "Cool."

Then, as if he were a child in a toy store, he reached into the computer drawer, pulled out his MSR206a, and said, "Here is my encoder. Over there is all my plastic." Then he reached under his computer keyboard, pulled out several counterfeit credit cards, and said, "What do you think?"

I knew Vincent was proud of his work, and honestly, since I had nothing but "fake" work to discuss, I replied, "This is excellent."

"Yes," Vincent said. "Thank you. Now, let's go. I have place to show you."

Vincent took me to his favorite bar, which I didn't consider a bar. I knew it as the "fishbowl." The concept was straightforward: ladies dressed in lingerie sat on one side, displaying a numbered tag, and on the other, men sat sipping their favorite drink, waiting to pick a number that interested them. This wasn't my kind of place.

As we ordered our favorite drink, Johnny Walker Blue Label, Vincent asked, "Any interest?"

I looked at Vincent and replied, "You know me, I prefer bars. This isn't my style."

Vincent nodded his head while saying, "Okay. We drink these and go."

Vincent's next stop was none other than the Garden of Eden. As we approached the entrance, Vincent leaned toward me and said, "This called seven levels of heaven."

I nodded while saying, "I've heard of this place." The irony couldn't have been better.

Vincent's eyes widened, and he replied, "Oh. We go to top. Best ladies there."

Once the elevator opened, I received an urgent message from ATSAIC Carrington: "Call me." It didn't take a scientist to figure out that the trip was being cut short again. I scratched my chin and said to Vincent, "It's my mom. I need to call her. I'll be right back."

Vincent said, "Okay. I be here."

When ATSAIC Carrington picked up, I said, "What's so urgent? You know I'm working."

ATSAIC Carrington was incredulous, "Call Montaña! He doesn't know how to call you and wants an update."

I became irritated and responded, "SAIC Montaña wants me to call him? Now? While I'm working?"

Irritated, ATSAIC Carrington replied, "I have two agents in Thailand. I have an SAIC who doesn't know how to use a mobile phone, so he calls me to tell me to call you to tell you to call him. This pisses me off! Call him now!"

Undiplomatically I responded, "It pisses you off? What about me? I'm in the middle of an op, but now I must call Montaña!"

After hanging up, I called SAIC Montaña. When he picked up, I asked, "What do you need?"

SAIC Montaña replied, "What are you doing?"

I was beside myself, "What am I doing?" I sarcastically said, "Working. What do you think I'm doing?"

I could hear Montaña smack his lips together before saying, "Yeah, but what did you accomplish?"

"Oh, I don't know," I replied. "I went to Vincent's residence, saw his carding plant, gathered carding intelligence, and built rapport. You? What have you done? And why am I calling you to brief you during an operation? I can do this tomorrow."

SAIC Montaña paused before saying, "Do you know what time it is? It's past midnight."

"Past midnight," I stated, "Who the hell cares what time it is? I'm not some child. Carders don't go to bed at midnight. Are you serious?"

"Shut it down! We leave tomorrow morning. I want you in your room within the next thirty minutes," SAIC Montaña demanded.

"Whatever," I replied and hung up.

As I approached the table, Vincent said, "Good, you back. Look." Vincent handed me a three-ring binder and continued, "You can get celebrities, newscasters, Playboy models. Anyone you want."

I flipped through the pages and asked, "Are you sure, celebrities? Newscasters? Even a Playboy model?"

Vincent enthusiastically shared, "Wages in Thailand are not the best, even they need more income."

I closed the book and said, "Are they even here?"

"No," Vincent said. "You pick one. They call. Thirty to forty minutes, they come."

I shook my head, "Okay."

"So, what you mom say?" Vincent caringly asked.

"It is my grandfather," I replied. "He took a turn for the worse. They aren't sure he will make it. She is a mess. I gotta head back tomorrow."

"Oh," Vincent exclaimed. "So sorry. What you think one more bar?"

"I don't know," I said as sadly as I could. "I'm not in the mood. I think I'm calling it a night."

Vincent patted my shoulder and said, "I understand. When you ready come back. I be here."

Chapter 34

You only have to RSVP!

During my trip back to the United States, I could only think about one thing: "How can I get SAIC Montaña to leave San Diego?" I felt he jeopardized the operation and more importantly, my life. He was a liability, a risk, and an operational burden. With every operation, my chances of ending up in an alleyway stuffed inside a dumpster increased.

Once I touched down in the United States, I prioritized spreading the word about SAIC Montaña's lack of operational judgment. For a fleeting moment, I thought ASAIC DuBois might return, but those chances disappeared the minute I entered the office. He was making a full-court press to be on a campaign and had given up hopes of going on future operations.

Instead, I called ATSAIC Carrington, who I knew would be fuming from the last mission. After he answered, I didn't waste a moment, saying, "I have to get this off my chest. There is no way Montaña can come on another undercover assignment. We talk about risk, safety, MY SAFETY, yet at every turn, SAIC Montaña jeopardizes it."

ATSAIC Carrington agreed, "I know."

Interrupting, I continued, "Really? Do you know? I get it, it sucks waking up to Montaña's five a.m. call, telling you to call me. But it's my ass on the line. Stepping outside in the middle of an op to explain what I'm doing should be a known no-no. Then, yet again, he kills the operations and tells me to go to bed."

Frustrated by the one-way conversation, ATSAIC Carrington jumped in: "Enough! My hands are tied; he's the SAIC. I don't like it any more than you." He took a deep breath before saying, "Let me make some calls."

I regained my composure and replied, "I apologize. It is so agonizing. Right now, I don't care. I'm telling anyone who'll listen. Now you know, in case anyone asks."

I hung up the phone and continued my campaign, calling anyone and everyone who would listen. Several weeks later, I learned two things. First, SA Rogers was promoted to ATSAIC. He would replace ATSAIC Sheehan, whom I was sad to see go, but Rogers had the ear of the new SAIC, John Tanzman. Second, SAIC Montaña was asked to not serve as the operational supervisor any longer.

Having leverage was more valuable than knowing carding cases, especially at SAIC Tanzman's level. I no longer needed to prove myself with every operation, explain the value as if each operation was the first, or fight the notion that "Russians don't meet." Quickly, I learned that there was an error in my judgment.

I had finished a conversation with Kaiser, who broke the "Bro" code and chased Maksik's side lady, earning him a red card and being kicked from his inner circle. Usually, I'd be one hundred percent on Maksik's side. However, I had different goals, which trumped the "Bro" code.

I built enough rapport to earn an invite and was excited to brief ATSAIC Rogers about this opportunity.

"Hey, I've got good news," I shared. "Kaiser, Maksik's ex-friend, invited me to Moldova."

DOI: 10.1201/9781003680390-34

"Moldova?" ATSAIC Rogers said. "Isn't that in Russia?"

"No," I said bluntly. "Moldova was part of the Soviet Union. Now an independent country."

"Okay," ATSAIC Rogers said. "When is he going?"

"Not sure, maybe within three weeks," I replied.

ATSAIC Rogers responded, "Let me pull the team together."

I knew Headquarters often moved slower than a Jawa Crawler, so I didn't waste a moment. I knew I needed approvals from the U.S. Embassy and the local police. Our office in Bulgaria covered Moldova, and a friend, Javier Gonzalez, was stationed there. Javier was a stand-up guy who you knew "had your back." I emailed him requesting that he call me when he was free. He called immediately.

"Hey Javier," I said. "I'm not sure if you're aware, but I've been running an undercover operation over the past year. I took the digital world and moved it to the real world."

Astonished, Javier said, "You mean to say you're meeting in person with cybercriminals?"

"Yes," I replied.

"Cool," Javier responded. "How can I help?"

"Well, that's why I wanted you to call," I explained. "A Carder named Kaiser invited me to meet in Chisinau, Moldova. You know the politics. Is it possible to work there?"

Javier replied excitedly, "You couldn't have picked a better time or location. I recently met with our counterparts, and our relationship couldn't be better. I'll talk with everyone and get back to you."

"That sounds great," I replied. "Also, I'm on a tight timeline. How quickly can you get an answer?"

Javier said, "Two days."

When I hung up the phone, I was confident the operation was on track, and I could say yes to Kaiser. Around this time, I heard that the new Diplomaticos had been released from prison. Sone had never met with him, but he was his best client. I thought, "What would I want to do if I had just been released? Travel."

I quickly sent Diplomaticos a message, "Privet, Freedom at last. ☺ Welcome home."

Diplomaticos messaged back, "Thank you, Brat. It is good to be out."

"I imagine you might be ready for a holiday?" I responded.

"My friend," Diplomaticos replied. "Yes, but money is tight. I'm also out of the business."

I had heard that, only for others to jump right back in, but it didn't matter. I had the evidence I needed to put together an arrest warrant for Diplomaticos. The only missing part was building the relationship so that I can plan how or where to arrest him. Knowing this I said, "Don't worry, Brat. Consider it my gift: a get-out-of-jail holiday to the Caribbean for you and Leon."

"That sounds nice, Brat," Diplomaticos replied. "Let me think about it."

Extraditions were lengthy and could become dicey. As an alternative, I thought, "If I can get Diplomaticos into international waters, the U.S. Coast Guard could board his boat and arrest him." The hard part was timing.

Because it was the Caribbean, and the threats of illegal drugs and migration were ever present, the U.S. Coast Guard patrolled the waters often. I contacted the Seventh District and introduced myself: "Hello. My name is Richard LaTulip, and I work with the Secret Service. I have a question."

"How can I help?" a representative replied.

I explained, "I'm planning an undercover operation in Punta Cana. If I get the defendants in international waters, what are the odds of having the U.S. Coast Guard board the vessel and arrest them?"

The representative replied, "Not implossible, but here is the issue. We're not always operating in the area and won't divert an asset unless you have a high-value target onboard."

"Basically, I'd need the targets at sea at the same time an asset was operating in the area, and even then, it wouldn't be guaranteed," I replied.

The representative said, "Yes, sir."

The odds of this working were so slim that it was almost not worth the phone call. Regardless, I needed to know the answer. A few days later, I got a call from Javier Gonzalez. When I picked up the phone, I answered, "Richard LaTulip."

Gonzalez replied, "Hey buddy, how's it going?"

"I'm fine," I replied happily. "But I'm more eager to hear some good news."

Javier's voice crackled, stating, "Well, then you'll be happy to hear the police in Moldova and U.S. Embassy support the mission. You only need to let me know the dates."

A bolt of energy shot into my arm. I replied, "I will. Thank you."

After I hung up, I ran to ATSAIC Carrington's office to share the news. I sat down and jubilantly proclaimed, "Moldova is a go. Everyone there has approved. Have you heard anything from Headquarters?"

ATSAIC Carrington looked puzzled, saying, "No, nothing, let's call them."

ATSAIC Carrington picked up the phone and called ATSAIC Rogers. When Rogers answered the phone, ATSAIC Carrington stated, "You're on speaker, and Rich LaTulip is here."

ATSAIC Rogers responded, "Give me one minute. Okay, I've assembled the A-team. I assume you're calling about Moldova. We discussed it and determined it was too dangerous. Also, there's no support from the U.S. Embassy or our local office."

Turning my head to the side, clearly puzzled, I said, "Too dangerous? Aren't all operations inherently dangerous? How's this one any different from all the others?"

ATSAIC Rogers said, "It's Moldova; it's not the best city, and close to Russia. Why would you even want to go? Besides, it's not a 'resort' destination."

Over the past operations, I often heard: "All Rich wants to do is take lavish holidays at expensive resorts on the government dime." I always replied, "Sorry, strangely enough, most people look to avoid holidays in Siberia and Russian cybercriminals won't come to Nebraska. They preferred locations with an appeal, gambling, women, beaches, something extraordinary."

Suddenly, it's: "Why does Rich want to go there? It's not a resort destination."

Confused, I replied, "I feel everyone believes I pick the place because I want to go. Don't get me wrong. It's nice to go to Phuket. But make no mistake, I pick it because it's a desirable destination. I didn't pick Moldova. Kaiser did and invited me."

"Yeah, I get that, but if the U.S. Embassy and police don't support it, there's no way we will," ATSAIC Rogers shot back.

Irritated, I asked, "You keep saying they don't support it. Who told you that?"

ATSAIC Rogers stated, "Jack Jones. Also, Moldova is next to Russia. It's too dangerous."

Irritated, I shot back, "Jack Jones? Who did you speak with at the U.S. Embassy? How about the police? Anyone? Because I spoke with Javier Gonzalez. You know, the agent assigned to Bulgaria who covers Moldova. Gonzalez spoke with the U.S. Embassy AND to the police. According to Javier, they all support the mission."

The line went silent, prompting me to ask, "Is anyone there? Did we lose you?"

ATSAIC Rogers responded, "No, no, we're still here. Let me call you back."

At that moment, it was clear to me that Jack Jones wasn't only the analyst but also the director. Jack Jones had garnered such a reputation that he didn't need to talk with anyone. He just talked, and they listened. Two days later, ATSAIC Rogers called the office. He only spoke to ATSAIC Carrington, but in the end, they approved the operation.

Unfortunately, the approval was too late. Kaiser's status was "Do Not Disturb." The indicator stayed this way for the next several days. When he replied, he said, "Sorry, I just got back."

But not all was lost; Diplomaticos was ready to travel, but not to the Dominican Republic. Instead, he invited me to Sharm el-Sheik. Once again, I put it in high gear and pushed forward with the approval process. ATSAIC Rogers was familiar with some of the agents assigned to the Rome Office. He would run point to get the approvals. However, the cracks in the foundation began to appear immediately.

I waited for news from ATSAIC Rogers, but everything was quiet. My patience wore thin, so I called ATSAIC Rogers and said, "Hey, how's it going? Do you have any news from Rome?"

The other side of the line was flat. ATSAIC Rogers stated, "Nothing good. The agent responsible for Egypt is on a protection assignment."

I replied quizzically, "What does that mean?"

ATSAIC Rogers stated, "No one is available to speak with the U.S. Embassy in Egypt or the local police."

Hearing this, I was beside myself and said, "Okay, then, can I do it? I'll fly to Egypt and speak with them directly."

I heard a deep sigh, and ATSAIC Rogers replied, "Sorry, that isn't happening. It's Rome's district, and only agents assigned to Rome can work with the U.S. Embassy."

I shook my head and responded, "What does this mean? Everything ends. What would happen if this were a protection assignment?"

ATSAIC Rogers didn't reply directly, "We must wait for Rome. Without their approval, my hands are tied."

Discouraged, I replied, "This is fucked up." Then hung up the phone.

In the operation's final death throes, I tried to get SAIC Montaña to make a phone call to get the operation back on track. Regrettably, I don't believe he ever lifted a finger. I was forced to sit on the sidelines. The Rome Field Office could have cared less. My only option was to tell Diplomaticos I couldn't join him in Sharm el-Sheik. As a consolation prize, once Diplomaticos returned from his holiday, he sent me a photo of himself on the beach. I could only lament that, once again, another opportunity was missed.

My frustrations couldn't have been higher. More and more, I thought about jumping on a plane, meeting Maksik in Ukraine, and afterward going to Headquarters to brief them on a successful operation. But I never got the nerve. I continued to follow procedures. Mainly, I complained to Rachel, whose advice was clear: "Stop talking about it and just do it. Fuck 'em." Unlike Rachel, I was still programmed to follow the chain of command.

Fortunately, there was some good news. In July 2006, the police from the Philippines called, stating they had identified Akihikatobe. The police worked with limited details and found the person and know where he was residing.

Because I provided the information, the police invited me to participate in executing a search warrant. In August 2006, I boarded a flight and headed to Manila to meet with the police. Upon arriving at the Ninoy Aquino International Airport, I was immediately transported into another world. The terminal, while functional, showed signs of its age and heavy usage. High ceilings and large glass windows aim to provide a spacious feel, but the crowds make the space feel congested.

I followed the airport signs, which were written in many languages, toward Customs and Immigration. Throughout my journey, I noticed scuffed floors, missing tiles, and dated seating—all signs of wear and tear. The lines at immigration were long. But in the distance, I noticed a sign marked "Diplomats." Since I was on official travel, I thought, "What the heck? Let's see if my official passport works."

I approached the Immigration Officer; he motioned me forward. I handed him my passport and answered a few questions. He flipped through the pages of the passport, located the required page, stamped it, and motioned with his head to the side, indicating I was free to proceed.

Once I had my bags, I headed for the GREEN lane—Nothing to Declare—and passed right through. On the other side, I was met by an Embassy driver. His job was to escort me to my hotel. Once I arrived at the hotel it was just the right time to shower, grab a quick dinner, and explore Manila's nightlife.

I initially thought it would be a short night, mostly because I had an early morning meeting at the U.S. Embassy. But my plans for an early night were quickly dashed. Inspired by the lively nightlife, I found the energy to stay up. The following day, due to the jetlag, I was fueled by drinking a lot of coffee.

The hotel wasn't far from the U.S. Embassy. Upon arriving, I noticed the high walls that separated the U.S. Embassy from the local street. The U.S. government had learned hard lessons from the bombings in Africa. High-threat countries were mandated to change the format. Standoff distances were increased, thus creating a more secure military-type compound.

Once inside, I was met by the Regional Security Officer. He escorted me to the meeting room. Once in the room, I was offered coffee, which I immediately accepted. Then I was introduced to Captain Miguel Bautista, the officer in charge of arresting Tobe. I approached Captain Bautista, extended my hand, and said, "Greetings, my name is Richard LaTulip."

Captain Bautista followed suit and said, "It's a pleasure to meet you. Please take a seat."

"Thank you," I replied.

Captain Bautista started the meeting, "Let me begin by saying thank you for all your information about Tobe. With that information, we were able to locate the person. We know where he is residing. It's located on a small island south and east of Manila."

Being unfamiliar with the Philippines, I inquired, "Do you need to fly to get there?"

"Yes," Captain Bautista said. "My team and I will leave tonight. We will make preparations. You should fly tomorrow morning. Once you arrive, we'll execute the warrants."

The following day came quickly, as the flight departed at five. Upon entering the lobby, I found the same driver waiting for me. Due to the early time, the drive was easy. But once we arrived at the airport, the congestion returned. People struggled to get their bags from the curb to the entrance. At first, when I saw the mass chaos, I thought, "I wasn't going to make my flight."

However, the pre-entrance baggage X-ray check caused the backup. Once inside and past security, I found a coffee stand; I depended on it to get me through the day. Because the flight was short, the airplane that would take me my final destination was a turboprop. Takeoff was quick; before I knew it, we were landing.

I deplaned and headed inside the airport, where I quickly found a taxi. It took me to the meeting location, where Captain Bautista and his team awaited my arrival. After the briefing, I joined Captain Bautista and drove to Tobe's residence. The drive wasn't too long, about thirty minutes outside the city center, but I understood the operation was planned to commence before the morning commute was in full force.

As the team arrived at the residence, Captain Bautista and I waited until we received word that the scene was safe. Once we received the green light, we headed to the residence. Akihikatobe's residence was primarily white stucco. The driveway had a gate that prevented unauthorized guests from parking inside the small compound. Once inside, I observed the team as they searched the residence.

While I meandered about, I watched over the team's shoulders. The team was briefed that the case involved the use of credit cards. I even briefed them on how Sone sent many

PlayStation 3s to Tobe's residence. I never thought I would be able to confirm his story. But as I entered his family room, I saw a stack of PlayStations. I wondered, "Could these be the shipped devices? If so, did Tobe save the shipping labels?"

I circled back into the kitchen and spent a few minutes watching the team search. I watched as they picked up documents, some of which were Western Union receipts, and set them aside. They didn't mark them as evidence; they just set them aside. So, I moved closer. To the best of my ability, I reviewed the Western Union receipts. It was clear the recipient was from Russia.

I couldn't stand quietly by, so I motioned for Captain Bautista to come over.

Pointing to the receipt, I said, "These are some documents I was talking about. Western Union receipts. Look here; the receiver is from Russia. Tobe may know this person, but it is only because they are working together in the carding business. This is the evidence I need."

Captain Bautista turned and barked commands to his team. Next, I pointed to the PlayStations: "See those in the corner. Here is the shipping label for at least one of those devices. Look here. It has information about my suspects from San Diego. This is also evidence."

Captain Bautista, shaking his head in agreement once more, provided further instructions to his team. I knew his team wasn't very experienced in financial crime cases, so I asked, "Do you mind if I help?"

Captain Bautista excitedly replied, "Not at all, please help."

With that, I set about retracing the team's steps. I pulled out receipts, documents, notes, counterfeit plastic, and other items of evidentiary value. When all was said and done, Captain Bautista approached me and asked, "Are you interested in working for us?"

I said politely, "Thank you for the offer, but I still have many years until I retire."

When I arrived in San Diego, I received a call from ATSAIC Carrington, who stated, "SAIC Montaña has been replaced." The new SAIC is Garrett Murphy. The name was very familiar, but it took me a moment to recall why I knew it. Then, I remembered meeting him several years before when he conducted the office inspection.

Over the next several weeks, I continued my conversations with Maksik. I knew travel wouldn't occur soon, but a trip to Macau was in the planning stages. I thought I could propose the opportunity, and if Maksik agreed, we could arrange it very quickly. Unfortunately, Maksik never agreed; instead, he offered to have me visit him in Ukraine.

I thought now may be a good time to propose unilateral operations in Ukraine. It was a logical next step, and since SAIC Murphy was new, he might have had more clout. The conversations between ATSAIC Carrington, ATSAIC Rogers, and me were positive; however, I would need the support of senior leadership to proceed.

About one week after settling in, a conversation with SAIC Murphy was inevitable because something was always pressing. The first meeting was between ASAIC DuBois, ATSAIC Carrington, and SA Grant Mason. I started explaining the past undercover assignments, the successes, the issues with the U.S. Attorney's Office, and the current goals.

Once I finished, SAIC Murphy said, "That's an impressive operation. It's far more extensive than I was briefed about before arriving here. I was instructed to 'close' Operation Carder Kaos—shut it down gracefully. But that's not going to work. Your proposal makes sense. Let me arrange a meeting with Headquarters."

About a week later, I heard rumors that they were seriously considering the proposed unilateral operation in Ukraine, to the extent that they scheduled a meeting at Headquarters. SAIC Murphy, ATSAIC Carrington, and I were to fly to Washington, to meet with SAIC Tanzman, ATSAIC Rogers, and several other essential supervisors.

ATSAIC Carrington and I were on the same flight to Washington, and at the time, I didn't even think about asking where SAIC Murphy was. My first thought was that he was on another flight, which was common considering mileage programs and personal preferences. Nonetheless, I expected SAIC Murphy to be at the same hotel when we landed.

When morning arrived, ATSAIC Carrington stood waiting for me in the hotel lobby.

I asked, “Do you know where Garrett is?”

ATSAIC Carrington smirked while shrugging his shoulders, “He isn’t coming.”

Confused, I asked, “I thought this was a meeting with the SAIC of CID?”

“We’ll see,” ATSAIC Carrington replied.

Upon entering the conference room at Headquarters, it was clear. The only attendees were the ASAIC of CID, ATSAIC Rogers, and others. SAIC Murphy and SAIC Tanzman were missing from the meeting. The message was clear: unilateral meetings in Ukraine were off the table.

The meeting became pointless, and I didn’t want to waste my breath. Whoever told SAIC Murphy to shut down my case must have reconnected with him and reminded him of that task. On that flight home, I knew I was fighting a losing battle. Nonetheless, I wasn’t going down without a fight.

Chapter 35

They wait for us in Ankara

During my flight back to San Diego, I felt disheartened by the lack of support from SAIC Murphy and others at Headquarters. I often reflected on how things could have turned out differently and how the outcome might have been more significant. If only those in leadership positions weren't immobilized by the fear that their supervisors might view the matter differently and hold it against them.

Years later, Darius Rookwood and I found ourselves at a bar, deep in conversation. As I sipped Johnny Walker Black Label, I couldn't help but think back to that meeting that never happened. The comment, "You're too close to see the bigger picture; leadership would never support unilateral operations in Ukraine," has always haunted me.

I turned to him and asked, "Question: If you had received a briefing about a unilateral operation in Ukraine, would you have given your approval?"

Without skipping a beat, Darius replied, "Had I been briefed? Yes, I would have approved it. If the Service wants to be a player, then we must be aggressive."

That night, Rachel and I went out to celebrate. We met several friends and drank well into the evening. Throughout the night, we played pool and threw darts, old pastimes from my college days. I thoroughly enjoyed the challenges, and Rachel was quite good at both pool and darts, which helped me sharpen my game. I attribute my skills to these consistent barroom games, which enabled me to beat Maksik in Thailand when we played pool.

However, like any other night, as the drinks flowed, something I said didn't sit well with Rachel. Instead of enjoying a fantastic night together, we ended up arguing. Rather than growing closer, we found ourselves on different paths, drifting farther and farther apart. Thoughts of ending our long-term relationship became increasingly common, but that's where it all stayed—just a thought. I didn't muster the courage to end the relationship, which was probably for the best.

When I woke up the next morning, I got ready and went straight to the office. My goal was to keep working on Maksik's hard drive. Each day, I uncovered more artifacts in the unallocated space. While I analyzed the evidence, SA Bander concentrated on unlocking Maksik's secrets.

"Hey, good morning," I said. "How's the search going?"

SA Bander replied, "I have a few potentials, but it's going slowly."

I said, "A few is better than zero. Keep working on it. We'll get there. Oh, by the way, for the next operation, I plan to install a keylogger on his computer. I want you to start testing how his AV will react. Will a pop-up appear when the computer is restarted? Do we need to step through the acceptance on his behalf to avoid problems? We can't afford to mess it up on game day."

SA Bander saluted and said, "I'm on it."

While SA Bander and I worked on testing software and searching for passwords, I continued to pitch Maksik about our next holiday. Months went by with little interest from

DOI: 10.1201/9781003680390-35

Maksik until one morning when I opened my undercover computer and found a message from him: "I'm ready for a break. 🙂"

I replied excitedly, "That's good news! 🙂 Where did you have in mind? 🤔"

Maksik answered, "I was thinking Antalya. Have you been?"

I said, "No, I haven't. I guess I can't be your tour guide this time. 🤪"

Maksik responded, "🤣 That's okay. We discover together."

After my conversation, I frantically made phone calls. I was particularly concerned about extradition. Was it even feasible? Türkiye was previously unknown to me; I had never given it much consideration before. The Office of International Affairs (OIA) representative, who is responsible for processing all legal matters related to Türkiye, informed me that extradition to Türkiye was indeed feasible and had seen successful cases.

With this in mind, I contacted Headquarters. From the first call, it was clear that this operation would be different. With ATSAIC Carrington next to me, I called ATSAIC Rogers and said, "I got all the information I need about Türkiye."

ATSAIC Rogers replied, "Good, the main question is, can we arrest and extradite him?"

"Yes, to both," I said. "But..."

ATSAIC Rogers interrupted me and said, "Then once Maksik arrives, we want him arrested."

"Why?" I asked.

"He's too valuable," ATSAIC Rogers replied. "What if the FBI arrests him? We have invested too much for that to happen."

I was confused and asked, "When did the FBI enter the race? Also, how would they arrest Maksik? It doesn't matter. Look, even if Maksik is arrested, I'm his friend. He'll come back to me. This fear shouldn't be the reason we arrest him."

"It doesn't matter," ATSAIC Rogers responded. "There isn't going to be another operation. Maksik must not leave Türkiye."

I knew it was pointless to continue arguing without top-level support. Instead, I accepted the outcome of the operation. However, with that acceptance, the first thoughts that entered my mind were from the movie "Midnight Express." This was how I was repaying Maksik's friendship—a Turkish prison. I put myself at ease, thinking that the conditions couldn't be that horrible; after all, it was just a movie.

Unfortunately, curiosity got the better of me. The next time I spoke with OIA, I asked, "Can you tell me about Türkiye? Are the prisons really that bad?"

The OIA representative replied, "They aren't ideal. The conditions are such that usually defendants get time-served credits. Typically, it's two to one. Sometimes more."

I hung up the phone, feeling terrible. Over the years, I couldn't help but develop genuine relationships with Maksik and others. I spoke with them frequently, vacationed with them, earned their trust, and, in an instant, I knew I was going to betray that trust.

However, telling ATSAIC Carrington, "I felt terrible. Let's not do this," wasn't an option. Feelings aside, it was my job to follow through with this.

The days were hectic; I assisted ASUA Peña in drafting the indictment, attended internal and external meetings, and continued chatting online. When news arrived from Türkiye, I felt indifferent. Half of me wished the police in Türkiye would deny my operation, but the other half had a job to do.

Ultimately, they supported the operation. However, there were conditions. For the operation to commence, they needed local victims. Without them, Maksik would be arrested upon arrival, and they wouldn't be allowed to install a keylogger. Therefore, the first question asked was, "Did I have any victims from Türkiye?"

We obtained an image of a mostly encrypted hard drive from the operation in Dubai. However, that partial view provided invaluable insight into the underground economy, the digital equivalent of breaking into Fort Knox. Arresting Maksik upon entry meant we would be seizing an encrypted computer, and nobody, least of all SAIC Tanzman, wanted that.

Because of this, acquiring Maksik's unencrypted computer became the top priority, more crucial than Maksik himself. Since providing the police with victim data was the only chance to ensure that Maksik wouldn't be arrested upon arrival we decided to share the data. Once the police had the data, they set about fulfilling their end of the agreement. The next step was to finalize our holiday plans.

Following extensive discussions, we chose a hotel near Antalya, Türkiye. It is a quaint resort town situated along the Mediterranean Sea and was well-liked among Russian tourists. We also agreed to meet there the last week of July.

I immediately passed this information to our local contacts to aid them in preparing their legal documents. I expected to meet them in Antalya, but they requested that I meet them in Ankara instead. Due to their request, ATSAIC Carrington, SA Grant Mason, and I departed San Diego on July 17, 2007.

The larger team, except for Sone, would meet about a week later. I never introduced Sone to Maksik, and they had never met in person. Therefore, there was little reason to invite him along. Besides, I was the only one who trusted and believed in him, and I knew ATSAIC Carrington preferred it this way. Sone was still considered a wildcard to him.

Upon landing in Ankara, we were greeted by U.S. Embassy personnel and escorted to the hotel. As we were dropped off, they advised, "Tomorrow, by nine am, we'll pick you up for your meeting with the TNP. Good night."

The following day, Meryem Demir met us. Meryem was the Regional Security Officer's FSNI. She was young, enthusiastic, and eager to assist. She had light brown curly hair about shoulder length. When she smiled, it lit up the room. From the moment we met, it was clear she had a bright future ahead of her.

Meryem and I bonded immediately. She was easy to talk to and had many questions due to her enthusiasm and interest in cybercriminal investigations. I was happy to answer them, knowing her support would be crucial to the operation's success.

The first meeting took place at a nondescript five-story office building. Meryem turned to me and said, "This is where the team works. Follow me."

We followed her into the building, where she assisted us with check-in. After this process was complete, an officer escorted us to the meeting room. Once inside, Meryem made eye contact with the lead investigator, Inspector Yusuf Aydin. "Rich, please meet Yusuf Aydin. He will be assisting you in your operation."

"Thank you, Meryem," I said as I extended my hand to Yusuf. "It's a pleasure to meet you."

"Likewise," Yusuf responded. "Please sit. Can we get you tea? Coffee?"

"Coffee, please," I said.

Yusuf started the meeting by saying, "I apologize. Senior Chief Inspector Mehmet Yilmaz was unable to attend today; he is on holiday and currently unreachable. However, I assure you that he will be briefed upon his return."

"Thank you for sharing," I said. "I assume in his absence, we still have your support."

Yusuf confidently replied, "Yes, of course. You have the full support of the police. Also, as we speak, the paperwork is being prepared and will be ready for Maksik's arrival. Do you have an exact date of his arrival?"

ATSAIC Carrington, not satisfied with Yusuf's answer, interjected, "Are you sure that this operation is approved, given that Senior Chief Inspector Yilmaz is not present?"

Yusuf, clearly uncomfortable by the challenge to his authority in front of his subordinates, declared, "You need not worry. Everything is under control."

There was already tension in the air. I looked at Meryem and could sense that she was uneasy too. Not sensing the tension, ATSAIC Carrington pressed on, "When will Senior Chief Inspector Yilmaz return? How can you guarantee his approval?"

ATSAIC Carrington was my supervisor and a friend, but his liaison skills needed improvement. Challenging Inspector Aydin in front of his subordinates cut against local culture. Nonetheless, Yusuf maintained his composure and sternly stated, "Your team can rest assured you are in good hands. You have our support and permission."

ATSAIC Carrington continued, "What about support? Can our agents be present during the operation? We must be close to ensure Rich's safety."

Yusuf confidently responded, "Yes, your team can be with our team during operations."

ATSAIC Carrington, seemingly happy, stated, "Okay, that's good. Thank you."

With that, Yusuf concluded the meeting by saying, "Tomorrow I will have more information. Once I have it, I will share it with Meryem."

I replied, "Thank you. We look forward to hearing from you. Take care."

Following that meeting, two key issues arose: Meryem had a negative impression of ATSAIC Carrington, and the Turkish team felt anxious about our partnership. Although it wasn't an ideal situation, I remained optimistic about changing the trajectory and improving our relationship over time.

The first person I spoke with was Meryem. I was interested in her culture and its rich history, and I thought this was an opportunity to distract her from the discomfort of the meeting. Meryem was happy to share and answer my questions, but she wasn't about to refrain from commenting on the meeting when the chance arose.

Meryem asked bluntly, "Are all Americans like ATSAIC Carrington?"

Meryem had only spent a few hours with ATSAIC Carrington and was already feeling uncomfortable with him. I was aware that Americans often carry a reputation for being challenging travelers and are frequently oblivious to foreign cultures. I encountered this repeatedly during my travels with colleagues.

Nonetheless, I remained as diplomatic as possible and responded, "ATSAIC Carrington is under significant pressure. This is the final operation, and all eyes are on us. I suppose it has him on edge."

Meryem nodded in confirmation and said, "I understand, and he should know Yusuf is doing everything he can to help."

I was relieved that she accepted the answer, but I knew it would only get worse if he didn't change.

The following day, Meryem welcomed us and took us back to police headquarters. During the drive, Meryem and I chatted casually. She asked if I had enjoyed my dinner and whether I had slept well. I provided her with a five-point review and suggested she visit the restaurant.

Once we arrived, Inspector Aydin and his assistant, Ahmet Kaya, greeted us. Ahmet Kaya was a younger gentleman with a slender build and jet-black hair worn in a ponytail.

Yusuf declared, "Assistant Inspector Kaya is our computer specialist. He will be happy to assist you with anything you need. Now, please follow me to the conference room."

While following Yusuf to the conference room, Ahmet and I briefly discussed cyber investigations. Like Meryem, he showed a keen interest in the subject. They eagerly absorbed the information, and I enjoyed sharing my insights.

Once seated in the conference room, Yusuf declared, "The team you see here will depart after this meeting to begin working with the local police directorate. They are responsible for policing Kemer, and we must collaborate with them. This is important because we haven't spoken with them yet, but we have a lot of preparations to attend to. Moreover, they will not know who any of you are; this is for your protection."

ATSAIC Carrington replied, "Thank you, Yusuf. We appreciate your support and professionalism. I'd like to confirm that we will be able to have an agent paired with your team, correct?"

With a huff of breath, Yusuf adjusted his shoulders and tilted his head as he looked back at ATSAIC Carrington and said, "Everything remains the same as the day before. Your team is in good hands."

As Inspector Aydin answered ATSAIC Carrington's question, Meryem leaned toward Assistant Inspector Kaya and whispered in his ear. I didn't understand what was said, but the look on her face told me she wasn't happy.

Wanting to change the topic and calm some nerves, I said, "Yusuf, we appreciate your support. Besides operational topics, I'm curious: do you have an update on if the keylogger can be installed on the target computer?"

Yusuf's eyes lit up as he answered, "Yes, we have everything. Do you know when he arrives?"

I replied, "I don't have flight details, but we plan to meet on July twenty-third and depart on the twenty-ninth. We are all staying at the same resort."

Stroking his chin, Yusuf remarked, "We have ample time. But as you know, it's essential to get him out of the hotel for several hours. What's your strategy?"

Immediately, I responded, "In Dubai, we went on an all-day desert safari. As we explored the desert, the team imaged Maksik's computer. I imagine that once we meet, I'll find another adventure. Once it's confirmed, I'll share all the details with everyone. Does that work?"

Yusuf nodded in agreement, "Yes, that works. Is there anything else?"

I shook my head and replied, "No."

Yusuf ended with, "Then we'll see you in Kemer."

After the meeting, Yusuf caught my attention and said, "I'm interested in any opportunities to train with the United States. It would be invaluable for my career. Do you think the Secret Service can sponsor me?"

"I don't know," I replied. "But I will talk to Headquarters. They'll need to be the sponsor anyway."

"Thank you very much," Yusuf replied.

Once we left their offices, Meryem escorted us to the U.S. Embassy, where we met Ronald Graves, the Deputy Chief of Mission, and John Sally, the Regional Security Officer. As we sat down, Ronald asked, "How is everything? Are you receiving the support you need?"

ATSAIC Carrington responded, "Yes, Yusuf and his team have been extremely helpful."

John jumped in and asked, "You mentioned installing a keylogger on Maksik's computer. Is this still in play?"

I replied, "Yes, Yusuf informed us today that they have everything needed."

John acknowledged with a nod and a smile, "That's great. Yusuf is a good man. You know he's seeking training opportunities in the United States. It would be helpful if you could assist him."

I chuckled and said, "Yes, I've already spoken to him. Once this is finished, I'll reach out to Headquarters."

"That's fantastic," John replied. "If you need anything else, feel free to ask."

"Meryem has been amazing," I responded. "If we need anything, I know who to turn to."

John nodded and said, "Right, I forgot she's going with you. I look forward to hearing all about it. Safe travels."

"I appreciate it," I replied.

On July 19, 2007, three days before Maksik's expected arrival, FSNI Meryem, ATSAIC Carrington, SA Grant, and I departed for Antalya.

Chapter 36

Antalya Türkiye

Traveling domestically is a breeze. There is no immigration or customs to pass through, only a direct route to baggage claim. After collecting our luggage, we exited into the main airport lobby, where Javier Gonzalez awaited us. It had been a while since I last saw him, and I looked forward to catching up with him.

As Javier and I caught up, Meryem organized our transport from Antalya. The hour-long drive hugged the coastline, offering breathtaking views of the Mediterranean Sea. Occasionally, seeking a change of scenery, I turned my gaze inward to view the coastal mountains. I couldn't help but think, "I could easily be in California driving along the PCH."

But as we drove, the time difference got the best of me, and I dozed off, only to be jarred awake as we crossed the resort's speed bump. I shook the sleep away from my eyes to view the beautiful Mediterranean-style resort. The structure's exterior was primarily composed of stucco, predominantly painted white with shades of blue. The design complemented the Mediterranean Sea and gave the resort a Greek feel.

Maksik and the U.S. team were set to arrive in a few days, so our schedule was relatively laid back for now. We had only one meeting scheduled that evening in ATSAIC Carrington's room to introduce ourselves and share any updates. Once it concluded, we all parted ways. But as I exited, Meryem approached me and asked, "Can you join me for dinner?"

Excitedly, I replied, "Sure, how about the Greek place?"

Meryem responded, "Yes, I'd enjoy that."

While walking to the restaurant, Meryem asked general questions about Americans, but then shifted to a more direct approach. She inquired, "Have I done something wrong?"

Astonished, I replied, "No, you're doing a great job. Why do you ask?"

"Your colleagues," Meryem explained. "They are mean. The way they talk and look at me is causing me a lot of stress. And your boss is so rude. At the Embassy, I do a good job, but I feel I can't do anything right here."

I rubbed my neck and said, "It's not you. It's them. They're Americans, and often we are bad travelers."

Meryem rubbed her forehead and said, "I understand about Americans, but why do your colleagues behave this way? Given all their travel, I thought they would be more culturally aware."

I bit my lip. I knew what she meant. It was something that bothered me. I replied, "Yeah, I don't have a good answer. I can only say from my first trip when others would say, 'Hey, how many scoots is that?' or 'I don't know, it's all monopoly money to me.' I was turned off."

"Scoots?" Meryem asked.

"Yeah," I replied. "It was a term they used for money. The 'monopoly money' comment is because, in Monopoly, the money is different colors."

DOI: 10.1201/9781003680390-36

Meryem furrowed her eyebrows and replied, "That's stupid. Why are you different? How come they can't be like you?"

"I'm sorry," I said empathetically. "When I talked about how my colleagues acted during my first trip, it created a dilemma within me. Right away, I knew I needed to get away. From that point on, I did my best to find one or two others who thought like me. The rest I worked with, but after hours, I stayed away from them."

Meryem, in despair, said, "I wish you didn't have to go."

Once dinner was over, it was clear that Meryem was unhappy with ATSAIC Carrington. I only hoped that their relationship wouldn't deteriorate further. But there wasn't anything more I could do. I had my job to focus on, and it was to concentrate on Maksik.

On July 23, I checked into my resort. I always felt that some leaders at Headquarters did everything possible to make me seem cheap, but on this trip, I upgraded my room. Besides, I knew Maksik had a family room, and I refused to appear as though I was broke.

I did my best to appear normal. Maksik knew I was traveling, so I stayed offline for a few days. I never knew if Maksik or others had hacked my undercover computer. Since I was only a Carder, I didn't take any special precautions to protect it. However, I kept my real and undercover lives separate, well, to a degree.

Separation was challenging to achieve, given that I was working from the San Diego Field Office using an undercover Internet line that, if anyone investigated, would have linked back to the area. Additionally, services like Western Union and my mailbox were a few blocks away from the office.

But this was all history now; luck had been on my side. To my knowledge, no one ever hacked my laptop. When I checked in, I presented my documents. In return, they gave me my hotel key and fitted me with a wristband. I wasn't a fan, but it was an all-inclusive resort, and the attendant placed it loosely on my wrist.

Later that afternoon, I walked around the grounds to familiarize myself with them. I checked out the pool, the garden, and the beach. The sea was beautiful, with waves crashing on a mostly pebbly shore. This was one aspect I wasn't fond of, as I had tender feet. I disliked walking on rocks to reach the water, but the heat and humidity were so intense that I knew this wouldn't stop me from swimming.

I knew Maksik would arrive soon, and having had enough of the heat, I headed back to the resort. As I walked back, I saw a sign that pointed to the resort spa. I decided to check it out since a visit with Maksik was possible.

As I approached the spa, I saw a stunning woman standing behind the counter. She had long, wavy black hair that fell gracefully onto her shoulders. Tall and thin, she had an exotic look. Once I saw her, I knew I had to enter and talk to her.

I approached the counter and said, "Greetings. Can you tell me about the treatments?

"We have many," she responded.

Her accent intrigued me, and I asked, "Where are you from?"

She replied, "I am Ukraine."

I said, "Really? I'm meeting friends from Ukraine. What's your name?"

With a smile, she replied, "Iryna. Are you American?"

"Yes," I replied.

Iryna curiously asked, "How do know people from Ukraine?"

"I met them online," I answered. But I was more interested in Iryna, so instead of explaining, I asked, "What brings you here?"

Iryna happily said, "I am summer helper. When the summer months end, I go back. But I like it here. The water is beautiful and warm. I come every summer to work."

We chatted for over an hour, and I would've invited her to dinner had she not been working. Instead, I promised to return and left gracefully. As I walked away, I glanced back to see if she was looking, a sign of interest. To my delight, I caught her watching me leave.

When I entered my room, I powered up my computer and logged into ICQ. After the application started, I checked for any messages from Maksik but found that his ICQ icon showed him as offline. I interpreted this as a sign that Maksik was still traveling. Not knowing when Maksik would arrive at the resort, I sent a message to the team: "Maksik offline. Unknown arrival time."

SA Mason replied, "Roger."

The waiting was the worst part. I never knew Maksik's exact arrival time, and it drove me crazy. On the one hand, I didn't want to sit by my computer—it seemed strange—but on the other hand, what choice did I have? So, I sat there, waited, and felt weird.

As evening approached, I observed Maksik's indicator change from "offline" to "online." My ICQ then came alive when Maksik messaged, "Greetings, we are here. ☺"

I wasn't sure if I should be the person who instantly replied or not, but I couldn't help myself and wrote, "Welcome ☺ Where are you?"

Maksik replied, "What is your room number?"

Hindsight, being twenty-twenty, I was fortunate that he asked me for my room number. All Maksik needed to do was ask at the front desk for "Richard Druc." Had he done that, the attendant may have told him, "There was no one at this resort with that name." But what if instead he asked for "Rich," and the attendant replied, "Richard LaTulip?" It could've exposed my last name.

Fortunately, Maksik performed the only "check-up" once. I remember speaking with Slimbady, who told me, "Maksik ask if you was cop."

Initially, when I read this message, I felt anxious. Still, I typed, "What did you tell him? ☺"

Slimbady replied, "I say, Surfrider, NOT cop. ☺"

The fact that Slimbady vouched for me meant I achieved my goal. I was a Carder, and had it not been for Sone, I may never have met Slimbady or achieved this status. Many stars aligned for me to reach this mark.

I messaged, "Building 4, room 416."

Maksik replied, "BRT ☺"

I immediately messaged SA Mason, "Maksik arrive. Meeting at my room."

Next, I double-checked my room to ensure that nothing—including my Secret Service credentials, passport, or other important documents—had been inadvertently left behind. While Maksik may not come into my room, double-checking wasn't a bad plan. There was no need to take unnecessary chances and mess everything up now.

Once I completed my sweep, I waited. While I waited, my blood pressure rose. Even though I had done this before, it felt different this time. I knew this was the last undercover operation, and on this occasion, there was no going back to Ukraine for him. My thoughts were freaking me out.

Then, there was a knock at my door. I knew who was on the other side. My blood pressure, heart rate, anticipation, and excitement collided, returning to normal. I became laser-focused, and everything shifted back to the mission at hand.

As I opened the door, I expected to see Maksik and Svetlana. Instead, the only familiar face was Maksik. A new girlfriend replaced Svetlana, and two new friends stood next to Maksik. Maksik, seeing that I was surprised, quickly said, "Rich, this is Maria."

I extended my hand and said, "Nice to meet you, Maria."

Maksik turned to his other friends and said, "This is Jacob, and this is Dmytro."

I said, "Jacob and Dmytro, nice to meet you."

Maksik looked at Dmytro and said, "I was trying to bring someone as big as you. Dmytro was my biggest friend, but unfortunately, you are still bigger." Laughing, Maksik continued, "I will keep trying. Maybe next time."

Jokingly, I replied, "Come on, I'm not that big, just a little taller. Are you guys hungry? Maybe a drink from the bar? It is all-inclusive." I then smiled and said, "Vodka is on me."

Maksik shrugged his shoulders while his friends nodded and said, "Let's go."

As we walked to the bar, Maksik and I discussed what was new in life, and I couldn't resist asking, "Did you pack $3,000 in your checked luggage?"

Maksik, embarrassed by my question, replied, "No, I learned my lesson."

Quickly, I surmised Maksik's new friends. Dmytro was muscular, carried some weight, and was shorter than I. He wasn't just Maksik's muscle, but I wondered about his role. I wouldn't be able to get information from him since he spoke little to no English. I then thought about wealthy Ukrainian culture; it was feasible that Dmytro was Maksik's driver. This could be his role.

Jacob was another story. He had a wiry build, like Maksik's, and was about the same height. He spoke excellent English and was very personable. He wore a Star of David necklace, which told me he was a Ukrainian or Russian Jew. Still, his role remained a mystery, but unlike Dmytro, I could speak with Jacob. I had time to figure it out.

Once we arrived at the bar, Jacob grabbed my attention. He was very much interested in U.S. politics. I did my best to stay in the middle of the road and not take a side. It was something I learned while working for the Secret Service.

As we sat and talked, I remembered I hadn't sent SA Mason an update. This prompted me to take out my phone and type a quick message: "At resort bar near pool."

Jacob tapped my shoulder as I typed and asked, "Did you get here early? Do they have a spa?"

I couldn't have planned it better and replied, "Yes, it's around the corner. Nice place."

Jacob looked at Maksik and said, "Let's do it tomorrow morning."

I replied, "Works for me."

Maksik replied in kind, saying, "Yeah."

Then Jacob leaned in and asked, "What do you think? Maria is much more beautiful than Svetlana. It's an upgrade."

I replied, "Yeah, I agree. Albeit I liked Svetlana. She was nice. But hey, I'm not in their house. If Maksik is happy, I'm happy for him."

At about midnight, the bartender announced, "Last call. We close in thirty minutes."

I looked at everyone and said, "One more round?"

Everyone nodded, and I replied, "We'll have one more."

We talked until about 1:00 a.m. Once everyone finished, Maksik said, "We will go to bed now. Meet for breakfast at eight?"

"Works for me," I said.

Walking to my room, I quickly typed a message to the team, "Maksik done for the night. Female is Maria, big guy is Dmytro and little one is Jacob."

The following day, I spoke with ATSAIC Carrington. He explained that they identified Maksik's colleagues. Furthermore no one was of record. Upon hearing the news, I was a little depressed. I thought for sure Jacob was a Carder. Regardless of the news, I planned to dig a little deeper today.

I walked down to the breakfast area and saw Maksik and his friends sitting together at a table. Once he saw me, he waved at me to get my attention. Seeing him waving, I waved back and headed to his table. I sat down and joined them. Jacob said, "Hey, we were all talking. Let's go to a club?"

I thought, "This could work. We'd be out for at least five to six hours." I replied, "Yeah. What club did you have in mind?"

Jacob said, "I have two. Let me research them, but we should go tomorrow."

I said, "Works for me. Thoughts?"

Maksik and everyone else nodded in confirmation. Tomorrow night, we're going to the club. I knew this was the break we needed. While we partied at the club, the team could execute the warrant. Once breakfast finished, we all headed to the spa.

I was excited to be going again. It was a chance to see Iryna, and I was looking forward to speaking with her once more. However, when we entered the spa, she wasn't there. I thought, "That's a shame."

Jacob and I approached and stated, "Five massages, please."

The attendant looked to see if there was availability. Once confirmed, she said, "Take a seat. Your masseuse will come shortly and escort you into the spa."

The masseuses came to get us one by one. Maria was chosen first; her masseuse was an Asian woman. Then Maksik was selected, followed by Jacob and Dmytro; all the masseuses were Asian women. I was the last person to be chosen, and my masseuse was a strong, tall, hairy Turkish man wearing only a towel around his waist. He looked at me and said, "Come with me."

I paused, unsure what to do. I didn't want to go at first, but then I got up and followed him. He brought me to the male changing room, handed me a towel, and said, "Strip down and put this on. When you are done, meet me here."

Taking a deep breath, I paused briefly before responding, "Alright."

As I changed, Jacob paused as he passed by and said, "I'm jealous. Did you see the size of his hands? I bet you're in for a great massage. Lucky man."

I thought, "Yeah, right, lucky man," as I headed out to meet my monstrous masseuse. He guided me to a larger room where everyone was already in their positions, receiving massages. The room was made of old Italian marble, and water gushed from fountains shaped like Greek gods and goddesses holding vases.

My masseuse placed a towel on the marble bench and said, "Lie down."

A marble bench with just a towel; I knew this wouldn't be comfortable. Nevertheless, I followed the instructions. The masseuse started with my legs. He bent, twisted, and contorted them while applying the right amount of pressure to the muscle. He then moved from my legs to my arms and then to my body, all the time applying pressure, pulling, turning, and twisting the various limbs.

At times, the pressure was immense. I looked over at Maksik and Dmytro, who, unbeknownst to me, were jealous of my massage. While they had their thoughts, I wondered, "Care to change masseuses?" Once the massage concluded, we moved to private rooms. Again, my masseuse escorted me. Once we entered the room, he said, "Give me towel."

I offered no resistance, saying, "Okay."

As I handed him my towel, he said, "Lie down." I thought, "Well, it's not a marble bench." Then he worked his magic, and by the end, I felt relaxed. Every muscle was as loose as it could be, but even with such a good feeling, I looked forward to getting out on the beach.

Once I changed into my resort clothing, I headed out to wait in the lobby. To my surprise, Iryna was there behind the counter. When she noticed me, she smiled and said, "You're back."

I was delighted to see her and said, "Yes, my friends and I stopped by for a massage."

Iryna looked down at the register and then exclaimed, "Oh, I see you had Mustafa. He gives firm massages. Too strong for me. How was it?"

I said, "You are right about strong massages. But it was good." Changing the topic, I asked, "What time do you get time off work?"

Iryna replied, "Sometimes seven, sometimes later."

"Well, we are going to a club tomorrow," I said. "Do you want to join us?"

Iryna's eyes darted left and right, and with a quieter tone, said, "I'm not allowed to date guests. Where is club? Maybe I can join, but not go with you. I would be in trouble."

Elated, I said, "I'm not sure yet, but if you give me your number, I can text you the details."

Iryna nodded and said, "Sure. Give me your phone." She typed her number into my phone and said, "Others use number too. What is your number? This way, I know it is you."

Maksik and Jacob emerged from the changing room as I wrote down my number and handed it to Iryna. Jacob gave me a look, which I understood meant, "I want to hear more about this." As we departed the spa, I grabbed Jacob's attention and said, "Her name is Iryna. She is interested in joining us at the club tomorrow night."

Jacob, surprised, said, "Does she have friends?"

I said, "No clue, but I will ask. Ah, who knows if she even shows up?"

Jacob replied, "You have a number. That's a start."

Just then, I got a message from ATSAIC Carrington, "Can you meet?"

I texted back, "Give me fifteen."

ATSAIC Carrington messaged back, "Meet at room number 1501."

I looked at Maksik and said, "I need to get online."

Maksik replied, "Yeah, me too."

I responded, "Meet for drinks later?"

Maksik shrugged his shoulders and said, "Yeah, say five?"

I replied, "Works for me. See you at five."

Chapter 37

Change of plans!

I pretended to walk to my room, but I turned around and headed for the beach once I was out of sight. Since both resorts were all-inclusive, my best option was via the beach. Fewer employees were watching these entrances. Once inside the resort, I headed to ATSAIC Carrington's room.

Grant, Javier, and Meryem were inside, and as I entered ATSAIC, Carrington could no longer hold back. He looked at me and said, "They are fucking us. They said we can't be anywhere near you during the surveillance. Apparently, Yilmaz returned from holiday and was unhappy that Yusuf hadn't briefed him. I knew this was going to happen."

I knew he was upset, but I did my best to calm him down. I said, "Can't we just be near the operation? It was how we operated in Thailand, Macau, and Dubai. Why is this a huge problem?"

ATSAIC Carrington, irritated, said, "Yusuf said. 'No. We must stay in our rooms.' Why the fuck do we have so many people? We were told we could participate in the operation. This is fucked up."

I understood his frustration, but one thing was clear: Yusuf didn't anticipate the changes Yilmaz implemented. As ATSAIC Carrington paced the room, Meryem interrupted and said, "Yusuf and Ahmet are coming to explain. They will be here shortly."

When Yusuf and Ahmet arrived, it was evident that ATSAIC Carrington was still upset. I did my best not to worsen the situation and asked, "What do you have for us?"

I wanted to minimize ATSAIC Carrington's speaking time as I knew anything he might say would only add to the tension. Yusuf explained, "I apologize; I'm unsure why Yilmaz is upset. I'm doing everything I can so that our promises are kept. But I caution you, there is only so much I can do."

Quickly, I asked, "What are your chances he allows the operation to proceed as planned?"

Yusuf looked down and said, "I don't have a good answer. Right now, your agents must stay in at the hotel."

ATSAIC Carrington had enough. "This is bullshit, Yusuf. You told us we would be part of the surveillance. I briefed Headquarters, and they AREN'T going to be happy. I have people I need to answer to!"

As ATSAIC Carrington continued ranting, Yusuf took it. However, his patience waned. Having heard enough, he motioned for ATSAIC Carrington to calm down and stated, "Trust me, I'm working on it. I'll have a final answer for you later tonight." Then Yusuf's telephone rang. Looking down, he saw the number and knew it was urgent. He said, "Excuse me. I need to take this."

As we waited, Ahmet approached me and said, "I hope you understand. This is out of our control. Yilmaz is the Chief. We have no choice."

I said, "Ahmet, I understand. We're not in the States. You have your own rules and people to answer to. My boss believes that a promise made by one is a promise made by all. He isn't

DOI: 10.1201/9781003680390-37

accounting for the fact that this is Türkiye. Things are different. Once he calms down, I'll talk to him."

Ahmet replied, "I'm happy you understand."

Once I turned away from Ahmet, Meryem said, "Can I speak with you?"

I responded, "Yeah. What's up?"

Meryem's facial expression was grave as she remarked, "ATSAIC Carrington is jeopardizing the Embassy's relationship with the police. He isn't respectful. I'm considering contacting the RSO to discuss these issues."

Hearing this, I began damage control, saying to Meryem, "Give me a moment. I'm figuring out how to handle the issue."

Sadly, I knew I could only do so much. ATSAIC Carrington was going to express his thoughts regardless of what I said. Concurrently, I understood the implications if the RSO were to step in. The entire operation could be shut down.

Meryem thought for a second before replying. "Okay, I trust you."

Fortunately, Meryem and I had a positive relationship. She believed in me and stood down, but I couldn't say for how long. I knew I had to get to work.

As Yusuf entered the room, he pulled Ahmet aside and spoke to him in Turkish. Afterward, Yusuf looked at our team and said, "We must step out. I will call later tonight."

As Yusuf and Ahmet turned to depart, I said, "Hey, before you leave, Maksik wants to go clubbing tomorrow night. The place is about forty-five minutes away. We plan to leave around eight. Will your team be ready to execute the warrant for the keylogger?"

Yusuf glanced at Ahmet before responding. Ahmet gave a slight nod, and Yusuf turned to me, saying, "Yes, we'll be ready."

"That's good," I said. "We also retrieved a password list from his old machine. Just in case we encounter a Windows password or something else."

Yusuf replied, "Okay, but as I said, I need to speak with Yilmaz."

Next, I addressed ATSAIC Carrington directly, saying, "The issue isn't with Yusuf or Ahmet; they aren't creating the problems. It's beyond their control. I can see they are just as upset as you. Anyway, I need to head back and meet Maksik for dinner."

As I walked back to my hotel, my phone buzzed. I looked down and saw it was an unknown number. "Hey, it's Iryna. Not sure if I can come. My manager says I must work hotel party."

I experienced a mix of sadness and happiness. I was sad that she couldn't come, but I was delighted that she reached out to me. Hoping she would join, I replied, "We'll be here all night. ☺ Join whenever you're done."

I knew the chances were slim, especially since our relationship was new, but it was worth a try. Besides, I was a guest and not someone worth losing a job.

When I arrived at dinner, my mind was a mess. To relieve some stress, I ordered a double vodka soda and lime. Maksik, Maria, Dmytro, and Jacob arrived as I started on my second drink. Being in high spirits, Jacob said, "What are you drinking? I want one."

I said, "Vodka soda lime."

"Perfect," Jacob replied.

The all-inclusive dinner was quick and rather tasteless. Once we finished, Jacob explained, "Tomorrow night, we go to Nera. I got a van and reserved a table."

"That's awesome," I replied. "Is it close?"

"Not too far," Jacob responded.

Yawning, Maksik said, "Maria and I are tired. We go to sleep now. See you tomorrow morning, Rich."

"Good night," I said.

This meant Jacob, Dmytro, and I were tasked with closing the bar at the resort. While drinking, Jacob suggested, "Hey, let's find out who's stronger. Arm wrestle Dmytro."

I wasn't looking for an arm-wrestling challenge with Dmytro; however, I also wasn't going to back down. It would be intriguing to find out if Dmytro was Maksik's muscle. I glanced back at Jacob and said, "I'm in if he is."

Jacob was thrilled and shared everything with Dmytro in Ukrainian. Dmytro nodded while squinting his eyes, replying, "Okay."

We locked hands while Jacob officiated. He held our hands steady and said, "Okay. I'm going to count to three. When I let go, you begin."

Both of us shook our heads in agreement. I could already feel Dmytro flexing his muscles, tightening his grip as we waited for Jacob's countdown.

I'd been drinking, but when your adrenaline spikes, momentary clarity and focus emerge. Jacob counted in English, "1, 2, READY, 3. GO!!"

We both moved closer to gain leverage. I think the word "ready" threw Dmytro off, which allowed me to gain the advantage. With momentum on my side, I curled my hand toward my chest and pulled it while leaning down. Once in this position, it was mostly over. I moved my shoulder forward; Dmytro struggled and made one last jolt, but it was all for nothing. I slowly pinned his hand down on the table.

Jacob was having fun and wanted us to arm wrestle again. "Best out of three," he proclaimed.

I replied, "I got lucky once. I don't want to push it. Besides, Dmytro's a strong man."

Continuing to arm wrestle Dmytro would yield nothing beneficial. I had no intention of showcasing my strength, which would only annoy him. I had everything to lose. Instead, I said, "Let's have another drink."

As we drank, Jacob indulged me by saying, "You know Dmytro and I don't work in the same line as Maksik."

Astounded, I replied, "No, not at all."

"Nope, we are only friends," Jacob replied.

When Jacob mentioned that, I didn't believe him. I thought, "They must be involved." Still, as dawn approached, we decided to call it a night.

The next day, we hung out at the beach, swimming. While wading in the water, Maksik asked, "How's the database? Did you make money?"

With all the excitement, I almost forgot about the database. I told Maksik, "I doubled my money. I'm happy."

"I am happy," Maksik replied. "You know why I do this?"

"No clue," I responded.

Maksik stated, "I do this because banks steal from us daily. Higher fees. More interest. They charge us for everything while they profit. I say fuck them. The little person should get their fair share. That is my reason."

I empathized with him and, to some extent, felt he was right. Bank fees had become absurd, not to mention the excessive interest rates. Over the years, they skyrocketed and continued to rise. The part I disagreed with was the hacking into a bank or processor and stealing the credit card data. Nonetheless, the entire banking industry was one-sided.

Having my chance to express how I felt, I replied to Maksik, "You're absolutely right and, to a small extent, a modern-day Robin Hood."

As night fell, we decided to return to our rooms to prepare for dinner and the club. The van was scheduled to pick us up at 9:00 p.m. to drive us to the club. It was approximately a thirty-five-minute drive from the resort to the club.

I was looking forward to hanging out with Maksik and my new friends. I was relaxing, but I also knew that time was drawing closer to the end. I figured that once the keylogger was installed on Maksik's computer, I had twenty-four hours before everyone screamed, "ARREST HIM!"

I tried not to dwell on it and thought, "I'd better check on ATSAIC Carrington." I was concerned the relationship was rapidly deteriorating. "Hey, how is it going?"

ATSAIC Carrington replied, "Not good. Still can't be with the Police."

"What are you going to do?" I replied.

"I'm sending the team anyhow," ATSAIC Carrington replied.

Well, that answered it: "The relationship was further declining."

When I finished speaking with ATSAIC Carrington, Meryem called. "Hey. How's it going?"

Meryem replied, "Do you have a moment to speak?"

I replied, "Of course. How can I help?"

Meryem responded, "Do you think the Secret Service would sponsor Inspector Aydin to come for training?"

At this moment, I already knew the answer. I had hoped the answer wasn't so pessimistic, but knowing ATSAIC Carrington was having challenges with Inspector Aydin, I feared that there was no way in hell. Regardless, I kept it positive and replied, "It is possible. I can also try to talk to some of my friends at Headquarters. Ultimately, they would be his sponsor since I'm in the San Diego Field Office."

Meryem seemed content and replied, "Thank you."

Needless to say, I feel she saw the writing on the wall. It wasn't going to happen. Since we were going to a club, I put on my club clothes: jeans and a button-down, long-sleeved shirt. Once I was ready, I headed to the bar.

While sitting at the bar, I thought it was an excellent opportunity to message Iryna. "Hey, about the head to the disco. You can still join us. ☺"

The message was brief, merely a gentle nudge. After finishing my drink, I made my way to the lobby to join everyone for the walk to the main gate, where the van awaited to take us to the club. As we walked, I removed the uncomfortable wristband. Taking it off made me feel much freer.

Chapter 38

An unexpected phone call

I gazed at the evening sky, absorbing the stunning celestial display. The stars and moon appeared particularly luminous tonight, likely influenced by my excitement for what lay ahead. While Maksik and I celebrated, the team would be busy installing a keylogger and imaging his computer. My task was straightforward: keep him occupied throughout the night.

While I contemplated and gazed into the endless void, Jacob tapped my shoulder and asked, "Ready to meet some Turkish girls tonight?"

I swiftly cleared my thoughts and stated, "I'm ready for that and more."

"Great," Jacob responded, "Then let's hop in the van."

I was so engrossed in my thoughts that I didn't even notice the van pull up. As I climbed into the van, I had to be cautious due to the cramped space and the many eyes on me. Still, I knew I needed to message the team. I angled my phone toward the vehicle and typed, "Departed."

The ride was enjoyable, but midway to our destination, I started to worry. I hadn't received a confirmation from SA Mason yet. I contemplated my options: wait or send another message? I knew that being too absorbed in my phone might arouse suspicions. At the same time, I recognized that this anxiety could be of my own making. Still, I needed an answer, so I decided to send another message: "Any update?"

After a brief pause, Meryem responded, "Still waiting."

Her message puzzled me. Still waiting? "For what?" I thought.

Memories of Dubai flooded my thoughts as I pondered, "Once again, I'm the insider. Why aren't they taking my cues?" I felt overwhelmed, wondering, "Does anyone trust me?"

As I was distracted, the last mile of the ride quickly passed, and the driver announced, "We're here," pointing to the left to indicate, "The club's entrance."

Without a line, we stepped inside. Cool air rushed forward as I entered, and I thought, "This will be nice; we'll escape the heat." Jacob spoke quietly with the hostess, who then turned to us and said, "Follow me."

She led us down a corridor to the main floor, but my excitement began to fade. The party was held in a large, open courtyard, and I found myself once again in the sweltering heat and humidity.

While we waited, I asked Maksik, "Do you want to get some drinks from the bar?"

Maksik shook his head and replied, "I told Jacob, 'Talk to the hostess.' I want to be here. Next to the dance floor."

I mused at the interaction between Maksik, Dmytro, and Jacob. It was clear that Maksik was the orchestrator; he had the money. Jacob and Dmytro were there to do his bidding as he stood over them, watching. Then I turned to Maksik, nodded, and replied, "Sure. This spot will be fantastic."

DOI: 10.1201/9781003680390-38

Shortly after Jacob finished talking with the hostess, several club staff arrived with our table and chairs. Once their task was done, one of them turned and said, "Your table."

Next came a group of ladies, one holding a liter of vodka while the others carried sparklers and mixers. I watched as our waitress arranged the table and poured our drinks. After everyone had a drink, I lifted my glass and declared, "To new friends and new adventures. Welcome to the party."

In less than an hour, the disco buzzed with a diverse crowd, each eager to celebrate, soak up the atmosphere, dance, and mingle. I felt restless, seated near the dance floor yet merely observing. It brought back memories of my eighth-grade dance, where I was just a spectator. However, things had changed; I was no longer the young, naive boy I once was.

Eager to explore, I looked at Jacob and said, "Shall we find some new friends?"

Jacob chuckled and replied, "I follow your lead."

I turned to Maksik and assured him, "We'll be back."

While Jacob and I scanned the crowd for someone to speak with, my phone vibrated. I tilted it to the side to read the message: "Made entry."

I could only shake my head in disbelief. I had been gone for over ninety minutes. I expected them to be in Maksik's room fifteen minutes after we left. Time is critical in forensics, and imaging a computer isn't an exact science.

As I contemplated the reasons why, a thought flashed in my mind: "Maybe the problem was ATSAIC Carrington." I knew Yusuf and he were not getting along, and Meryem could barely stand being near him. For her, it was like watching a car wreck in slow motion. Bodies were everywhere, but Meryem didn't want to overstep her authority. She was between the proverbial rock and a hard place.

But on that night, from the word "go," the temperature rose. Inspector Aydin wasn't budging on the Secret Service's participation. Despite his warning, ATSAIC Carrington sent them anyway. Meanwhile, curiosity got the better of me, and I messaged Meryem asking, "Why did they wait?"

Meryem replied, "They wanted the first bottle to arrive."

While Jacob and I hunted for ladies, the Secret Service team searched for Maksik's laptop. Since there were multiple guests, they needed to be sure. Eventually, it was located in the main suite, save for one issue: Maksik had upgraded his laptop since the last meeting.

Racing against time, SA Bander opened the lid. The keyboard illuminated, and the computer powered on. However, as the screen came alive, a wave of fear washed over them. Instead of the anticipated Windows splash screen, they were met with PGP. The blinking cursor awaited the input of the passphrase.

Panic broke out. Everyone was at a loss for what to do next. Tensions were running high since Yusuf knew that ATSAIC Carrington had sent his team. Anger bubbled over, and Inspector Aydin shouted his order, "We have no alternatives. Maksik will be arrested tonight."

ATSAIC Carrington quizzically asked, "Can the hard drive still be imaged?"

SA Bander interjected, "Yes, but since the hard drive is encrypted, copying it can take hours. I just don't know."

Inspector Aydin signaled to Ahmet. They quickly convened to discuss their next move. Their conversation was brief. Afterward, Inspector Aydin addressed the team, stating, "Assistant Inspector Kaya will coordinate with the local police. Advise your agents."

Ahmet immediately contacted the local police and informed them that their assistance was needed to arrest an international cybercriminal. ATSAIC Carrington called Headquarters to inform them of the complications. Yusuf reached out to Senior Chief Inspector Yilmaz to notify him of the changes. SA Bander called me.

Jacob and I had just come back to the table to refill our drinks when my phone rang. Recognizing the number, I glanced at Maksik and said, "I'll be right back. It's my team."

Unaware of the recent developments, I was in a good mood and replied, "Mr. Bander, how can I help you?"

Doug replied, "I have some bad news. The computer is encrypted. The police want to arrest Maksik tonight."

The news sobered me, and I replied, "Doug, we planned for this; pivot to the hardware option."

Doug, feeling embarrassed, responded, "Yeah, I forgot about that. Give me twenty minutes. I'll call you back."

I'm miles away. I have my job to do, yet here I am guiding them on how to do their job. Frustration immediately set in, but I needed to put this out of my mind. I returned to the table and did what I could to "appear" normal.

I held my phone in my hand while waiting for Doug's call. Scenarios ran through my mind; I didn't want the operation to end. I felt we still had options, and only once those were exhausted should we arrest Maksik. I hoped for reason to prevail over panic.

I sat there with a thousand-yard stare when Maksik noticed me and asked, "Everything okay?"

I shook my head and said, "Huh? Oh yeah, everything's fine. They ran into a small problem. Nothing major, but they'll call me back. You know, if I'm not there babysitting, shit happens."

Maksik laughed, "Yeah, same here. Consent problems, it's all day and night."

Then it struck me: if nothing changes, they will arrest Maksik tonight. I thought, "I should warn him," but instead reminded myself, "You have a job to do." I was conflicted; do I go left or turn right? I knew what I must do as a billboard popped up in my mind with three words, "You're a DICK!"

Three years of building trust, friendship, and memories. In an instant, I was throwing it all down the drain. Not knowing what else to do, I raised my hand and high-fived Maksik, saying, "It's my guys. Be right back."

When I was far enough away, I answered, "Talk to me!"

Doug sighed and said, "I talked to Carrington. They don't want to take the risk. They believe he'll notice."

"What risk?" I asked. "Maksik will be drunk. He won't even notice that someone touched his machine."

Doug replied, "Well..." I cut him off, saying, "Besides, Maksik's girl always pokes around in his stuff. When he wakes up the next morning, he'll likely blame her. He trusts me and doesn't suspect anything."

Doug, conveying as much empathy as he could, stated, "I understand. However, the decision has been made. There's nothing more to do. Maksik will be arrested tonight. Sorry."

It was over. Three years of clawing my way into a top-tier hacking organization would be cut short tonight. I had never met the hackers, yet I knew that, given time, I could. I resolved to head back to the table to enjoy the little time that remained. The inevitable was waiting just on the other side of the door.

Time passed slowly, yet, like every night before, it inevitably continued its march. We had already drunk two liters of vodka when our waitress approached us. "Compliments of the bar," she said, handing us a bottle of champagne. "Thank you for joining us tonight."

Surprised but not complaining, I grabbed the bottle and began pouring drinks. I knew my time was growing shorter. I couldn't shake the thoughts of betrayal from my mind. Ignoring them, I raised my glass and said, "To good friends."

Maksik, Maria, Jacob, and Dmytro followed my lead and raised their glasses, saying in unison, "To good friends."

With five of us drinking, finishing the bottle didn't take long. Maksik glanced around at the mostly empty bar, then turned to me and asked, "Shall we go?"

I replied, "Might as well, it's dead here."

Having overheard the conversation, Jacob said, "I'll call the van."

No one ever told me when Maksik would be arrested. The likely reason was that everything was still being figured out. Needless to say, this kept me on edge. I constantly looked around, expecting that any moment the police would swoop in and arrest us. But inside the club, nothing. Not a single sign of a police officer.

Breaking the silence, Jacob gestured to everyone and said, "Come on. Van is here."

Standing up, I thought, "It's happening outside." I was now moments away from being exposed. I trailed behind Maksik as he took the lead. Once we emerged outside, I quickly scanned the surroundings. I glanced left and then right, but once again, saw nothing.

"Where are they? We are out in the open, intoxicated and oblivious. It's perfect." But as I stood back waiting, nothing happened. Instead, everyone leaped into the van except for me. Maksik noticed I wasn't inside, looked back, and said, "Are you getting in?"

I looked around and then replied, "Yeah, of course."

As we departed, I peered into the shadows, searching for someone out of the ordinary. Yet no one was there. I was shocked that the van was allowed to pull away. During the drive, my mind oscillated, with thoughts ranging from "You are a traitor" to "You're doing your job."

To calm my mind, I considered how this could unfold. I pictured a police car stopping the van, but as we drew closer to the resort, there were no police vehicles around. Doubt crept in about whether it would happen, so I grabbed my phone, tapped out a message, and texted Grant, "Is this still going ahead?"

Grant replied, "Yes."

"Yes? Well, it better happen soon. We're almost back."

The driver slowed down and veered onto the hotel's driveway, approaching the gate. He stopped abruptly because entry was prohibited. We all got out of the van and started walking toward our rooms when suddenly, police emerged from the bushes, guns drawn, shouting, "DON'T MOVE!! YOU ARE ALL UNDER ARREST!"

Maksik and I raised our hands in disbelief. I watched as the color drained from Maksik's face. Jacob instantly reacted, shouting, "What? UNDER ARREST? I want to know why!"

I anticipated this, but I also thought I would encounter familiar faces. However, only men in uniforms were present. The majority donned ill-fitting, tattered uniforms. Their badges sagged on their shirts, and sweat stains became visible when they lifted their arms.

I stood there absorbing everything around me. The intoxication had me feeling relaxed. Maksik and Dmytro were stunned. Maria was in tears, while Jacob was shouting. It struck me like a freight train that I wasn't fitting in. As an undercover, it was my role to "fit in." In that instant, I adjusted my attitude and demeanor.

An officer pointed at me, yelling, "MOVE!"

I pushed back and asked, "Why? What the hell did I do?"

The officer seized my elbow and shoved me toward Maksik and Dmytro, growling, "Stand here."

With a disgusted and defiant look, I snarled back, "Don't touch me!"

The Lieutenant assessed us all and declared, "No one moves."

He then directed his officer, barking commands in Turkish. Once done, the officers snapped to attention and began searching us. When it was my turn, the officer glanced at my wrist. With a puzzled expression, he asked, "Where is your wristband?"

I responded, "Wristband? I'm not sure what you mean."

Unhappy, he proceeded to search me. After finding nothing, he asked firmly, "Where is your wristband?"

I smartly responded, "As I mentioned, I don't know what you're talking about."

I understood what they sought. My wristband was securely stored in the tiniest pocket of my jeans. Few people utilize it because of its size, but that's where I conceal it. After all, I didn't want to lose it.

Frustrated yet satisfied, the police marched us to Maksik's room. It was here that I began to recognize some familiar faces. Yusuf and Ahmet stood next to the hotel manager, who needed to open the hotel rooms. Seeing the manager, I was relieved that Iryna hadn't met me.

Upon entering, Yusuf gestured toward the chairs and instructed, "Take a seat."

We were all seated around the living area, able to see each other, but not close enough to talk privately. The hotel manager paced back and forth before finally stopping to confront me. He sneered, "Who are you? Why are you here? Where's your wristband?"

Instinctively, I acted on my first impulse: to lie. Facing the hotel manager, I said, "My name is Rex Hayden. I only met everyone tonight. Since I didn't have a place to stay, they said I could crash here."

The hotel manager snapped back, "No. No, tell me, what's your room number?"

I shook my head and replied, "I'm not staying at your hotel. You can look it up."

The hotel manager asked, "What's your name again?"

"Rex Hayden, H-a-y-d-e-n. Good luck," I said sarcastically.

Inspector Aydin turned to Maksik and asked, "How do you know him?"

Maksik, shifting his gaze, looked at me and then at Inspector Aydin before saying, "We met him tonight. His name is Rex, and I offered him to stay here."

"That is correct," Jacob added, "His name is Rex. We met tonight."

The hotel manager appeared furious as he exited the room. I heard him communicating via radio, mentioning my name to his team. He seemed to think he could locate my room number. However, Rex Hayden was a fictitious identity. Unless someone coincidentally booked a stay under that name, he wouldn't find my room.

Jacob grew furious and shouted, "Hey! You! Yes, you, I'm Jewish. I need to talk to my embassy. I will sue you and everyone involved. I demand you release me."

Inspector Aydin replied, "Calm down. You will have the opportunity to speak with your embassy."

Infuriated, Jacob stood up and attempted to leave the room. Immediately, an officer stood and blocked his path. Inspector Aydin yelled for him to sit down. Defiantly, Jacob held his ground and didn't move.

I snapped back, "You can't tell him what to do. He isn't under arrest. This is fucking bullshit."

Nodding in agreement, Jacob said, "Yes, yes, what are the charges? What am I being arrested for? You can't hold me here. I want to speak to my embassy now."

"I agree," I said. "What are the charges? Where's your warrant?"

Inspector Aydin glanced at Jacob and barked, "SIT DOWN!" He then focused on me, stating, "We have your warrant, and if you give us a moment, I'll show it to you."

Maksik sat still, gazing at the wall. His posture was perfect: head aligned with his shoulders, arms straight at his sides, hands placed neatly on his legs, and both feet firmly on the floor. At that moment, he brought to mind Stonewall Jackson, known for his rigid, upright sitting stance.

Jacob was slumped over his knees, his hands supporting his head. Dmytro leaned back, letting the wall support his head. Maria cried as she looked toward Maksik, longing to be near him to provide comfort.

Inspector Aydin returned with official documents and confronted Maksik. He handed over the papers, stating, "This is the search warrant. You are charged with hacking and stealing credit card information. Additionally, this is an arrest warrant for the unlawful sale of that data."

Maksik appeared exhausted as he clutched the papers. When Inspector Aydin concluded, Maksik slightly leaned forward and placed them on the table. Once I could view them, I exclaimed, "What are those? Seems like scribbles on paper. How do I know that isn't your shopping list?"

Hearing this, Jacob stood up and declared, "This is bullshit, I'm leaving." As Jacob moved toward the door, Ahmet and another officer seized him. Jacob was forcibly dragged to another room. Immediately, I thought, "That's not going to be good."

While they dealt with Jacob, others searched the bedrooms, pulling out three computers, a few jump drives, and Maksik's counterfeit badge. It was laid out for Maksik, Dmytro, Maria, and me to see. Since I had seen it before, I knew the police were following their policies that aimed to reduce corruption.

Eventually, Jacob returned, but this time he was handcuffed. After he sat down, Ahmet and his partner seized me and pulled me aside. I was unclear about their intentions, but I immediately assumed they would tell me to "tone it down."

Once Ahmet felt safe that no one could hear us, he said, "Are you okay?"

"I'm okay. But what about me?" I inquired. "Am I being overly aggressive? I don't want to upset you."

Ahmet shook his head, saying, "No, you're fine. But your boss calls every minute. We have already informed him that you are okay, and once our work is complete, we will call him again. But he keeps calling. It is very annoying. My question is, do you want to be taken away now or stay?"

I was caught up in the moment and said, "I want this to appear natural. If I have to sit here for hours, I will sit here for hours."

Ahmet smiled and said, "Yes, it is normal for everyone to be present during our search. Afterward, everyone is transported to the station for processing. Once we complete your processing, we will walk you in front of everyone. However, we will escort you through the back door instead of jailing you."

I nodded my head and stated, "Let's do it."

Ahmet held my arm behind my back and guided me back to my chair. We spent the next hour observing the police complete their processing. Evidence was placed in black garbage bags and subsequently loaded into a van. After that, Inspector Aydin stated, "Now, you will be taken to the police station for processing."

The hotel manager stood quietly in the background, but just as they were about to escort me to the police car, he remarked, "You are forbidden to ever return to this hotel."

Squinting my eyes, I said defiantly, "Your hotel is a shithole; I wouldn't come back even if you paid me." Yet I was already planning how to return to get my luggage without him seeing me. I knew that would be challenging.

Chapter 39

My second time in handcuffs

I was the last to leave the hotel. My drivers were Yusuf and Ahmet. I sat in the backseat, handcuffed. It was early morning, and the sun rose as Yusuf pulled away. As Yusuf drove, he looked in the mirror and asked, "How are you?"

I said, "Yes, I'm good, but how is Carrington?"

Yusuf laughed, "Carrington, he is angry. He wants updates every minute. I told him to be patient; you are okay. But he called nonstop, so I stopped answering his calls."

Laughing, I said, "I'm sure I'll hear all about it."

When I arrived at the station, two police officers escorted me inside for processing. The building was approximately three stories in height and primarily constructed from adobe, with a clay tile roof. The markings were in Turkish; if I weren't there to be processed, I would never have known it was a police station.

Inside, the walls, along with the floor, showed their age. The paint was layered in dirt, and the middle of the hallway wore through to the wood. Offices were lit by fluorescent lamps that hung precariously from an aging drop ceiling.

The desks were straight from the 1950s. They reminded me of my grandfather's auto shop. Made from metal, they were heavy; they squeaked when the drawers were opened. This all aside, the worst part was that there was no air-conditioning. With the sun rising came the oppressive heat and humidity.

Keeping to their word, I was paraded before Maksik and Jacob. For my plan to work, they needed to see me. I was seated on the other side of the station, ensuring plenty of distance between us. I never saw Maria or Dmytro, but they were unimportant, and I wasn't worried that I didn't.

My processing lasted about thirty minutes, and when it was finished, they walked me past Maksik again. The difference was that this time, I disappeared into the bowels of the station. Here, everything got darker. As I passed each cell, I witnessed each person's predicament. Their cells were small, filthy, and emanated a foul odor. I immediately felt sorry for Jacob and Maksik.

Once I was past all the cells, we turned right. A guard stood next to a door at the end of the corridor. The police officer spoke in Turkish, then turned, pulled keys from his pockets, and opened the door. On the other side were Ahmet and Yusuf, who said, "Greetings, please turn around."

I spun around, and Yusuf removed the handcuffs, saying, "How was it?"

I ran my hands through my hair, saying, "I think I'm still drunk. Other than that, I'm good."

Ahmet then asked, "Did you get the bottle of champagne at the club?"

Surprised, I said, "Yes, was that from you?"

Ahmet said, "Yeah, we were nervous you would leave too soon. We needed more time."

DOI: 10.1201/9781003680390-39

Yusuf chimed in and said, "Also, we never told the local police who we were. I had to explain to the Chief you were a U.S. Agent and not a criminal. Had I not, you'd be in jail right now."

My eyes widened as I said, "Thank you for that. I'm not sure those cells would have been as comfortable as my hotel room."

Laughing, Inspector Aydin said, "No, I don't assume so. But here is where we say goodbye. Ahmet and I have tons of paperwork. This police officer will give you a ride. Oh, and be on standby. We only have seventy-two hours before Maksik must appear before the Magistrate."

I shook hands with Ahmet and Yusuf and said, "Okay, thank you."

While being driven back to the hotel, I texted ATSAIC Carrington: "Heading back. Where should we meet?"

ATSAIC Carrington replied, "My room."

After being dropped off, I went to the beach, knowing this route was best to bypass the hotel staff quietly. I navigated to Carrington's room once past the guards and on the property. Upon entering, I was greeted by the whole team, who expressed their excitement at my arrival, asking, "How was it being in a Turkish prison?"

I chuckled in response, saying, "I wasn't exactly in a prison cell."

ATSAIC Carrington chimed in, "What the fuck was Yusuf's problem? He wouldn't answer my calls."

Upon hearing Carrington's words, Meryem could only shake her head in disbelief.

I said, "They were busy. A lot of politics were at play between them."

SA Mason asked, "What happened once they arrested you?"

I responded, "I mean it was normal. Everyone was searching and gathering evidence. Maksik and I sat there watching. Interestingly, all the evidence was placed in black trash bags."

"Black trash bags?" SA Mason questioned.

"Yes," I quipped. "Let's hope the laptops don't get destroyed."

ATSAIC Carrington said, "What do you mean, get destroyed? That laptop was the only reason we're here."

I shrugged my shoulders and said, "Nothing to do now, I was arrested."

"About that," ATSAIC Carrington replied. "Why did they keep you? Why didn't they take you out the back door?"

"They asked," I responded. "But I wanted it to be real. Ahmet told me that I would need to stay put. Which I did."

Meryem chimed in, hugging me, "I'm just glad you're safe."

"Thank you," I said. Then I asked Doug, "What happened with Maksik's computer?"

Doug explained, "When I opened Maksik's computer, the PGP splash screen appeared. Everyone saw it and realized the hard drive was encrypted. That's when Yusuf panicked. I suggested the hardware solution, but couldn't say whether Maksik needed to approve anything. That's when Yusuf decided to shut it all down."

"I understand," I replied. "Anyway, sucks that none of our passwords from your list worked."

As I spoke, I scanned the room and noticed only blank stares. I immediately asked, "You tried the passwords, right?"

Sheepishly, Doug replied, "No. I forgot about them."

"You mean to tell me, after all that work, no one thought to try any of the passwords?" I questioned.

ATSAIC Carrington jumped in, saying, "A lot was going on. It's over. I'm just glad you're safe."

I knew ATSAIC Carrington was frustrated with Headquarters. He was tired of the headaches, the travel, and the constant back-and-forth. He wanted this to end, which meant tremendous pressure off his shoulders. Ultimately, he only wanted to return to San Diego and work on counterfeiting cases. These cases were straightforward and uncomplicated for him, and they produced easy office stats.

"I guess you're right," I replied.

Rather than quarreling or finding fault, I considered it a good time to get my luggage. I turned to ATSAIC Carrington and stated, "Look, before Maria, Dmytro, and Jacob are released, I should head to my hotel and check out."

ATSAIC Carrington pondered momentarily before replying, "Do you believe it's safe? Can't you retrieve your luggage later?"

"Why wait?" I stated. "After all, I was arrested. It's only natural for me to grab my stuff and run."

ATSAIC Carrington nodded and said, "Okay, get your stuff."

On my way to the beach, I took my wristband from my pocket and showed it to the employee to confirm my guest status. Walking by the pool, I looked down, attempting to steer clear of everyone. My only thoughts were about avoiding being seen.

Regrettably, Maria and Dmytro were standing by the pool. They instantly spotted me and waved. Inside, I screamed, "You've gotta be kidding me." I realized there was no escaping them now. I waved back and approached them. Once I got closer, I asked, "Hey, how are you doing?"

Maria remained motionless; her expression vacant. I prompted, "Have you seen Maksik?"

There was still no response, so I continued, "Jacob?"

Dmytro merely shrugged, offering no words.

I realized that nothing I said was being understood. Then I had an idea: Iryna speaks both English and Ukrainian. If she were working, she could act as a translator.

I gestured for them to follow and said, "I have an idea."

As I entered the spa, I felt fortunate to see Iryna at work. When she saw me, her smile lit up her face, but her expression changed when she realized I was in my club clothes. With a hint of concern, she asked, "Is everything okay?"

Who wants to hear, "I got arrested." But what options did I have? I took a deep breath and said, "No, we were all arrested last night. Can you translate?"

Iryna, worried, replied, "Yes, certainly. What do you want me to say to them?"

"Awesome," I replied. "Tell them that after the police searched the room, we were taken to the station for processing. I was released about thirty minutes ago, but Maksik and Jacob are still there. I only returned to get my luggage and leave."

While Iryna translated my words, I noticed a worried expression on Maria's face. When Iryna finished, Maria asked her questions. Then Iryna turned to me and said, "She asked if the police would let him go, and if you know why they arrested him?"

I had clear answers to both questions. Instead of truthfully stating, "No, he isn't going to be freed, and they know who he is, which is why they arrested him," I lied, saying, "No, I don't know. But they must know him. They didn't know me, and I was released. Look, I'm not staying here. I'm outta here."

Knowing I had nothing more to say, I bid farewell, saying, "Good luck and be careful."

Next, I looked at Iryna. I couldn't reveal the truth yet—that this was a major undercover operation, and I was a Secret Agent—though that would have been pretty cool. Instead, I said, "I enjoyed meeting you and wish we could've spent more time together. Can I call you? I'd love to meet you sometime."

It was the most awkward pick-up attempt, and I anticipated her response would be, "fuck off." Instead, Iryna hesitated before replying, "Yes, you can call or message me. I'd like to keep in touch."

Elated, I said, "Awesome, I will be calling soon," then I turned and headed to my room. I focused on keeping my head down and avoiding the manager. Once I arrived at my door, curiosity and concern overtook me. I wondered if they had uncovered my secret and cleaned out my room.

I cautiously inserted the key into the slot and saw a green light flash. I opened the door and peeked inside. Everything was just as I had left it. Either Yusuf informed the manager to let it go, or they never uncovered the situation. Regardless, I had no intention of staying and discovering the truth. I quickly packed everything into my bag and departed.

For the last eight hours, I had been running on adrenaline. But once I was checked into my new room, exhaustion took over. I set my alarm and collapsed into bed. Because we were on a clock, sleep was a commodity I couldn't afford.

When my alarm finally went off, I woke up feeling disoriented. Unsure of my surroundings, I shook the sleep from my mind and remembered: we had arrested Maksik. I picked up my phone and noticed a message waiting for me from ATSAIC Carrington: "Meeting in my room at six." I looked at the clock and realized it was only five, so I knew I had time.

Being in the same hotel made meeting easier, as there was no need to sneak past the guards. I slowly walked over to Carrington's room, and when I entered, I immediately made eye contact with Yusuf and nodded. Then, I walked toward Meryem and asked, "How are you holding up?"

Meryem inhaled deeply and said, "It's been stressful, but I'm good."

I softly said, "Hang in there. We're almost done," as Yusuf started the meeting. "Maksik and Jacob will be brought to our facilities in Antalya. Once they arrive, we can start our work in better conditions." Yusuf then turned to me, stating, "As Rich is aware, the local offices aren't comfortable."

I chimed in. "Anything is likely a step above."

Yusuf continued, "My team will work nonstop over the next seventy-two hours. Maksik's and Jacob's computers are encrypted, and our goal is to get those passwords."

Still troubled by my previous discussion with Doug, I interrupted Yusuf and asked, "Since we're talking about passwords, what was your reasoning behind arresting Maksik? We had agreed to install a keylogger on his computer—that was our plan for that evening."

Yusuf sternly replied, "Once I saw the PGP log-in screen, I determined the operation was compromised. I had no choices."

"No option?" I snapped back. "Maksik was intoxicated; he couldn't possibly remember the state of his computer. And accidents occur; computers reboot without warning all the time. Additionally, we discussed how my team tirelessly worked to create a password list. I was informed that not a single password was entered that night. Who knows, one of those passwords might have been the key. Finally, even if we had waited and they discovered the truth, four people aren't just going to vanish without a trace."

Yusuf scratched his head and replied, "You're right, and I'm sorry, but you weren't here. Regardless, it doesn't matter now. We need to concentrate on retrieving their passwords."

ATSAIC Carrington injected, "You're still handing over Maksik's hard disk drive, encrypted or not, correct?"

Yusuf appeared visibly annoyed but responded professionally, "We will honor our promises. Meryem knows the details of our office in Antalya. From now on, we meet there."

ATSAIC Carrington sarcastically remarked, "Just like our surveillance participation."

With that, the room fell silent, and Yusuf and Ahmet said, "We will be in contact."

In the days that followed, we endured an arduous journey to Antalya to collaborate with Ahmet. Upon seeing him, Ahmet remarked, "We interview Maksik and Jacob constantly, day or night. They only get short breaks."

I was concerned and asked, "Is this legal?"

Ahmet, recognizing Americans' views on Turkish prisons, assured me, "No one has been brutal with Maksik or Jacob. This is not Midnight Express. We only speak to them. Nothing else."

I felt relieved and responded, "That is good news." However, there was no way for me to verify Ahmet's statement. During this entire time, no one was ever allowed to visit Maksik.

Ahmet leaned in and stated, "Needless to say, we still lack his passwords. You must share his details with me. This will create the impression that we fully know his operations."

I started sharing all the necessary information while Ahmet carefully took notes. Once he had enough details, he remarked, "This should work. I will be in touch."

The next day, Meryem contacted me and said, "Ahmet called me. He told me they have Maksik's PGP password."

I said, "That's great! Did they pass it to you?"

Meryem replied, "Yes! Additionally, he mentioned that Maria and Dmytro visit the office every day and that we must be cautious so we aren't seen."

After obtaining the password, I asked SA Bander to verify it against our password list. Tragically, it turned out to be password number twelve.

Although Maksik hadn't been formally charged, time quickly slipped away, and pressure increased. As a result, Yusuf and Ahmet worked around the clock. Adding to their stress, the next time I saw Ahmet, I couldn't resist saying, "Did you notice that password was number twelve on our list?"

Ahmet sighed and said, "Yes."

"We shut down a viable operation for nothing," I continued.

"I know," Ahmet conceded.

While working with Ahmet and his team, I also texted Iryna. Since I was no longer a guest, I couldn't stop by the spa to talk to her. My only hope was to arrange a meeting on the beach. Unfortunately, she worked long and unpredictable hours that kept us from meeting. Each day brought new hope, yet time was slipping away, and I quickly lost faith in it.

Later that evening, Meryem joined me for dinner. Our conversation started pleasantly and lightly, but she quickly shifted to a more significant issue. "I don't like your colleagues. They lack communication skills and are disrespectful. You get it, why don't they?"

I understood her point, and I concurred. Many of my colleagues lacked diplomatic skills. For instance, when traveling abroad, they frequently referred to a country's currency as "scoots" or "monopoly money." To me, this demonstrated a lack of respect and was demeaning to locals. It put me off so much that I often chose to keep my distance from them.

To help alleviate some tension, I said, "I don't have a perfect answer. I understand how off-putting some people can be. Surprisingly, despite all their travel, one would think they'd pick up some culture. Yet, it seems to escape most of them, so I usually socialized with a few colleagues."

"That's unfortunate," Meryem remarked. However, her expression changed as she added, "After this concludes, my friends and I will sail the Aegean Sea. We have one spot open. We'll be away for a week. Would you care to join us?"

Since my time at Indiana University, I have longed to learn how to sail. Unfortunately, my drinking habits prevented me from enrolling in sailing classes. As a result, I had no choice but to sign up for scuba diving and volleyball instead. Today, that all changed. I had a chance to sail on the Aegean Sea. Along the way, who knows, I might learn how to sail.

My instinct was to blurt out, "YES!" Instead, another thought railroaded my instinct. My extension in Thailand nearly sent ATSAIC Carrington off a cliff. With Maksik now arrested, I assumed he would be livid if I "stayed" in Türkiye to sail. Therefore, I replied, "Thank you, but unfortunately, with Maksik's arrest, I have too much work to do."

After dinner, I realized I had let Meryem down and missed my opportunity to sail the Aegean Sea. The next day, we met with Ahmet, who had some exciting news to share with me. "Maksik is nearly broken," he exclaimed. He shares more information by the hour, and Jacob has already provided his password."

Astonished, I asked, "Really? What is it?"

Ahmet said, "You won't believe, it's Americansliketopay."

"That's hilarious," I responded, laughing.

The drive to and from Antalya became a contentious issue. Everyone was weary from the extra hours spent in the van. I was the only one advocating for us to remain at our resorts —what motivated my stance? The possibility of seeing Iryna. Despite our cheerful messages, we never met. With my optimism fading, I finally relented and suggested, "Let's move to Antalya."

The next day, we checked out and drove to Antalya. Driving there felt quite disheartening. Maksik had been arrested, and the operation was drawing to a close. I was closing a chapter in my life that had been both stressful and rewarding, yet also exciting and exhausting.

As I traveled to Antalya, I gazed into the endless void, pondering my next steps. My joy felt diminished by my sorrow. Adding insult to injury, my phone vibrated about twenty minutes after leaving, and I presumed it was another message from Ahmet.

I wasn't rushing, but when I checked the message, it was from Iryna. She had written, "I'm at the beach. Join me. ☺" I shook my head in disbelief and thought, "What luck do I have? As I depart, Iryna invites me to the beach."

I considered my choices: stopping the van and returning, or suggesting we stay another night. Neither was a viable option as it was already too late. With no real choices, I responded, "☹ I left today. I can't join you. 😭"

After arriving in Antalya and settling in, we met with Yusuf and Ahmet. They appeared rejuvenated, and Yusuf joyfully announced, "We got it—Maksik's password. He will be charged and transported to Ankara today. We'll head to Ankara to meet you and finalize our business together."

ATSAIC Carrington said, "Yusuf, with all due respect, you promised us Maksik's hard disk drive. Where is it?"

Yusuf said, "We will discuss this with you in Ankara."

Unsure how this would play out, I leaned in and asked Ahmet, "What are the odds we get the hard disk drive?"

Ahmet responded, "I wouldn't be concerned. However, I must admit, I enjoyed collaborating with you. However, as you know, not everyone is happy."

I responded, "I understand. Any assistance you can provide is truly appreciated."

Ahmet raised his hand and remarked, "I nearly forgot. It was remarkable. Even under immense pressure, Maksik and Jacob stayed true to the story throughout the interview. They defended you. I exhausted every tactic to break them, yet they remained committed."

It felt like a knife piercing my heart. As if my actions weren't terrible enough, Ahmet insisted on sharing how, despite everything, they defended me like true friends. Even though I was doing my job, I realized that once they learned the complete story, they would despise me, and rightfully so.

The team and I had dinner and drinks that night. We all reminisced about our successes, challenges, possibilities, and the headaches that came with them. It was during this conversation that I had a eureka moment. I replied, "I've figured it out. What if you and your friends were arrested? You'd go online and tell your closest friends. This is what I should do. I could even promote the idea of establishing a Maksik defense fund. People might easily blame me for Maksik's arrest if I remain silent. Thoughts?"

Jack Jones replied, "That makes sense. It's common for Carders to assist one another."

I nodded and responded, "Great. I'll begin tonight. I'll inform everyone that Maksik was arrested in Türkiye."

We caught the morning flight to Ankara to meet with Senior Chief Inspector Yilmaz and his team. For them, it was a moment to celebrate. Unfortunately, not everyone shared this sentiment. ATSAIC Carrington viewed it as a mission marked by broken promises.

I had mixed emotions about the operation. I never felt Ahmet or Yusuf did anything with ill intent. Instead, they were victims of Inspector Yilmaz's decision, destined by their roles to follow his orders. When we arrived, Inspector Yilmaz gleefully declared, "Welcome, my friends. Our operation was a great success. My team now prepares Maksik's drive. But first, Yusuf and Ahmet will take you on a cultural tour. Safe journeys, my friends."

Senior Chief Inspector Yilmaz left the room, and Yusuf said, "Please come with us."

Yusuf and Ahmet graciously escorted us to various cultural sites throughout Ankara while ATSAIC Carrington appeared annoyed. During one of the stops, Yusuf approached ATSAIC Carrington and me and said, "I'm seeking some training in the United States. I was hoping you might be able to sponsor me. Is this possible?"

ATSAIC Carrington listened and unemphatically replied, "Yes, I'll check on it."

Soon, a brown van arrived, and the driver waved at Ahmet. Ahmet approached the van and conversed with the driver. After their discussion, Ahmet walked over to Yusuf and handed him a package. Yusuf grinned and turned to ATSAIC Carrington, saying, "As promised, here's Maksik's hard disk drive. That hard drive cost two million dollars—the price Maksik paid to make it disappear."

ATSAIC Carrington received the hard drive and responded, "Thank you, Yusuf. It was a pleasure collaborating with you." Ahmet then led us to our van and instructed the driver to take us back to our hotel.

No sooner Yusuf was out of sight than ATSAIC Carrington looked at me and said, "There is no fucking way I'm asking to sponsor him for anything."

Hindsight is a bitch. Over time, because of ATSAIC Carrington's unwillingness to sponsor Inspector Aydin, it likely led to their default on the promise to hold Maksik for one year before extraditing him to the United States.

Instead, Türkiye prosecuted Maksik and sentenced him to thirty years in prison. The news made national headlines. I found out later Inspector Aydin turned to the FBI, who eventually sponsored him, solidifying a reliable relationship. Additionally, due to the perceived insult, Inspector Aydin refused to directly assist the Secret Service. Because of one person's anger, the Secret Service lost a valuable partner that day.

Chapter 40

Where do we go from here?

News travels fast. A Carder, named ChaO, posted "Interesting news from Türkiye... Maksik's hard disk drive was decrypted and contained a gold mine worth of data." ChaO continued that Maksik was fighting extradition to the United States, but time would tell if he could beat the rap. He ended with, "That's all from my Turkish pigeons... :-)."

After a long flight and plenty of time to think, I knew I had made a mistake by not accepting Meryem's invitation. She offered me a once-in-a-lifetime trip, and I said, "No, thank you." To this day, I lament that decision.

At the home front, the relationship between Rachel and I was becoming more volatile. We both were heavy drinkers, which didn't help our situation. Then there was Taylor. Rachel and he often burned the midnight oil, drinking while I preferred to stumble off to bed.

The fights came easily; a joke was sometimes all that was needed. If I were a stronger person, I would have ended the relationship. I didn't dare to break it off. When times were bad, I ignored the obvious and focused on prolonging the undercover operations. At its worst, I thought about Dok Mai while limping along in Rachel's and my relationship.

Online messages, such as the one from ChaO, helped spread the word about Maksik's arrest and its seriousness to the online community. I helped push the message by telling Slimbady, Kaiser, Mona, and others. My message was basic: "Maksik and I were arrested in Türkiye, but ultimately, after questioning, they released me. Maksik, on the other hand, was still being held."

I advocated for raising a defense fund for Maksik and even sent several thousand dollars to Kaiser. I'll never know if the money was used to hire lawyers, but sending it gave me "hope." Hope that maybe my operation could survive Maksik's arrest. In a narcissistic way, I did it to help convince myself that the case would go on. In addition to contributing to Maksik's defense fund, over the last months of 2007, I met with Delpiero, Danny, Vincent, and Slimbady in Macau and Bangkok.

Concurrently, the Belarusian police were hard at work. Diplomaticos caught their attention again, and while investigating him, they came across my investigation. Despite strained diplomatic relations, their case was important, and SA Mason and I were invited to help. I jumped at the chance because I knew Diplomaticos was still connected, and this intelligence could prove valuable.

Upon meeting Igor, I assessed him as an honest man who was genuinely interested in doing the right thing. I had an unanswered question, so I asked, "Do you recall an inquiry about one year ago regarding whether an inmate could use a cell phone from prison?"

Igor looked at me and replied, "Yes, I recall. However, such things aren't possible in Belarus."

I handed him a jump drive and said, "Well, you may want to review this. On that drive, you'll find conversations between Diplomaticos and me while he was in prison."

DOI: 10.1201/9781003680390-40

Igor's eyebrow raised as he handed the jump drive to his investigating officer. Igor briefly provided instructions in Russian. He then turned to me and said, "Okay, wait here. We will have questions."

Over the next two days, SA Mason and I worked with Igor and his team until they were satisfied there was enough evidence to prosecute Diplomaticos. The next day, we departed for San Diego. Immediately, I contacted AUSA Peña and asked, "Is the indictment for Delpiero done? Can we proceed with the Interpol red notice?"

AUSA Peña replied, "Yes, everything is ready."

Since Delpiero wasn't a citizen of Thailand, Lieutenant Colonel Chaiwat confirmed that once the extradition request was approved, they would search his residence and arrest him pending extradition to the United States. I was elated, so I sent a message to Dok Mai: "I am coming to Bangkok."

Dok Mai replied immediately, "When you come?"

"In one week," I wrote back.

Dok Mai responded, "Message me when you here. 😮"

Time flew by, and before I knew it, I arrived in Bangkok. After I checked into the Grand Hyatt Erwan, I messaged Dok Mai. "I am here. Where are you?"

"I at nearby bar. You come here," Dok Mai replied.

My answer was short, "Okay, see you soon."

I threw down my cell, undressed, showered, and changed. I was ready in a flash. Then I headed to the lobby to grab a taxi.

Once I walked in, I saw Dok Mai near the bar with three of her friends. She immediately noticed me and, unable to hold her excitement, ran toward me, leapt off the ground, and into my arms. Luckily, she wasn't more than ninety-five pounds, as I stumbled slightly from the force but held on tight. Seeing her again overwhelmed me, not just because I was spending time with her, but because this was my last trip to Thailand.

From the beginning, Dok Mai was there. Whenever I was in Thailand, she was my faithful partner in crime. Instead of saying anything, I kept it to myself. I couldn't bring myself to tell Dok Mai. I wanted Dok Mai to be happy, to believe I would return.

Ultimately, I believe Dok Mai knew the truth. She read me like a book. Instead of dwelling on the depressing stuff, we put it all into a closet and threw away the key. We chose to focus on each other rather than these details. It was time to celebrate our being together.

Taking charge, I asked the bartender, "Do you have Johnny Walker Black?"

The bartender replied, "Yes."

"How much for the bottle?" I asked.

"Two hundred," replied the bartender.

I quickly replied, "I'll take the bottle."

We sat at a table and quickly got caught up in our lives. Dok Mai opened her world to me, showing me her affection. We sipped on whiskey, and the evening went with it as we did. Before long, the bartender said, "Last call."

Once that happened, Dok Mai and I finished our drinks and left together. We had long-awaited business to attend to. Hand in hand, we made our way to my hotel, walking through the lobby and into the elevator. The anticipation between us was undeniable—we hadn't seen each other in months, and the desire to reconnect was palpable. As I escorted her toward my room, our pace quickened, driven by the moment's intensity.

The moment we crossed the threshold, restraint vanished. Behind closed doors, freed from any pretense, our passion erupted. As our bodies collided and our lips locked, Dok Mai pressed against me, driving me back toward the bed with an urgency that left no room for hesitation.

Each step backward for me and a step forward for her was a chance for our hands to explore our bodies. Their mission was clear. Once alone, the only item between us and a physical connection was our clothing. Quickly, I untucked her shirt, then fumbled, trying to unbutton it. It was too late, as my heel touched the bed. Dok Mai took charge.

She shoved me back so that I would fall backward, only to be caught by the ever-so-soft bed. Knowing her mission was intent and focused, I raised myself on my elbows. I was gazing at Dok Mai, who fiercely stared back at me. Knowing I was watching, she took her time slowly undressing herself. She toyed with me as she undressed. Passion building inside drove me toward her, only for her to push me back down. Dok Mai wanted me to lie on my back and watch her.

She took complete control, legs wrapped around my waist; leaning over, she took my hands and pinned them beside me. I lay still, fully acknowledging Dok Mai's dominance over me. She drove, and I enjoyed it. Feeling delightfully relaxed, we held each other, and gently, we drifted off into a blissful sleep together.

When I woke up the following day, I showered, got ready, and said goodbye. It was our last meeting together. As I stepped through the grand doors of the Grand Hyatt Erawan, I was met with warmth. The sky was hazy, and the morning air was thick with humidity. Immediately, I began to sweat, but I relished the moment.

I knew my next stop was a meeting with the police. They would be my sword of justice and execute the warrant at Delpiero's residence. Unlike Maksik, I felt a sense of accomplishment. I harbored no guilt or second thoughts. Partly, it was because I knew the case was over, and partly because our relationship was mostly online, save for a single meeting.

Notwithstanding those feelings, I knew Delpiero was a big player in the carding world. Whatever was on his computer would be significant. It didn't matter if it benefited me or another case. Those critical details could be the break needed today or tomorrow.

However, as I approached Delpiero's residence, I thought about the undercover operation. It seemed like a lifetime ago, but I wondered if Delpiero would be angry, surprised, or shocked. The last time I saw him, I was a Carder. Today, I was a Secret Service Agent.

As I stepped out of the van and onto the quiet suburban street, Delpiero's residence stood out slightly. It was a two-story house painted primarily white with a clean, almost sterile appearance. I adjusted my raid jacket and followed the lead Lieutenant Colonel Chaiwat.

We walked up the short driveway past a meticulously maintained garden. The front door opened to reveal a neat interior where everything seemed to have its place. I was immediately struck by the contrast between the ordinary suburban exterior and the high-stakes operation unfolding within.

Inside, the house was modern and well-lit, with white walls that matched the exterior's color scheme. The furnishings were minimalistic but stylish, suggesting Delpiero had a taste for the finer things or wanted to appear that way. The living room to the right was furnished with a sleek black leather couch and a glass coffee table, on which lay a single magazine about technology trends.

Entering the living room, Delpiero sat on the couch, hands cuffed behind his back. We locked eyes momentarily, but quickly, Delpiero looked away. I didn't say anything to him; I knew I would have my moment. Over the next few hours, the police searched Delpiero's residence.

Once they finished, Delpiero was led away to a waiting van. Before he got in, he looked back at his house one last time. I wondered what went through his mind. I turned toward Lieutenant Colonel Chaiwat and said, "Nice work."

Lieutenant Colonel Chaiwat nodded and said, "Thank you. Now let's go talk to Delpiero."

We arrived at the police substation near Delpiero's home. Lieutenant Colonel Chaiwat led me down a narrow hallway, my footsteps echoing off the tiled floor. Suddenly, he stopped, turned toward me, and said, "Please, sit down. Delpiero will be here momentarily."

Inside the room, the air feels different—quieter, more distracting, and emanating a unique odor. The walls are painted a neutral shade of green and beige, which neither distracts nor comforts, but simply exists. At the center of the room stands a simple wooden table pressed against the far wall, its surface clear except for a few sheets of paper and a telephone. Around the table are four plain chairs, two on each side, facing each other like silent adversaries.

Lieutenant Colonel Chaiwat sits beside me, placing a notepad and a pen on the table. He sits with a steady, measured gaze as Delpiero is led into the room. The officer directs him to sit across from me. He sits quietly, head slightly bowed, a look of despair covering his face.

"Delpiero," Lieutenant Colonel Chaiwat begins, his voice calm and authoritative, "we need to ask you some questions."

Interrupting, I said, "Before we begin, I must read this to Delpiero."

Lieutenant Colonel Chaiwat replied, "Please, proceed."

I turned toward Delpiero and said, "My name is Richard K. LaTulip. I have a document with your Miranda Warnings, in English and Chinese. I'm going to read it to you in English. Are you familiar with these basic rights?"

Delpiero quietly replied, "Not really."

"That's okay," I said. Once I finish, you must read the Chinese version. When you complete it, you can ask questions, but ultimately, you have two options. Option one is to agree to speak with me now, or option two is to decline to talk to me. Do you understand?"

Delpiero nods and diligently looks down at the paper. Taking his time, he reads both the English and Chinese versions. Once he finishes, he asks, "May I have a pen? I will speak with you."

Delpiero takes a deep breath and retells his story to me, but he portrays himself as a victim, insisting another person—a more sinister person—tricked him. He assures me he isn't the man I think he is.

I rubbed my forehead as I looked down. When I looked back up, I said, "You understand. We met. You introduced yourself as Delpiero. We talked about our business together. We talked about Maksik. You told me he invited you to Phuket. You said he visited you afterward and explained how you didn't trust me, which is why you refused to come. Does that ring a bell?"

Delpiero turned white, blood vanishing from his face. He knew there was no point in playing games and replied. "I am Delpiero."

Delpiero eventually secured legal counsel who, unfortunately, had another agenda: delay extradition. Years would pass, and the entire time, Delpiero remained in a Thai prison. The conditions inside were notoriously harsh. The facilities are rudimentary at best. Access to clean water and sanitation was limited, exacerbating the risk of diseases.

Due to poor conditions, the U.S. government allows for any time served to be counted as double or, in extreme cases, triple time. All the while, I believed Delpiero's lawyer kept him there and used him as a continued source of income. Stringing him along for about five years until the money ran out. The Secret Service, feeling horrible about his situation, passed word, "If you agreed to extradition, you would already be free."

Hearing that Delpiero agreed to extradition. Once he arrived in the United States, he was brought before the U.S. Magistrate Judge. The entire process was ceremonial. Delpiero pled guilty, was sentenced to time served, and was ordered deported. Thus ended the extradition saga of Delpiero.

Delpiero's situation was considered successful because he was extradited from Thailand despite his health problems. Others were not so successful. Fidel, was on Interpol's red notice list like Lifestyle before him. But unlike Lifestyle, when Fidel entered India, no one was home to answer the phone.

Part of Interpol's requirements is that a participating country must have a point of contact available 24/7 to confirm a "hit." In May 2010, the Secret Service received such a notice. Sadly, the call went to voicemail.

Two days after Fidel entered India, I received a call from AUSA Peña. "Hey, did you know Fidel is in India?"

Puzzled, I asked, "What? When?"

AUSA Peña replied, "A flash notification was sent two days ago, but no one replied. Therefore, they released him. The only good news is he's still there and will depart in five days."

I was beside myself. The one responsibility is to be available and answer the call, and even that can't be guaranteed. I responded, "Thank you. Let me call Headquarters and prepare the paperwork. At least we may get him on the way out."

When Fidel attempted to leave India, he was detained. The difference was that our team answered the phone, and Fidel was arrested. Unfortunately, he was only in possession of his passport. After holding him for several months, his lawyer requested a bond, which was approved and set at 15,000 Rupees. That was the last time he appeared in an Indian court.

Diplomatic communications between the United States and Türkiye related to Maksik couldn't have been colder. Even the U.S. Attorney stepped in and asked about Maksik's extradition status. I never received an official answer as to the Turkish response. However, it wasn't long afterward when it came across the wire. The headlines read, "Maksik sentenced to thirty years in Turkish prison."

To this day, I remain unsure if Türkiye has ever officially responded to or replied to my extradition request. Then again, I'm not sure they are required, and I also believe the Ukrainians never replied to the United States about Script's electronics.

Operation Carder Kaos would never be officially recognized or nominated by the Secret Service for any prestigious awards. However, pieces of it that were farmed away would be recognized. For example, the hacking case of Dave and Busters was nominated to receive a reward from the Department of Justice. I was one of several nominees because the evidence and most targets were from Operation Carder Kaos.

The ceremony required me to travel to DC, where the Secretary of Homeland Security presented the team with the group award. Since I was in town, I was invited to meet with AD Alex Johnson, known for his love of counterfeiting. He was old school and was nearing the end of his career. New cases, such as anything involving electronics, eluded his comprehension.

Now was my opportunity to brief him on a significant operation I had woven together. I entered his office, and he said, "Agent LaTulip, please sit. I understand you put together a magnificent case. Tell me about it."

Proudly, I said, "Sir, it was a lot of work not only by me but by the entire San Diego Field Office. It all started with a Carder named Sone. He introduced me to a large network, spanning from Eastern Europe to Southeast Asia, of people hacking into databases and selling stolen intellectual property. Maksik was the most prolific vendor of this data."

AD Johnson looked left, right, and up at the ceiling as I spoke. Having heard enough, he interrupted me, saying, "Did you know, in LA, we stopped one of the last counterfeit printing press machine cases? Those were the days."

It was clear that cybercrime was incomprehensible to the old guard, who had still longed for the days of counterfeiting—a globally insignificant crime. Under his leadership, the Secret Service was stuck in neutral, fighting yesterday's crime. To progress forward, it would have to wait for a new crop of leaders.

Index

For Product Safety Concerns and Information please contact our
EU representative GPSR@taylorandfrancis.com Taylor & Francis
Verlag GmbH, Kaufingerstraße 24, 80331 München, Germany